The Life and Music of Gérard Grisey

Eastman Studies in Music

Ralph P. Locke, Senior Editor
Eastman School of Music

Additional Titles of Interest:

Aaron Copland and the American Legacy of Gustav Mahler
Matthew Mugmon

CageTalk: Dialogues with and About John Cage
Edited by Peter Dickinson

Claiming Wagner for France: Music and Politics in the Parisian Press, 1933–1944
Rachel Orzech

Claude Vivier: A Composer's Life
Bob Gilmore

Composing for Japanese Instruments
Minoru Miki
Translated by Marty Regan
Edited by Philip Flavin

The Courage of Composers and the Tyranny of Taste: Reflections on New Music
Bálint András Varga

The Dawn of Music Semiology: Essays in Honor of Jean-Jacques Nattiez
Edited by Jonathan Dunsby and Jonathan Goldman.

Elliott Carter's "What Next?": Communication, Cooperation, and Separation
Guy Capuzzo

Gay Guerrilla: Julius Eastman and His Music
Edited by Renée Levine Packer and Mary Jane Leach

The Sea on Fire: Jean Barraqué
Paul Griffiths

A complete list of titles in the Eastman Studies in Music series
may be found on our website, www.urpress.com.

The Life and Music of Gérard Grisey

Delirium and Form

Jeffrey Arlo Brown

UNIVERSITY OF ROCHESTER PRESS

Copyright © 2023 Jeffrey Arlo Brown

All rights reserved. Except as permitted under current legislation, no part of this work may be photocopied, stored in a retrieval system, published, performed in public, adapted, broadcast, transmitted, recorded, or reproduced in any form or by any means, without the prior permission of the copyright owner.

First published 2023
Reprinted in paperback 2025

University of Rochester Press
668 Mt. Hope Avenue, Rochester, NY 14620, USA
www.urpress.com
and Boydell & Brewer Limited
PO Box 9, Woodbridge, Suffolk IP12 3DF, UK
www.boydellandbrewer.com

ISBN-13: 978-1-64825-068-2 (hardcover)
ISBN-13: 978-1-64825-084-2 (paperback)

ISSN: 1071-9989 ; v. 191

Library of Congress Cataloging-in-Publication Data
Names: Brown, Jeffrey Arlo, author.
Title: The life and music of Gérard Grisey: delirium and form / Jeffrey Arlo Brown.
Other titles: Eastman studies in music; 191.
Description: Rochester : University of Rochester Press, 2023. | Series: Eastman studies in music, 10719989; 191 | Includes bibliographical references and index.
Identifiers: LCCN 2023008412 (print) | LCCN 2023008413 (ebook) | ISBN 9781648250682 (hardback) | ISBN 9781805430728 (pdf) | ISBN 9781805430711 (epub)
Subjects: LCSH: Grisey, Gérard. | Composers—France—Biography.
Classification: LCC ML410.G923 B76 2023 (print) | LCC ML410.G923 (ebook) | DDC 780.92—dc23/eng/20230224
LC record available at https://lccn.loc.gov/2023008412
LC ebook record available at https://lccn.loc.gov/2023008413

A catalogue record for this title is available from the British Library.

For my two grandmothers,
Mary Barber and Dorothy Brown

"I see nothing but infinities."
—Blaise Pascal, *Pensées* (1670)

Contents

List of Illustrations ... ix
Acknowledgments ... xi
1 The Lost Voice (1946–61) ... 1
2 The Carnal Shell (1961–65) ... 11
3 The Rhythm of Love (1965–67) ... 28
4 Exchange Beyond Language (1968–70) ... 46
5 The Silence that Attracts (1970–72) ... 70
6 The Sensual Embrace (1972–74) ... 92
7 Ultimate Fusion (1974–78) ... 108
8 Astarte (1978–79) ... 125
9 Extreme Pleasure, Extreme Pain (1980–82) ... 147
10 The Grains of Sound (1982–86) ... 171
11 Absolute Love (1986–88) ... 203
12 Seduced by the Star (1988–91) ... 218
13 Suggestions of the Infinite (1991–96) ... 231
14 Nut (1996–98) ... 258
15 Berceuse ... 276
   Appendix ... 281
   Bibliography ... 283
   Index ... 297

Illustrations

Illustrations follow p. 138

1. Grisey with his first Hohner accordion.
2. Grisey as an altar boy.
3. Grisey in his accordion-soloist days.
4. Grisey in his room at Sainte-Marie de Monceau in Paris, ca. 1965.
5. Grisey and Jocelyne Simon at their wedding on June 26, 1970, at the Institution Sainte-Marie in Anthony, a suburb of Paris.
6. Grisey and France Detry with Raphaël and Detry's son Renaud in Brittany, ca. 1989.
7. Grisey (on vacation in Italy with France Detry), ca. 1990.
8. Sommeliers Gérard and Raphäel Grisey uncorking a rare vintage.
9. Grisey (on vacation in Morocco with Mireille Deguy), ca. 1992.
10. Gérards Grisey and Zinsstag at the thermal baths in Vals, Switzerland, ca. 1996.

Acknowledgments

It takes a village. I'm so grateful to all the people who supported this project over the last four years. Without them, *The Life and Music of Gérard Grisey* could not exist.

This biography would not have been possible without the essential scholarship of Guy Lelong, Jérôme Baillet, Liam Cagney, François-Xavier Féron, Jonathan Goldman, and many others. I hope *The Life and Music of Gérard Grisey* lives up to the high standards of their work.

I was lucky to receive a grant from the Robert B. Silvers Foundation at the very beginning of this project, allowing me to conduct interviews in person and providing valuable encouragement. The Paul Sacher Foundation generously awarded me a two-month research scholarship to live in Basel while doing archival research. I'm particularly grateful to Angela Ida De Benedictis and Michèle Noirjean, who led me through Grisey's archives and patiently helped me decipher the composer's frequently baffling handwriting. I'd also like to thank Marianne Diessner, who was an invaluable help with logistics during this busy time.

My composition teachers Reinhard Febel and Georg Friedrich Haas encouraged me to dive deeper into Gérard Grisey's music when the only thing I knew about it was that I liked it.

My colleagues at *VAN Magazine* are an inexhaustible source of inspiration. I'm especially grateful to Hartmut Welscher, who took a risk on me as a music journalist when few other people would have, and Olivia Giovetti, whose hard work allowed me to take time off to write this book.

I am endlessly indebted to all the interviewees who participated in this project. If I came to understand Gérard Grisey the man—even incompletely—it is thanks to them. I am especially grateful to Jocelyne Grisey, Raphaël Grisey, France Detry, Mireille Deguy, and Gérard Zinsstag, all of whom welcomed me into their homes and spent hours answering intimate questions with candor and insight.

The team at the University of Rochester Press—Sonia Kane, Ralph P. Locke, Chris Adler-France, Julia Cook, and Laurence Cole—have been a joy to work with. They have also improved the book immeasurably; I'm humbled that they believed in it.

Carine Kuntz, Laura Knoops, Teadrak Kongsombut, Boris Kauhl, Fritz Wiemann, Conrad Winslow, Michael Amico, Yair Klartag, Arash Yazdani,

William Dougherty, Ryan Beppel, Andrew Trovato, Madeline Warner, Alex Piasente, Noémi Makkos, Maria Kallionpää, Luis Velasco-Pufleau, Jay Schwartz, Oliver Liedloff, Noel Schneider, Jared Carl Millan, my sister Zoe Brown, and many more have been sources of moral support, inspiration, care, and kindness in the years I've spent absorbed in this project. I couldn't have written *The Life and Music of Gérard Grisey* without each of them.

Finally, I would like to thank my parents, Peter Brown and Jennifer Barber. They spent countless hours improving this book, expertly editing the text several times over and giving me invaluable advice on questions as small as commas and as large as form. Most importantly, they have always believed in me.

Chapter One

The Lost Voice (1946–61)

In the daytime, the French town of Belfort is luminescent. The small squares and narrow streets of the old center glow from the pale pink sandstone mined from the nearby Vosges mountains. The sandstone gives the whole sleepy, provincial town an otherworldly atmosphere. Belfort feels like a place out of time, a sense heightened by the slow speech and lilting accent of its people.

The calmness of current-day Belfort, in the eastern region of Franche-Comté near the Swiss border, belies its martial history, a function of its strategic position between iterations of French, German, and Austrian power. Monuments to heroic deeds in times of war can be found around almost every corner and on every square. Towering over the city, visible from nearly everywhere in the old town, is the citadel of Belfort, made of the same Vosges sandstone found below.

On November 3, 1870, Prussian forces led by General Udo von Treskow surrounded Belfort. His French counterpart, Aristide Denfert-Rochereau, declined an offer to surrender. The siege of Belfort that resulted lasted through a brutal winter, and the city eventually fell to the Prussians, on February 18, 1871. The Belfort garrison had held out for an astonishing 103 days. In 1880, the Alsatian sculptor Frédéric-Auguste Bartholdi, who also made the Statue of Liberty in New York Harbor, completed his *Lion de Belfort* in commemoration of the siege. It is built out of the same luminescent sandstone which comprises the fort itself.

Further monuments to Belfortian bravery abound in the city. In 1993, Belfort dedicated a sculpture and the Place Anne Frank to the liberation of the Jewish victims of the Nazis and their Vichy collaborators in World War II. The sculpture shows a man, his head held high, his arms spread, his chains broken. Gérard Grisey's father, whose bravery in the face of mortal danger fits well into the history of this town, played a part in the liberation of France. This, in turn, shaped the composer's earliest artistic and psychological development.

CHAPTER ONE

On June 19, 1940, the Nazi tank unit Guderian thundered into Belfort and occupied the city. Throughout World War II, Resistance fighters in the region attempted to sabotage Nazi logistical sites. Frequently they were caught. One hundred prisoners of war from the Resistance were executed by firing squad at the Nazi-controlled fort in nearby Besançon and, after liberation, the bodies of murdered partisans were found throughout the region. In all of France, the number of executed Resistance fighters has been estimated at between 12,000 and 20,000.[1]

According to family lore, these were the risks that Jules Henri Grisey braved as a member of the Resistance. Born on June 11, 1899, to a family of farmers, Jules Henri was raised by his mother and three older sisters. His own father was largely absent. Jules Henri didn't have much chance to enjoy his childhood: he left school at age twelve to provide for the women, working on farms and often sleeping in barnyards. After joining the Resistance, he participated in train robberies and bridge sabotage operations against Nazi logistical sites. One family story, later recalled by Grisey's wife Jocelyne Simon, involves Jules Henri sheltering a German deserter from the Wehrmacht.[2] In another, which Grisey told Simon and his son Raphaël, Jules Henri found himself in a village with several other Resistance operatives. He had to leave briefly, and when he returned, every single one of his comrades had been arrested.[3] It was a story that burned itself into Gérard Grisey's psyche. Much later, he had a vivid dream, which melded this story with the impression that his father had committed a terrible crime:

> Trial in a large room full of people. Twenty death sentences. Defendants scattered everywhere, mostly men. One woman, however, with what is perhaps her child. Two of the men have committed a murder. [Among them] a man of a certain age (like an adventurer) and my father ... I try to prove that he was in the Resistance; this may help with a presidential pardon. I look at all these men who will die tomorrow morning.[4]

Jules Henri's narrow escape from the Nazis may be apocryphal—like many of the war stories that wend their way through generations. But it made a primal impression on Gérard Grisey, providing an essential clue to his relationship with his father.

The diaries of a Belfort citizen give a sense of the knife-edge danger prevalent in the city shortly before Gérard Grisey's birth in 1946. "The nights

---

1   Fenby, *The History of Modern France*, 310.
2   Interview with Jocelyne Grisey, who is introduced in Chapter Three. Jocelyne Grisey still has a knife with a swastika on it, which the deserter presumably gave to Jules Henri.
3   Interview with Raphaël and Jocelyne Grisey.
4   Paul Sacher archive.

have become noisy," the anonymous chronicler wrote. "The patrols are shooting and killing. The railway is heavily guarded. Very young German soldiers, insufficiently in control of themselves, are standing guard. Every night, before we get ready to go to bed, there's a ceaseless racket of weaponry and exploding grenades."[5] The last few months of the German occupation of Belfort were among the most brutal, with widespread deprivation and extortion. However, the Allies were making progress across France, and, in late November 1944, the First French Army under General Charpentier liberated Belfort. The first Allied regiment to enter the city was a unit of Moroccan soldiers, nicknamed *les chocs*. A young Gérard Grisey later wrote of seeing "two young Algerians speaking in their language" in Belfort—were they actually the children of Moroccan soldiers, like him the offspring of parents who had fought for liberation?

Belfort, the perennial site of Franco-Prussian competition, was also the last refuge of officials from the collaborationist Vichy regime in France; in the fall of 1944, the Allies drove them out of the country. The victorious General Charles de Gaulle was swept into power, beginning a period known as *Les Trente Glorieuses*, the Thirty Glorious Years. And while this period was full of political scandal, moral stagnation, and colonialist violence perpetrated by French forces, most prominently in Algeria, it was also a period of state-powered economic growth, with concurrent gains in equality and quality of life. De Gaulle

> presided over an extraordinary swing to the left. ... The state took over the commanding heights of industry and finance. The welfare system was substantially expanded and access to credit was reorganized to better serve social needs. Measures to encourage families were introduced, boosting the population by 3 million in ten years.[6]

Jules Henri Grisey was married to another woman when he met Lucie Monna. Monna was married, too: her husband was a Frenchman of Italian origin named Pierre Frédéric Lanza. Like Grisey, Lanza fought in the Resistance. But Lanza had been captured by the Nazis and brought to a labor camp in Berlin. Monna probably feared the worst. Lanza eventually returned to Belfort; still, Monna stayed with Grisey and divorced her first husband.

Monna and Lanza had a daughter named Josienne. She was about nine years old when her mother met Jules Henri Grisey. Josienne found him kind, but refused to call him *papa*, settling on the variation *pépé* instead. (She

---

5   Bischoff and Pagnot: *Belfort, 1307–2007*.
6   Fenby, *The History of Modern France*, 319.

also kept Lanza's name.) One day, out of the blue, Monna announced to Josienne that she now had a little brother.[7]

It all happened very fast. Gérard Henri Grisey was born on June 17, 1946, around 7 p.m.[8] On September 28, 1946, Jules Henri Grisey and Lucie Monna were married. This was a necessary step, as Gérard Grisey would have been considered an illegitimate child during the first three months of his life. Jules Henri, a tall, stern-looking man, was forty-seven when his son was born; Monna, an elegant, tanned woman with precisely set brown hair, was thirty-nine.

The Griseys made their home in the rue d'Offemont, in the village of Éloie, about twenty minutes by bus from the center of Belfort. The rue d'Offemont winds up from the small center of the village, cutting into a landscape of forests and misty ponds, ideal settings for a child's enigmatic games. Today, the occasional shot from hunters rings out in the quiet. It's a beautiful but probably somewhat lonely place.

Jules Henri Grisey opened a garage called Renov'Accu that specialized in car batteries. He repaired vehicles and Monna helped with the bookkeeping. The new family lived in a two-story house with the garage and a small gas station on the bottom floor, and an apartment above it, beneath a slanted roof. In an undated photograph, taken on a sunny day, the house looks cozy and bright, with a white-and-red color scheme, the flowers on the balcony in full bloom.

Jules Henri didn't like to talk about his experiences in the war. But there is some evidence he was traumatized by what he had seen. Gérard Grisey described his father as an angry man whose fits could involve hurled hammers. One time, the little boy broke one of Josienne Lanza's treasured dolls; she started hitting her new brother in retaliation. Jules Henri settled the dispute by throwing the doll into the fire.[9] In another rage, Jules Henri threw out all young Gérard's toys—a story the composer frequently repeated. Monna, whom Grisey called Mammalou, was strict. She insisted that her son be clean and well-mannered even as a small child; she liked to dress him in elaborate outfits and curl his pretty blond hair. "His hair was beautiful, mine was terrible," Josienne Lanza said, a trace of jealousy in her voice, nearly eighty years later.[10] She loved him, but sometimes felt that he was the favored child.

---

7   Interview with Lanza.
8   Birth certificate from the city of Belfort.
9   Interview with Lanza.
10 Ibid.

Lucie Monna treated Gérard "like a little doll."[11] Every Sunday, the Griseys would go to a local café, and Gérard would be forced to sit around while "the grownups drank, talked, ate."[12] One of Grisey's girlfriends, France Detry, remembered of Monna: "She was not an affectionate mother. I remember her nails. She had nails like an eagle. Claws. She was not a tender person, not at all. This is probably the reason why Gérard was looking for tenderness in every woman."[13] But Grisey cared deeply for his parents. In a journal entry from when Grisey was eighteen years old, he wrote, "From my mother, I got my extraordinary sensitivity and a certain delicacy. From my father, I got intelligence and a passionate character, always focused on the goal. I love them both, of course, but feel closer to my mother: the harshness of my father takes away my confidence."[14] Crucially, Grisey's parents supported him when it came to the big decisions, especially his pursuit of music.

The family member to whom Grisey felt closest was his maternal grandmother, Anastasie Eugénie Marie Poulot. Poulot was always around during the workday to watch the children. She had a beautiful singing voice. In two later, undated written fragments, Grisey described a connection between his earliest memories of his grandmother and his subsequent love of music. In the first version, writing in the third person, Grisey described himself as a "blond and pale little boy," the sole listener to his grandmother's songs. She provided a safe haven against "the violence of his father, the exigencies of his mother, and the indifference of his sister." One day, his grandmother disappears from her bed. He can't hear her voice, and he is without refuge in the Belfort winter, "a desert of ice." Music is his only consolation. "For the first time," Grisey realizes, "the music of the sacred and the erotic, of the inaccessible and the tender, are united."[15] In these four terms, Grisey defined his calling as an artist.

In the second draft of this memoir about his grandmother, Grisey wrote maybe the most incisive extant portrait of his childhood. Vivid and painful, reminiscent of Marcel Proust's description of losing his own grandmother, the short essay is also imbued with a real sense of the magical possibilities of sound:[16]

---

11   Interview with Raphaël and Jocelyne Grisey. Raphaël, Grisey's only child, was born in 1979. See Chapter Eight.
12   Interview with Detry. Detry, who met Grisey during his time teaching at the University of California at Berkeley, is introduced in Chapter Ten.
13   Ibid.
14   Paul Sacher archive.
15   Lelong, *Écrits*, 411.
16   The musicologist Liam Cagney first noted Grisey's talent as a writer. "Synthesis and Deviation," 86.

At night, a little boy can't fall asleep. He is afraid. He calls out to his grandmother, who is sleeping in the next room. She answers him. He calls out again. She answers. He continues the game, thinking that she will get tired. But no, he hears the voice answering until sleep takes him. In the evening, maybe at night too, he hears the cries, the hoarse breathing, the wheezes.

They come from his parents' bed. He is afraid at night.

In the daytime, he sees blood on towels. Blood means you're sick ...

Thus there is a violence of the daytime and a violence of the nighttime ...

But in the daytime, seated in his grandmother's lap, he listens to her sing. She is nearly blind, she is melancholy, but she sings very well. She is absolute, limitless love, tenderness that will last forever, that will always protect him from father's violence and mother's demands. (When he is to be punished, he takes refuge behind a big armchair, a place of infinite protection.)

Thus there is a tenderness of the daytime and a tenderness of the nighttime ... A sound for the day, and a sound for the night ...

Later, with the accordion he got for Christmas, he reproduces the songs he hears from his grandmother, imitating them as best he can.

One day, his grandmother doesn't get out of bed. He paces around and looks at her pale, drawn face. He is told to embrace her and be silent. The voice loses its expression. They aren't speaking, they are whispering ...

Later they retreat to the countryside. When they return, he gathers a bouquet of wildflowers for his sick grandmother. They enter the house. Immediately, he runs to the end of the corridor and opens the last door on the left.

The bed is empty and unmade.

He takes refuge in the bathroom and stays a long while, his forehead pressed against the wall. He must be pulled away, then it is explained to him that all the people are in black because grandmother is in the sky.

After a long time, he plays the songs again.

"If only your grandmother could hear you!" his mother tells him.

Winter comes. Where is that voice? Where is that special tenderness, that place of infinite safety? The cold is everywhere, and nothing can protect him.

Soon his father punishes him more harshly that he could have imagined: no more toys; the shelves are cleaned out and remain empty. An unprecedented violence has devastated his world.

All his dreams have been annihilated except the magical sounds of his accordion.

Then he gets sick. Ear infection. Three times, they mutilate his ear with a needle. Violence, again and again, forever. He screams, so does his father. Until he weakens. His father feels sorry for him, his mother fusses over him, both fear for his life.

When he feels better, he writes big notes on music paper, because he's been told that's how to make sound permanent. He plays, he writes, he plays, he writes, but his teacher tells him, smiling, that what he writes doesn't correspond to what he plays and that he has a lot to learn.

So he learns, because he knows that only the magic of sound will ever be able to evoke the lost voice.[17]

The large armchair where Grisey's grandmother would sit, behind which the child hid, is still in the possession of Mireille Deguy, who was Grisey's girlfriend at the end of his life.[18] It's gray-beige, and tassels hang down from its front. It's easily large enough for a child to hide behind; a small boy could even have crawled beneath it to disappear.

Grisey never forgot the violence of the medical intervention on his ears. For his friend, the composer Julian Anderson, a series of attacks from Grisey's piece *Dérives* (1973–74) are a musical recreation of this traumatic ear infection.[19] The full orchestra plays cutting chords, the textures made jagged by harmonics, distorted electric guitar, and groaning strings. On the thirty-first attack, the winds create a "*sss*" sound, like parents comforting a suffering child. This passage is followed by complete silence and immobility.

It's impossible to know whether, as a young boy, Grisey truly thought about music the way he described it as an adult. The memoir-essay above has a hint of exaggeration or, as the musicologist Liam Cagney has written, the retroactive myth-making that can result from psychoanalysis.[20] Nevertheless, as Grisey's later diary entries showed, his relationship to music was always profound. It was his way of smuggling love across the boundary between life and death.

When Grisey was four and a half or five years old, he begged his parents for an accordion. They obliged him with a small cardboard instrument.[21] Delicate, with a red rim and ornamented blue sides, it made—and still makes—a sound. Grisey, however, was adamant that he wanted a real

---

17   Lelong, *Écrits*, 369. The text is also available in the Paul Sacher Stiftung archives. My translation.
18   Deguy, whom Grisey met in 1991, is introduced in Chapter Thirteen.
19   Interview with Julian Anderson, who became friends with Grisey in the 1990s. "Just a thought," he said, but the connection is convincing.
20   Cagney, "Synthesis and Deviation," 78.
21   Raphaël Grisey still has the instrument.

accordion; he threw the cardboard one out the window.[22] So Grisey's parents bought him a new instrument. It dwarfed his body.

Grisey's first accordion teacher was a local popular performer named Rudi Valli. Grisey quickly showed an impressive aptitude for the instrument. As a headline in the local newspaper boasted, "Gérard Grisey, Five Years Old, Plays 'The Blue Danube' On His Accordion."[23] It's even possible Grisey learned to read music notation before he learned the alphabet.[24] Years later, in 1961, as Grisey began seriously considering music as a career, he bought a professional-quality Hohner Morino piano accordion from Valli for 2,300 francs.[25]

Grisey always associated the accordion with his humble origins. But, for the musicologist Jonathan Goldman, the instrument strongly influenced his early musical development.[26] Certain acoustic properties of the accordion would later make their mark on Grisey's mature compositional style. These include the accordion's characteristic decay; the way the instrument's chords meld and the dynamic swells that enliven its sound; the respiratory rhythms of its bellows; and its two distinct sound sources, reflected in the composer's interest in musical space.[27] William Schimmel, an accordionist Grisey met later in Philadelphia, agrees with Goldman about the importance of the instrument for Grisey. "I really believe that the accordion greatly influenced his composition philosophies," he said. "I can attest to the fact that the accordion can function as a 'composing oracle'—it contains everything one needs."[28]

Grisey attended elementary school at the Institution Sainte-Marie in central Belfort, in the Faubourg des Ancêtres, overlooking the Savoureuse river that runs narrowly through the town. The squat schoolhouse building, its entrance watched over by a small statue of its namesake in an alcove, is of the same pale pink color of Vosges sandstone as so much of the rest of the city. This school was run by a Catholic order known as the Marianists, a group founded on the heels of the French Revolution, which pitted the monarchist church against the secularist uprising.[29] The Institution Sainte-Marie in Belfort opened in November 1875, in the wake of the Franco-Prussian

---

22 Interview with Detry.
23 Raphaël Grisey has the clipping.
24 Interview with Raphaël and Jocelyne Grisey.
25 Goldman, "Gérard Grisey, Accordionist," 14.
26 Ibid, 23.
27 The point about dynamic swells is a little less convincing because swells are very common in twentieth-century music.
28 Interview with Schimmel.
29 The Marianists, "A Short History."

war. The school originally served as a refuge from the Prussian occupation. According to an official history, "By entrusting their children to the Marianist order, the families, all from Alsace, were expressing in a spirit of resistance their attachment to the French language and culture which were prohibited at that time in the occupied territories."[30] In this way, too, the perpetual conflicts between France and Germany permeated the atmosphere of Grisey's youth.

Although Grisey's parents were not fervently religious, the choice of a Catholic institution made sense in a city recovering from the trauma of World War II. Many—though far from all—French Catholics had been active in the Resistance, which gave the formerly monarchist church a new political legitimacy in De Gaulle's Fourth Republic. Catholicism became associated not just with the spiritual, but also with the material salvation of the working class to which Jules Henri belonged. There was a renewed association between Catholicism and intellectual inquiry in the country, with a flourishing of religious-philosophical journals and the elevation of Catholic artists and thinkers such as the paleontologist, theologian, and writer Pierre Teilhard de Chardin and the poet Paul Claudel, figures who became vital inspirations in Grisey's teenage years. For those searching for moral guidance after the horrors of Vichy France, religion became an attractive beacon.[31]

Cagney discovered an academic yearbook in Grisey's archives that gives a sense of the faith-oriented atmosphere at the Institution Sainte-Marie. A notice reminds parents of "their responsibility to maintain their children's spiritual life during the summer holidays," and the yearbook includes a chronicle of events that took place during the third term, such as "a retreat for students to the Abbey of Notre-Dame d'Acey," as Cagney notes.[32] Because Grisey's parents were not religious, it seems likely that his ardent Catholic faith first blossomed at the Institution Sainte-Marie, where belief and education went hand in hand.

The yearbook Cagney unearthed also attests to the young Grisey's scholastic aptitude. In the 1956–57 school year, when he was ten and eleven, Grisey received the equivalent of A grades in religion, French, written composition, reading, recitation, history, and geography, with his only Bs in math and spelling. Though, as Grisey later told it, he never seriously considered becoming anything other than a composer, he would not have lacked for options. His wide-ranging intelligence did influence his aesthetic development: Grisey remained a voracious reader his entire life, with a vivid interest

---

30 Institution Sainte Marie de Belfort, "Historique."
31 Godin, "French Catholic Intellectuals and the Nation," 45–46.
32 Cagney, "Synthesis and Deviation," 87.

in all kinds of subjects, many of which flowed subtly yet decisively into his musical output.

Grisey made his first forays into composition at a remarkably young age. The earliest surviving score, from 1955, when he was nine, is titled *Fête en Alsace* (*Alsatian Celebration*).[33] Grisey decorated the manuscript in yellow, blue, red, and green pen, writing proudly at the bottom: "This score was written by G. Grisey, age nine." A simple piece—probably for accordion—it contains two sections, one an attenuated, descending line in C major, the other a livelier melody in F major. The phrases are in clean, periodic structures of eight, sixteen, and thirty-two bars, and the melodic writing shows an understanding of the fundamental tonal principle of secondary dominants. In other words, the piece displays a basic grasp of musical structure, impressive in a nine-year-old. His writing is childlike but clear, including the "big notes" mentioned in his essay on the death of his grandmother.

In December 1957, the now eleven-year-old Grisey completed his next piece, again likely for accordion (or piano).[34] Titled *Merlin*, it is also in C major, using the simplest chords in tonal music. Like *Fête en Alsace*, the melody is enriched by occasional passing tones. It also includes slightly more rhythmic complexity, with dotted quarter-eighth note patterns giving the thirty-five-bar piece a bouncy flair.

The following August, Grisey completed the first draft of an *Étude harmonique*, a third C major study with a repeating, sixteen-bar bass line, harmonized with slightly more complex tonal chords than in the previous two pieces. Grisey practiced a simple modulation, into A minor, and explored parallel motion in the two voices, while still making a beginner's classic mistakes in voice leading: parallel octaves. (He revised the piece in September 1961, as a fifteen-year-old.)

Grisey was a talented young composer. But he did not belong to that class of prodigies who seem to effortlessly grasp the refinements of tonal style, improvising works at the piano in the manner of, say, early Mozart.[35] The effort necessary in his early years would prove useful to him later. In his late teens, he would more easily break free of classical idioms, testing the waters of contemporary music through promising early compositions.

---

33 Paul Sacher archive.
34 Ibid.
35 For example, the young composer Alma Deutscher.

Chapter Two

The Carnal Shell (1961–65)

As an adult, Grisey made frequent notes describing his dreams and state of mind. These jottings are often impossible to read. When they are legible, they offer valuable insights into his psychology. One such document, undated though likely from the mid-1990s,[1] contains what seems to be a list of the desires and fears that motivated his id, in his own perception (or that of a psychoanalyst):

- Rivalry with and imitation of my father
- Fear of solitude (death of my grandmother), fear of death
- A taste for pleasure, discovery, beauty
- Substitution of one woman for another (if not pornography, fantasies, images)
- A taste for risk, challenges, exceeding one's limits (going all the way)
- A taste for play and the good things in life
- Fear of homosexuality (= violence)[2]

The first item on the list is classically Freudian. The fourth item, Grisey's awareness of his own need to be surrounded by women, will become relevant, both biographically and musically, in his adult life. To the contemporary reader, it is Grisey's "fear of homosexuality," and the "equals violence," that raises questions about his childhood.

But none of Grisey's many friends, lovers, and confidants could recall the composer mentioning that violence had been done to him. His written archives make no further mention of any such traumatic event. Guy Lelong,

---

1 In 1993, Grisey began seeing a psychoanalyst regularly.
2 Paul Sacher Stiftung archive.

a writer and openly gay friend of Grisey's later in the composer's life, said that Grisey was not at all homophobic.[3]

The abstract idea of rape makes the occasional appearance in Grisey's journals and in his writings on music. In one diary entry from the early 1980s, he wrote in a mysterious poem, "The Unknown rapes me."[4] In his 1982 article "Le devenir des sons" ("The Becoming of Sound"), he said that "musical form has something terrifying about it: it contains voyeurism and rape ... ."[5] He was pointing out that if we don't want to see an image, we can close our eyes; if we don't want to hear a sound, we can't close our ears, because they don't have lids. Sound penetrates us whether we consent to it or not. Like sex, sound is a pleasurable experience that must be entered into willingly. Otherwise, this experience is distorted into violence. Throughout his life, Grisey was extremely sensitive to unwanted noise.

🌿 🌿 🌿

Grisey finished his studies up to one year before the *baccalauréat* at the Collège St. Marie, where the upper classes of the Institution Sainte Marie were taught. A certificate from the Académie de Besançon, the governing educational body for the region of Franche-Comté, dated June 20, 1961, confirms his achievement of the *Brevet d'études*. He also took additional courses in French literature at a school called the École Universelle.[6] He seems to have been a good student.[7] But by this age—just fifteen—Grisey had already decided he wanted to become a musician, which probably explains the paucity of information preserved about his non-musical studies.[8]

Grisey kept a diary between 1961 and 1966.[9] This text gives great insight into his inner life, while all but ignoring practical details. The handwriting is conscientious throughout—the correct cursive of the French student—and the journal has two epigraphs on the inside cover. "To the one whom I learned to love," reads the first, referring to God. "How wonderful it is to live! / And how immense is the glory of God! / But how wonderful it is as well / To die when the time is right," reads the second. These two quotations summarize the main themes that preoccupied Grisey throughout his

---

3   Interview with Lelong.
4   Paul Sacher archive.
5   Lelong, *Écrits*, 31–39.
6   Hohner-Konservatorium archive.
7   Interview with Jocelyne Grisey.
8   Ibid.
9   All quotations from Grisey's diary are from the Paul Sacher Stiftung archives unless marked otherwise.

youth: his relationship with God and the Catholic Church; his first experiences of falling in love; and his rather romantic idea of death.

The second epigraph reflects Grisey's fascination with the idea of martyrdom. The quotation is from *La jeune fille Violaine* (1892), a play by Paul Claudel that explores the ideas of intention and sacrifice.[10] The teenage Grisey returned continually to the necessity of self-sacrifice in his diary. "I will consecrate myself to music," he wrote in February 1962. "It will be my life, my goal, my best way of serving God." The necessity of giving oneself up to God dovetailed with his musical aspirations. He would repeat this sentiment often, as if following the extortion of Psalm 150: "Praise Him with the ram's horn's blast / praise Him with the lute and lyre. Praise Him with the timbrel and dance, / praise Him with the strings and flute."[11] For the young Grisey, music and God were two sides of the same coin.

By the time Grisey began his journal in 1961, his Catholicism was fully formed. As mentioned, he didn't get his fervent religion from his parents. Lucie Monna and Jules Henri Grisey sent both children to church, but more out of social obligation than religious feeling. Josienne stopped going as soon as she could.[12] Grisey was a genuine believer, as his diary proves. A photo from his confirmation shows the boy, age thirteen or fourteen, in an elegant robe, with a beatific expression on his face.[13]

Grisey's Catholicism could be dogmatic. In June 1964, he wrote:

> My parents aren't Christians: they were both divorced before they remarried. Therefore, I'm from a sinful union, and I often have the intuition that my life will be no more than an immense martyrdom for their mistakes! My religious education doesn't come from them, and I've suffered a lot from their incomprehension concerning this and their lack of instruction and, in particular, their lack of idealism.

At the very beginning of his journal, this Catholicism made an early adolescent crush more complicated. From a distance, in silence, he fell in love with a girl from church. His notion of relationships was idealistic. "I dream of a girl who knows how to understand me, who loves me for my work, my music," he wrote in January 1961. "A man and a woman who walk, side by side, hand in hand, toward a goal, toward a powerful ideal. With the purity of my youth, its happiness, its triumphs ... we will love one another in Christ."

---

10 Société Paul Claudel, "La jeune fille Violaine."
11 From Robert Alter's translation of the Hebrew Bible.
12 Interview with Lanza.
13 Photograph in the private archives of Lanza.

Grisey continued to compose works of juvenilia. Between 1960 and 1961, he wrote a brief *Fuge en sol mineur*, a thirty-eight-bar piece for piano in two voices.[14] Stylistically, it's closer to a Baroque invention than a fugue. Despite a few minor outliers—for instance, an improper melodic resolution and a final phrase in awkward octaves—the study shows a good grasp of the basics of the genre. His theme contains a striking downward fifth motive which serves as an effective aural marker. The piece shows obvious competence and potential, but Grisey later crossed out his dating of the work, writing in pencil over it: *Nul*. His perfectionist streak was already emerging.

In 1962, as a sixteen-year-old, Grisey's main preoccupations—God, sacrifice, music, purity, and love—were increasingly worked out in his diary. He devoted very little space to the trials of daily life, instead cultivating a self-image as a tormented, sensitive artist. From a line in September 1962, in which Grisey admonished himself to "love those who mock you," it appears he was bullied at school. "Sometimes, I ask myself if I wasn't born to be a martyr," he wrote. "I'm overwhelmed by injustice, mockery, pettiness, to the point where I'm beginning to doubt my personal courage. Yes, I'm not sure of anything anymore ..." He continued to look to the writings of Claudel for solace. In a diary entry from December 1962, Grisey copied out the entirety of Claudel's rhapsody "Sainte Cécile," about the patron saint of musicians. Grisey observed, "Oh, P. Claudel! You knew so well to tell us that youth is made for heroism and not for pleasure."

Grisey's struggle with the competing demands of "purity" and puberty continued throughout 1962. By secular standards, Grisey was harsh with himself about his thoroughly normal sexual awakening: "My God! Me, who thought that purity was solidly established in my soul! What temptations I still have! Even in my dreams! But I must not succumb; no, I do not want to be like other men." He channeled his schoolboy crush into somewhat purple language, calling a girl's eyes "mirrors of purity." In October 1962, Grisey reflected on Alain-Fournier's classic sentimental novel *Le Grand Meaulnes*. In the novel, a schoolboy gets lost while riding in a carriage, and ends up at a strange, fairytale-like wedding, where he falls in love with a mysterious girl. After he departs, he is unable to find the castle again, and despairs.[15] This was the part of the book that Grisey enjoyed, writing, "We see a young girl, once, and we search for her ceaselessly. She occupies all our thoughts. We have no rest until we see her again, until we speak to her ... we love her!" Grisey was less interested in the second half of the novel, in which Meaulnes finds the girl again and marries her. The character is unable to settle down, instead disappearing in search of ceaseless adventures.

---

14   Paul Sacher archive.
15   Alan-Fournier, *Le Grand Meaulnes*.

From the very beginning of his diary, Grisey intended to become a musician. That resolution hardened in 1962: "It's done. The die is cast. I'm throwing myself into music." He worked on several pieces that year.[16] Between February and June, he composed a Prélude in C-sharp Minor for accordion. In what seems like an attempt to sound like Chopin, Grisey opens the work with a C-sharp minor chord in eighth notes: a descending melody clashes satisfyingly with the root of the chord. In comparison to Grisey's surviving pieces from the late 1950s, the Prélude shows more care in its dynamics and tempi. A fifty-nine-bar Andante Maestoso is followed by an *allegretto* section, with fast sixteenth notes in the right hand and a simple, blocky chordal accompaniment in the left. Grisey wrote out the names of the chords beneath them, indicating his youthful process of familiarization with the most basic materials of tonal music. While the score to the Prélude shows hints of Grisey the later, perfectionistic artist—there are visible revisions on the manuscript—the work did not yet display the easy familiarity with tonality that Grisey achieved in time for his professional education.

The same year, Grisey composed a *Petit Caprice* in A Major for two accordions, a work he dedicated to his mother. A simple and somewhat inorganic set of variations on a childlike eight-bar melody, the piece still shows flashes of promise, especially one variation in which the motives of the tune are broken down and passed between the accordions. The section would not be out of place in an early Haydn string quartet. But the most mature piece of these years is a set of three Études for accordion, which he began in June 1962 and probably finished in early 1963. Each movement is characteristic: the first is a Perpetuum Mobile in E minor; the second, an Andante with an undulating inner line; and the third, a Religioso piece and probably the most memorable of the set. It contains a simple two-bar phrase in A minor which resolves in a manner familiar from Bach—an idea which, when repeated and developed by the composer, could get stuck in our heads. Grisey was making rapid progress. Compared to the Prélude and the *Petit Caprice*, the Études show increasing competence and comfort in a tonal idiom.

In June 1962, Grisey wrote endearingly, "I can't prevent myself from thinking of O. Messiaen and J.S. Bach, these men who understood that music is about more than just making a lot of money" (as if anyone became a classical composer to get rich). Grisey made specific notes on Bach's Magnificat in D Major, BWV 243, a brightly contrapuntal work for choir and orchestra that Grisey called a "pure marvel," saying it gave him visions of the City of Zion.

A journal entry from January 1963 shows that Grisey's Belfort education was somewhat provincial. "I finished *The Diary of Anne Frank*," he wrote.

---

16 Paul Sacher archive.

"What an extraordinary young girl! And here I was thinking that purity and moral bravery were only possible among Christians!" Whether or not the discovery that Jews can be brave played a role, in 1963 religious doubts began creeping with increasingly regularity into Grisey's diary. In February, he wrote, "I realized with terror that I don't know how to pray anymore." He criticized what he saw as the superficial, materialistic Christianity as practiced by the "working classes." Yet, when he was sad or lonely, Grisey still turned to God, writing prayers in his diary.

Grisey continued to try and reconcile what he was taught about sexual sinfulness with his infatuations. In January 1963, he wrote, "I think I'm going crazy, because I've fallen in love with two girls at the same time!" A diary entry from February 1963 shows Grisey's nascent hedonistic side, which he would embrace as an adult. It also gives us a hint as to why his music is so deeply grounded in the perceptive capabilities of the human body. Maybe Grisey was able to invent such sensual music because he knew the denial of the body so intimately and was drawn to an alternative:

> How beautiful a woman's body is! I always end up mute from admiration when I see one of those statues in the Renaissance style which depict the beauty of the body ... I also admire the strength and power that resides in the male body, but not with the same ardor; that's normal. God created man with a body and a soul and I simply wish for the body to be guided by the fingertips of the soul, for the body to give thanks to the soul. Why bully the body? Why crush it? Perfect happiness exists only in the perfect harmony and union of body and soul. God created a carnal shell for man, which is beautiful and worthy of admiration.[17]

Maybe this early grappling with the topic of sensuality allowed Grisey to refuse to "bully" or "crush" the ear in his mature music.

On April 18, 1963, Grisey went on his first date. The journal entry is both joyous and abashed. Grisey wrote that he and the girl, named Bernadette, encountered a group of soldiers. Grisey became anxious that the soldiers were watching the teenagers on their romantic walk. In further diary entries, the young composer, seemingly irrational, agonized about the fact that someone might find out that he and Bernadette were dating, and admonished her when she told her friends about him. Faith was a part of his anxiety: he noted that Bernadette "lacked religious fervor," and wrote later that "flirting is a caricature of love." It also becomes obvious from Grisey's diary entries that Bernadette wasn't particularly interested in the classical music that gave his life meaning, despite Grisey's rhapsodizing about how wonderful it would be if they could share it.

---

17   Paul Sacher archive.

In May 1963, Grisey wrote, referring to his relationship with Bernadette, "It seems to me that our love won't be able to find its fulfillment, its sublimation, except in death, death in unison, like that of Tristan and Isolde or Pelléas and Mélisande." Throughout the year, he continued in this melodramatic vein. He longed for "the infinite tenderness of two beings who love each other, scattered in an unloving universe," and added, "How sweet it would be to die together!" In August, he wrote that he wanted to fall asleep in Bernadette's arms like a child hearing a lullaby. In September, Grisey recounted how a friend told him that he and Bernadette were from irreconcilable social and intellectual milieus. "Society! Society! This monster," he wrote, like so many sensitive teenagers throughout history. But Grisey acknowledged his own exaggerations in another diary entry. After writing that he longed for death, he compared himself to the unhappy old man in La Fontaine's fable: the man begs to die, so Death obliges. Then the man realizes he isn't ready—"Do not draw near, O Death!"—but it's too late.[18]

Meanwhile, in diary entries from the same year, Grisey showed a more specific engagement with individual compositions by masters of the art form. Rather than appealing to the power of music in general, he analyzed specific works through listening. Maurice Ravel became a role model. In an entry on the sweetly melancholic *Pavane pour une infante défunte* from 1899, Grisey wrote that the work reminded him of the Royal Monastery of San Lorenzo de El Escorial, outside Madrid, describing how, in his vivid imagination, a child danced in a black robe, and "the sun played across the gothic stained-glass windows." (It's not clear whether Grisey visited the site with his parents as a child, or, more likely, learned about it during his religious education.) Grisey also took notes on thematic variation in Nikolai Rimsky-Korsakov's *Scheherazade*, op. 35, and heard Richard Addinsel's *Concerto de Varsovie*, a piece in the style of Rachmaninoff, popular in World War II-era England.

April 1963 was the first time Grisey mentioned his own attempts at composition in his diary. He was beginning to wrestle with essential questions: How important is training versus inspiration? Could he compose first and learn the rules later? Did a working-class boy from Belfort have a chance at a career in classical music? "I have no knowledge in harmony, but I compose ... mental abnormality?" he wrote. "I know nothing. I write with my instrument; my compositions are like improvisations that I write down ... And what do I care about the rules, what do I care if my works are worth nothing! I write music that sounds beautiful to me and that's all that matters." Grisey's insistence on his right to pursue composition despite having no theoretical background soon faded, however. By September 1963, he

---

18 Jean La Fontaine, *Fables*.

had written that he had decided to wait, if impatiently, to learn music theory before pursuing composition in earnest.

On a hike that same month, Grisey saw a little lake in the mountains, which was "all black." He wondered if he would ever be able to express in music the lake's "surprising beauty." In the same diary entry, Grisey made an observation that appeared to prefigure his interest in human perception and sensuality as the foundation for his style of music. "I'm receptive to everything that strikes the senses!" he wrote. "Everything engraves itself on me, everything penetrates me, everything obsesses me ... The dead leaves at the foot of a wall, the sound of passing trucks, the taste of champagne, blasphemy ... I bathe in all of these as if they were my own blood." As a teenager, Grisey was on the path to understanding that perception is an anatomical system, a series of places in our bodies, and that he would have to compose with the needs and capacities of the human organism in mind.

In September 1963, Grisey also began lessons in harmony. Cagney has determined that these classes took place at what was then called the École Municipale de Musique de la Ville de Belfort, where Grisey studied with Richard Ciapolino, a composer and an ex-prisoner of war. Ciapolino described Grisey as a "down-to-earth student, friendly and full of talent, who displayed an extremely acute aptitude for music and composition."[19]

The same month, Grisey attended the Coupe mondiale, or world accordion championship, in the West German spa town of Baden-Baden. There he met a Canadian performer named Joseph Macerollo. The musicologist Jonathan Goldman describes the two as "drawn to each other by their growing disillusionment with the world of accordion competitions and what they perceived as the empty virtuosity that they fostered." Still, Grisey performed a flashy arrangement of Gershwin's *Rhapsody in Blue* for the occasion and got ninth place.[20]

In November 1963, Grisey wrote that he wanted to achieve "the precision and the mysticism of Bach, the sweetness and emotion of Chopin, the sensitivity and the finesse and the mysterious geometry of Ravel ... How much patience it'll take before I'm able to express myself and make myself understood using the magic of sounds." These three composers were Grisey's musical heroes, composers whose clarity, perfectionism, and sensuality echo in Grisey's adult works. As Grisey progressed more tangibly toward a musical career, he became aware of the societal and financial disadvantages he would need to overcome. "What difficulties!" he wrote later that month. "Sometimes I think that destiny herself is opposed to my musical career," and later, "I'm looking in vain for a guide." On December 30, 1963, on

---

19   Cagney, "Synthesis and Deviation," 89–90.
20   Goldman, "Gérard Grisey, Accordionist," 16.

vacation in Germany with his parents, he wrote about his uncertainty for the upcoming year. Would his musical ability match his desire? What would his artistic future bring?

※ ※ ※

In order to further his musical studies, Grisey decided he would need some competence in German. This was most likely a pragmatic choice: his teenage diary didn't show a particular interest in German culture or composition, apart from the music of Bach, a universally admired artist. Instead, Grisey was probably already thinking of attending the Hohner-Konservatorium in Trossingen, about 125 miles across the German border from Belfort, a music school sponsored by the accordion maker of the same name. (As mentioned, Grisey owned a Hohner.) Around the age of fifteen, Grisey began student-exchange visits with a German boy named Franz-Josef Bade, who was a little younger and lived at Heidbergweg 28 in Essen-Kupferdreh, a suburban area next to a winding lake called the Baldeneysee.[21] They had four visits to each other's families in total. On their first meeting, in Essen, Bade went to pick up Grisey at the train station. Barely able to communicate at the time—neither spoke the other's language—Grisey and Bade lugged two suitcases on the half-hour bus ride to Kupferdreh. Something was missing. The next day, they returned to the train station to pick up a large package: the accordion. "I'm not a small guy, but it was very heavy," Bade said.[22]

Grisey spent most of his time shut up in his room, practicing his instrument. Bade described himself as "a normal fourteen-year-old who played soccer," while Grisey showed little interest in hanging around with the local kids. That, added to the language barrier, made it difficult for the two boys to connect. Still, they managed to bond over a shared Catholic faith—Bade, who lost his faith soon after, was an avid reader of Pierre Teilhard de Chardin. Bade has a clear memory of Grisey praying. That spirituality seemed, to him, part and parcel of the composer's art. The boys also shared a similar sense of humor: Grisey was shy, but he could also be funny. "You had to force him a little bit, but he could joke around," Bade recalled. Grisey "had a good sense of irony," he added.

If Grisey's intention was to *learn* German, he didn't get very far. But he did achieve that most essential of German bureaucratic tasks: obtaining a certificate, dated September 1965, which claimed that Grisey's command of the language was "adequate, though with a noticeable French

---

21 Hohner-Konservatorium archive.
22 Interview with Bade.

accent."²³ According to Bade, this was a favor done by a teacher at the local Helmholtz Gymnasium, or high school, for Bade's father. (The name of the school was prophetic; in 1863, the German physicist and doctor Hermann von Helmholtz had published a book called *On the Sensations of Tone as a Physiological Basis for the Theory of Music,* a foundational work of musical acoustics.) Grisey probably didn't attend classes at the Helmholtz Gymnasium more than a few times, however.

During Bade's visits to Grisey's home in Belfort, he noticed right away that the young musician didn't seem to fit in at all in his environment. Bade and Jules Henri connected over their shared love of "tinkering" with cars. Bade spent most of his time with Grisey's father and with other teenagers from the neighborhood. The differences between the two boys were stark enough that adults often mixed up their nationalities. "Between us, the grownups always thought that I was the French one and he was the German," Bade said. "I was a little darker ... and I was a little more extroverted, and he was blond and very precise."

Jules Henri never made Bade feel unwelcome or out of place in Belfort, even though Bade's own father had served in the Nazi Wehrmacht in World War II, during the occupation of France. Bade pointed out that some French families exaggerate their connections to the Resistance partisans. The fact that Jules Henri never mentioned it could make it *more* likely that he fought against the Nazi occupation.

It was never clear to Bade who had supported Grisey's love of music; by that point, Grisey's grandmother had long since died. It was not the sort of family to engage in amateur music-making. They didn't own a piano.²⁴ Even to a teenage boy with a limited grasp of French, it was obvious to Bade that Grisey was the odd one out.

※ ※ ※

On January 20, 1964, at age seventeen, Grisey received word that he had been accepted to the Hohner-Konservatorium in Trossingen. In his diaries, he never mentioned the application process, keeping with his tendency to avoid the details of daily life in favor of meditations on love and God. But, in a resumé from this period, Grisey wrote that he had studied piano for two years without a formal teacher; harmony, up to cadences and modulations; ear training in one voice; and solfege, where he had started learning the viola clef.²⁵

---

23 Paul Sacher archive.
24 Interview with Lanza.
25 Hohner-Konservatorium archive.

Trossingen is a pretty, small town in the southwestern region of Baden-Württemberg, nestled between rolling hills and the Black Forest; in their soft dialect, the locals often drop the "N." As mentioned, the city is best known for the accordion firm Hohner, which was founded in 1857 by a trained watchmaker named Matthias Hohner and quickly became a leading European manufacturer. It is hard to overstate the presence of the Hohner name in Trossingen. There are at least three streets named after various Hohners. Besides the Hohner-Konservatorium, which still exists today, there is a Hohner accordion factory, a Hohner villa, and a Hohner museum.

Grisey's move to Germany happened quickly; he began his studies in Trossingen in February 1964. He moved into a room in Tuningerstrasse 51, staying with a Frau Wöhr.[26] He soon became homesick. "My parents are gone and I remain, lost, not understanding what is happening, with an inexplicable fear twisting my stomach," he wrote on February 2, 1964. He described his loneliness, and occasional bullying from other students in Trossingen—all on an abstract, even philosophical level. Ultimately, he decided to immerse himself in his studies: "I've discovered the consoling power of music. It's extraordinary ... I never would have thought it. I still feel the vocation, the calling, to one day be a composer vibrate within me—meanwhile I patiently work on my harmony." Grisey also found solace through weekends at home in Belfort, where he was able to see his parents and Bernadette. But he knew he would have to stick it out in Trossingen to become a musician and did so: an early sign that Grisey was willing to prioritize his musical development over nearly everything else.

Like many talented musicians who go on to conservatory, Grisey was at first overwhelmed by the amount of material he would have to master. In May 1964, he wrote, "I even sometimes doubt my suitability for the vocation of composer. What will I become if this faith is lacking?" In June, he added, "When I see the immense work that must be done to become a worthy creator, I feel discouraged: I find my intelligence too limited to acquire all the science required of the composer nowadays." Nevertheless, his friend in Trossingen, the Swiss accordionist Hugo Noth, told Goldman that Grisey was "the finest accordionist" at the Hohner-Konservatorium.[27] In 1964, Grisey recorded three works for an LP titled *Contemporary and Original Music for the Accordion* on "the Pennsylvanian label Kaibala, founded by the Latvian-born accordionist Victor Naruns," Goldman writes.[28]

---

26 Ibid.
27 Goldman, "Gérard Grisey, Accordionist," 17.
28 Ibid, 19. See also https://www.discogs.com/release/12129362-Stanley-Darrow-Gerard-Grisey-Mogens-Ellegaard-Contemporary-And-Original-Music-For-The-Accordion.

The German composer Hans Brehme was an important figure at the Hohner-Konservatorium. According to his publisher, he "shaped the accordion, more than any other in his time, as a legitimate concert instrument."[29] Brehme was a post-tonal composer especially influenced by Max Reger.[30] As Jonathan Goldman notes, Grisey "arrived too late in Trossingen to study with the composer Hans Brehme," but the young performer did later record two of Brehme's works on the accordion.[31] (Brehme was a card-carrying Nazi who joined the party in 1933.[32])

Even at this time, Grisey was focused on accordion performance and composition. He managed to get out of classes on rhythmic training for children and accordion repair so he could focus on music theory.[33] It seems Grisey didn't write any original pieces in 1964.

Besides his accordion work at the Hohner-Konservatorium, Grisey took composition at the Staatliche Hochschule für Musik, a five-minute walk away toward Trossingen town hall, where his musical education would broaden beyond his main instrument. With his teacher, Helmut Degen—a largely forgotten composer who came recommended by the director of the Hohner-Konservatorium, Armin Fett—Grisey analyzed classics of the repertoire such as Beethoven's Piano Sonata in C Minor op. 111; Wagner's "Prelude" to *Tristan und Isolde*; Schubert's song "Der Doppelgänger"; and Arnold Schoenberg's *Farben*.[34] That same year, Grisey also made his first acquaintance with the serial music that dominated contemporary classical music at the time. Grisey was already unimpressed by the genre, or at least his idea of it. "New music seems to have lost all sensitivity. It speaks to our intelligence. The serial musician is more of a scientist than a poet," he wrote.

During his stay in Trossingen, Grisey's religious feeling went through somewhat of a rebirth; not that he had ever abandoned Catholicism, but in a time of distress he found consolation in traditional expressions of religious feeling. He composed a text called "Elegy to Joan of Arc" in a style reminiscent of Claudel, who hadn't figured in his diary for some time, and wrote, in May 1964, "If only God could give me the strength to bear my sad fate until the day his inspiration would enlighten me, then my music would be a song of love and thanksgiving. But between the lines, we would always distinguish a few tears." Grisey still missed his mother and Bernadette terribly.

---

29 Knauer, "Der Pianist und Komponist Hans Brehme."
30 "Hans Brehme."
31 Goldman, "Gérard Grisey, Accordionist," 17.
32 Landesarchiv Baden-Württemberg, "Brehme, Hans Ludwig Wilhelm."
33 Hohner Konservatorium archive.
34 Paul Sacher archive.

He wrote, melodramatically, "I finally understand the immense suffering of a soldier, a prisoner, and an exile."

In July 1964, Grisey received his grades from his first semester at Trossingen. In an educational irony comparable to Albert Einstein failing math, Grisey got a C in acoustics.[35] Besides that, he averaged Bs, with an A on the accordion. The subjects included rhythm training, improvisation, conducting, ear training, music theory, music history, an introduction to musical form (*Formenlehre*), and courses in instrumental pedagogy.

On September 6, 1964, Grisey departed to North America from Paris for another world accordion championship. It was likely his first time on an airplane, and he took delight in describing the minutiae of the experience before, during, and after the flight, such as the make of the aircraft (a Boeing) and the stewardess's safety demonstration. But Grisey also showed his mystical bent as he contemplated the experience. Having arrived, he wrote, "I would like to remain on the plane and fly forever. I felt a presence there that I no longer have here: that of the infinite." A few days later, he wondered, "Why do time and distance exist?"

As the accordionist William Schimmel recalled, Grisey stopped off at the Neupauer Conservatory in Philadelphia, an accordion school founded by Jacob C. Neupauer, an educator and accordionist who played in the Philadelphia Orchestra under Eugene Ormandy.[36] Schimmel was studying accordion and composition at the time:

> [Grisey] performed his arrangement of *Fêtes* [from the *Nocturnes*] by Debussy. We were amazed. When he reached the first climax, he threw on the musette stop where one of the reeds is slightly out of tune. This could have been one of the first steps that would lead to his "spectral music." ... I could tell then that he was more interested in the sounds that he was making rather than [accordion virtuosity].

In the world of competitive accordion playing, Grisey maintained a certain arrogant streak. "We, at one point, congratulated each other on accordion contest winnings, but it was a fiercely competitive scene," Schimmel said. "We never really bonded as friends, but we were cordial. A few of us from the conservatory asked him who he thought was the greatest contribution to France since Brigitte Bardot. He answered, '*Moi!*'"[37] This may have been Grisey's way of hiding a certain insecurity. He hated touring. In North America, the loneliness Grisey knew in Trossingen returned: "I feel like I did in Germany, deprived of human company," he wrote.

---

35   This was *befriedigend*, or a 3 out of 6, on the German scale. Paul Sacher archive.
36   Sally A. Downey, "Jacob C. Neupauer, 93, a musician and educator."
37   Interview with Schimmel.

Grisey continued on to the world cup finals in Toronto. What most occupied his thoughts during the world cup was not the competition itself, in which he got third place (just a point and a quarter away from winning[38]), but his flirtation with a Québécois girl around his age named Guylaine Charon.[39] Their connection had the intensity of a summer camp romance. They talked about their dreams: Grisey's goal of becoming a musician; Charon's intention of moving to Chile to become a missionary. They discussed their "adolescences, their problems," and visited a church together. Grisey's later insouciance and confidence with women was starting to develop. "We leave each other in the elevator. Her gaze dazzles me with friendship and tenderness. I burp suspiciously," he wrote. Grisey was trying to show that he didn't care about Charon when he clearly did.

Hijinks aside, the flirtation left an impression on both Charon and Grisey. They exchanged letters for the next three years. While in New York after Toronto, Grisey drafted a letter to Charon which was full of suffering. He believed that Charon was "the only person in the world who understands me completely," adding that he felt "like a stranger in this world." He could not understand how God could be so cruel as to put Charon and Grisey in the same place, have them realize their connection, then tear them apart forever. Charon was slightly more pragmatic. "Those two days were wonderful, but all joy must come to an end," she responded. "I'm attached to you like I am to a friend. I think you felt more than friendship for me. Am I wrong? You suffer because you think that life is over, that you will never be met with understanding."

Cagney believes that Charon and Grisey bonded because they both had depression.[40] But it may have been something less medically definitive: the two shared the simultaneous grandiosity and banality of teenagers, for whom meditations on the nature of evil intersect with mundane anecdotes about summer camp and which classes at school they dislike. Charon and Grisey were both interested in Catholic writers such as Claudel and Georges Bernanos, whose works deal with themes of purity, martyrdom, and sublimity, and whose play *The Fearless Heart* was adapted into the opera *Dialogue des Carmélites* by Francis Poulenc. As Charon, who was studying to become a teacher, became less secure in her faith, Grisey's constancy continued to impress her. "I admire you very much, I admire the force of your soul," she wrote. "I admire that you believe so strongly in the Mass."

Charon was also sensitive to Grisey's desire to follow a musical path. She praised his abilities and ambition:

---

38   Hohner-Konservatorium archive.
39   Cagney identified her last name. "Synthesis and Deviation," 99.
40   Cagney, "Synthesis and Deviation," 99.

You told me about music and your vocation as a composer. You seem so convinced [of your suitability for the vocation] that I am certain that you will succeed: where there's a will, there's a way. You have a truly "musical soul." You perform a piece with such intensity that anyone who listens to you remains troubled. I believe it's because of your great sensitivity which you express in your music. Maybe one day you will resemble a great artist like Beethoven, Brahms ... I really think your compositions are extraordinary.[41]

This foreshadowed Grisey's mature relationships. He frequently needed his partners to be convinced of his exceptional abilities. This might explain why Grisey worried to Charon that he would never find someone else who "met him with understanding." In June 1965, Charon sent him a record, *Le fou de l'île*, with songs of the Québécois *chansonnier* Félix Leclerc, whom she called a "great poet." But Grisey had little interest in popular music, as he focused on the classical canon that formed the fundament of his composition studies in Trossingen.

As both young people moved on from high school to college, their connection ebbed, and their letters became less romantic and more like familial exchanges of the latest news. In the final letter of their correspondence, Charon announced that she had married a psychology student. "I hope that one day we'll meet again," she wrote. "But at that moment, I will introduce you to my husband." Grisey's romantic hopes were dashed, and it seems Charon never heard from him again.

After the Coupe mondiale in Toronto, Grisey spent a further two months at the home of Stanley Darrow, an accordionist and former member of the U.S. Air Force, in Westmont, New Jersey. Darrow had paid for Grisey's trip to North America. In exchange, Grisey taught some of Darrow's younger students, and the two worked on a commercial recording at Darrow's home and academy, the Acme Accordion School. Little else survives about Grisey's experience of suburban, post-war America, living with an older married couple—except that Grisey performed several concerts, but was anxious about his exams in music history and music education back in Trossingen.[42] Grisey dedicated a later piece, the *Passacaille* for accordion, to Darrow's wife.

Grisey came back to Belfort in November 1964. From there, he returned to Trossingen to continue his studies before applying to conservatory. Grisey didn't keep a diary in 1965. However, he did compose a *Suite en mi* for flute, oboe, and bassoon.[43] The brief, four-movement work, taken along with the *Passacaille* written the following year, marks the transition between Grisey's juvenilia and his early works of apprenticeship. The *Suite en mi* is composed in

---

41 Paul Sacher archive.
42 Hohner-Konservatorium archive.
43 Paul Sacher archive.

a free-tonal idiom reminiscent of several composers, none quite as much as Paul Hindemith. Grisey's piece shows a fairly sophisticated compositional working-through of his ideas. The suite isn't in E minor or E major, but uses the pitch E as a tonal center. (This note is also the tonal center of *Les espaces acoustiques*, though Grisey always denied that it had any special significance.) In the first movement, a march, Grisey introduces the motivic theme of the piece: a perfect fifth that will appear in different forms in each subsequent section. Here it is integrated into the main, strident melody, and spun out in a more lyrical second section. Over a dissonant march rhythm reminiscent of Darius Milhaud, Grisey states both his main and secondary melodies. The young composer was thinking in clearly defined if simple forms, a fact even more obvious in the second movement, a *passacaglia* where the bassoon carries the bass line—further developing the perfect-fifth motive—and the flute and oboe elaborate on top of it. The final variations of this movement closely resemble the earliest, suggesting a mirror-like form. In the third movement, a *Scherzino*, Grisey tosses, Beethoven-like, a broken fifth between the instruments. The fourth movement, marked *Moderato*, with much use of irregular time signatures, implies a basic twelve-tone structure, with oboe and bassoon playing overlapping rhythmic cells while not doubling any of one another's pitches. (The flute fills in the rest, while also repeating a few notes from the other instruments.) The final bars of the composition include the buzzing sound of flute fluttertongue, which appears to be Grisey's first use of an extended instrumental technique.

Overall, the *Suite en mi* is a huge leap forward from Grisey's juvenilia, and a promising piece from an eighteen-year-old. It shows that Grisey was no longer composing intuitively or at his instrument, instead working with clear, abstract forms in mind. His wind scoring is largely idiomatic, and his handwriting is impeccable, a fact which must have endeared him to his teachers and his fellow students—rhythmic division markings in the flute part imply that the *Suite en mi* was at least rehearsed by Trossingen students.[44]

If Grisey suffered from professional doubts and loneliness when he began his studies in Trossingen, the adults who encountered him seemed uniformly impressed with his talent and work ethic. In May 1965, Wolfgang Jacobi, an accordionist and professor of composition at the prestigious Staatliche Hochschule für Musik in Munich, wrote to Grisey praising his "admirable musicality and virtuosity," along with some tips for performing Jacobi's *Capriccio* for accordion. Jacobi wrote a letter of recommendation for Grisey that summer, noting that the young musician had "mastered his instrument, the accordion, with rare comprehensiveness and masterfulness, and is remarkable not just for his virtuosity, but also for his unusual musicality and reliably good taste."[45]

---

44 Paul Sacher archive.
45 Ibid.

Grisey's grades improved in his second year at Trossingen. His State Exams took place in two-day chunks in February, March, and July 1965. He passed them with distinction on July 7, with honors in piano and button accordion, the piano, and ear training. He also raised his grade in acoustics to a B.

Grisey's talent was equally noticed in the field of composition. In a letter of reference dated August 18, 1965, Degen, his composition teacher, praised Grisey in no uncertain terms:

> Considering his great talent, he was able to finish his studies in traditional composition relatively quickly and move on to free composition.[46] Even though he was at the beginning of his studies, Grisey has powers of invention and expression, and compositional talent, in both formal and sonic matters, and is starting his path to developing a personal language. I consider Grisey an unusual talent, who proved his ability in my subjects as well as on his instrument—a fact I was able to witness several times.[47]

Not one to rest on his laurels, Grisey spent six days in July 1965 at a "Sommer-Arbeitswoche" (summer working-week) for accordion teachers, sponsored by a German umbrella organization for accordionists. He learned new repertoire for the instrument, practiced the mouth harmonica, and conducted an accordion orchestra.[48]

It was this combination of ability and relentless hard work, showing a rapid development from his childhood compositions, that made the entrance examinations at the Conservatoire National Supérieur de Musique in Paris attainable for Grisey. These exams, which test entrants' abilities in music theory, style copies, ear training, analysis, instrumental performance, and other subjects—contained in the French umbrella term *écriture*—are some of the most rigorous music entrance exams in the world.

Grisey also applied to the Hochschule für Musik in Munich.[49] He was accepted to both and chose Paris, based on the allure of Olivier Messiaen's legendary composition class. In a letter to Armin Fett, the director of the Hohner-Konservatorium, Grisey wrote, "Finally I made it and have been accepted into the Paris Conservatoire. The exam lasted five hours, with [dictations] in soprano, alto, tenor and bass clefs." He added, "I've never seen a big city like this." On December 12, 1965, Fett wrote to Grisey to congratulate him. Fett continued, "I hope you won't give up the accordion for good."[50]

---

46   "Traditional composition" is *Strenger Satz* in German.
47   Paul Sacher archive.
48   Ibid.
49   Interview with Jocelyne Grisey.
50   Hohner-Konservatorium archive.

Chapter Three

The Rhythm of Love (1965–67)

In November 1965, Grisey moved to Paris. His new living quarters were at 20 rue de Monceau, in the eighth arrondissement. This address housed a Catholic *lycée* for children ages eleven to nineteen called Sainte-Marie de Monceau, now Lycée Fénelon Sainte-Marie. Grisey was almost certainly connected to the institution through his Marianist schooling in Belfort and was granted a tiny room of about sixty-five square feet and regular meals in exchange for doing small chores like sweeping classrooms, erasing blackboards, and washing dishes on the weekends for the nuns who lived on the premises (the lay teachers and the students lived elsewhere). On the outside, the building was a drab and dirty white, but at least it had a large communal balcony, and there was a piano in the dining room that he could practice on.[1] A photograph from this period shows the slender, fine-featured young composer sitting at a desk, his chair rubbing up against the bed, with pictures of Greek antique art on the walls, a record player, and at least one LP with music by a Boulanger sister.[2] The school was centrally located, and, for a boy from a working-class family, free room and board in Paris were not to be taken for granted.

On February 13, 1966, after a year and a half of silence, Grisey returned to writing in his "old journal." At the Conservatoire National Supérieur de Musique he primarily attended courses in *écriture*. Though taught in many conservatories, Paris has undoubtedly one of the most difficult *écriture* programs in the world. Grisey would focus on this musical scaffolding for the next three years. His routine was rigorous, his focus almost single-minded: "I get up early and I go to Mass when I'm able. Then from 8:30 to 11:30, I compose. In the afternoon: accordion, piano, reading, studying scores,

---

1   Interview with Jocelyne Grisey.
2   Either Lili or Nadia, it's not visible in the photograph. Private archive of Jocelyne Grisey.

counterpoint, etc. In the evening: letters and listening to records." On March 9, 1966, he admonished himself to "Work. Work, yes, work like the bees, with application, without looking to the right nor to the left, without comparing myself with others, without waiting to see the result nor what is left to do."[3] Evidently, Grisey found the difficulty of his studies at the Conservatoire less intimidating than invigorating.

As a young teenager, Grisey was preoccupied by his nascent sexuality, but also by religious ideals of purity. In the literature of his youth, sex—understood to be within marriage—was often portrayed as a transcendent gift from God, rather than as a simple earthly pleasure. As a conservatory student, he continued to reflect on this potent physical blessing. In a diary entry from February 13, 1966, he imagined God and love as contained in rhythm, an aspect of his music he wanted to focus more deeply on. In one entry, he addressed God directly, saying he saw rhythm as "Your creation, the pulsations which are Your self. You are Rhythm, oh my God; you are absolute rhythm, the rhythm of eternity, of love." This idea took on a tangible, physical aspect when, in the spring of 1966, Grisey fell in love with the woman who became the central figure in his romantic life for the next sixteen years.

❦ ❦ ❦

Jocelyne Simon, with dark hair and a shy smile, was the last to arrive of the four au pairs in residence that year at Sainte-Marie de Monceau (the other two were Austrian), coming to live at the school a few months after Grisey. Raised in Châlons-en-Champagne, Simon was the oldest of three children, born nine months after the death of her parents' first infant daughter from meningitis. Simon's father died when she was five years old in a railroad accident, and her mother remarried, creating a new family of six siblings. Her circumstances, like Grisey's, were modest. Her parents discouraged her from finishing her *baccalauréat*, suggesting she become a secretary. Instead, she spent a year selling tickets for the French railways, working on her degree via a correspondence course, and saving for university in Paris. She decided to study social work.[4]

Grisey and Simon quickly became friends. The two students explored Paris, going to museums and concerts and spending time with the Austrian au pairs. They also exchanged ideas and books from their respective degrees—Grisey developed an interest in psychology from Simon. Slowly they became "more intimate," Simon said. On February 14, 1966, Grisey

---

3 Paul Sacher archive.
4 Interview with Jocelyne Grisey.

wrote in his diary, clearly referring to Simon, "You cried in my arms the whole night ... I could have devoured you with tenderness." He hoped that Simon could soothe his selfishness and convince him that true love and true friendship existed, referring to an unexplained event in November 1964 which had convinced him that love was not for him.[5] Grisey still had doubts about his own temperament. "A friend just wrote to me that my way of giving myself, of loving, is to close myself up in a room and sacrifice my small self to make music for mankind," he wrote on March 15, 1966. "I have the need to be loved, [to be secure], but I don't feel the express need to be giving." This conflict between the desire to love the world through composition, and the desire to be loved by individual women, was one that Grisey never completely resolved.

Simon, though a baptized Catholic, was not especially religious. Grisey however understood his blossoming relationship with her in spiritual terms: as a gift to be enjoyed in unity with God. He wrote that his relationship with Simon was like "bathing all my being in tenderness and sweetness." His reflections on sexuality continued to emphasize the metaphysical, symbolic eroticism of Catholic thought. He added, "As with women, I believe that men will never find in sexual union all they expect. They will never completely sate that thirst. The man wants to lose himself in her, to cease existing ... He never succeeds." For him, it followed that love was a sublimation of death: "The greatest lovers of history and literature were united in death because life wasn't enough—it couldn't support their love. Love stronger than death." (In music, this idea most strongly recalls the archetypical lovers of Wagner's *Tristan und Isolde*.) And yet Grisey acknowledged the innocent side of his and Simon's sexual relationship too: "Sleeping side by side like two children, hand in hand, body against body ... full of the idea of carnal love, sensuality, and the search for pleasure."[6] Much later, Simon recalled this experience and its relevance for Grisey's work. "Sometimes, he spoke of his physical desire, the breath, the beating heart," she said. "It was important for his music."[7]

Grisey and Simon were experiencing all the intensity of young love. On March 18, 1966, Grisey wrote that he had become "obsessed" with desire and thirst for Simon. In this period, he compared sex to "vibrating in unison" and the body to a musical instrument; he also wrote to a friend that "while it's true that music is the most immaterial of all the arts, we remain deeply, physically—I was going to say sensually—attached to the material that

---

5   Probably Grisey losing his virginity to another woman.
6   "*Recherche de plaisirs*" in French. Paul Sacher archive.
7   Interview with Jocelyne Grisey.

is sound and that we knead like craftsmen working with clay."⁸ Throughout the spring of 1966, Grisey vacillated between romantic ecstasy in his relationship with Simon and a hypersensitivity to perceived slights from her. "What heartbreak, what shame in a refused kiss!" he wrote on March 21. In another diary entry, he wrote, "Right now, I'm afraid of being face to face with her. I'm not sure of anything anymore, I doubt myself, what she is thinking, everything ... She told me of her hesitations ..." He added, "I would like to work, but not to think."

In his diary, Grisey also recorded striking experiences from daily life, though few prosaic details. One day, he struck up a conversation with a Hungarian barber about the music of Béla Bartók. It was the type of interaction which despite its relative superficiality he preferred infinitely to "those conversations around the table going from money to social status, from social status to politics, all falling back down to social success and, of course, money." He continued, "They predict an unhappy future for me! *Wait until you have no home, nothing to eat! You don't know what money represents!* No, it's true, I ignore it. Or at least, I don't ignore it, but I apply myself to detaching myself from it every day." He heard a performance on the Baroque composer François Couperin's organ at the Église St-Gervais-St-Protais and felt the first breezes of the spring. On April 8, he noted presciently, "I would like to be able to succeed at once in my artistic and in my sentimental lives. Even if the two are difficult to reconcile, I will apply myself to the whole so that one does not make the other suffer."

Grisey's time with Simon involved frequent discussions on the nature of God. On May 2, 1966, he noted that Simon had visited a church, which he felt put her at the beginning of a more heartfelt Christian path. On May 12, the two had a "minuscule philosophical discussion" on proofs of the existence of a higher power that left Grisey both doubting his faith and feeling guilty for this doubt: "Oh Father, forgive us! Forgive us our intelligence, this incalculable power which You put in us. Forgive us if we use it against You." As a youth, Grisey had occasionally felt his Catholicism shaking; now the seeds of an intellectual doubt were planted.

Simon and Grisey were a good fit for one another; Simon was a sensitive, intellectual young woman, with an interest in art and Grisey's compositions. She supplemented her courses in social work with night classes in psychology. The two swapped journal entries: on May 19, 1966, Simon wrote, "I like to watch him play, I could go for hours without getting tired, following his hands ... striking or caressing the keys of the piano, listening to this music which he is mastering." On June 1, they celebrated Simon's birthday in the Latin Quarter. While Grisey could not quite surmount his occasional

---

8   Paul Sacher archive.

doubts about their relationship—in July, he saw a film about a married couple who grew apart and feared for a future in which he and Simon would do the same—they were profoundly in love. Subtly, this love was making its mark on Grisey's aesthetic thinking. On July 4, he wrote, "The body is only a translation; that of the marvel [of love]. It is nothing but an instrument, put on the path, which gently accomplishes its release and the recollection of your tenderness."

As the 1966 academic year wound down for the summer, Grisey returned to Belfort. There he worked on a new composition, a Magnificat. He was also practicing the piano and the accordion and reading, part of a program of personal enrichment he'd decided to undertake during his vacation.[9] As the text for his work, Grisey chose the Magnificat from the *Missel biblique de tous les jours* in Latin.[10] Maybe the composition of the piece was an effort to shore up the faith that his conversations with Simon had caused him to doubt; in his letters to her, he frequently wrote of the vital spirituality he felt while working. On June 28, he told her, "This morning I worked on my Magnificat; very little, but enough to put me in a state of unique interior exaltation. I was nearly happy, transported." Just two days later, he finished the third section of the piece, noting that he felt his skills improving: "Day after day, I feel ever more competent, increasingly sure of myself." And yet he was aware of the difficulty of his task: on July 5, he added, "Composition requires a concentration so profound, a preoccupation so complete, that life can only delay everything (at least that's the case for me) …" The slow process of composition and the utter devotion it required became one of the most defining aspects of Grisey's mature work.

On July 8, 1966, Grisey spent an afternoon with a friend he identified only as Prezman. The two engaged in passionate discussions on art and music, with Prezman praising Grisey's sketches for the Magnificat as "splendid." Meanwhile, Prezman confided in Grisey that he felt stifled by the atmosphere of material luxury in which he lived. This was a phenomenon foreign to Grisey's working-class background. But his letter to Simon betrayed no trace of jealousy. All he wrote was: "It's worth thinking about, isn't it? …"

A few days later, Grisey took a trip with his parents to Bagneux, a small city with historic churches, gardens, and cemeteries ten miles outside Paris. He hadn't overcome his youthful contempt for the lives of his parents. "I can't understand how one can go through life without joy, without a goal, without love, glued to habits," he wrote to Simon. "I believe I like my solitude better, as hard as it is, than the presence of these man-insects buzzing around a source of light." He withdrew into his faith—he believed that he

---

9 Lelong, *Écrits*, 293.
10 Paul Sacher archive.

had once again felt the "profound creative presence of God" in him—and into his music. Still, the Magnificat wasn't progressing, so he turned his attention to a different work, the *Passacaille* for accordion solo.

Grisey completed this *Passacaille* extremely quickly. On July 12, 1966, he told Simon he'd worked on the piece the entire morning, from eight to noon, and had forgotten to eat breakfast. Unlike the Magnificat, whose composition process continued into 1967, it appears Grisey finished the *Passacaille* within a month. Along with the *Suite en mi*, this student piece is the bridge between his juvenilia and his early apprentice works.[11] Some four and a half minutes long, it's a sophisticated composition by a twenty-year-old composer in a freely atonal idiom reminiscent of Hindemith. The bass line is a nine-bar melody characterized by dissonant upward leaps and given mild grit by the addition of a major second on top of each pitch in the buzzing low range of the accordion. Throughout the piece, Grisey plays with this melodic theme. At certain moments he hides it so that the listener is only reminded of the bass by stray major seconds; at others, all his material is clearly derived from the first idea, but he frequently varies the length of the phrase so that the point where it repeats comes as a surprise. In one structurally impressive section, Grisey inverts his bass line while stripping it of its characteristic major seconds; adds the same line on top, displaced by an eighth note, in a sort of canon; and ornaments it with dissonant flourishes. The *Passacaille* is a striking work by a young composer with an obvious gift for the craft. It closes with a *misterioso* restatement of the bass theme, the ubiquitous major seconds of the first statement replaced by unsettling minor seconds—a far more dissonant interval. This conclusion gives the last working-through of the passacaglia theme a memorable, bitter aftertaste.

The *Passacaille* was first recorded in 2007 by the accordionist Mikko Luoma.[12] On listening, too, the piece holds up well; the passacaglia bass exerts a sort of magnetic force on the composition's variations, unifying them without resorting to pedantic repetition. It doesn't sound anything like Grisey's adult works, but it shows competence and imagination. Grisey himself did not consider his *Passacaille* an important work in his larger development. Unlike the Magnificat, he hardly mentioned it in letters to Simon, and later rejected it completely, calling it, in a much later letter to an accordionist, a "*Jugendsünde*," or "sin of youth."

---

11   Paul Sacher archive.
12   Luoma, *The Virtuoso Accordion*. For details of this and other recordings of Grisey's music, see the appendix.

Shortly thereafter or in parallel, Grisey completed the Magnificat, also a student work in a free, atonal idiom.[13] Some rhythmic sketches on the "*stretto* of the final fugue" for the work on a loose program page of an accordion Coupe mondiale in Versailles, from September 1966, survive. The marked-up flyer is a striking illustration of the way Grisey's interest in the accordion was waning as his passion for composition waxed.[14]

The Magnificat is scored for female voices, piano, percussion, and four winds: flute, bass clarinet, saxophone, and horn. It opens with an ominous unison D in the horn, bass clarinet, timpani, and piano. A sinuous piano line rises from the low to the high register of the instrument and arrives, interrupted by interjections in the other instruments, at a dissonant, *fortissimo* tremolo on a major ninth. The voices enter with the Latin text in a quiet but busy atmosphere of piano glissandi, percussion *tremoli*, and wind figuration. This leads to a longer elaboration of Messiaen-like melodic ideas in a slow section marked "like a fragment of a choral." What follows alternates between the bitonal (G major and F-sharp major chords overlapping) and the Webernian (chords of fourths and tritones).

The *Passacaille* is a more convincing work, though: shorter and for a single instrument which Grisey knew inside-out, it is more detailed, and the structure of the work also seems clearer and better controlled. Grisey had reached a stage in his development as a composer where his ambition outmatched his skill. On July 10, 1966, he wrote to Simon, "I finally finished the three first parts of the Magnificat. At the moment ... drought concerning what is to follow." He didn't mention the piece again in his letters to her.

A compositional goal Grisey set for himself the same day—which he didn't attempt to realize in his *Passacaille* but did achieve later in life—was "the mystical simplicity and poetic purity of the masters of the Middle Ages," like the transparent music of the medieval troubadour Adam de la Halle. On July 16, Grisey had composer's block, so he set about reading a book on Freudian psychoanalysis. The ideas of the Viennese intellectual took root early on in Grisey's thinking and later informed his musical aesthetic as well as his fascination with his own dreams.

A journal entry from the same month, titled "Response to a friend" and addressed to a woman named Christiane, details Grisey's emerging view of the role of the artist in society. Christiane had wondered to Grisey whether "the artist doesn't more or less lose his sense of reality?" Grisey, maybe replaying an unsatisfactory verbal argument in his journal, acknowledged the

---

13 Cagney, "Synthesis and Deviation," 103. Cagney writes that the Magnificat was completed in April 1966, but Grisey mentions working on it later into the summer (compare Lelong, *Écrits*, 294).

14 Paul Sacher archive.

removal of the artist from the routines of daily life, and the necessity of his egocentricism. For him, the role of the artist was to create "a mirror where we see our most authentic aspirations, or, better: a sensible approach toward a better world with an open door to Love, the Infinite, and Being."

On July 19, 1966, Grisey spent the entire day composing—a first for him—observing the profound fatigue that "enveloped my body and my spirit" after. (He was too tired even to take a walk.) He identified this fatigue as resulting from the banalities of daily life. But he also felt a profound belief in righteous isolation and the importance of his personal mission, comparing himself to Antoine de Saint-Exupéry in the memoir *Wind, Sand and Stars*, where the writer describes flying mail planes in the early days of aviation. It is unsurprising that the book resonated with Grisey. Saint-Exupéry wrote eloquently of feeling detached from other people while entrusted with a mission essential to them; he was a thoughtful critic of the small-mindedness of middle-class French life. In his memoir, Saint-Exupéry also made a statement that applies perfectly to Grisey's mature compositional method: "All man's industrial effort, all his calculations and his nights spent poring over drawings, all these visible signs have as their sole end the achievement of simplicity."[15]

Grisey was feeling alone yet marked by destiny; this emotion was heightened by the simple fact that he was missing Simon while at home for the summer. On July 21, 1966, he told her that he spent the day looking forward to their reunion. He quoted the Song of Solomon to her: "Set me as a seal on your heart."[16] It was a natural text for a young man with a combined interest in sexuality and spirituality to turn to; he praised the poem for its "marvelous parallel between the love of a man and a woman and the Union of God and man."

Earlier that month, Grisey had had two powerful, spiritual experiences. On July 5, 1966, he wrote, "I saw the Father the other day," and he began to read Jean Guitton's *Essai sur l'amour humain (Essay on Human Love)*, which posits continuity between sexual and divine love. Three days later, Grisey attended Mass and "felt profoundly the creative presence of God." Throughout the summer, he missed Simon terribly. But their meeting, at the end of July, was far from a simple pleasure. "We collided from the very first moments," he wrote. "I felt a sudden desire to leave, to go far away, to leave her with her cries and her young girl's inhibitions ... For my part, I have other things which torment me, this is all too much."[17] Later that evening,

---

15   Saint-Exupéry, *Wind, Sand and Stars*, 31.
16   Alter's *Hebrew Bible*.
17   This entry is dated "Mardi 2.7.66," but the preceding entries are for the 21st and 24th, so there's probably a number missing. Paul Sacher archive.

Grisey continued, the two reconciled. They soon felt closer than ever before. Yet Grisey's doubts were not completely assuaged. "I don't understand anything anymore," he wrote, in the same diary entry. "I know that she isn't playing with me, so why these incessant reversals, this instability? What is she looking for?"

In late August 1966, Grisey traveled to Barcelona, probably with his parents. He listened to Debussy's tone poem *La Mer* and Bartók's *Music for Strings, Percussion, and Celesta*, whose first movement he also identified with the sea. (Two of Grisey's later compositions, *Vagues, Chemins, le Souffle* and *D'eau et de pierre*, were both inspired by water images.) But Grisey was uncomfortable with the idea of relaxing and doing nothing. On August 22, he called the idea of vacation "cowardly," "abnormal," and "greedy." On August 29, he noted that he was "beginning to miss music terribly."

Grisey returned to Paris in the fall. As a young composer with an as-yet undiscovered personal aesthetic, he wrote that he felt like Christopher Columbus. If the explorer "had heard proof of the existence of a new continent before he left, he would never have gone, he would never had discovered anything."

For three months in 1967, Grisey enrolled in Henri Dutilleux's composition class at the École Normale de Musique, a thirty-minute Métro ride from the Conservatoire National Supérieur but a short walk from Grisey's living quarters in the Rue Monceau.[18] Dutilleux was an idiosyncratic choice of teacher for Grisey. Born in 1916, Dutilleux's breakthrough works were his First and Second Symphonies, both composed in the 1950s.[19] As his biographer Caroline Potter writes, "The very fact that Dutilleux wrote two works entitled 'Symphony' in the 1950s suggests that he was distant from the integral serialist preoccupations of the European musical avant-garde and in particular of [Pierre] Boulez." The Second Symphony, titled "Le Double," divides the orchestra into two groups, an idea that Grisey used in many of his works, including in the crucial *Dérives* for orchestra. Dutilleux's Symphony, though gestural, almost linguistic in a way that Grisey would later reject, is a polished work of a dark, rich hue. (Entangled wind lines in its first movement recall the second section of Grisey's *Partiels*.) Harry Halbreich, the Belgian musicologist who later became a champion of Grisey's music, once praised Dutilleux's Second Symphony as "a lunar garden, its luxuriances finely draped with an aura of mourning,

---

18   Cagney, "Synthesis and Deviation," 104.
19   Potter, *Henri Dutilleux*, 9.

sumptuousnesses surrounded by latent illusion."[20] Dutilleux was an adamantly independent composer who resisted the magnetic pull of all stylistic schools and as such was performed by more prestigious orchestras in the United States than in France.[21]

Dutilleux's free idiom and skepticism toward the dogmatic serialism of the period resonated with Grisey. In a diary entry from October 9, 1967, Grisey parroted one of Dutilleux's main convictions, that pitches or chords have "a pivot or magnetic force of attraction."[22] In Grisey's words: "I consider atonality to be non-existent. From the moment where two different notes sound one after the other or simultaneously, *a relationship* is established. All music possesses one or several tonal centers, veritable poles of attraction." Another important musical concept that Grisey adapted from Dutilleux was that of *métaboles*, as Cagney has convincingly shown.[23] Cagney defines this technique as "a process of recurrence of a given sound object or musical figure whereby each time said object/figure reappears it is modified" in its sonic properties. Dutilleux pioneered the idea in his orchestral piece of the same name, a five-movement work in contrasting moods which was commissioned by the Cleveland Orchestra under George Szell and premiered in January 1965.[24] Both Cagney and the composer Julian Anderson locate the *métabole* process in Grisey pieces: Cagney in *Vagues, Chemins, le Souffle,* Anderson in *Partiels*. These pieces were composed years after Grisey's studies with Dutilleux concluded; as is often the case with important musical influences, it took time for Grisey to digest and apply them in a way that meshed with his own interests.[25]

Dutilleux had been appointed to the position of professor of composition at the École Normale in 1961 by the legendary pianist Alfred Cortot; Dutilleux apparently preferred the institution to the more prestigious Conservatoire de Paris because it offered flexible hours.[26] In his courses, given once or twice a week, he taught orchestration, analysis, and composition. Francis Bayer, Dutilleux's student from 1969 to 1970, tells Potter:

---

20   Gervasoni, *Henri Dutilleux*, 789.
21   Anderson, "A Provisional History of Spectral Music," 448.
22   Potter, *Henri Dutilleux*, 14.
23   Cagney, "Synthesis and Deviation," 111–113.
24   Potter, *Henri Dutilleux*, 14.
25   Anderson, "A Provisional History of Spectral Music," 453. Anderson finds a chord on the harmonic spectrum at the beginning of Dutilleux's *Métaboles*, but the seventh, ninth, fifteenth, twenty-second, and thirty-second partials are used on the tempered scale, which changes the sound significantly.
26   Potter, *Henri Dutilleux*, 15.

> The student had to play his or her own piece at the piano (Dutilleux disliked sight-reading), and then Dutilleux would sit in silence for ten or fifteen minutes before talking about something specific in the piece, which would inevitably have repercussions for the entire work. He never discussed his own music and never tried to direct the students' ideas ... [27]

This was a style of teaching reminiscent of Messiaen, though Messiaen's approach could be even more gnomic and guru-like.

Also valuable for Grisey were Dutilleux's wide interests. He insisted that his students study the visual arts, literature, and different streams of music. On May 8, 1967, Ivan Wyschnegradsky, a wildly inventive French composer of Russian extraction, made a presentation to Dutilleux's class.[28] Wyschnegradsky wrote microtonal pieces based on quarter, third, and even twelfth tones. He also developed a system of chord generation in which the octave was never repeated, and a light spectrum analogous to his microtonal concepts. It's unclear whether Grisey participated in this masterclass.

According to Cagney, Grisey later intentionally downplayed the influence that Dutilleux had on him as a student, possibly preferring not to get on the more powerful conductor and composer Boulez's bad side by publicly identifying with his rival Dutilleux.[29] However, Grisey and Dutilleux stayed in touch occasionally. In 1969, Dutilleux wrote to Grisey telling him to see the film *Dieu a choisi Paris* (*God chose Paris*), which celebrated the artistic heritage of the city and starred the iconic New Wave actor Jean-Pierre Belmondo. In 1975, Dutilleux wrote, in a recommendation for Grisey's (unsuccessful) Fulbright application, that Grisey's "temperament is marked by depth and even a certain gravity, as shown in some of his scores. The moment has come for him to discover new horizons."[30] In 1988, the two composers exchanged cordial New Year's greetings; in 1992, Grisey told Dutilleux that the latter's five-movement, exquisitely colored cello concerto *Tout un monde lointain...* "was an absolute masterpiece which transcends all the aesthetic categories of our time."[31] Maybe the then-evident differences in the two composers' aesthetics made it easier for Grisey to unambiguously praise Dutilleux's composition. "As you can imagine, I'm grateful for what you wrote to me," Dutilleux responded. "For, without your having imagined it, I have always paid close attention to your development, your

---

27 Ibid.
28 Gervasoni, *Henri Dutilleux*, 823–24.
29 Cagney, "Synthesis and Deviation," 108.
30 Paul Sacher archive.
31 Cagney, "Synthesis and Deviation," 108.

personal trajectory delighting me in what you have created these past twenty years, in a direction, to be sure, that is far removed from my own."[32]

Cagney locates a sense of hurt here: for him, the phrase "without your having imagined it" implies that Dutilleux "felt Grisey had perhaps neglected to give proper due to his old teacher."[33]

This ambiguity is reinforced by a tribute Grisey wrote for Dutilleux in 1994, which Cagney and Anderson both read as backhanded. Grisey praised Dutilleux for his subtle innovations in twentieth-century music while also recognizing his technical mastery, which feels to them like faint praise. Then again, Grisey concluded, "Perhaps one day we will be capable of according the rank of innovator to Henri Dutilleux in a history of music which will not only be that of musical language"[34] (meaning a history of broad stylistic trends). And if Grisey's tribute to Dutilleux was half-hearted, a 1988 tribute to Messiaen was equally so. It mostly eschewed heart-on-sleeve praise of the composer in order to show how quiet, difficult to please, and mysterious Messiaen was.[35]

Although Dutilleux's teaching certainly influenced the young Grisey, his real master was Messiaen. Still, Grisey's studies with Dutilleux were productive. They helped give him the confidence to forge a personal language in the calcifying serialist climate in France, orienting him at the beginning of the aesthetic path toward his mature voice.

※ ※ ※

Now even busier with his studies in Paris, where he'd voluntarily added Dutilleux's composition class to his studies in *écriture* at the Conservatoire National Supérieur, Grisey felt increasingly ill at ease during breaks. He spent the 1967 spring vacation at home in Belfort. (Breaks were becoming the only times he wrote letters or in his journal.) On March 27, 1967, Grisey wrote to Simon that he was "dragging his slippers around the apartment," flitting between various demanding works of literature and the gossip magazine *Paris Match*. Among these books were an unnamed orchestration treatise, a work by Pierre Teilhard de Chardin, and Stendhal's classic novel *The Red and the Black*. "In short, I'm vegetating," Grisey wrote. "It's horrible."

Even if Grisey had trouble concentrating on his Stendhal, he probably recognized some parallels between the book and his own life. An ambitious,

---

32 Paul Sacher archive.
33 Cagney, "Synthesis and Deviation," 108.
34 Anderson's translation from "A Provisional History of Spectral Music," 449.
35 Lelong, *Écrits*, 227.

intelligent, and handsome young man from a poor family in the eastern regions of France makes his way out of his village and into the world, where he learns about power, sex, and the machinations of high society, only to find himself desperate and isolated in the cutthroat world of the capital. Julien Sorel, Stendhal's protagonist, listens to the "full-bodied and masculine sounds" of church bells, and on the spot decides to become an artist.[36] Sorel didn't succeed; Grisey did. The two men, one fictional, the other real, shared a similar, often heedless ambition. In the same letter, Grisey wrote, with real insight into his own personality, "I dream often, perpetually ill at ease, ravished, obsessed with my art. I feel extremely insensitive to the rest, extremely detached ... Why? Even if my attitude seems strange or even cruel to others, I don't have the right to act otherwise. It isn't in my power anymore."[37] Months before his twenty-second birthday, Grisey had recognized two of his distinctive adult character traits: protective selfishness and extreme focus. These are maybe necessary for an artist, but would weigh on his relationships throughout his life.

In a letter from the same vacation, the composer complained of the predictability of his days, which he compared to an "old, dreary sky." He had, however, been on a "delicious" solitary walk. Again, he missed Simon dreadfully. The two were reunited later that month, on April 24, 1967. "My *Hymne* is two-thirds finished," he wrote in his journal.[38] "Forgiveness, contact between me and Jocelyne like never before."

On June 26, 1967, once more in Belfort for the summer, Grisey took up letter writing. Unable to compose, he nonetheless found "the Poem" for an unspecified piece: Claudel's *Cinq Grandes Odes*. Grisey's reference to the specific text is slightly garbled,[39] but he was struck by the phrase "*Va t'en!*" (It can be translated as "Get away from me," though "Go forth," "Get out," or "Beat it" all come closer to its striking rhythm.) This gave Grisey an idea for a musical rhythm; he wanted to compose a piece on ideas of God, the material world, and carnal love. Claudel's long poem, written between 1900 and 1908, takes the form of a conversion: the narrator rejects his previous admiration of polytheistic muses and gods like the Egyptian Isis and Osiris in favor of "the one true God." Structurally, the work builds in fervor, gradually but powerfully. The section that Grisey wanted to set was the coda to the fourth *Grand Ode*:

---

36   Stendhal, *The Red and the Black*, 206.
37   Paul Sacher archive.
38   It seems he never completed this piece.
39   He refers to the "Epode du Magnificat" of the *Five Great Odes*. The Magnificat is the third Ode, but the section opening with the line "*Va t'en!*" is the Epode of the *fourth* Ode, titled "The Muse Called Grace."

> — Get away from me! I desperately turn towards the earth!
> Get away from me! You will not take the cold taste of the earth from me,
> This obstinacy with the earth that is in the marrow of my bones and in the pebble of my
> substance and in the black pit of my entrails!
> ....
> Whoever has bitten the earth keeps the taste between his teeth.
> Whoever has tasted blood will no longer feed on bright water and ardent honey!
> Whoever has loved the human soul, whoever has once been compact with another living soul, is caught there forever ... .[40]

Entitled "The Muse Called Grace," this ode is structured as a dualistic argument between the Poet, enamored of this world and its pleasures, and the Muse, who urges him to remember his holy responsibilities.

This specific section is in the voice of the Poet. Claudel's line, "Whoever has loved the human soul ... is caught there forever," dovetails nicely with Grisey's contemplation of his relationship with Simon. In fact, there is much here that mirrors Grisey's personal and aesthetic interests in 1967. Lauren Bergier, a translator of the *Cinq Grandes Odes* into English, argues:

> There is no more conflict between paganism and Christianity in Claudel's Ode than there is in the art of Michelangelo, or of Poussin ... . There is no Puritanism in these verses. It would be more appropriate, rather than speaking of "antagonism" between the views of the poet and his Muse, to speak of the exchange as being agonistic, like an athletic contest that brings out the best in both athletes; and also, to a great extent, as erotic.[41]

It's a view of religion that echoes Grisey's teenage comments about the beauty of the female body, encountered through the religious *and* sensual art of the Italian Renaissance.

Besides these common interests, Bergier notes the prevalence of sea imagery in Claudel's language. The poet had composed the work during two maritime voyages to China. Similar imagery surfaced in Grisey's later two works *Vagues, Chemins, le Souffle* and *D'eau et de pierre*. The word *Souffle*, which can mean wind, breath, and the flow of the Holy Spirit, is particularly prevalent in the *Odes*.[42] That term resurfaces in *Vagues*; Grisey also assigned great importance to the rhythms of human breathing, observing it with wonder.

---

40   Bergier, "Paul Claudel's Cinq Grandes Odes," 175.
41   Ibid, 177.
42   Ibid, 1.

But the piece that resulted from Grisey's encounter with this text—maybe a preliminary version of the later *Deux Madrigaux*—was never finished. In his sketches, Grisey worked largely with a trio of percussion (including tam-tams, vibraphone, and xylophone), baritone, and piano. However, the occasional note on orchestration implies that he was thinking of a larger ensemble. The extract from *La muse qui est la grâce* is another transitional piece, moving from the crafted free tonality of the *Passacaille* to a sound world which, while apparently not composed with tone rows, recalls the serialist idiom of Pierre Boulez and Karlheinz Stockhausen (in a simpler, less refined form). Grisey's jottings showed he was thinking in terms of repeating formal blocks and intervallic procedures, but the initial result is half-baked, with many clichéd atonal gestures. And while he was becoming more confident in his use of rhythmic complexity, the vocal writing is awkward, caught halfway between difficult melismatic atonal flights and uncomfortable droning on a single pitch.

Back in Belfort at the beginning of July 1967, Grisey had arranged for a piano to work on, but it didn't arrive when expected. In the meantime, he set about reading Gustave Flaubert's *Madame Bovary*. Like Stendhal's *The Red and the Black*, Flaubert narrated the rise and fall of Emma Bovary, a naive yet ambitious character in provincial France, ravished by romantic illusions and the false promises of society. Grisey preferred Flaubert's book, writing that it contained "the most beautiful French prose that I know," and calling the author "a musician, an architect and a painter all at once." (One startling example of Flaubert's musical ear is a bit of punctuation in a line from the town's sleazy pharmacist: "The wine glasses!!! whispered Homais."[43]) Grisey described the novel as "discreet" and "suggestive." This fragment of dialogue is an illustration of those qualities; it also has musical value, showing the power of a very soft sound performed with the utmost intensity.

On July 6, 1967, in the continued absence of his piano, Grisey spent his time sitting on his terrace and meditating on the *Deux Madrigaux*. Three days later, Grisey complained about his inertia and inability to work. "Today, everything I added seems destined for the trash can," he wrote. "It's terrible. I'm advancing like a snail." On July 11, he realized, to his horror: "*I don't feel like composing!*" On summer break from one of the most demanding *écriture* programs in the world, supplemented by additional classes with Dutilleux, Grisey couldn't give himself a day off: "I committed violence toward myself, forced myself to work in the afternoon," he wrote. "I was almost crying. Then suddenly, the idea came and reignited all of my poor imagination."

---

43 Flaubert, *Madame Bovary*, 301.

The following evening, Grisey wrote in a letter to Simon that he went with a musicologist, an organist, and a doctor to check out a local organ.[44] They made recordings and improvised together in the style of "pseudo-Ravel, Debussy and Messiaen," but ended the night with something altogether more fun: "drinking champagne and listening to bawdy songs." He concluded the letter with another strikingly accurate bit of insight into his personality, especially relevant later in his career: "I believe the only time that I'm fundamentally mean and ruthless is when I'm prevented from working."

Continuing his fascination with Claudel, Grisey studied a book called *Paul Claudel poète-musicien*. He discussed the poetic form of the alexandrine in letters to Simon and listened to Mozart's opera about erotic obsession and moral comeuppance, *Don Giovanni*. But mostly, he was wrestling with the composition of the *Deux Madrigaux*, overwhelmed by the abyss of the empty page.

❧ ❧ ❧

Abandoning his idea of setting the "Epode" from the fourth poem of Claudel's *Cinq Grandes Odes*, Grisey instead chose texts by the Christian philosopher Pierre Teilhard de Chardin for his *Deux Madrigaux*. As mentioned, Grisey had been interested in Teilhard de Chardin's works since his teenage years. The new excerpt was a passage from de Chardin's *La présence du Christ dans le Monde* (*The Presence of Christ in the World*). The essay, divided in short chapters that alternate between poetic prayer and prose, affirms the presence of Christ in all aspects of the universe, while admitting certain modern points of view. De Chardin was a "Christian humanist," a Jesuit, and also a scientist, a Darwinian paleontologist. He admired the beauty of ancient Egyptian art; explored the intersection of geography and genetics; and made frequent use of sexual imagery to describe the power of his faith. "Lord, it is you who, through the imperceptible goading of sense-beauty, penetrated my heart," he wrote in *The Presence of Christ in the World*.[45]

Despite the change of text, the instrumentation of the *Deux Madrigaux* is similar to the sketches for *La muse qui est la grâce*—baritone, piano, and two percussionists.[46] For the form of the work, Grisey had a programmatic idea in mind. Despite the change in text, this idea was still closely connected to Claudel's dialogue. On July 22, 1967, Grisey summarized his idea for Simon: "The poet, in the grip of his muse, which is none other than Grace,

---

44   Sadly, not named.
45   de Chardin, *Hymn of the Universe*, (translation Bartholomew).
46   Paul Sacher archive.

refuses one last time the terrifying embrace, covers his ears and turns back to the earth. [His aim is the] supreme evocation of carnal and human love."[47] Years before Grisey's music achieved its powerful sensuality, summoning physical intimacy through sound was his explicit goal.

The first movement, titled "Un son très pur" ("A Very Pure Sound"), was dedicated to Jocelyne Simon. The text is excerpted from the fifth chapter of de Chardin's essay:

> A limpid sound rises amidst the silence; a trail of pure color drifts through the glass; a light glows for a moment in the depths of the eyes I love ... Three things, tiny, fugitive: a song, a sunbeam, a glance ...

In this short excerpt, de Chardin poetically raises ideas of great interest to Grisey at this time: communication between souls; penetration and sexuality as the "final depth where all the faculties of man are so closely bound together as to become a single point"; and the deceptive nature of our "sense-perceptions."[48]

The resulting composition is brief, about two and a half minutes, in an A-B-A1 form. The central motives of the first section are a vibraphone cluster and a vocal melody that vaguely outlines a C minor seventh chord, interrupted by dissonant interjections in the outer range of the piano and archaic, wooden percussion. The second section includes a low piano recitative with shorter, softer interjections; Grisey unifies the two sections by repeating the vibraphone cluster throughout. In the repeated A section, he adds piano glissandi and white-note clusters, also transposing the characteristic vibraphone cluster up a minor third. The movement closes with this cluster in its original position. This disjunct music tries to evoke the fragments of perceived light in de Chardin's poem.

The second movement of the *Madrigaux*, "Hymne à la matière" ("Hymn to Matter"), was dedicated to Jean-Marie de Miscault, a Marianist priest who taught in Hauts-de-Seine, outside Paris. For Grisey, this movement was "more classical" than the first, and "certainly very close to Stravinsky and Jolivet."[49] He composed it mostly at the piano in Belfort (which had finally arrived). The four-and-a-half-minute piece opens with a soft baritone melody in an implied D harmonic minor, featuring prominent augmented seconds. Besides this tonal echo, Grisey appears to be imitating the *sound* of serialist music without using actual serial techniques: he gives atonal lines to essentially the whole ensemble, relying on the standard intervals of tritones and major sevenths, but specific pitches and intervals repeat enough to rule

---

47   Lelong, *Écrits*, 302.
48   de Chardin, *Hymn of the Universe*, (translation Bartholomew), 79.
49   Lelong, *Écrits*, 302.

out a twelve-tone row. The *Deux Madrigaux* have never been performed. And while it's unlikely that this second movement's overlapping atonal lines coalesce into a satisfying texture, Grisey is consciously attempting to shape his climaxes, increasing and decreasing density and volume and releasing at different paces, trying to control the flow of musical tension. The movement concludes with a reprise, the augmented seconds transposed. Three overlapping, descending piano lines are left to resonate.

Deux Madrigaux represents an improvement on Grisey's Magnificat from the previous year, but is still an early student work. Cagney has correctly observed that Grisey's later student pieces, beginning with *Échanges* (1969), display a striking mastery of the maximalist, serialist aesthetic of the time.[50] They were not close to the composer's mature voice. But even this merely competent imitation required work. Despite the anguish that went into the composition of Grisey's madrigals, the result is fragmentary and a little timid.

As was his custom, Grisey didn't write letters while he was in Paris. He was busy with his studies and had Simon with him. His last letter from 1967 was dated December 26, from Belfort, where he spent Christmas with his family. Grisey attended Midnight Mass but found the ceremony lacking. Though his faith in God was not yet truly shaken, he found the ritual a bit pathetic. "Our old *curé* hummed a Franco-Latin jargon in falsetto, to which [the others] responded with Gregorian chants, all this for a dozen curious people gathered at the back of the church," he wrote. "I was ashamed, yes, ashamed, of such a liturgy, such a massacre that could only awaken a smile of pity in the audience."[51] On the cusp of the fateful year of 1968, Grisey was beginning to find more power in the rituals of the concert hall than in the ceremonies of the provincial Catholic church. Meanwhile, he continued to read widely. To deepen his education, he studied Freud, the fervent Catholic poet Léon Bloy, and the surrealist Paul Éluard. For fun, he read the classic French children's comic *Astérix et Obélix*.[52]

---

50 Cagney, "Synthesis and Deviation," 110.
51 Paul Sacher archive.
52 Lelong, *Écrits*, 303.

Chapter Four

Exchange Beyond Language (1968–70)

Grisey's *écriture* classes at the Conservatoire National Supérieur were a constant in his student years. Several exercise books from that time remain: Grisey practiced figured bass accompaniment, counterpoint, harmony, and orchestration in notebooks that ran into the hundreds of pages.[1] In a later interview, Grisey complained of this education, at once boring and difficult and destined to produce a generation of traditionalist-copycat composers:

> The term "French music" automatically evokes the specter of the Conservatoire National Supérieur de Musique de Paris, including its entire catalog of *écriture* classes. One produced there—it's not that long ago—a mixture of different styles, including among other characteristics a strong dose of Fauré. This was meant to allow you to pass your examinations, perfectly anonymous, but also undeniably "anonymously French"![2]

Still, Grisey was a proficient and motivated student, and successfully mastered the requirements of the Conservatoire. He received first prizes in history of music (1966), harmony (1967), fugue and counterpoint (1968), and second prize in piano accompaniment (1970). The latter was especially impressive considering the piano wasn't his first instrument.

The only letters Grisey wrote between 1968 and 1970 were again during his breaks in Belfort. These letters were typical of the composer's youth: he avoided the prosaic in favor of the abstractly spiritual. On February 17, 1968, Grisey meditated on death in a letter to Jocelyne Simon, returning to a theme of his teenage years. "Death, too, so close and so far ..." he wrote:

> Sometimes I look in the mirror and think that it will all rot away soon. There is something in me that "knows," that rather feels that it is petrified of eternity, which cries out to the Other Side. Isn't that the soul? If music

---

1   Paul Sacher archive.
2   Lelong, *Écrits*, 239.

can be the product of this part of us, it should therefore be the only language of men.³

On April 10, from Belfort again, Grisey told Simon that he was reading Blaise Pascal's *Pensées*. The book contains much that appears relevant to Grisey's aesthetic. For Pascal, human nature was at its core a process of constant change, an idea that fits neatly into Grisey's later goal to write music of a "pure sonic becoming, mutating ceaselessly."⁴ A famous passage in Pascal also parallels Grisey's later idea of the different planes on which his music operated, from the microscopic to the cosmic. "What is a man in the infinite?" Pascal wrote. "Let him lose himself in wonders as astonishing in their minuteness as the others in their immensity." Grisey would make use of this concept in later works such as *Le temps et l'écume* (1988–89).

At the same time, Grisey analyzed Arnold Schoenberg's *Variations for Orchestra*, op. 31. The work, composed from 1926 to 1928, is coloristic and brooding—even frightening in its surprises. But however instructive certain aspects of the piece may have been to the young Grisey—its orchestration, its different perceived tempi colliding—the overall philosophy behind the *Variations*, as articulated by its composer, represented an aesthetic against which Grisey would soon explicitly rebel. In 1931, Schoenberg delivered a radio lecture on the piece in advance of a performance in Frankfurt. "I vary material incessantly, repeat almost nothing that is unaltered, jump quickly to quite remote variations," Schoenberg said, "and take it for granted that an educated listener will be able to work out the intervening stages for himself."⁵ (Especially the idea of jumping "quickly to quite remote variations" contrasts with Dutilleux's *métabole* idea.) As a mature artist, Grisey championed the repetition of unaltered material, locating the need for predictability in the human brain. He also explicitly composed processes in his music that were meant to cover all the intervening stages between one musical form and another.

Still, Schoenberg's musical arguments were deeply rooted in the classical tradition, and the *Variations* have a certain moderate flow of information that makes the work intuitively pleasurable. Pierre Boulez, who based his aesthetic on the structural rigor of Schoenberg's pupil Anton von Webern, sometimes overloaded this flow of information, and became, rightly or wrongly, the main figure whom Grisey criticized aesthetically.

Grisey's next composition was a work of scenic music for Sophocles' play *Antigone*, set for choir, flute, bass clarinet, violin, viola, percussion, and clarinet. The exact date he completed the piece is unknown, but it was

---

3   Ibid, 303.
4   Pascal, *The Thoughts of Blaise Pascal*, 20.
5   Jenkins, *Schoenberg's Program Notes and Musical Analyses*, 299.

probably in the spring of 1968, since by the summer he'd already moved on to *Échanges*. In a later letter to Simon, he tacitly admitted that he had rushed the composition of *Antigone*.[6] This hastiness was a mistake he never repeated. The work consists of a Prelude and six settings of text from the Greek play's choir passages. The most impressive aspect of the piece is Grisey's new approach to the instrumentation of the clusters: by choosing very dissonant pitches but orchestrating them with lots of space between, he makes translucent what would otherwise be forbidding blocks of sound. Another good orchestration idea is the blend of piano clusters and the choir singing with closed mouths. In other ways *Antigone* is very much a student work: the vocal writing is repetitive and therefore uncomfortable for the singers, while most of the atonal melodic lines meander. The orchestration is sparing, with scattered percussion—a technique likely meant to give the music a certain archaism, but which results in a thin and fragile sound. A useful stage to pass through for the composer, but probably not an intriguing work for the listener, *Antigone* may be most important for helping Grisey realize he would need to take his time for every piece he wrote.[7] The low quantity and high quality of his later oeuvre suggests that he took that lesson to heart.

On March 20, 1968, a Trotskyist student group based at the Sorbonne led a demonstration against the Vietnam War in front of an American Express branch near the Paris Opéra, between the upscale second and ninth arrondissements. Some two hundred protestors showed up, some of whom flung projectiles. One of the demonstration's organizers was arrested. In response, on March 22, the Trotskyists occupied a room at the university in Nanterre, outside Paris, where they interrupted a classical music concert to call for their comrade's release.[8] At the tentative forefront of the sexual revolution in France, the students were also protesting rules which forbade opposite sex couples from being in dorm rooms together at night. The students felt the prevailing ideology of Gaullism that had created the Thirty Glorious Years had lapsed into traditionalism with an authoritarian streak.

During their all-night discussions on March 22, the Nanterre students proposed "anti-imperialist days" to take place on May 2 and 3, 1968. On May 3, students occupied Sorbonne buildings in the Latin Quarter, on the left bank of the Seine, and began holding meetings and sit-ins. The police

---

6   Lelong, *Écrits*, 307.
7   *Antigone* has never been recorded.
8   Abidor, *May Made Me*, 19.

arrived that afternoon. They clashed with the students, battles that later escalated to so-called Bloody Monday, with officials counting 422 arrests and 345 wounded police officers. But the students sought allies among France's working class, and the demonstrations metastasized into massive strikes. On May 8, some ten thousand people demonstrated in Nantes; on May 20, somewhere between six million and ten million people went on strike throughout the country.[9]

During the student protests, a copy of Bartholdi's statue *Lion de Belfort* in the Latin Quarter became a focal point for speeches. It's tempting to wonder whether Grisey, who attended some of these demonstrations, noted this or saw a symbolic meaning in the coincidence.

One group of students, who called themselves the "cultural commando unit," began to occupy theaters in Paris, declaring that "since the National Assembly has become a bourgeois theater, all bourgeois theaters should be formed into national assemblies."[10] On May 15, the students occupied the Théâtre de l'Odéon, in the sixth arrondissement, where they supplied political pamphlets to the audience and held long discussions. Luminaries such as the writer Louis Aragon and the philosopher Jean-Paul Sartre both showed up to speak to protesters at the Odéon and at the Sorbonne.

Together, Simon and Grisey attended such meetings. But their attitude was not quite as militant as that of their comrades. At one point, some of the students, thrilled by the immediacy of violent revolution, decided to burn down the Opéra national de Paris, seeing it as a symbol of the bourgeoisie. But Simon and Grisey stayed put. They didn't want to participate in burning the opera house down.[11] The young composer venerated culture and could not countenance its destruction, no matter the political background. Boulez's 1967 exhortation to "blow the opera houses up" couldn't have been far from Grisey's mind.[12]

The revolutionary atmosphere of May 1968 was felt at the Conservatoire National Supérieur as well, if in a less fervent, more assimilationist form. The musicians at the Conservatoire came largely from the kind of respectable backgrounds that provided access to excellent music education and had little to gain from revolution.[13] Physical distance was also a factor. The

---

9 Ibid. See Abidor's "Timeline of Events."
10 Singer, *Prelude to Revolution*, 166.
11 Interview with Raphaël and Jocelyne Grisey.
12 Kohda, "Boulez in his own words."
13 The bassist Joëlle Léandre has said, "When I arrived in Paris for classes at the Conservatoire National Supérieur, there were 1,400 students and only 45 [working class students] in the school." Barry, "Becoming Sound: An interview with bassist Joëlle Léandre."

Conservatoire, on the Right Bank in the eighth arrondissement, was far from the core of the protests.[14] But, on May 10, during the violent Night of the Barricades, Conservatoire headmaster Raymond Gallois-Montbrun "decided to summon several students in the middle of the night to defend the building, which he believed was under threat by the 'Red Guards' of the Sorbonne." There were no such attacks, though the students used the opportunity to flip the power dynamic, organizing and discussing how to join the movement.

Their concerns were mostly prosaic, focusing on the facilities, the canteen, and other practical matters. But the more radical students made aesthetic demands as well: famously, during a demonstration on May 13, one sign read "No more Gounod—Xenakis!" Though the Conservatoire was officially closed, students met there to talk, spray graffiti slogans, and eat ("The canteen was never as good as it was then," the composer and later director of the Conservatoire, Alain Louvier, joked.[15]) On May 19, the students who had not already gone home for the summer voted for a general strike. On May 22, members of a far-right group called Occident, already agitating against student protestors, attacked the Conservatoire. They hit a student composer with an iron bar and caused chaos in the lobby, until "the concierge scared them away by firing a pistol in the air," as one student at the time recalled.[16]

Boulez, the firebrand, was not in Paris during the events of May 1968. More significantly for Grisey, Messiaen was. The composer's traditional Catholic piety was accompanied by a profound political conservatism. "He was not at all reassured by what was happening," said Messiaen student Louvier. "Messiaen was a very Gaullist person and preferred to stay in the background." The musicologist Noémi Lefebvre said that Messiaen was "a little scared" by the revolutionary energy flowing through the Conservatoire.[17] According to Messiaen's later assistant, the composer Betsy Jolas, this fear was more extreme: "He was terribly scared to the point that he had tried to get himself appointed to another conservatory."[18]

Grisey came to believe that his small role in the wider clash of cultures—because he wasn't a Messiaen student yet, this encounter may have been as slight as Messiaen seeing Grisey with long hair and hippyish clothes and associating him with more radical protesters—caused lasting harm to his musical career. In 1991, Grisey told Julian Anderson that his music was never played

---

14   Laspière, "Mai 68 au Conservatoire de Paris."
15   Ibid.
16   Ibid.
17   Interview with Lefebvre.
18   Interview with Jolas.

in the United Kingdom "because Messiaen never mentions me." Grisey thought that Messiaen never completely trusted him, a feeling that Grisey attributed to his involvement in the events of May 1968. Jean-Luc Hervé, who became Grisey's student in the 1990s, recalled that Grisey confided in him: "He thought Messiaen didn't like him. He said that he thought that Messiaen was a little bit of afraid of him ... It was the time of '68. [Grisey] had long hair, and Messiaen thought he was a *révolutionnaire*. Messiaen was a very reactionary man."[19]

For the composer and conductor George Benjamin, who studied with Messiaen after Grisey, the reasons for the lack of warmth between Messiaen and Grisey were more complicated. The political theory is "pure surmise," he said. It could also have been Grisey's work, which Benjamin believes Messiaen found too "mechanical." "It was almost the only case when [Messiaen] didn't love a student," Benjamin said. "But Grisey never turned against him. He just wondered why he didn't love his music."[20] Simon also doubts that the events of May 1968 caused a rift between the legendary teacher and his student. Even if Messiaen was not always enthusiastic about Grisey's compositions, he encouraged Grisey to follow his own aesthetic instincts, granting him a sort of musical *laissez-passer*.[21] Grisey would later adopt the same practice with his own students. One day much later in his life, Grisey was walking in Paris with a friend when he pointed to the sky and told her, "Messiaen is up there, playing his organ."[22]

Whether by temperament or from a desire to protect his musical career, Grisey, though doubtlessly inspired by the youth culture of May 1968, was more of a passive observer of the reform movement at the Conservatoire. Louvier was highly active in the events, but "I don't particularly remember Gérard Grisey," he said. "He probably participated in the discussions of the 'commissions,' notably in composition, but I don't recall any particular traces." Grisey was not a student representative, nor did he serve on the committee founded to advise the Conservatoire after the school year resumed. "I think that his actions in 1968 were more discreet and less visible than other composers," Louvier continued.[23] Simon's family was touched by the troubles of the time—a cousin had died in the war of Algerian independence—but she remembers Grisey as somewhat disengaged and not particularly well-informed when it came to politics.[24]

---

19 Interview with Hervé.
20 Interview with Benjamin.
21 Interview with Campion.
22 Interview with Doderer.
23 Interview with Louvier.
24 Interview with Jocelyne Grisey.

As mentioned, May 1968 at the Conservatoire was a milder version of the other movements sweeping France. But it did lead to some lasting aesthetic changes at the institution. Édith Lejet was studying composition at the time and had noted a certain aesthetic backwardness at the conservatory: while it prepared students "admirably" for tonal composition, it largely left students up to their own devices in a contemporary idiom. "I was not introduced to the [aesthetic] thought of Boulez, Stockhausen, Berio, Ligeti, Xenakis and others as part of my studies," Lejet told Lefebvre. "Our achievements in the field of the Conservatory didn't give us any real keys to understanding them."[25] (All she remembers about Grisey is that he was going through a hippy phase during May 1968.[26])

Among other improvements, Pierre Schaeffer, the pioneer of *musique concrète*, became a permanent member of the Conservatoire faculty after May 1968, teaching a course that came to be known as the class on "musique électro-acoustique et recherche musicale." It doesn't seem that Grisey participated in this class. Still, the musical environment in which he was developing his aesthetic had become significantly richer thanks to the uprisings.

Grisey would also personally benefit from another reform to the conservatory structure. The Prix de Rome was a legendary scholarship for French students to work in Italy; the prize was first awarded in 1663 under Louis XIV and had been expanded in 1803 to include music students. Previous winners included Hector Berlioz, Claude Debussy, and Lili Boulanger. After 1968, as Lefebvre recounts, students "demanded to be judged by the entirety of their work," as opposed to old-fashioned exercises in fugue and cantata composition.[27] The reform, enacted in June 1970, ranked competitors on recordings of their compositions, reports from senior composers who heard live performances of the works in question, and an interview with a panel. The title Prix de Rome was officially abolished by the French government in 1971, but composers from the Conservatoire were still granted analogous scholarships to the Villa Médicis in the Italian capital.

For the musicologist Eric Drott, the political upheaval of May 1968 had a direct effect on the rhetoric of what would be known as the spectral movement. He reads in their later manifestos "a rhetorical gambit that gained widespread currency in the years following May '68 ... the 'neither/nor/but' structure ... a means of conceiving a way past some perceived social antinomy." In Grisey's writings, this structure presented as neither a continued exploration of serialism, nor a return to tonality, but a third way

---

25 Lefebvre, "Mai 1968 au Conservatoire," 20
26 Interview with Lejet.
27 Lefebvre, "Mai 1968 au Conservatoire," 22–23.

forward, researching the musical integration of acoustic phenomena. Drott argues that this approach is itself political:

> In attempting to formulate a capacious idea of the musical work, one that could accommodate and to some extent reconcile the entire gamut of sonorities, Grisey imagines musical form as a kind of federation of equal yet non-identical entities – a rainbow coalition of sounds, as it were (recall in this regard his call to respect the different "races and ethnicities of sound.") The musical work's capacity to acknowledge and embrace difference without distorting it becomes a potent emblem of social and cultural tolerance.[28]

But as the anecdote about the opera house shows, Grisey was far from understanding himself as an explicitly political artist. While his musical philosophy may allow a political interpretation in an abstract sense, Grisey was more preoccupied by the development of his music than he was by the concrete calls for justice of that heady, chaotic time.

In the summer of 1968, Grisey began to compose a new piece, *Échanges* for prepared piano (piano with objects in the strings that change the timbre), assigned to two players, and a double bass. It was completed by the following year and is a major improvement on his other works from this time. The *Deux Madrigaux* and *Antigone* were somewhat haphazard attempts at composing in the contemporary idiom; by contrast, *Échanges* is a polished, professional piece, though not especially original. (It was retroactively acquired by Ricordi, Grisey's publisher, in 2006.[29])

Grisey was aware that he found himself at a turning point. On July 20, 1968, he wrote to Simon to ask her what she thought of the title. "At the moment, I'm certain of being right," he continued. "I'm taking all the time necessary for this dangerous bend in my art … I'm experimenting with many new procedures. How much progress made, what a path traveled so far! Sometimes it seems to me that I'm raising a veil and that a field of immense possibilities is revealed to my eyes."[30]

Échanges opens with an exploration of the overtones of a piano string. Tempting as it is to interpret this as an overture to the spectral style, it should be treated as one extended technique among many, as the other elements of *Échanges* are more like reflections of then-contemporary trends: Webernian tritone-seventh chords, dissonant clusters, a texture of dialogue rather than coalescence. There are also small nods to the idiosyncratic style

---

28   Drott, "Spectralism, Politics, and the Post-Industrial Imagination," 58.
29   Cagney, "Synthesis and Deviation," 109.
30   Lelong, *Écrits*, 307.

of Messiaen: fragmentary, almost modal melodies and plaintive minor thirds in the bass; a clear tonal center on a B♮. The piece is the work of a student, but an accomplished and highly competent student whose technical skill was growing by leaps and bounds.

The duality implied in the title *Échanges* was a preoccupation for Grisey. The musicologist Lars Heusser sees this concept in the instrumentation and the differences between the busy piano and the more melodic bass material, with the second piano player, who plays inside the piano, in "a sort of intermediary role." Heusser adds, however, that "the piece is not based on a clear alternating structure or a coherent formal direction."[31] In fact, an analysis of the rhythmic structure of the piece does show a clear formal conceit—however, it is imperceptible to the listener and rather composerly. Grisey, perhaps taking inspiration from Messiaen's taste for prime-number rhythms, constructs an interplay of prime, non-prime, and free rhythms throughout the piece.[32] Grisey's mature music would continue to make use of elaborate structures; he would soon improve on his ability to make these structures tangible.

In early July 1968, Grisey returned from the tumult of Paris to his home in Belfort. As in earlier summers, he used the time to compose, read books, study scores, and otherwise broaden his cultural horizons. Away from Simon, he again wrote her frequent letters, leaving a valuable record of his intellectual development at this crucial time.

On July 6, 1968, Grisey was reading André Malraux's 1933 novel *La Condition humaine*. The book follows Communist resistance fighters and their French sympathizers and imperialist opponents in the period of the Chinese Civil War. (Malraux, himself a Resistance operative during World War II, had been named Minister of Culture under Charles de Gaulle. He later had a highly public falling-out with Boulez.[33]) Malraux's book

---

31 Heusser, "Il est donc temps de rendre la complexité efficace."
32 The first and last sections of the piece alternate between prime and non-prime rhythmic groupings and free time, which Grisey indicates in the score. Within the first section, these values are also mirrored: 2-3-3-2-4 (=14); Fermata; 3-2-2-3-1 (=11); etc. The three following sections each focus on one "type" of time: the second section is quasi recitativo, in a sort of pulseless time. The third uses almost exclusively rhythmic groupings of prime numbers; the fourth, exclusively non-prime numbers. The final section returns to an interplay of prime and non-prime groupings: 1-3-2-2-3 (=11); Fermata; 4-2-2-3-3-2 (=16). It is doubtful whether any of this can be heard.
33 Parouty, "Boulez, l'Inflexible."

compares the revolutionary cause to opium, seeing in both an intoxicating numbness that leads to pointless suffering, and implicitly criticizes the Marxist idea that religion is the opiate of the masses—all relevant topics in the aftermath of the May upheavals. "It is the whole man of the twentieth century who emerges from it, desperately anguished, searching in vain for a way out," Grisey wrote. "This cry of anguish seems to me to be a pressing call from God. Contrary, undoubtedly, to the author's will, everything in this book is about eternity."[34] Grisey added, "I'm thinking a lot about suffering right now. Maybe because of this book, or because I feel too happy and ... fragile." The reasons for his happiness were manifold. He was calm and took pleasure in composing. He was also getting along with his parents, especially his father. The two men talked about "the revolution, the birds, the forest" and, Grisey added, "I restrict myself to that, because if I get away from it I perceive the gap."

Grisey was a quick reader: by July 13, 1968, he'd moved on from Malraux to Simone de Beauvoir's *Memoirs of a Dutiful Daughter*. "I'm learning a lot about femininity, about the style of education in the first half of this century," he wrote. "I could never have imagined that the sexual, racial, and social taboos of the bourgeoisie could be so far away." De Beauvoir and the young Grisey also had several things in common: musical grandmothers and love for the novel *Le Grand Meaulnes* and the works of Claudel. De Beauvoir captures the appeal of the Catholic author to the young Grisey: "I loved Claudel above all else," she wrote, "because he celebrates in the body the miraculously sensitive presence of the soul."[35]

The next day, Grisey had a powerful experience with Mozart's String Quartet No. 19 in C Major op. 10, "Dissonance." The aspect of this piece that most struck him was a formal logic his own best works would also achieve: "The form is born with the idea, at once spontaneous and constructed in advance."[36] In the middle of this optimistic time, Grisey still felt the constrictions of his background. To Simon, he bemoaned the lack of money that prevented him from buying recordings of the complete Mozart pieces.

On July 22, 1969, Grisey finished the de Beauvoir memoir and moved on to Camus (he didn't say which Camus book he'd read). He appreciated the existentialist writer's "conception of the absurd," but generally found the philosophy lacking: "The more I deepen my understanding of his ideas, the more I seem to be returning to God(!)"[37] Still, his reading Camus was

---

34   Lelong, *Écrits*, 304.
35   Ibid, 290.
36   Ibid, 306.
37   Ibid, 307–8.

a reflection of his broadening interests, moving from religious writing and music to "everything," as he acknowledged on July 26: "Politics, jazz, poetry, philosophy, the growth of trees, the lives of animals, everything concerns me." This was a defining characteristic of the artist as an adult. No narrow specialist, Grisey had "total culture."[38]

Picking up on this interest in poetry, Grisey spent the following day "dreaming a little" on the long poem "Pluies" ("Rains") by Saint-John Perse, the nom de plume of Alexis Leger, a French poet-diplomat who won the Nobel Prize in Literature in 1960. Though Grisey never composed a work based on the text, it shares the solemn cadences and cathartic structures of Claudel's *Cinq Grandes Odes*, presenting beautiful images of waves, seas, and breezes, natural phenomena that inspired the composer explicitly throughout his life. Grisey felt a profound sense of musical mission in the summer of 1968. On July 28, he wrote to Simon, "What can I do if not write, write again and forever, a bit of music, until my last breath?"

On August 5, Grisey wrote to Simon from Marseille, where he probably traveled with his family.[39] "The girls are really very beautiful," he told Simon. "All the Parisians are nothing compared to a group of Provençal girls at the beach." Intentional or not, the remark echoes Proust's narrator, who is enchanted by the "young girls in bloom" at the fictional beach town of Balbec.

But, as in previous summers, when Grisey had struggled to relax while on vacation, his stay in Marseille was not simply "down time." More than the girls on the beach, the thing that captured his attention was a television program on the horrors of the civil war in Biafra, Nigeria. The conflict was a result of decolonization—an issue to which the politics of May 1968 may have sensitized Grisey—and its humanitarian cost was catastrophic. In his letter to Simon, he raged against the indifference he saw around him. "I am truly scandalized by the reactions here," he wrote. "*They just have to manage; tomorrow we will be beaten up for something else; they are too lazy to work; we don't make war when we can't stand it; why don't we [kill] them when they are dying, they will suffer less; they just have to have fewer children*, etc."[40] The following year, Grisey would channel this outrage into *Mégalithes*, his only explicitly political composition.

Nature continued to make a powerful impression on Grisey. In his last letter from the summer of 1968, dated August 7, Grisey wrote, "I abandon my body to the sea, to the waves, merge with this icy water, rich with all the salt of the earth. My eyes are troubled at the sight of the sun and the

---

38   Interview with Julian Anderson.
39   Lelong, *Écrits*, 309. It's dated to July, but that's probably a mistake.
40   Ibid.

dizziness comes, in this swirl of gold, light and foam." He was immersed in a sensual experience.

Grisey abandoned his first instrument, the accordion, around the same time that he entered Messiaen's prestigious composition course, in the 1968–69 academic year. Jonathan Goldman discovered a letter, dated 1969, from Grisey to his Canadian accordionist friend Joseph Macerollo, which explained Grisey's thought process. Grisey wrote it in English, which he didn't know well yet:

> I could never tell to musicians of the Paris Conservatory that I am accordionist without hearing them laughing. Messiaen knows something about electronic accordion but he doesn't like it at all ... I am not playing accordion any more. My way is another one. I compose, which need [*sic*] a lot of time and I play a little piano ... I didn't write any work for accordion during these past four years because I don't know anybody in France who would be able to do it. Maybe did you hear of the *Passacaglia* I wrote a few years ago. It's a youth's essay and I would like everybody [to] forget it. My style has changed; I am now very close of people like Ligetti [*sic*] or Stockhausen.[41]

Given Grisey's bursting schedule at the Conservatoire, it was a logical decision for him to abandon an instrument which he felt couldn't help him on his path as a composer. But this decision also illustrates the class dynamics into which the young composer was thrust there.[42] The institution was an elite place; of Grisey's close artistic fellow travelers, many had intellectual backgrounds. Giving up the accordion was a way for Grisey to fit into his new environment.

Goldman writes that Grisey then took concrete steps to "avoid being identified with the humble instrument, a perennial object of scorn in certain art-music circles," adding that his roots with the instrument have been "expunged from his own artistic narrative." Grisey was not above retroactively manipulating various aspects of his career in order to pave his future way.[43] But he still retained an emotional attachment to his original instrument.[44] In 1989, Grisey lent his Hohner Morino VI piano accordion to a

---

41 Goldman, "Gérard Grisey, Accordionist," 12.
42 Interview with Raphaël Grisey.
43 Cagney, "Synthesis and Deviation," 373.
44 Grisey declined at least two invitations to write for accordion as a mature composer, citing especially its inability to perform non-tempered music. Paul Sacher archive.

Trossingen non-profit, which in turn loaned it out to a talented German accordionist whose family didn't have the means to buy him his own instrument. When the non-profit asked Grisey if he would be willing to sell the instrument to the young German, he declined, "for whatever sentimental reasons."[45] One day around this time, Grisey encountered a teenage beggar who was playing an accordion in the Paris Métro. Grisey had to leave the train; he was so moved that he was close to giving the teenager all the cash he had.[46] Although Grisey stopped playing the accordion, it remained a part of him.

※ ※ ※

In the 1968–69 academic year, Grisey was accepted into Messiaen's renowned composition class at the Conservatoire de Paris. Born in 1908, Messiaen's background was so artistic that his mother, the poet Cécile Sauvage, dedicated a set of poems to him while he was still in the womb; Messiaen was admitted to the Conservatoire de Paris at the age of eleven.[47] In other ways he had much in common with Grisey. Both men were fervently religious despite their parents, and both were great admirers of Claudel. Both saw composition as a spiritual calling.

In May 1940, Messiaen was serving as a medical auxiliary in the French Army. (He was rejected as a soldier due to poor eyesight.) He was on the way to Nancy when he was captured by German forces. He was sent to a Nazi prison camp in Görlitz, Germany, where he famously composed his overwhelmingly powerful *Quartet for the End of Time* for instruments that the prisoners had at hand. The piece was performed on January 15, 1941. Just a few months later, he was freed and allowed to return to Paris.

Messiaen started out teaching harmony at the Conservatoire in occupied Paris. One of his earliest students was the ferociously talented and opinionated Boulez. Messiaen was so impressed with Boulez that he followed his own student in composing with "twelve-tone entities," though Messiaen's music remained unmistakably his own.[48] Messiaen later "assiduously" supported Boulez's prominent new-music concert series, the Domaine Musical, and the two men were among the most powerful figures in French music—Boulez probably the most powerful of all.

Paris was liberated in 1944. In April 1945, Messiaen attracted controversy on the music scene of the newly freed city with a performance of his

---

45 Ibid.
46 Interview with Detry.
47 Griffiths, *Olivier Messiaen and the Music of Time*, 19.
48 Ibid, 143.

vitally prayerful *Trois petites liturgies de la présence divine* for piano, ondes Martenot, vocal ensemble, and chamber orchestra. Critics found it harmonically "cheap," repetitive, and "exotically sensual" (this last trait apparently a bad thing).[49] In the fall of 1947, Messiaen was given a new assignment as a teacher of analysis at the Conservatoire, a role which he defined broadly and held until after Grisey's entrance to the *écriture* courses at the Conservatoire in the spring of 1966. No wonder the young Belfortian dreamed of entering this class: by Grisey's teenage years, when he first formulated this dream,[50] Messiaen had already taught such legendary figures as Karlheinz Stockhausen and Iannis Xenakis.[51] In October 1966, two years before Grisey officially became his student, Messiaen's role as the Master—if not the professor—of composition at the Conservatoire de Paris was recognized, and he was finally given bureaucratic permission to teach that elusive subject.[52]

Messiaen held his classes three times a week, for three (and even four) hours at a time.[53] They were roughly divided between analysis; presentation of student pieces; and lessons on technical subjects that interested Messiaen throughout his career, including "Hindu and Greek rhythms, neumes, instrumentation, and so on."[54] In the fall of 1968, Messiaen "arrived in class more energized than ever," the musicologist Jean Boivin writes. "But he still spent long moments examining, nearly as an aside, the works of the individual students, and if his references to the repertoire were still frequent, they became increasingly fleeting."[55]

Messiaen's composition classes combined his unparalleled mastery of the repertoire with a memorable—and sometimes impenetrable—guru-like style of teaching. This peculiar style stuck with Grisey long after his years of apprenticeship with Messiaen were finished. Some twenty years after joining Messiaen's course, in 1988, Grisey recalled:

> Whenever I think of Olivier Messiaen's teaching, the first word that comes to mind is: silence.
>
> In the uncertainty of his first phase, every young composer starting out looks for a master, a father or a guru, from whom he expects advice and criticism.

---

49 Ibid, 113.
50 Lelong, *Écrits*, 239.
51 Boivin, *La classe de Messiaen*, 103.
52 Ibid, 151.
53 Cagney, "Synthesis and Deviation," 154.
54 Ibid.
55 Boivin, *La classe de Messiaen*, 161.

I was attentive to the least word of encouragement or the most scathing critique. I was quickly disappointed. He would slowly and attentively read my scores, and then: some sibylline words, murmured between two pages.

Doubtlessly, my music was still a bit further away, and I needed to continue searching.

With his silence, Messiaen put me inexorably back in touch with myself, with my true music, with the critiques which only I could formulate.[56]

In 1971, a documentary, *Olivier Messiaen et les Oiseaux* (*Olivier Messiaen and the Birds*), was made, which illustrates this dynamic of the Zen master and his disciples. Messiaen plays the piano and discusses an excerpt from Debussy's opera *Pelléas et Mélisande* while the students, including Grisey, crowd in a circle around him. They look simultaneously eager to absorb his knowledge and acutely afraid of saying the wrong thing in response to his questions.[57]

For the 1968–69 academic year, a Canadian student auditing Messiaen's class kept meticulous notes, allowing Boivin to reconstruct the remarkably broad range of topics discussed.[58] In the fall of 1968, Messiaen covered technical subjects such as magic squares, in which numbers are distributed in a grid so that their sum is the same when added horizontally, vertically, and diagonally, a technique Grisey used to generate durations for his 1970 work *Initiation*;[59] antique Greek and Hindu rhythmic structure; fugue; melody; irrational rhythmic values; and Gregorian chant. Besides critiquing student works, Messiaen analyzed Claude Le Jeune's *Printemps*; Chopin's Étude op. 8 no. 5; Polish composer Krzysztof Penderecki's *Passion of St. Luke*; Xenakis's *Metastasis*, *Pythoprakta*, and *Eonta*, a work for two trumpets, three trombones, and piano whose oppositional structure, use of external resonators, and performative elements all found their ways into Grisey's music;[60] Wagner's *Ring* cycle operas *Das Reingold* and *Die Walküre*; and Alban Berg's *Lyric Suite*. There were also scattered philosophical talks and lectures on themes such as Russian Spiritism, an occult movement.

With this packed and fascinating schedule, it's no surprise that Grisey didn't write much in his journal at the beginning of the 1968–69 academic year. In January 1969, however, he wrote to Simon from Belfort to describe both his restlessness at home and the solace of his work. "I never feel at rest or at peace," he told her. "My lonely work, whenever I have the courage to

---

56 Lelong, *Écrits*, 228.
57 Pavlović, "Messiaen on Debussy and color."
58 Boivin, *La Classe de Messiaen*, 162 and 443–47.
59 Lelong, *Écrits*, 143.
60 Grisey took the piece with him for further study during his summer vacation in 1969.

devote myself to it, gives me great joy. Everything is ready, everything has a shape. All I can do is compose and the task will be long."[61]

After the Christmas break, on January 8, 1969, Messiaen's course went back into full swing. Technical topics in the new year included "magic and mathematics," on numerical principles with musical applications, such as palindromes; Xenakis's stochastic music, which generates random series of musical objects based on a given material; Chinese music; and the art of the oratorio. The works analyzed were remarkably contemporary: Stockhausen's *Gruppen*; Penderecki's Cello Concerto and *Fluorescence*; Betsy Jolas's String Quartet no. 2; further Xenakis works; Ligeti's *Atmosphères, Volumina*, and *Apparitions*; Boulez's Piano Sonata no. 3 and *Structures* for two pianos; Varèse's *Amériques*; Pierre Schaeffer's *Solfège de l'objet sonore*; and Berg's Violin Concerto. Among the few older works Messiaen discussed with his students were the madrigals of Monteverdi and Gesualdo and the final two operas from Wagner's *Ring* cycle, *Siegfried* and *Götterdämmerung*. As if this wasn't enough, the class examined Chinese philosophy through the lens of the I Ching, an essential influence on John Cage; birdsong; internal listening, or the inner ear; and chance processes in music. They also discussed Messiaen's own *Réveil des oiseaux*, in April 1969—though the group had covered many of their teacher's favorite topics, this was the first time they had explicitly talked about one of his pieces.[62]

Still kept busy with this rich program, Grisey hardly wrote in his diary. There are just two entries for the year 1969. On March 16, the composer again felt the presence of God, which moved him to tears of joy. He begged the Lord to not allow him to forget the moments "in which You reveal yourself as a living person." On April 23, he had a similarly transcendent—yet more ambiguous, almost cruel—experience while listening to Mozart's Requiem. The work reminded him of lines from Rainer Maria Rilke's *Duino Elegies*:

> For beauty is nothing
> But the beginning of terror, that we are still able to bear,
> and we revere it so, because it calmly disdains to destroy us.[63]

In these lines, beauty and violence are adjacent phenomenon, the one impossible without the other. "Strange thoughts are coming to me," Grisey wrote. He even considered destroying the music he'd written so far. Having survived the *écriture* program of the Conservatoire de Paris and achieved his dream of studying with Messiaen, Grisey—briefly, at least—confronted an

---

61 Lelong, *Écrits*, 310.
62 Boivin, *La classe de Messiaen*, 162.
63 Rainer Maria Rilke and A.S. Kline (translator), *The Duino Elegies, Poetry in Translation*.

artistic void. On June 11, 1969, Grisey, a "shy presence" in Messiaen's class, introduced a piece of his to his colleagues for the first time.[64] There is no record of which work he showed or how it was received.

❧ ❧ ❧

In 1969, alongside his studies with Messiaen, Grisey enrolled in a one-year course at the Centre International de Recherche Musicale, a Parisian institution founded three years earlier by the experimental musician Jean-Étienne Marie.[65] Marie taught subjects such as acoustics, sound engineering, and experimental music analysis, where he emphasized the potential of *musique concrète* and microtonal composition to transcend what he considered the ossified categories of serial music. Like Messiaen, Marie gave introductions to various mathematical topics with potential applications to music, such as logarithmic curves and geometrical progressions, concepts that Grisey later integrated into his structural planning for his compositions.[66] Marie also introduced Grisey to the technique of composing with sum and difference tones. Starting with two "generator" frequencies, which are added or subtracted from one another, composers could generate never-ending chains of acoustically related harmonies. Grisey would later call these harmonies "the shadows of sound" because of their latent numerical relationships.

Cagney locates further influences that Marie's course had on the young Grisey: Grisey's fascination with acoustics and psychoacoustics; the notions of "contracted" and "dilated" time, or how a listener perceives time as flowing differently based on the density of musical events happening within a given chronological period; his predilection for dividing orchestral forces into independent groups; and his interest in the philosophical works of Gilles Deleuze.[67] In Messiaen's composition course, Grisey breathed the atmosphere of the canon and studied prominent works of contemporary music that aspired to canonical status. With Marie, Grisey came closer to the cutting edge.

❧ ❧ ❧

The composer Michaël Levinas,[68] Grisey's fellow student at the Conservatoire National Supérieur, dates the origins of spectral music—a

---

64   Cagney, "Synthesis and Deviation," 175.
65   Cagney was the first musicologist to discover the extent of Grisey's connection to Marie. "Synthesis and Deviation," 191–203.
66   Ibid, 194.
67   Ibid, 198–200.
68   Levinas declined to be interviewed for this book.

term that describes Grisey's work, but that wasn't coined until 1979—to the Darmstädter Ferienkurse in the summer of 1972, when the young composers heard a revelatory performance of Karlheinz Stockhausen's *Stimmung* for six voices.[69] Questioning this too-neat origin story, Cagney points out that the Paris premiere of *Stimmung* took place in December 1968, and that Grisey probably heard the performance.[70] A work which Cagney doesn't mention, but which strongly supports his thesis, is Grisey's unperformed, unpublished *Répons* for three voices. The title refers to the call-and-response between a solo singer and a church choir in the Catholic liturgy. The piece has been dated to 1969.[71] (Boulez named a work for large chamber orchestra *Répons* in 1981.)

Répons was composed specifically for the Abbey of Notre-Dame du Bec, in the city of Bec-Hellouin in Normandy. The abbey was completed in 1060 and housed a Benedictine order. It was ransacked in 1792 during the French Revolution, and repurposed as a depot for Napoleon's army; after housing soldiers during World War II, it was returned to the Benedictine order in 1948. With that history, the abbey had weathered many of the same swings from religion to secularism as France itself.

On the manuscript, Grisey wrote: "I am open to the Lord, always and everywhere." *Répons* lasts about an hour and is obviously inspired by *Stimmung*. A bass, a tenor, and a mezzo-soprano sing minute-long measures on a single chord, of an A, D, and E♭—a Webernian fourth and tritone, as if to distinguish itself from Stockhausen's overtones. The text of *Répons* consists of vowels which are supposed to change imperceptibly. The singers are also told to open and close their mouths, and to vary their pitches by a quarter-tone higher or lower. Grisey's piece builds from *pianissimo* to one *forte* section a minute in length. And that's it: an extraordinarily simple piece.

Without a performance, it's hard to tell if *Répons* achieves the slow, transcendent hypnosis of *Stimmung* or if it becomes boring and self-serious. But Grisey's debt to the Stockhausen work is unmistakable.

Grisey had not forgotten the horrors of the war in Biafra which had left such an impression on him in July 1968 (the war continued until January 1970). In 1969, Grisey completed *Mégalithes*, a piece for four trumpets,

---

69 Cagney, "Synthesis and Deviation," 205.
70 Ibid, 238.
71 By the musicologists of the Paul Sacher Stiftung. The work's similarity to *Stimmung*, along with its explicit religiosity, makes this a good guess. The score is also in the Paul Sacher archive.

four trombones, six horns, and tuba. A megalith is a prehistoric monument made from stone, and Grisey's piece is intended as a kind of archaic witnessing to tragedy. The moral content of the composition is clear from the very first page. It is marked "in memory of the victims of Biafra" and bears an epigraph from Lanza del Vasto, an Italian Catholic writer, peace activist, and disciple of Mahatma Gandhi.

With *Mégalithes*, Grisey began using aleatoric sections, bits of musical material from which the performers can choose freely. Cagney ties this to Boulez's Piano Sonata no. 3 specifically and the anti-hierarchical climate in France after May 1968 more generally, seeing Grisey follow fashionable trends in new music.[72] There are nine "sequences" of music in *Mégalithes*, lasting between seven seconds and three minutes. These sequences can be performed in nine different orders.

Other elements of Grisey's later music appear in this piece for the first time: the use of sustain lines to denote held pitches; complex layered rhythms such as five against eleven; the requirement for both the conductor and the musicians to remain completely silent and immobile while performing grand pauses. Though both *Échanges* and *Répons* worked occasionally with quartertones, *Mégalithes* uses them more expansively; still, these additional notes are used as ways of varying or "dirtying" the usual twelve pitches, rather than as the new harmonic thinking they later came to represent. As in *Antigone*, the chords in *Mégalithes* are largely comprised of dissonant clusters that have a certain translucency, since they are voiced with plenty of space between the intervals. Grisey's composition shares a similar instrumentation, as well as a kind of violent austerity, with Xenakis's *Eonta* from 1963–64, which, as mentioned, Grisey studied both in Messiaen's class and again in late August 1969, after he completed his own work.

Grisey never heard *Mégalithes* in his lifetime. The world premiere took place at the Lucerne Festival in 2009 under the conductor Martín Baeza Rubio. Reviewing the concert, *Guardian* music critic Tom Service wrote:

> It's music of massive, monumental power, as you'd expect from the title: clusters of gigantic dissonance thrown around the auditorium (the players perform all over the hall), which coalesce into huge sonic pile-ups and then break apart with ear-splitting energy. It was a performance of roof-shaking intensity, and revealed an important addition to the Grisey canon.[73]

To contemporary critics, the sound of the piece and its origins in human tragedy are immediately perceptible. Music critic Simon Cummings writes that *Mégalithes* is "rough-hewn, jagged, solid, implacable—it isn't difficult

---

72 Cagney, "Synthesis and Deviation," 171.
73 Service, "Lucerne Gets to Grips with the Alphorn."

to find parallels with the dreadful human impact wrought by and upon the Nigerian people—and yet, there's beauty in the music too."[74]

Political music is a notoriously finicky genre; it can easily collapse into the superficial or the didactic. From that standpoint, Grisey's achievement with *Mégalithes*—which does neither—at the age of twenty-three is impressive. It was his first and only explicitly political work, as his later pieces focused on the miracles of human perception.

On July 15, 1969, Grisey applied to the Fondation de la Vocation prize, aimed at people under thirty who were already excelling in their given field, with his compositions *Antigone* and *Échanges*.[75] He also applied to a masterclass in Siena, Italy, at the Accademia Chigiana, an institute for advanced musical studies, with *Échanges* and *Mégalithes*. Jocelyne Simon handled the work of preparing and mailing the materials.[76]

Grisey was accepted to the course and traveled to the historic Italian city at the end of the month. The composition course was led by the Italian composer Boris Porena, whom Grisey described as "a nice guy, but a hardcore serialist with all the dogmatism that implies." In Grisey's letters to Simon, the composer appeared more interested in the history, art, and natural beauty of Siena than in the specific content of the masterclasses. He spent hours examining Lorenzetti frescoes, Donatello sculptures, and the late-medieval and Renaissance paintings in the Pinacoteca Nazionale. He also attended the horse races at the Palio, with their trumpets, bells, and tambourines, and praised the landscape of the region, with its "sweetness of life, its cypress groves, shadowy hills, secret, calm little houses, ochres and greens ..." Grisey also asked Simon to send him a life of the Dominican mystic Catherine of Siena, whose presence he said was palpable throughout the city. His religious feeling was awakened by the potent Catholic poetry of the place. Of a Duccio altarpiece, he wrote: "I stood for thirty minutes, fascinated, by the infinite serenity and ecstatic sweetness of this Virgin, under which Duccio dared to write: 'Holy Virgin, protect and bless our city of Siena and give salvation to Duccio who painted you so well.'" Continuing his practice of artistic education in the summer, Grisey also studied music such as Mozart's *Exultate* and *Jubilate*, pieces in which he noticed an "interior tension and passion, controlled and cast in a language that does not tolerate the slightest excess." On the piano, he practiced Debussy's profoundly

---

74 Cummings, "Gérard Grisey – Mégalithes (UK Première)."
75 Cagney, "Synthesis and Deviation," 177–178.
76 Lelong, *Écrits*, 310.

mysterious 6 *Épigraphes antiques*, a work originally composed for piano four-hands, which can also be played by one pianist. The work did not so much influence Grisey as enter his aesthetic marrow.

Grisey's project during his three weeks in Siena was to compose a short new work. The piece that resulted from this assignment was *Charme* for solo clarinet, dedicated to another participant in the festival, the Spanish clarinetist Jesús Villa Rojo; Villa Rojo had shown Grisey some multiphonics, like "chords" for a melodic instrument, which intrigued him, according to a later program note.[77] Grisey finished the work between August 7 and August 22, 1969—a short time period for any composer but especially compressed for Grisey who, after the let-down of his rushed process in *Antigone*, had become slow and patient. "I've worked enormously on [*Charme*] this week, and it was with some difficulty that I managed to deliver it," he wrote in a letter to Simon from the end of the Accademia Chigiana masterclass.

The power of the resulting piece, *Charme*, lies in the way it manages to sound like electronic music while using only a single acoustic instrument. This is especially true of the *mobiles*, aleatoric elements which the musician must select and insert at different places. These contain the multiphonics Villa Rojo showed Grisey in Siena; Grisey's notes on these multiphonics are among his sketches for *Charme*.[78]

In that sense, *Charme* is more a part of the electronic music lineage than it is a traditional clarinet piece. In 1959, Karlheinz Stockhausen had expressed a desire to write music that sounded like nothing else before. "Electronic music sounds best when it only sounds like electronic music," Stockhausen wrote, "meaning that, as far as possible, it should only contain sounds and connections between sounds that are unique and free of association, and make us believe that we'd never heard them before."[79] With *Charme*, Grisey hit on a paradox explored more thoroughly in the work of his eminent colleague and later friend Helmut Lachenmann: that acoustic music on traditional instruments can, through careful deconstruction, also result in the kinds of unplaceable, foreign sounds that Stockhausen associated with advanced musical technology.

Besides this paradox, which results mostly from Grisey's precise dynamic markings and effective use of the clarinet multiphonics in his *mobiles*, *Charme* is a conventional work of its time. It sets up a duality between serialist passage work and the static mobiles which confront the primary material and

---

77 In this program note, Grisey says he was an "assistant" at the Accademia Chigiana, but according to his letters, he needed to apply for a scholarship after he'd already arrived in Siena.

78 Paul Sacher archive.

79 Stockhausen, *Elektronische und instrumentale Musik*, 140.

gradually take over the sound of the piece entirely.[80] In Grisey's sketches, a table of subtly varied rhythms exists as well; however, the final version of the piece is composed in spatial notation, with the notes to be played proportionally within a specified number of seconds.

In his later program note, Grisey describes the form as "a dialogue between two *personnages* … a third *personnage* resolves all conflict: silence." This dualist form, built out of contrasting musical ideas, recalls his writings on his relationship with Simon, highlighting the unknowable nature of other people. Silence, the last character, is the mediator, and especially important, as Grisey urges the performer to keep absolutely still when not playing—as in *Mégalithes*.

Cagney notes that Messiaen used the term *personnage* to denote "distinct and mutually contrasting musical figures undergoing transformation in sequential repetitions."[81] In Messiaen's conception, these figures then "act upon" one another, one changing the length of the other, for example. Grisey used the term more simply to refer to two separate and distinct musical ideas, but this technique was clearly inspired by the master artist.[82]

In 1974, after a later performance of the piece (paired with Alban Berg's *Four Pieces for Clarinet and Piano*, as well as other works), the critic Jacques Lonchampt wrote in *Le Monde*, "The young clarinetist seemed less happy in Gérard Grisey's *Charme*, an interweaving of pointillist sounds, fluctuating sounds and silences, rigorously weighed and written, from the almost imperceptible murmur to the brutal cackle—which do not however manage to be 'charming.'"[83] With hindsight, Grisey did not consider *Charme* an important work. In his later program note, he wondered, "What to say about this work from my youth, except that it refers to serial procedures from which I later radically distanced myself?" Despite its effective elements, the work was tainted by its association with the serial music Grisey was coming to disdain.

In July 1970, Grisey also began composing a new work, *Perichoresis*, his last piece explicitly inspired by his understanding of Christianity, completed in March 1970 (and revised in the summer of 1973).[84] The title refers to the simultaneous oneness and three-ness of the Father, the Son, and the

---

80   Heusser, "Il est donc temps de rendre la complexité efficace," 99. He refers to the pitch material as a *"zwölftöniger, lagenfixierter Vorrat"* (twelve-tone, fixed-range pitch set). The pitches only repeat in their original octave. Besides that, I couldn't discover the precise serial procedure which generated the pitches of the work.
81   Cagney, "Synthesis and Deviation," 163.
82   Ibid, 169.
83   "L'Itinéraire de Murail à Méfano."
84   Paul Sacher archive.

Holy Spirit.[85] As Grisey himself wrote in the program note for *Perichoresis*: "The title means mutual exchange, a deep relationship, beyond language and thought, between two or more people. Three groups, three characters, three colors, three rhythmic cells confronted ..."[86] Again, Grisey turned the sensual connection between entities into an ineffable musical form of dialogue and interpenetration.

Perichoresis is scored for three groups of instruments: viola, bass clarinet, tenor trombone, and a pianist with two players in the first group; two flutes, B♭ clarinet, tuba, and harp in the second group; and trumpet, English horn, bass, and percussion in the third group—an instrumentation which matches the program of the Holy Trinity. Every player also has a large aluminum sheet on which to create noise effects. Each group is assigned a color—black, blue, and red—and notated in its respective color in the score.

The work is highly complex, with a remarkable level of detail. At the same time, it includes aleatoric elements, like *Mégalithes* and *Charme*. There is an unresolved contradiction between the painstakingly detailed notation on the level of individual instruments and the undetermined elements in the form of the piece. But there are several signs of Grisey's emerging aesthetic in *Perichoresis*. The piece shows his interest in the precise notation of dynamics in his scores, with a viola swell determined to a sixth of a beat. Another hint is the contrast between pitch and noise, which the composer teases out between the groups using the aluminum sheets and atonal chords. As Cagney argues, *Perichoresis*, despite a certain Stockhausian pointillism, also "contains some strikingly quasi-tonal passages" that "evince a tentative effort to reassert harmony into a post-serial idiom."[87] A minor third between an F♯ and an A in the flute, clarinet, and harp is a particularly clear example (the same interval that appeared in the bass melody of *Échanges*). *Perichoresis* also contains chords which reappear at irregular intervals but which are close enough together to give the listener a feeling of predictable pulse. Finally, in his sketches, Grisey worked out the timing of the composition on graph paper, helping him to visualize the form of his piece, a method he continued to use, and which helped him develop his keen sense of dramaturgy.

On the evening of June 16, 1970, *Perichoresis* was premiered at a concert of student works at the Conservatoire National Supérieur. The work opens with noisy breath sounds. With hindsight, the texture in which *Perichoresis* spends its first three minutes is pure late-1960s serialism, featuring more than a few clichés of that genre. Initially isolated glissandi gather into a satisfying, if too short, texture in the first third of the composition, and a

---

85   Otto, "The Use and Abuse of Perichoresis in Recent Theology."
86   Lelong, *Écrits,* 134.
87   Cagney, "Synthesis and Deviation," 174.

robotic, high-bow-pressure string line has real wit. But Grisey's use of bells is too portentous for the music they solemnly introduce, and *Perichoresis* tends to meander. In the final minutes of the piece, Grisey hints at his future development by devoting sustained attention to a single pitch accompanied by near-white noise, setting the two later structural poles of his music in a juxtaposition that is most interesting in the context of what came next.

A series of written "appreciations" from faculty members of the Conservatoire following the concert give a sense of how this technically advanced but somewhat derivative student composition was received. Georges Hugon, a teacher of harmony at the Conservatoire and a composer who, like Messiaen, had studied with Paul Dukas, wrote simply and a bit passive-aggressively, "I can't judge Monsieur Gérard Grisey's musical qualities based on what he had us hear." The composer Michel Zbar was more expansive. While noting a certain "disorder in the internal argument of the score," he enjoyed its texture and imagination:

> The sonic material, interesting through its variety, its constant renewal, its very richness, permanently ensures the pleasure of listening. I would like to hear it again, because there are certainly multiple facets to the work. A furious bubbling, in opposition to [areas] of finesse, contributes to a constant tension for the listener.[88]

With this critique, Zbar was on to something essential. Grisey's most powerful pieces combined rigor in their internal argument with sensual pleasure in the ways they sounded. Grisey hadn't achieved this in *Perichoresis*, but he was working toward it.

---

88   Paul Sacher archive.

Chapter Five

The Silence that Attracts (1970–72)

In April 1970, Grisey read *Gravity and Grace* (1947), by the legendary theologian and philosopher Simone Weil.[1] It was auspicious reading for the young composer: Weil, a devout Catholic from a Jewish background, was a profound religious thinker who also "had a deep veneration for the great Hindu and Taoist writings," as her editor Gustav Thibon writes.[2] In additional to her ecumenicalism, Weil held a near-religious veneration for art. For her, as for Grisey, faith and musical listening were close to the same thing. Weil writes:

> When we listen to Bach or a Gregorian melody, all the faculties of the soul become tense and silent in order to apprehend this thing of perfect beauty—each after its own fashion—the intelligence among the rest. It finds nothing in this thing it hears to affirm or deny, but it feeds upon it. Should not faith be an adherence of this kind?[3]

In other ways too, Weil's work dovetailed neatly with Grisey's instinct toward a less dogmatic, more mystical and sensual version of his Catholic faith. *Gravity and Grace*, written in aphoristic style, contains many ideas that Grisey integrated into his aesthetic, especially the equivalence between "extreme attention" and prayer and the insight that "Time does us violence; it is the only violence."[4] (The second idea resurfaces much later, in Grisey's *Quatre chants pour franchir le seuil*.) Weil had a carnal understanding of Christianity that aligned with Grisey's own: in *Waiting for God*, she writes, "God has provided that when his grace penetrates to the very center of a

---

1   Paul Sacher archive.
2   Weil, *Gravity & Grace*, XI.
3   Ibid, 129.
4   Ibid, 82.

man and from there illuminates all his being, he is able to walk on the water without violating any of the laws of nature."[5]

Grisey wrote far fewer diary entries in the 1970s, making it impossible to trace his month-by-month development as in the previous decade. But the ones that do exist contain important aesthetic reflections. Reading Weil, Grisey emphasized the humanist distinction that Christ had not suffered for God but suffered for *mankind on behalf of* God. Returning to a theme of his youth, he also noted Weil's injunction to "be only an intermediary between the uncultivated ground and the ploughed field, between the data of a problem and the solution, between the blank page and the poem, between the starving beggar and the beggar who has been fed." In *Gravity & Grace*, Grisey found a model for his spiritual understanding of his art.

On June 17, 1970, Grisey wrote an aesthetically essential diary entry that may have been inspired by Weil's elevation of attention and perception. While he had barely begun composing his earliest "nascent spectral" pieces,[6] he was able to formulate spectral ideas quite clearly in words:

> Never build a form only on abstract rhythmic structures but also on directly perceptible sound impacts (rhythm, intensity, timbre etc …).
>
> Everything must contribute to the shaping of the form. Not only the rhythmic cutting but also the color, intensity, density, pace, and other internal modellings of the sound as well as the micro-rhythms must underline the form of a work.[7]

This diary entry was the formulation of a goal; it would take at least another two years before he came close to achieving it in sound.

On June 26, 1970, Grisey and Simon were married. Their engagement had taken place the year before when Simon was introduced to Grisey's parents. They were young—Grisey was twenty-four—and his parents, who had also married young but remarried later, didn't seem thrilled. Especially Lucie Monna: according to Simon, Monna accepted her, but may have been hoping that Grisey would hold out for a "more brilliant" woman. Simon recalled a story that shows this side of Monna. "One day, on vacation, we went to visit Gérard's parents," Simon said. "Some of [his parents'] friends came over. One of them asked [Gérard Grisey], 'So, how is your job as a professor of philosophy?' The mother had told them that. It sounded more

---

5   Weil, *Waiting for God*, 141.
6   Cagney's apt phrase.
7   Paul Sacher archive.

prestigious!" Monna told Grisey that she would give the couple her blessing "if he was sure that's what he wanted."[8]

The two young people were deep in their studies at this point, Grisey with Messiaen, Simon finishing her degree as a social worker and taking psychology courses at night. There wasn't much money to lavish on the wedding, so they had a simple ceremony. It took place at the Marianist Institution Sainte-Marie in Anthony, a suburb south of Paris, in a modern chapel with brick walls and plastic chairs. In attendance were their parents, a priest, and a few other family members and university friends, fewer than twenty people in total.

In photographs from the wedding, Grisey's parents look well put-together and proud. Simon is beautiful, her dark hair in a precise bun, her wedding gown with a hood that recalls a monk's habit. Grisey, clean shaven, wears a tuxedo with a bow tie. In one shot, Simon looks adoringly at him, and he in turn looks at the camera, a flicker of doubt or indifference on his face.[9]

By the fall of 1970, the Griseys had moved into a new apartment, in the rue de l'Hôtel de ville at Cité des Arts in the Marais, which housed government-subsidized apartments for artists. Though not free, as at the rue de Monceau school, the cheap rent, as well as two scholarships that Grisey was soon to receive, meant that the young couple was able to lead a modest but stable adult life. The only drawback was the lack of proximity to their friends. In the rue de Monceau, the couple had lived near the Conservatoire, where they often ran into acquaintances. In the Cité des Arts, there was a high turnover, with artists from around the world coming and going, making it more difficult to form lasting friendships.

Between August and October 1970, Grisey composed a new work called *Initiation* for an ensemble of baritone, trombone, and bass. A duality of two irreconcilable ideas—one "pointillist, aleatoric," the other "linear, rigid, and hierarchical"—forms the structural core of the piece.[10] The text for the baritone is phonetic and "constituted of the names of divinities pertaining to different mythologies and religions," as Grisey wrote. (The list includes over forty gods, including from the ancient Egyptian pantheon.[11]) This choice shows Grisey's growing interest in non-Christian religions and his attempts to compose music that functioned as a sort of non-denominational musical

---

8 Interview with Jocelyne Grisey.
9 Photos in the private archive of Jocelyne Grisey.
10 Lelong, *Écrits*, 134.
11 Paul Sacher archive.

ritual. In his program note, he described the goal of the work as "apprehending the Essential through the magic of sound; penetrating further into the mysterious layers of being."[12] This language echoes the connection between the spiritual and the sexual in Weil's writing.

Initiation is structurally and aesthetically similar to *Perichoresis*. Lars Heusser hears a "pendulum-like motion" in both the density of events and the vertical reach of the chords of the first section of *Initiation*; each increases toward a middle point before ebbing away.[13] The second section is based on irregular durations using the magic square principle that Messiaen introduced to his composition class in the 1968–69 school year. The third is highly aleatoric; in the final section the composer creates a duality again, this time between sound and silence, as in the previous year's *Charme*.

These structural games are not immediately audible to the listener. In *Initiation*, what stands out are not the carefully plotted (though overly complex) formal elements, but rather Grisey's ear for timbral combinations: *sprechstimme* mixed with dry *col legno battuto*; the baritone's low register mixed with bass glissandi, or his falsetto blended with high harmonics. There are also trombone attacks, which start off as shocking and become predictable through repetition.

Initiation was premiered soon after its completion, on November 20, 1970, at the student composers' concerts at the Conservatoire de Paris, as *Perichoresis* had been. The preparations did not go smoothly. Georges Couroupos, a fellow composer and friend of Grisey's at the time, told Cagney that Grisey had been overly harsh on the baritone, a Greek singer named Spyros Sakkas, for singing wrong notes.[14] It is the first—though far from the last—recorded instance of Grisey reacting badly when he believed that musicians weren't taking his compositions seriously.

The written "appreciations" of *Initiation* from students and professors were notably positive this time. One classmate called *Initiation* "sensitive, original, and intelligent music announcing an authentic creator." For another fellow student, the piece was "more substantial" than a work by Grisey's classmate Tristan Murail. "A mysterious impression emerges from this work which is obviously related to the text," the student wrote. "However, the magnitude (and the implications) suggested by such a subject bring out the very sympathetic, but very young side of the author, who perhaps made the mistake of tackling it prematurely?"[15] The most sensitive criticism came from Georges Hugon, the professor who had found *Perichoresis* impossible

---

12   Ibid.
13   Heusser, "Il est donc temps de rendre la complexité efficace," 101.
14   Cagney, "Synthesis and Deviation," 175.
15   Paul Sacher archive.

to judge. The first time the Conservatoire harmony teacher heard *Initiation*, it annoyed him; the second time, its details awoke his curiosity; after listening a third time, he wrote, "It seems that, through sonic effects that are sometimes quite extraordinary, M. Grisey allows us to glimpse unfathomable depths."[16] Hugon declared himself won over.

Initiation is clearly a student piece. However, as the reactions to it suggest, it was at least a skillful product of its time. Grisey was rewarded for his hard work and craft: on October 1, 1971, *Initiation* won him a working scholarship of 5,000 francs from the seventh annual Biennale de Paris. The scholarship was donated by an American foundation called Theodoron through its president, a Chicago doctor named Sol Roy Rosenthal. Grisey wrote a thank-you note to Rosenthal that included a few lines in English, a language Grisey barely knew. "I just speak a few words English [*sic*] but enough to end this letter with it and to thanks you [*sic*] from the bottom of my heart for the help and the trust which the Foundation Theodoron gived [*sic*] to me," Grisey wrote.[17]

If Grisey had spoken harshly to the baritone Sakkas, the latter didn't seem to hold a grudge. In the summer of 1970, Sakkas, who was studying at the Mozarteum in Salzburg, invited the Griseys and a group of other conservatory friends to his home on a small Greek island between Icaria and Samos. The island had little more than a hundred inhabitants, and its traditional houses were built on the hill. Jocelyne remembers this vacation in idyllic terms. "It was a very simple life," she said. "When we went up to the hill they gave us fruit, pancakes, a very warm welcome. In the evening all the people of the village would go down to the beach with a radio and we would dance."[18] Besides this, the young musicians spent time sailing and lounging on Sakkas's boat. It seems plausible that Grisey turned this experience into the aesthetic one that underpinned his later piece *Dérives*, which means drifting or tacking; in his program note, he referred to the need of a boat to constantly correct its course as a formal model for the work. Grisey and Simon returned to Greece for one more summer but found the place changed. Tourists had arrived, and the simple hospitality that Simon remembered was gone.

In November 1970, Grisey received the Prix de la Vocation, from the competition he applied to over a year earlier with Simon's help. Thirty young French people across various fields, including an oceanographer, a paleontologist, and a mountain guide, had been selected from thousands

---

16   Ibid.
17   Ibid.
18   Interview with Jocelyne Grisey.

who applied to receive a scholarship of 10,000 francs.[19] Even if some of the other winners came from more baroque circumstances of poverty than Grisey did—one woman was born to a rural family as one of eleven children—it must have been a huge financial relief to the young couple.

On December 1, 1970, an award ceremony took place at the Maison de l'ORTF (Office de Radiodiffusion Télévision Française), with Claude Pompidou, wife of the French President Georges, presenting the checks. Cagney discovered a local newspaper report about the prize. The reporter called Grisey's parents for an interview. "It's brilliant for him," they said. "Although we're not musicians we helped him as much as we could to succeed, and it's with joy we note that his talent and his desire to succeed in his vocation are today recognized."[20]

A few weeks later, Grisey wrote in his journal about Ambrogio Lorenzetti's 1344 painting *The Annunciation*, which he'd probably seen during his time in Siena in 1969.[21] The work depicts an angel and the Virgin, facing one another across a gold backdrop. Though the figures are flat, rendered in the medieval style, the floor is shown in perspective; light golden letters flow between them. What interested Grisey in this painting was the theme of duality and separation between two beings:

> The emptiness, the silence that repels and attracts two forms apparently made to fit together ...
>
> The eye goes from the Virgin to the Angel and from the Angel to the Virgin, only encountering a recess in the decor necessitated by the superposition of their silhouettes. There is an abyss between them.
>
> ... See for a possible musical correspondence. Silence would be conceived not as caesura nor even as *arsis* or *thetis* [the stronger and weaker parts of musical measure] but as the separation imposed between two objects dependent on each other, as if magnetized.

Grisey was fascinated by this visual demonstration of the insurmountable space between people that defines the human condition.

The next day, Grisey worked out an important point, corresponding concretely to his current compositions. He wondered whether it was possible to create dynamism, structure, surprise, and drama with an aleatoric form. This mirrored a debate that had already raged for years at the Darmstädter Ferienkurse. In 1957, Boulez had accused John Cage of using aleatoric strategies "in order to conceal a fundamental weakness in compositional technique." Luigi Nono had added later that aleatoric composers put "chance

---

19   Cagney, "Synthesis and Deviation," 177. See also https://fondationdelavocation.org/les-laureats.
20   Cagney, "Synthesis and Deviation," 178. Cagney's translation.
21   Paul Sacher archive.

and its acoustic results forward as a discovery, being afraid of their own decisions and the freedom that they imply."²² Grisey was coming to realize that he would have to face the same terrifying freedom.

Grisey continued to study in Messiaen's composition class from 1970 to 1972. Details of the topics and works analyzed are less readily available than for the 1968–69 school year, but Messiaen foregrounded the works of post-war new music titans.²³ In 1971, the Italian iconoclast Luciano Berio visited Messiaen's course to discuss his 1960 piece *Circles*, for female voice, harp, and two percussionists. In 1972, Stockhausen came with his recently completed *Trans* for orchestra in tow. According to Grisey's classmate Tristan Murail, Messiaen also analyzed his own richly evocative *Chronochromie*, *Sept haïkaï*, and *Couleurs de la cité céleste*—though the students had to specifically ask their teacher to do so, which Murail chalked up to Messiaen's "coquettishness."²⁴ It was a stimulating atmosphere where works were listened to multiple times, scores studied, and aesthetic questions posed.

In 1971, French-American composer Betsy Jolas, a former Messiaen student twenty years older than Grisey, became Messiaen's assistant. She tried to cover areas that Messiaen stayed away from, such as Indian music and preserial Webern. Jolas noticed Grisey right away. She found him handsome: more importantly, she was interested in his artistic progress. "At the time, he seemed less intellectual" than his classmates, she recalled. "He didn't seem to be so preoccupied with figures and calculations and things like that. He seemed more rooted in nature."²⁵ Early on in her time as Messiaen's assistant, she introduced Grisey to Boulez; Boulez was interested in the students from this most prestigious composition class in France. They seemed to get along.²⁶

As mentioned, Boulez was probably the most powerful musical figure in France in the twentieth century, a status that continued to grow throughout—and beyond—Grisey's lifetime. Boulez started out as a radical serialist composer, writing in 1952 that "any musician who has not experienced …

---

22   Kurtz, *Stockhausen: Eine Biografie*, 135.
23   Boivin essentially skips from 1968 to 1974. Boivin, *La classe de Messiaen*, 166–168.
24   Ibid.
25   Interview with Jolas.
26   Ibid.

the necessity for the dodecaphonic language is useless."²⁷ In 1956, he began an illustrious conducting career that lasted until his death in 2016. (His influence was so inescapable that, according to one friend, Grisey and his friends later had a standing agreement that anyone who mentioned Boulez's name at dinner had to go out and buy the others a bottle of wine.²⁸)

Between 1969 and 1972, Grisey took the occasional teaching gig, leading courses in ear training for young students at *conservatoires d'arrondissement* (local music schools) associated with the main Conservatoire National Supérieur.²⁹ Between 1971 and 1972, he also taught orchestral score reading at the Sorbonne. Either these were private lessons, or Grisey had a third teaching gig during this period as well: a letter to Grisey dated February 1972 shows a list of students for whom he was responsible, along with lesson times and rooms.³⁰ In his early twenties, Grisey was already teaching for his financial survival, an additional pressure on a composer who couldn't rely on his parents for long-term monetary support. He would teach for the rest of his life.

In this period, Grisey sketched out three works he never finished. In various stages of completion, they show the composer's increasing preoccupation with space as a musical parameter, as well as some early, conceptual seeds of the spectralist aesthetic. One of these pieces was a sketch, in the form of a verbal synopsis, for two orchestras, one onstage and the other backstage. Grisey's piece was to use echoes as a structural principle—an acoustic phenomenon that continued to interest him—but besides that, little about this abandoned orchestra piece is known. (Cagney considers this idea a knock-off of Stockhausen's *Trans*, introduced in Messiaen's class.³¹) A string quartet from the same period was left in similar condition, with the note G passed around the group as "quarter tone variations gradually slip in, as well as harmonics, occasional sweeping arpeggios in the overtone series, and sum and differences tones," Cagney writes.³² The idea of a tone rotating in a circle with quarter-tone variations also recalls a through-composed Doppler effect.

Of the three drafts from this period, a work called *Rosace pour une méditation* reached the most advanced stage, though it still wasn't anywhere near completion.³³ The term *Rosace* refers to rose windows, prevalent in the

---

27 Quoted in Kohda, "Boulez in his Own Words."
28 Interview with Wintle.
29 Paul Sacher archive.
30 Ibid.
31 Cagney, "Synthesis and Deviation," 345.
32 Ibid, 346.
33 Paul Sacher archive.

Gothic cathedrals of northern France. Like *Répons* from 1968, *Rosace* was explicitly inspired by the beauty of Christian architecture.

Grisey never settled on an instrumentation for the piece: he considered percussion solo, different combinations of brass, and an ensemble of trombone, clarinet, flute, viola, and bass. The sketches show various possible circular or spiral shapes for the ensemble setup, with a central melody ornamented and varied in its parameters passing among the instruments. In one version, Grisey imagined placing a voice at the center of this vortex.

In his sketches, Grisey made a note to himself to "see the periods of the breath / see the periods of the cardiac rhythm." Another section is marked "like the breathing before falling asleep." It's difficult for us to carefully observe our own breath right before falling asleep, so maybe Grisey was awake in bed with a lover when he got this idea, contemplating the gradual winding-down of the human body.

※ ※ ※

Between 1970 and 1972, Grisey composed *Vagues, Chemins, le Souffle* (*Waves, Paths, the Breath*), for two symmetrical orchestras and solo clarinet. On October 16, 1972, the Ministère des Affaires Culturelles announced that it would commission the work from the young composer for an honorarium of 9,000 francs.[34] That year, Grisey bought a copy of Émile Leipp's *Acoustique et Musique* and German acoustician Fritz Winckel's *Vues nouvelles sur le monde des sons*.[35] Since *Vagues, Chemins, le Souffle* is the first Grisey piece to deal concretely with musical acoustics, it's worth defining a few terms important to the composer's work. Many naturally occurring sounds are made up of multiple sound waves.[36] This combination of waves constitutes the *spectrum* of a sound. In the *harmonic* spectrum, these sound waves, called partials, are discrete from one another. Theoretically at least, partials are whole-number multiples of the lowest frequency, the *fundamental*, measured in Hertz (Hz). The melody or harmony created by the lower partials played in order creates an instantly recognizable sound: an octave from the fundamental (first partial), a fifth from there (second partial), a fourth (third partial), and so on. This discovery dates to Pythagoras and can be demonstrated by dividing a vibrating string into equal-sized sections.

In an *inharmonic* spectrum, the other frequencies can be in different relationships to the fundamental, and they are continuous—they bleed into one another—rather than discrete. Roughly, our ears perceive harmonica spectra

---

34 Ibid.
35 Cagney, "Synthesis and Deviation," 350.
36 Sine waves, which occur in sound and in light, have only one frequency.

as pitch and inharmonic spectra as noise, though this perception takes place in shades of gray. Analogous to the scale between harmonic and inharmonic sounds is one between periodic and aperiodic rhythms. Periodic rhythms are regular and predictable, like the heartbeat, while aperiodic rhythms are irregular and unpredictable.

Instrumental sounds, being made of imperfect instruments, contain noise in them. The timbre of an instrument depends on its construction; acoustically, its sound is shaped most decisively by the formants, usually the second- and third-strongest partials in the sound. Computers can show the full spectrum of a recorded sound. Beyond the neat theory of the harmonic series, they demonstrate that partials are constantly in motion—especially at the beginning and end of a note on an instrument.

With close listening, we can often hear some of the inner partials of a sound. In general, when the musical events in a section of a piece are sparse or highly predictable, our perception is free to examine each sound in detail. In Grisey's terminology, this means that time is "dilated." Our perception gains the ability to go inside the sound and perceive it in microscopic grains, observing overtones and subtle timbral changes. Grisey liked to compare this kind of listening to the examination of tiny organisms under a microscope. From these facts of psychoacoustics, Grisey forged his poetic idea of the births, lives, and deaths of sound.

Vagues, Chemins, le Souffle was Grisey's last piece under the direct tutelage of Messiaen. Grisey appealed to his teacher for help securing a performance of the piece. On October 3, 1971, Messiaen wrote Grisey a warm letter inquiring after his health—Grisey had been in the hospital for an unspecified operation—and saying that while he wouldn't be able to attend the prestigious Royan Festival due to Conservatoire obligations, he would talk to the artistic director, Claude Samuel, to recommend Grisey's work for performance there.[37] Messiaen's vote of confidence was enough. Samuel scheduled the piece for the final concert of the Royan Festival in the spring of 1972, to be performed by the Orchestre de l'ORTF.

The title of the work contains three discrete images, all of which provided poetic inspiration for Grisey throughout his life. In the summer of 1968, he had written to Jocelyne about "abandoning his body" to the waves (*Vagues*) of Marseille. *Chemins* summons the idea of Christian pilgrimage or the Egyptian *Book of the Two Ways*, which describes the passage of the dead through the underworld (and is featured in later pieces). Most important is *le Souffle*, which means "breath"—literally but also figuratively, as in the animating force of life. Grisey's first title for the piece was *Transe*, which

---

37 Paul Sacher archive.

Cagney associates with an attempt to create a hypnotic effect.[38] (Grisey probably abandoned the title after realizing Stockhausen had a piece with almost exactly the same name.)

In preparation for *Vagues, Chemins, le Souffle*, Grisey took copious notes and created plans to organize "rhythm, rhythmic density, density of instrumental timbre, space ... intensities, pitches, and general dynamic curve."[39] This reflected a trend in Grisey's style of composing, begun in *Initiation* and *Perichoresis*, that continued for the rest of his life. It's an intriguing paradox between Grisey's method and the sounding result: a hypersensitive musician, he composed so schematically as if to almost eliminate emotion—until the listener hears the work, with its immediate and visceral impact.

The literal shape of the piece—like a giant S—recalls Iannis Xenakis's primal, spatialized 1966 orchestral piece *Terretektorh*. It is also reminiscent of *Spiegel I-VII* (1960–61), by the Austrian composer Friedrich Cerha, in which massive blocks of sound flow in parabolas around the orchestra. Grisey was soaking up the trends in contemporary music that most reflected his interests in the primordial, sculptural, and dynamic.

Vagues, Chemins, le Souffle bears an epigraph from the Brihadaranyaka Upanishad, a Hindu religious text and one of the Ten Principal Upanishads (it was particularly beloved by the German philosopher Arthur Schopenhauer). What most struck Grisey in his reading of the Upanishads was the texts' treatment of the ear as a holy organ associated with space. Hearing is central to the creation of the universe, and death and deafness are practically the same thing: "He is becoming one, he no longer hears."[40] The specific epigraph in *Vagues* is, "It carried Hearing across. When it was delivered from death, it became the Spaces ..." The work, with its motion of sounds between instruments, is an attempt to literally carry hearing across a space. It is also a sonic demonstration of the invisible yet impenetrable barrier between people: in his program note, Grisey wrote of his intention to "envelop the listener in sound, with each person having a different listening experience depending on the place he chooses."[41]

The piece is in three parts without breaks. *Vagues* includes suggestively named aleatoric modules ("somber," "heavy," "morbid," "clear"), where the musicians choose what to play from the given material. There are also string glissandi with tightly coiled tremolos moving in the middle of the texture, and what appears to be a musical representation of the physics of waves. The wave shape comes from the orbital motion of

---

38   Cagney, "Synthesis and Deviation," 212.
39   Ibid, 216.
40   *The Brihadaranyaka Upanishad,* trans. Johnson, 139.
41   Lelong, *Écrits,* 135.

water molecules, which rotate while passing through the wave's peaks and troughs. In pages of *Vagues*, a constellation of pitches moves up and down on a macro level, while each individual pitch, like a water molecule, has a unique trajectory.

Chemins has the character of a development, as if the section is following different paths suggested by the material introduced in *Vagues*. Ideas from the aleatoric modules at the beginning of the work are reprised, as are hints of the ebbing waves in the flutes and clarinets. Unpitched sounds are tossed around the space. Scales take over from single held pitches, then surge into the timbre of a massive tam-tam crescendo.

The aleatoric modules return in the final section of the piece, *le Souffle*. (One of them features the overtone series.) So do the waves. The piece concludes on a brief C-E major third—a pointed tonal statement in the context of new music at the time. Grisey conceived of this structure as a triptych: from a still, static texture, to dynamic motion and back again.

Despite the refined structure of *Vagues, Chemins, le Souffle*, Grisey's complicated aleatoric elements, involving significant independent responsibilities from each player in a large orchestra, all but guaranteed that the piece would cause problems in performance. In the end, it wasn't premiered at Royan in 1972: the orchestra went on strike. Cagney guesses that the complexity of Grisey's score was one of the reasons the musicians walked out in the first place.[42]

Vagues, Chemins, le Souffle was finally premiered in late October 1975. The composer Jonathan Harvey reviewed the concert:

> One of the real revelations of the festival was a 35-minute orchestral work by the 29-year-old French composer Gérard Grisey: *Vagues, chemins, le souffle*. It was written in 1971–72 while Grisey was still studying with Messiaen and it possessed a breadth of resourcefulness bordering on opulent. Though the usual traces of Stockhausen, Xenakis, Boulez, Amy etc were discernible, an entirely original sense of drama and poetry was unfolded, expressed both in exquisite gesture and progressions over larger spans ... *Vagues* created a sensation of musical dizziness with string glissandos turning round a false axis as if in a distorting mirror, the wind instruments taking off from the glissandos' points of arrival with their own material. *Chemins* grew from pointillism to a tutti of trills, and *Le souffle*, the most lyrical section, was a colour-mirror of the first one with its waves of breath rhythm. Spatial effects (which, like string glissandos, were elsewhere a cliché of the week) were intended to be very elaborate, the orchestra to be set in S-formation throughout the audience. I suppose that no one but God and Grisey was sorry that this did not prove practicable, as we could, with

---

42   Cagney, "Synthesis and Deviation," 257.

the normal seating, hear clearly all that occurred. There is no doubt that Grisey will be an exciting composer to watch.⁴³

In *Le Monde,* the critic Gérard Condé wrote that the work

> contains touching things, often of the most naïve kind … One senses an idea here: that the soloist has more weight than the mass, but this weight must be controlled within the ensemble in which it is placed. The extreme division of the strings, on the other hand, proves in the long run to be much more decorative than effective.⁴⁴

Not everyone was excited. In *Le Figaro,* Pierre Petit found the work "sad, interminable, monotonous, lugubrious."⁴⁵ Either way, it was a valuable opportunity for Grisey to hear such an ambitious work, allowing him to learn what worked and what didn't from his complex score. As Condé wrote prophetically: "Let us hope that Gérard Grisey will be able to say later, when speaking of this score: 'At that time, I did not know how to compose.' (The admission is from Beethoven)."

Cagney has argued, against the consensus of most Grisey scholarship, that *Vagues, Chemins, le Souffle*—rather than the later *D'eau et de pierre*—contains the decisive seeds of the spectral style. Among the sketches for *Vagues,* Cagney discovered a "small scrap of manuscript paper" marked as a *"spectre harmonique."* The corresponding section of the work is *Chemins,* where Grisey uses a series of so-called resonance chords; *le Souffle* also opens with a series of these chords.⁴⁶ But in his summary of this phenomenon, Cagney admits the sticking points of his claim. "Although Grisey did not use a sonogram to calculate the chord's content, or microtones to accurately simulate its partials, the harmonic spectrum is still the declared auditory reference point," he writes. "These therefore appear to be the first quasi-spectral chords in Grisey's oeuvre."⁴⁷ One point that supports Cagney's argument is that Grisey frequently used "good enough" models of the harmonic spectrum in his pieces—even late ones—that were based on mildly expanded equal temperament, not accurately simulated partials. But other aspects of *Vagues, Chemins, le Souffle* tend to contradict this understanding

---

43   Harvey, "The ISCM Festival."
44   Condé, "La dernière charrette de la S.I.M.C."
45   Quoted in Cagney, "Synthesis and Deviation," 258.
46   Resonance chords are soft echoes of attacks from instruments such as bells or vibraphone. Using Paul Sacher archive documentation, Cagney shows that Grisey probably got this idea from Boulez's *Pli selon pli* (though Messiaen also worked with a similar idea).
47   Cagney, "On *Vagues, Chemins, le Souffle* (1970–72) and the Early Use of Resonance Chords in Grisey's Oeuvre," 54.

of the work. First, though Grisey uses chains of chords based on the harmonic spectrum, they don't have the structural function they would have in Grisey's mature compositions (in the later *Dérives*, these chords are specifically conceived as resting places for the ear). Second, Grisey himself always played down the importance of chords based on the harmonic spectrum for the spectral style. Third, maybe the most important stylistic element of spectral music is the perceptible process—an audible transformation from one musical state to another—which *Vagues* doesn't have. Finally, in the hypercomplex and often, as Cagney rightly notes, overloaded style of the piece, the chords based on the harmonic spectrum don't exactly strike the ear. *Vagues, Chemins, le Souffle* is not a spectral work by most of the criteria that Grisey himself recognized.

In January 1972, Grisey traveled to Rennes to deliver his first public lecture on his compositions, titled "Music and Space."[48] In the presentation, he returned to the theme of listening in the Upanishads. Grisey said:

> From a physiological point of view, the organ of the ear has two functions: hearing and [equilibrium]. In ... the Upanishads, (Baranyakaa and Chandogya), we find some curious phrases which tell us that the Hindus knew about this double function of the ear. When those texts speak of the transformation after death of our organs—the Voice becoming Fire, the Breath becoming the Wind, Sight becoming the Sun, the Mind becoming the Moon—it is asserted that Hearing becomes space ...[49]

In order to "illustrate ... the possibilities of moving sound spatially" in his lecture, Grisey wrote three short, occasional studies for what Cagney plausibly surmises were the instruments on hand: clarinet, baritone voice, bass clarinet, piano, flute, trombone, vibraphone, English horn—and bongos.[50] As in the earlier sketches for a string quartet, various elements are rotated around the audience: percussive speech in the baritone on phonetic or nonsense text, combined with bongos; flurries of atonal grace notes; trills and tremolos; swells; and the interval of a minor third. Grisey turned off the lights at one point to heighten the effect.[51] By emphasizing the motion of sound, Grisey was showing its physicality. Sounds can dance through space like human bodies.

The same month, Grisey developed a concept for an installation-like work with the provisional title *Projet de sculptures sonores*.[52] Containing elements of music, sculpture, and performance art, the sketch shows Grisey's artistic

---

48   Cagney, "Synthesis and Deviation," 211.
49   Ibid. Cagney's translation of Grisey's lecture text.
50   Ibid, 226.
51   Ibid.
52   Paul Sacher archive.

thinking in a new light. While incomplete and wildly impractical to realize, his idea also had intriguing potential. It has never been performed.

Grisey's concept of "sounding sculptures" requires five to eight multicolored "blocks" of at least nine cubic feet, made out of light materials such as papier-mâché or plastic. These blocks were to be "of variable forms, abstract but sufficiently evocative of totemic, human, or animal forms." The sculptures were then to be situated in a "transitional space" or a concert hall, where they would be placed in relation to one another so as to realize "a coherent ensemble in the space."

The twist was that the performing musicians would play *inside* these sculptures, which would also be lit from the inside. The sound needed to be perceived as coming exclusively from inside the blocks; the musicians would also "provoke" vibrations of the sculptural material. The score, which Grisey notated verbally, is made up of seven sections, starting in "ink-black night." The blocks are gradually revealed; the colors of the lighting change; musical characters with distinct aural tags emerge from each block, interspersed with silence. "Find a *time* and a *different appearance* for each block," the composer wrote. Grisey didn't decide on an instrumentation; it seems he wanted it to remain flexible, but his notes require at least one low brass instrument and a horn. This sketch is an exception from Grisey's obsession with duality in this period. Rather than two irreconcilable entities, there are seven, each trapped in its solitary sonic existence.[53]

Grisey also made sketches for another installation-like composition for seven instrumental groups sometime during this period, tentatively titled *Atelier I*.[54] At the center of his concept was the idea of an *Appel*, or call, performed by a main small ensemble and echoed by the other groups, scattered as far as possible from one another in the performance space. Written out mostly in verbal cues, the idea was promising, but would have had a better chance of being performed if Grisey had fully notated it. For the *Appel* group of instruments, Grisey composed simple permutations of a seven-note row. The musicians were supposed to order their sequences by the degree of tension; apply the pitches to a series of "relative durations"; and pass these scraps of musical material to the members of other groups. The members of these other groups, called *Échos*, were instructed to imitate or "contradict"[55] the material played by the *Appel* group while simultaneously subjecting it to a series of improvised but complex variations organized according to the

---

53 Ibid.
54 Ibid. The Paul Sacher musicologists date them to 1976, but the aleatoric elements and presence of a serial structure in the sketches strongly indicates that Grisey developed this idea earlier than that—possibly as early as 1969.
55 By playing soft and slow after hearing loud and fast music, for example.

typically serialist parameters of sound, pitch, timbre, volume, and articulation. While the concept of *Atelier I* is intriguing, its performance is a musician's nightmare. Like the *Sculptures sonores*, this work was never realized.

❧ ❧ ❧

In 1971, Grisey took part in the Villa Médicis competition at the Conservatoire de Paris. The reforms to the process made after May 1968 had been implemented the previous year, and instead of being sent away to Fontainebleau to compose a fugue and a cantata, Grisey's works were judged by a panel of contemporary composers. On June 23, 1972, Grisey got news that would change the arc of his aesthetic life. Olivier Messiaen sent him a telegram: "You received the Prix de Rome // Come with Madame tonight 8:30 Chinese restaurant in the Rue Jean Mermoz Paris 8 // Affectionately Messiaen."[56]

The prize was a vote of confidence from the French musical establishment: even if Grisey had not yet developed his own voice, his craft and raw talent convinced them to give him the award. One of the members of the jury for the Prix de Rome was Xenakis; in a recommendation Xenakis later wrote for Grisey, he noted how impressed he'd been with Grisey's student works. "He has an outstanding imagination in music," Xenakis wrote, "and is one of the most gifted young French composers."[57]

In the spring of 1972, Grisey received another commission from Claude Samuel, who was leaving the festival at Royan to start a new one, the Rencontres Internationales de Musique Contemporaine Metz, in the northeast of France.[58] Despite the debacle with *Vagues, Chemins, le Souffle*, Samuel was willing to give him a second chance. Grisey began composing *D'eau et de pierre* in April 1972 and completed the work the following October.

The musicologist Jérôme Baillet has termed *D'eau et de pierre* "the pivotal work between apprenticeship and maturity, the Conservatoire de Paris and the stay at the Villa Médicis."[59] For Cagney, it is "the composition that extends like a rope bridge over the ravine between Grisey's precocious but derivative student compositions and his accomplished, mature masterworks."[60]

---

56 Paul Sacher archive.
57 Ibid.
58 Ibid.
59 Baillet, *Fondements d'une écriture*, 9.
60 Cagney, "Synthesis and Deviation," 261.

Cagney has located the origins of *D'eau et de pierre* in a prior work planned for clarinet and tape. Grisey began his research for the techniques to be used in this piece at the Conservatoire de Pantin, an experimental music school in the suburbs of Paris, where he examined the spectrum that gives the clarinet its timbre. This piece was Grisey's first that began with such concrete acoustic research. Cagney argues that Grisey abandoned the idea of the clarinet piece, adapting these sketches for two orchestral groups, after receiving the Metz commission.[61] Grisey's plan was to work with two elements in the style of Messiaen's *personnages* which act upon one another.

D'eau et de pierre means *Of water and stone*. When a rock lands in water, it pushes water molecules out of the way. The molecules closest to the water's surface rush back to fill the space, causing ripples and forming peaks and troughs (like waves on the ocean). This image also has spectral implications. The shape of the waves that make up sound are visible in water as they aren't in air; the stone is like the instrument that excites air molecules. But the concept of his work was at least partly spiritual as well. In his program note, Grisey wrote:

> From water and stone was born an aesthetic emotion, in this case the one provoked by the reading of the Upanishad which conceptualizes the interaction between the two Hindu principles of Purusha and Prakiti. This interaction has been transposed into two elements, mineral and water, hence the title chosen for this piece.[62]

Prakriti and Purusha stand very roughly for body and spirit, the solid stone and the ungraspable water.

This program is set somewhat literally into music. As Baillet observes, the stagnant water—less dynamic than the waves of *Vagues, Chemins, le Souffle*—is associated with a (tempered) harmonic spectrum on an F.[63] The rock is represented by an "aspectral pitch agglomerate" which falls metaphorically into the water, causing the harmonic spectrum to change.[64] Like standing water returning to its original state, the water group then slowly returns to the original harmonic spectrum. These instruments "react momentarily to the sudden, violent instrumental aggressions in the form of frequency differences, then little by little return to the reference spectrum," Baillet explains.[65]

---

61 Ibid, 276.
62 Lelong, *Écrits*, 136.
63 Baillet, *Fondements d'une écriture*, 9.
64 Heusser, "Il est donc temps de rendre la complexité efficace," 91.
65 Baillet, *Fondements d'une écriture*, 9.

In Grisey's original, 1972 program note, he describes his work as dramatizing

> the antinomy of two elements: the one static, calm, eternal, receptive, from the point of view of the organization of pitches, durations and timbres—the form of a spiraled circle which could begin at any point in the score; the other dynamic, aggressive, vigorous, composed of absolutely autonomous, permutable sequences.[66]

As mentioned, Grisey often pondered the unbridgeable gap between people, an idea reflected in the dualistic conception of so many of his pieces. It seems plausible that the two elements of *D'eau et de pierre* were related to the profound differences in his and Jocelyne's characters, and the unpredictable ways those two entities reacted to each other. *D'eau et de pierre* is dedicated to her.[67]

For Cagney, who argues for the "nascent spectralism" of *Vagues, Chemins, le Souffle*, *D'eau et de pierre* is still further along in the path toward a spectral style, because of its "process of gradual deviation by which a given sound figure changes in appearance." That is an essential element of Grisey's mature music. But another key aspect is missing here: total control. *D'eau et de pierre* continues to use aleatoric techniques.

In the fall of 1971, Stockhausen had come to Messiaen's composition class, where he presented his concept of *Veränderungsgrad*, or degree of change. This concept became essential to Grisey's musical thinking; *D'eau et de pierre* was his first piece to make use of it. Stockhausen had first explained the concept in 1955:

> A repetition has the lowest *degree of change*, a completely surprising event the highest.
>
> Furthermore, our experience of time depends on the *density of change*: The more surprising events happen, the shorter the time feels; the more repetitions there are, the longer it feels [This corresponds to Grisey's idea of temporal contraction and dilation.] But surprises can only occur when something unexpected happens: based on the events that have come before, we begin to expect a certain type of change, and then something different from what we expect happens. In the moment, we are surprised: our senses are extraordinarily stimulated, in order to adjust to and integrate the unexpected change. That means that after a short time, a constant change of surprises will become just as boring as constant repetition: we stop expecting something specific and can no longer be surprised ... [68]

---

66   Cagney, "Synthesis and Deviation," 315.
67   Lelong, *Écrits*, 136.
68   Stockhausen, "Struktur und Erlebniszeit" in *Texte zur elektronischen und instrumentalen Musik*.

Stockhausen developed this thesis from an analysis of Anton von Webern's String Quartet no. 2, where the rhythmic regularity of the second movement creates a highly surprising effect in contrast to the amorphousness of the first. In Messiaen's class, the exemplary composition was Stockhausen's own sensual and mysterious *Carré*, from 1958–59, for a setup of four orchestras and four choirs. In this piece, his treatment of the idea of degree of change can be heard clearly at several points, without studying the score. Stockhausen passes an individual pitch or a chord from one part of the ensemble to another, working with a low degree of change: the movement of a note from one location to another.

In *D'eau et de pierre*, Grisey uses Stockhausen's idea to morph the sounds of the water group gradually after the impulse of the rock material. The music departs from and returns to the F harmonic spectrum through the stepwise modification of its parameters. This conceptual process is at least as important as the presence of the harmonic spectrum in the composition.

D'eau et de pierre was premiered on November 27, 1972, at the Théâtre Municipal in Metz. The ensemble was the Ensemble Européen, under the direction of Michel Tabachnik, who also led the group in Marek Kopelent's *Intimissio*, Xenakis's brass trio *Linaia-Agon*, and Paul Méfano's propulsive *Signes/Oubli*. The reviews were largely positive, though one critic found Grisey's piece too long, another "overly simplistic." In the *Saarbrücker Zeitung*, the German critic Albert-Peter Bitz wrote, "When one leaves the appeal to Indian philosophy aside, there is nothing more than the primitive poetry of programmatic ideas."[69]

Despite the prestigious circumstances of the commission and premiere of *D'eau et de pierre*, and its essential place in Grisey's musical development, Cagney notes that the work has largely been forgotten—in accordance with the composer's wishes.[70] No recording of the work is currently available, though it was performed at La Scala in 2019.[71]

In the summer of 1972, Grisey attended the twenty-eighth edition of the Internationale Ferienkurse für Neue Musik in Darmstadt on a half scholarship worth 300 Deutsche Mark.[72] According to Michaël Levinas, who was also there, Grisey attended following Messiaen's explicit encouragement.[73]

---

69   Quoted in Cagney, "Synthesis and Deviation," 322–23.
70   Ibid, 324.
71   Email from Grégoire Lorieux of Ensemble L'Itinéraire, February 11, 2022.
72   Archive of the Internationales Musikinstitut Darmstadt.
73   Levinas, "Rupture et Système," in *Le Temps de l'Écoute*, 34.

The composition professors included the puckish Mauricio Kagel, the John Cage disciple Christian Wolff, and three of Grisey's musical heroes, Stockhausen, Ligeti, and Xenakis. The eccentric Romanian proto-spectralist Horatiu Radulescu was also invited; his *Flood for the Eternal's Origins*, for global sound sources, was performed at the festival.

Grisey spent most of his time at Darmstadt with two Canadian composers: the flamboyant gay maverick Claude Vivier, who came from a working-class background like Grisey's, and Walter Boudreau, a saxophonist and conductor as well as composer, whom Grisey had already met briefly in Messiaen's class at the Conservatoire in 1971. The three bonded over the miserable quality of the food served by the festival, which Boudreau described as "cooked in the devil's kitchen itself." Since Vivier was having an affair with a waiter at an Italian restaurant, the three friends met there instead of in the canteen. (All three composers found lovers at Darmstadt.) They got special treatment, and, over pasta *con le verdure*, salad, and wine, they philosophized, discussed the presentations and music they heard, and considered their artistic destinies.

Boudreau remembered Grisey as sweet, quiet, and intelligent, with a goofy style of dress that reminded Boudreau of a "musketeer." Even then, Grisey showed an independent streak. While Vivier was captivated by Stockhausen and Boudreau was aesthetically aligned with Xenakis, "Gérard was a kind of outsider," Boudreau said. "He was slowly brewing his witches' brew," already "obsessed" with the harmonic spectrum.[74]

Not everything about the festival was interesting: Boudreau recounted attending lectures by German structuralists, "where you'd spend the whole morning looking at blackboards full of numbers on how to arrive at a horrible chord." The three young Francophone composers dismissed Radulescu, who had an egocentric and esoteric streak, as a "con artist."[75] Xenakis's lectures contained insights about the parameters of sound that Grisey took an interest in, but also got bogged down in abstract math. According to Levinas, Grisey presented the score of *Vagues, Chemins, le Souffle* to Ligeti, who told Grisey that "although it had a certain *maladie*, it wasn't yet Grisey's own particular *maladie*"—meaning a unique aesthetic obsession. Ligeti recommended that Grisey study the work of acoustician and composer John Chowning—also present at the festival—and Hector Berlioz's classic *Treatise on Orchestration*.

The activities at Darmstadt that year were dominated by the larger-than-life personality of Stockhausen, who convinced the three young musicians of his musical brilliance while putting them off with his ego. (At one point,

---

74 Interview with Boudreau.
75 Cagney, "Synthesis and Deviation," 209.

during a workshop, Stockhausen denied Boudreau permission to go to the restroom. "Sir, if I stay here, I'm going to pee on you," Boudreau answered, storming out to applause from the other students.) Stockhausen analyzed *Mantra* and most importantly *Stimmung*.

Stimmung was performed at the festival on August 3, 1972, followed by a workshop on extended vocal techniques. This contemplative work's sounds inspired Boudreau, Vivier, and Grisey to imitate the piece while walking around Darmstadt; one tram driver threatened to eject them if they didn't cut it out.[76] But they weren't mocking. "We were in awe of *Stimmung*," Boudreau said. "We never *made* fun. We *had* fun singing *Stimmung*."[77]

As mentioned, *Stimmung* was premiered in December 1968. The work was inspired in part by the singing babble of Stockhausen's then-infant son.[78] (In the *Three Essays on the Theory of Sexuality*, Freud argues that adult eroticism is shaped by physical sensations of infanthood; babbling could count as one of those sexuality-adjacent pleasures.[79]) *Stimmung* had marked a new era in Stockhausen's compositional output. The music is simple, consisting of an overtone chord up to the ninth partial over a low B♭, with the various vowels and their unique formants causing different overtones to emerge from the texture. The text is made up in part of erotic poetry written by Stockhausen to his then-lover Mary Baumeister ("My phallus is my soul / when I immerse you. / Right at the tip / is where I sit ...[80]"); the composition is an hour long. In a technique that is most directly recognizable in Grisey's later work, the tempi in the piece are organized to correspond with the proportions of the harmonic spectrum. (According to Levinas, Grisey took careful notes on this specific aspect of the composition during the lecture.[81]) More broadly, *Stimmung* spoke to Grisey's interest in trance and the combination of the religious or mystical and the erotic in music.

The discussions at the 1972 edition of the Darmstädter Ferienkurse were pointed as usual, with the older composers accused of "conspiring to exclude the young." Ligeti, for his part, claimed in a lecture that the younger generation of composers were simply producing imitations, and that there was little new music worthy of his attention at the festival. Despite the greater

---

76 Gilmore, *Claude Vivier: A Composer's Life*, 71.
77 Interview with Boudreau.
78 Kurtz, *Stockhausen*, 209.
79 For example, see the second essay, where Freud describes the "rhythmic character" of aspects of infantile sexuality. Freud, *Drei Abhandlungen zur Sexualtheorie*, 85.
80 Chang, "Stimmung."
81 Cagney, "Synthesis and Deviation," 302.

care Ligeti showed in his private lesson with Grisey, these polemics stuck with the young composer.

Levinas later described Darmstadt in 1972 as the birth of spectral music.[82] As mentioned, important elements of spectral thought were present in the music that Grisey composed before he attended the festival that year. Still, Grisey, Vivier, and Boudreau felt marked by destiny. For Boudreau, Darmstadt in 1972 was a turning point; the three young composers would remain friends even as their artistic lives followed vastly different arcs. "If I could, I'd like to step in a time machine and go back to Darmstadt and sit at the table next to us and listen to our conversations," Boudreau said. "I think I would cry, because we were really intense. And we each made our way."

---

82 Levinas, "Rupture et système," 34.

Chapter Six

The Sensual Embrace (1972–74)

On October 1, 1972, Grisey and Jocelyne arrived at the Villa Médicis in Rome. Located in the center of the city, the gardens alone consist of seven hectares, crowning a stunning sixteenth-century villa. For Grisey, who had already documented his fascination with the art and culture of the Italian Renaissance during his 1969 visit to Siena, it must have been an inspiring setting. Freed from financial worries and teaching, he was able to read, listen, spend time with the other artists at the French and other academies in the city, and compose.

Most importantly, Grisey got to know Tristan Murail. The two young men had been acquaintances, but not more, in Messiaen's class. Their closer encounter in Rome had lasting consequences for both of their musical aesthetics.

Murail was born in Le Havre in 1947. His family background contrasted starkly with Grisey's: Murail's father was a journalist, poet, and painter, and his mother was a writer (Murail's three siblings also became writers). In 1963, the Murails moved to Paris so that Tristan could prepare appropriately for his *baccalauréat*. Murail's university education reads like a summary of the most prestigious institutions in Paris: economics at the Sorbonne, Arabic at the École nationale des langues orientales vivantes, political science at the Sciences Po—a sort of finishing school for the country's bureaucratic elite— and composition in Messiaen's class. In this class, Murail was considered the top student, while, as mentioned, Messiaen kept Grisey at arm's length.[1]

Besides the different worlds from which the two composers originated, they also had divergent natures. "Murail is, at his root, this funny combination of super romantic and complete scientific positivist," said Joshua Fineberg, the American spectral composer, who was close with both men. "And Grisey was almost the opposite. He had the mystical where Murail was

---

1 Cagney, "Synthesis and Deviation," 119.

rational, and he was kind of modernist where Murail is romantic."[2] In their overlapping year at the Villa Médicis, from 1972 to 1973, a friendship began to develop.

One day, Grisey and Murail went for a walk on the grounds. Murail told Grisey that, having experimented with small composer-collective projects, he was planning to create a new group with attached ensemble. This collective became Ensemble L'Itinéraire, which, more than any other institution, helped establish spectral music as a viable aesthetic movement. According to Murail, however, Grisey didn't want to be part of the collective. He attributed this to Grisey's unwillingness to be "compromised."[3] That tracks with Grisey's personality: when it came to his career, Grisey was "naturally and healthily selfish, like an animal," as the novelist Christopher Isherwood once described a character named Otto.[4] Grisey was wary of any distraction that could eat into his composing time, as the administrative duties of supporting Ensemble L'Itinéraire surely would have.

Cagney suggests Grisey had a further careerist motivation for declining Murail's invitation. Several aspects of L'Itinéraire were set out in direct opposition to Pierre Boulez's concert series Domaine Musical, which might have caused Grisey to worry about getting on the bad side of France's most powerful musical figure:

> Given ... Grisey's openness to the Boulezean faction in Paris, his reluctance to associate himself with Dutilleux (an enemy of Boulez's) and his being programmed at the Domaine Musical around this time, one can conclude that Grisey put priority on his own career progression over any group project, and that since his career progression may well involve being on the right side of Boulez, the main power-broker in French new music, he did not want to be too closely associated with a new collective that might be seen as a rival to the Domaine Musical.[5]

Hugues Dufourt, the composer and member of Ensemble L'Itinéraire, said that "Grisey had a perfectly defined status" within the group: he was "the guest of honor ... the thinking head." But Murail did much more to promote L'Itinéraire, and the composer Roger Tessier was responsible for securing its financial future.[6] As much as Grisey's music would come to be defined by a movement, he always saw himself as a singular composer.

Besides Murail, Grisey also had fruitful encounters with the other artists at the Villa Médicis. The painter François Rouan and the poet Christian

---

2   Interview with Fineberg. Murail didn't respond to interview requests.
3   Cagney, "Synthesis and Deviation," 365–73.
4   Isherwood, *Goodbye to Berlin*, 93.
5   Cagney, "Synthesis and Deviation," 373.
6   Interview with Dufourt.

Gabriel Guez Ricord both helped guide Grisey's trajectory at this crucial juncture. Rouan had arrived in Rome in October 1971 for a stay of three years. In this period he made a series of paintings titled *Les Portes* (*The Gates*). These are abstractly patterned works in which strips of canvas are cut up and woven together; they exert a sort of gravitational pull on the eye. The *Les Portes* series "relied on subtle plays of elements appearing and disappearing, upon repetitions and the sense of how the smallest element is incorporated into a larger dimension," the art critic Mick Finch would write in 1995.[7] Finch's description could equally well have been written about Grisey's spectral music, with its telescoping in and out of the harmonic spectrum. The composer perceived the connection. Rouan recalled that although he did not have a musical background, the two men had frequent conversations about the content of their works:

> Gérard as a patient teacher tried to make me understand that his work was not unrelated to what he perceived in my work at that time, *Les Portes*. Lugubrious paintings, non-figurative on the threshold of monochrome but trying to re-introduce the sensitive experience of a certain thickness in the plane of the gaze.[8]

Rouan and Grisey stayed in touch after the two artists left Rome. In 1978, Rouan moved to Laversine, in northern France, where Grisey visited him once. "I then was able to understand that in his writing he himself was trying to keep together different layers of sound that were subtly intertwined," Rouan said. The two men then fell out of touch. But Grisey hadn't forgotten Rouan's work. Nearly a decade later, he took a student to see one of the artist's exhibitions.[9]

Born in 1948 in Marseille, the poet Guez Ricord was a prodigy—he won the Prix Paul Valéry at the age of seventeen. However, Ricord was in fragile physical and mental health, and by the spring of 1974, he left the Villa for an emergency stay in a closed psychiatric facility. He returned in the summer of 1974 as the partner of his girlfriend, who had also received a scholarship at the Villa Médicis. Much later, Grisey recalled the brief but powerful impression the poet left on him:

> I met Christian Guez-Ricord at the Villa Médicis from 1972 to 1974 and we often talked about a possible common work. Then our paths diverged and my research took me away from vocal music for a while. His death, which occurred in 1988 at the end of a tragic life, upset me. Even more so these few verses, like the silent climax of a dense, mystical work, heavy

---

7   Finch, "François Rouan."
8   Interview with Rouan.
9   Interview with Fishman-Johnson.

with Judeo-Christian images, almost medieval in its unceasing quest for the Grail.[10]

Grisey also met the reclusive Italian composer Giacinto Scelsi at some point during his stay in Rome, probably in 1973 or early 1974. Born into the aristocracy in 1905, Scelsi composed his early works in a twelve-tone idiom. According to legend, he had a crisis in the early 1950s, brought about both by composer's block and his separation from his first wife. In 1959, he composed *Quattro pezzi su una nota sola* (*Four pieces on a single note*). This work uses microtonal, dynamic, and timbral variations to make these single notes as exciting to listen to as other vastly complex scores. In the 1970s, Scelsi was living in a luxurious apartment overlooking the Roman Forum, surrounded by Eastern art objects and books, with a baby-blue four-poster bed. Unlike Grisey, Scelsi composed entirely intuitively, improvising and recording his pieces on an instrument called the ondioline.

One day, Murail brought the Griseys along to Scelsi's apartment. Grisey remembered the Italian as "a small man with white hair and a blue, melancholy expression" who presided over the view of the Forum "with the exquisite politeness of a great lord allowing his *orangerie* to be admired." Tea and cakes were served, and the three composers listened to two of Scelsi's compositions on an old Grundig reel-to-reel tape recorder. Grisey remembered that the first piece they heard was Scelsi's String Quartet no. 1 from 1944 (though this was more likely one of the later quartets[11]). The second work they heard was *Anahit*, Scelsi's masterpiece for solo violin and eighteen instruments, a "lyric poem dedicated to Venus" (the Roman goddess of love, sex, beauty, and fertility) which by some obscure magic turns highly dissonant microtonal beatings into music of radiant luminescence.

In a memoir-essay titled *Autoportrait avec L'Itinéraire,* Grisey recalled:

> I liked this music from the outset, in which I saw a confirmation of my own discoveries concerning the internal tensions of sound and the extreme dynamism that results. The radical difference and the essential freshness of this music strengthened me on my path while showing me that it was not without peril.
>
> I saw Scelsi several times afterwards because I liked him and he liked me back. But it was not always easy to insert an authentic dialogue in the interstices of his ritual monologues, a clever mixture of oriental wisdom,

---

10 Lelong, *Écrits*, 176.
11 The First Quartet is a thirty-minute work in a Webernian idiom, while the three next pieces for the same instrumentation are intricate, tense explorations of microtonal variations, beatings, natural harmonics, and other phenomena which fascinated Grisey.

banalities, and memories that this guru distilled, luckily not without humor, in perfect French.[12]

Like Olivier Messiaen, Scelsi was a mysterious figure whose strength of presence and magnetic musical ideas seemed to attract and repel Grisey at once.

❦ ❦ ❦

D'eau et de pierre was the apotheosis of "nascent spectralism" and the last of Grisey's pieces with aleatoric elements. *Dérives* marked the beginning of the composer's mature output. At least, the composer himself saw it that way. While *Périodes* and *Partiels* would become more famous, Grisey continued to analyze *Dérives* in the following decades, using it as a prototypical example of spectral thought.

Grisey began *Dérives* at the Villa Médicis in 1973 and finished it on September 17, 1974. The residency gave him the time he needed to work on this massive piece. Over twenty minutes long, it is scored for a large orchestra, with an independent *petit ensemble*, consisting of flute, clarinets, saxophone, bassoon, horn, accordion, and strings.

Dérives begins with a musical joke. The orchestra pretends to be tuning to an A, but the slight differences in their interpretation of this note are through-composed and expanded into larger microtonal variations, rather than being eliminated through the tuning process. The audience doesn't know that the composition has already begun. Edgard Varèse used a similar joke in his 1947 composition *Tuning Up*, but Grisey couldn't have heard it, because the piece remained unfinished, not being completed and premiered until 1998. Besides, the ideas are different. Grisey's opening reflects on the jarring shift between the noisy world and the cocoon of the concert hall. In Varèse's piece, the tuning to the A is blended with the typical orchestral tics of string noodling and loud brass warmups, plus one of Varèse's favorite instruments, the siren.

Even on the first listen to the first minute and a half of *Dérives*, it is clear that Grisey is breaking new aesthetic ground, rejecting the hyperactive serialism of much of the music around him and, building on the transparency of *D'eau et de pierre*, giving his sounds space to breathe. The fine-grained texture of the opening is interrupted by a terrifying, dissonant orchestral chord that retains its scare factor even on repeated listenings.

The structure of *Dérives* is based on Stockhausen's degrees of change concept. The central perceptual "pole" of the piece is a chord based on the harmonic spectrum of an E♭. From there, the piece uses processes of

---

12 Quoted in Lelong, *Écrits*, 204–5.

imperceptible changes to "tack" toward different textures, then back to the spectrum, which Grisey conceived of as a resting place for the listener's ear.

As in *Vagues, Chemins, le Souffle* and *D'eau et de pierre*, Grisey used an aquatic metaphor as an explanation for the structure of *Dérives*. In his program note for the piece, as mentioned, Grisey was thinking about the adjustments a boat makes in its forward path. He wrote:

> Drifting is like the course of a boat which, wanting to go from one point to another, finds itself obliged to constantly correct its course. The whole piece evolves around an ideal trajectory, from which one slowly moves away to a certain point; one comes closer to it after having somehow tacked. The maximum distance is silence. This ideal trajectory is defined by immediately recognizable auditory markers: the points of junction, or rather fusion, between the sequences of the small ensemble and those of the large orchestra. These instants make us hear a spectrum of harmonics that constitutes the axis of *Dérives*. The density of events is almost nil ...
>
> [The focus becomes] the passage from one object to another and its evolution. This in no way prevents one from controlling the nature of the sound object that we manipulate, but it only takes on its meaning in time, inserted in a context that defines it.[13]

Grisey concluded, "The road traveled is more important than the vehicle."

Another of Grisey's descriptions of *Dérives* gives a more visual (and quite poetic) impression of the piece:

> The image I wish to leave to those for whom the sound is insufficient would be that of a sea progressively agitated by a formidable storm whose waves solidify little by little, finally letting one hear only the isolated cracks of the icebergs overlapping ... then silence occurs, the ultimate point of this drift. But I insist on the fact that this image came to me well after this sequence was composed!

For the musicologist François-Xavier Féron, *Dérives* marks the moment where the harmonic spectrum stops being a collection of notes to be inserted into a composition and becomes a series of proportions with an influence "over a large number of compositional actions, in addition to the temporal structure of the piece."[14] In a similar way to the rhythmic form of Stockhausen's *Stimmung*, Grisey uses the proportions of the harmonic spectrum to structure his durations in whole-number ratios.

Dérives is constructed in sixteen parts, Féron notes, with a total of eight sequences, each with a section in the orchestra and in the ensemble. (The

---

13   Lelong, *Écrits*, 136.
14   Féron, "The emergence of spectra in Gérard Grisey's compositional process," 349.

two groups overlap in the fourth section.) Each of these sections is made up of one deviation from the E♭ harmonic spectrum. Grisey sketched out the plan for the work in detail before he began composing, a method of working established in earlier pieces that he continued for the rest of his life. "The piece had begun taking shape before a single note was written," Jocelyne told Féron.

Despite the accuracy of Grisey's planning for *Dérives,* the sonic effect of the piece is anything but didactic illustration. In the first third of the work, the texture shimmers intangibly, like a tapestry that changes slightly every time you look away and back. This texture coalesces first into a unison and later into the violent orchestral hits that reminded the composer Julian Anderson of the treatment for Grisey's ear infection as a child. The dryness of the ensuing silences stands in stark contrast to the resonances of Grisey's harmonic-spectrum chords. A rich, shifting texture gives way to fantastically well-orchestrated glissandi and upward scales that are unabashedly Debussyian. A few minutes from the end of the piece, Grisey's childhood instrument, the accordion, makes an appearance, intertwined with pizzicato strings. Maybe the most striking quality of *Dérives* is the way the sounds seem to change first incredibly slowly, then all at once.

The final section of the work is exciting, with at least six different musical elements colliding in a complex texture.[15] While each idea in the finale is related to an acoustical phenomenon, the combination of all of them together is an effect of Grisey's own creation. The result is an orchestral sound with seemingly bottomless depth. It's fitting that the piece ends by dissolving upwards, like water evaporating.

Jérôme Baillet also thinks that *Dérives* represents a turning point in Grisey's oeuvre. It's the piece where the composer finally breaks from the influences of his contemporaries and achieves his own way of working. Baillet writes:

> *Dérives* marks the birth of a style which, by its management of the temporal unfolding, distinguishes itself from the fragmentation of the music of Messiaen or serial composers, from Stockhausen's *Momentform* or Morton Feldman's music, as well as from Scelsi's contemplative scores ... The model of Ligeti's music is outmoded in the sense that a simple permanent change of texture is not enough to create a directed and perceptible path between one moment and another.[16]

Even with hindsight, Grisey saw *Dérives* as one of the most important turning points in his oeuvre, a fact he made clear in a letter from 1984 (while admitting to the piece's imperfections). "*Dérives,* Rome, 1972: I was

---

15   Ibid, 355.
16   Baillet, *Fondements d'une écriture,* 10.

in crisis, and this piece was a key work, an opening, a ramp, the beginning of a musical thought that I developed thereafter and that others have imitated since," he wrote. "I did not know, then, the importance for my thought of certain moments of this uneven score."[17]

Dérives was premiered on October 31, 1974, at the Salle Wagram in the seventeenth arrondissement, by the Orchestre National de France under the baton of Reinhard Peters, who was filling in for the indisposed Pierre Vozlinsky. As before the premier of *Vagues*, a strike by the orchestra was feared, but this time it didn't come to pass. It was an ambitious program: the central works were two masterpieces, Schoenberg's *Four Orchestral Songs* op. 22, from 1913–16, and Ligeti's Requiem from 1965. Alongside *Dérives*, the orchestra also played Niccolò Castiglioni's 1973 hall-of-mirrors composition *Inverno In-Ver*. *Le Monde* critic Anne Rey wrote of Grisey's piece:

> This "acoustic experiment" begins on the impassive rivers of a long continuum, then drifts by slow impulses or violent rebounds to plunge into silence or into chasms of sound. The course evolves thanks to the dynamism of the timbres, but immobilizes the duration of the successive states of balance or mutation. This anthropological attitude applied to the constitution of complex orchestral sounds is perhaps quite similar to the approach of electroacoustic music composers.[18]

Though Rey didn't quite say whether she liked the piece, she did perceive its form clearly, correctly noting the origins of its structure in acoustics. The piece was also performed for Radio France's "Perspectives of the 20th century" series in March 1980. The critic Roger Tellart praised its "beautifully lyrical nature" in *La croix*, with the caveat that "the energy drops a little at the end, where we expect a conclusion that doesn't really come."[19]

In early 1974, Grisey composed *Périodes* for flute, clarinet, violin, viola, cello, bass, and trombone. This timeline overlaps with the composition of *Dérives*. According to Féron, *Dérives* was close to finished by the time Grisey began *Périodes*, with only the final edits and the laborious copying process remaining.[20] Grisey worked on the copying with an assistant

---

17   Personal archive of Detry.
18   Anne Rey, "Musique plus."
19   Cohen-Levinas, *L'Itinéraire en temps réell*, 416.
20   Féron, "The emergence of spectra in Gérard Grisey's compositional process," 349.

named Alexandre Rabinovitch-Barakovsky, a pianist and composer who came to Rome especially for the job in the summer of 1974.[21]

This parallel composition process is explained by the fact that *Périodes* was commissioned by the newly formed Ensemble L'Itinéraire for a performance in June 1974 at the Villa Médicis. *Périodes* was one of fourteen world premieres created by the ensemble as part of its first season. The other works included pieces by Alain Louvier; L'Itinéraire founders Murail and Roger Tessier; Messiaen's assistant Betsy Jolas; and fellow Villa Médicis resident Michel Zbar. "Despite being busy composing *Dérives*," Grisey "gratefully accepted the commission," Cagney writes.[22] As a twenty-seven-year-old composer in the early stages of his career, Grisey was far from having the luxury of declining any paid commission, irrespective of the stage of completion of *Dérives*.

Despite the chronological closeness of the two pieces, there is audible progress between *Dérives* and *Périodes*. If the former work represents the first sophisticated application of key ideas of spectralism to a composition, the latter shows those ideas being shaped into a piece of concision, effectiveness, and remarkable beauty. For Cagney, *Périodes* marks Grisey's first unqualified compositional success. He compares it to Debussy's *Prélude à l'après-midi d'un faun* and Boulez's *Le marteau sans maître*.[23]

The composition opens with an E in the viola, marked *forte*, played on three of the viola's four strings; the note is then varied microtonally in a manner reminiscent of Scelsi's *Anahit*. But the most striking feature of *Périodes* to the listener is the quicksand quality of its harmonics. The fundamental, based on a trombone E, sounds frequently, and yet the pitches that Grisey uses to suggest its harmonic spectrum follow their own trajectories, like the energies that make up sound itself. Rather than *demonstrating* the acoustic phenomena that inspired him, the effect of *Périodes* is of the composer releasing these phenomena into their medium, the air, in which they are born, live, and die.

Grisey was aware of the magnitude of his achievement. In his diary, he wrote:

> Today, May 11, 1974, I finished my piece *Périodes* after three months of suffering and torture! No other work up till now has cost me so many tears. For three months I've been isolated and have done nothing but work on this score from morning until evening ... killing myself. But it is done, and its import is great, since I've finally come back to an awareness of the importance of the Ternary in duration (tension and fall; or [inhalation],

---

21 Interview with Jocelyne Grisey.
22 Cagney, "Synthesis and Deviation," 395.
23 Ibid, 396.

[exhalation], repose), of the heartbeat (quasi-periodicity) and of the spectrum of harmonic partials.[24]

This set a pattern for Grisey's compositional process for the rest of his life. Never content to imitate himself, he dedicated himself to every piece with obsessive energy. Each new work felt like utter reinvention.

The quasi-periodicity of the human heartbeat that Grisey describes affirms the centrality of other people's sensual experiences to his compositional process. As Grisey noted, and as Féron shows in his analysis of *Périodes*, the formal scheme of the work is based on an equally vital physiological process, the breath.[25] To define musical states analogous to this process, Grisey used the explicit connection between the regularity of periodic rhythms and the harmonic spectrum and the irregularity of aperiodic rhythms and the inharmonic spectrum, or noise. Inhalation is represented in the sections of the work where a process moves steadily toward a climax of tension characterized by aperiodic rhythms and inharmonic sounds. Exhalation is represented by a process that proceeds in the opposite direction. To delineate this motion, Grisey adds moments of periodic and harmonic rest, moments for the ear and the brain to recoup their concentration. Baillet writes that this structural use of regularity was a historically striking choice: it had been a "taboo notion in post-War European music which Grisey rediscovered for its universal character."[26]

As in *Dérives*, Grisey chose a harmonic spectrum on the note E to form the resting point of *Périodes*. In his later program note to the work, the composer claimed that he had based this harmony on a spectrogram of that pitch in the trombone. Féron, citing difficulties in the timeline, casts doubt on this claim; he believes that the spectrum in *Périodes* is something closer to a "sonic archetype." Féron adds that Grisey chose the low E because it lay in a comfortable range for him to score its harmonics, not for a symbolic reason.[27] (If there was going to be one, in the mode of Bach or Shostakovich, the note G would have been a more obvious choice, because his initials were G.G.)

To create his harmonic spectrum on the note E, Grisey chose partials up to the twenty-first, largely the odd ones—the evens would have given him a limited palette of repeated pitches—and transcribed them from frequency tables, approximately, into musical notes. (These were transcribed

---

24 Lelong, *Écrits*, 365.
25 Féron, "The emergence of spectra in Gérard Grisey's compositional process," 358.
26 Baillet, *Fondements d'une écriture*, 11–12.
27 Féron, "The emergence of spectra in Gérard Grisey's compositional process," 357.

in quarter-tones, plus "slightly" raised or lowered notes, a more accurate—though still imperfect—rendering of the harmonic spectrum than is possible with equal temperament.) Grisey then used a series of calculations deriving from the numbers of his chosen partials to "control the musical processes," Féron explains.[28] But the individual processes remained the products of the composer's vivid acoustical imagination. A tangling series of scales sounds like a psychedelic version of Ravel.

In another element common with *Dérives*, *Périodes* contains a brief theatrical moment that plays with the onstage ritual of tuning. In the newer work, this moment takes place toward the final third, interrupting the processes of the piece rather than playfully easing the listener into the composition. The violinist and the violist attempt to tune up, remaining a quarter-tone apart until they come together on a melodic upward major second. In the process they exchange "brusque" looks (the violinist, clearly in character) until the violist has finally found the correct pitch (also in character). There is something of Grisey's light sense of humor in this moment, as well as a hint that he knew the kind of troubles that awaited him as a composer of microtonal music.

The final page of *Périodes* is simultaneously the opening of the next work in what would become the cycle *Les espaces acoustiques*. Featuring a harmonic spectrum based on the same trombone E that anchored the rest of *Périodes*, this moment would become the most recognizable seconds of music in Grisey's entire oeuvre.

In May 1974, Grisey finished *Périodes* and gave the score to Ensemble L'Itinéraire. In June, the group premiered the piece in Rome under Boris de Vinogradov alongside works by Claude Ballif, Solange Ancona, Roger Tessier, and Stockhausen. In a later essay, Grisey recalled discussing *Périodes* with Scelsi and Murail. Scelsi said he'd enjoyed the piece.

"Even the joke in the middle?" Grisey asked.

"That's more questionable," Murail said. The theatrical section "is a bit of dirtiness that needs to be cleaned up within the piece."

Scelsi told Murail that Grisey "surely has his reasons."[29]

As Cagney notes, it was "an anecdote illustrating the basic difference in Grisey and Murail's respective aesthetics."[30] The Paris premiere of *Périodes* took place the same year. In *Le Quotidien de Paris*, Gérard Mannoni praised

---

28   Ibid.
29   Lelong, *Écrits*, 203–4.
30   Cagney, "Synthesis and Deviation," 400.

the "very rich sound world" of *Périodes* for its "alternation of the meditative and the explosive."[31]

In May 1976, Grisey had the opportunity to discuss *Périodes* on television. While music critics and colleagues may have been impressed by the new work, casual viewers were probably lost. In a screed against the elitism of French television published in *Le Monde*, Claude Sarraute wrote, "It was very difficult to follow the rare comments, incomprehensible to anyone who has not studied harmony, which Gérard Grisey made during the rehearsal of his latest work: *Périodes*." She added, "Here again, we should have been enlightened, attracted instead of repelled. Is it a service to these creators to keep the uninitiated away from them?" Sarraute clearly had an axe to grind. But she had also perceived that Grisey was not an effortless promoter of his own music, a fact that dogged him for his entire professional life.

Around this time, a thorny musicological issue emerges: was Grisey or Murail the first composer to write pieces in the genre that later became known as spectral music? Julian Anderson remarked that, for a time, Grisey and Murail were as close aesthetically as Picasso and Braque.[32] For Cagney, Murail's earliest spectral piece is *Tigres de verre*, from 1974; for Anderson and Baillet, it's *Sables* for orchestra, from 1974–75.[33] These pieces overlap closely with *Dérives* and *Périodes* in date of composition.

Some say Grisey was the first spectralist. "Gérard had something of a guru about him. He had a way of influencing people, and he influenced Murail for a very long time," Dufourt said. "In my opinion, Murail didn't become free from his influence until *Gondwana* [1981], if he ever did."[34] The question of who came first is beyond the scope of this biography. Its premise also deserves a critical eye. Musical styles are not singular inventions like the lightbulb, to be patented and manufactured. What is known as the "spectral movement" that originated at the Villa Médicis is a group of individual artists inspired by the stuff of sound, working largely on their own. The imitations came later—everyone imitates, like Grisey with his Stockhausen copies. Grisey and Murail, as well as the other composers who came to be associated with them, like Levinas and Dufourt, did write music that sounded similar at times. They are probably best understood as composers who walked a path together for a while. Furthermore, great art is not the result of originality alone: it requires craft, dedication, patience, intuition. This is a theme that reappears throughout Grisey's life. He rarely wrote the newest piece on an idea or phenomenon, but often the most powerful.

---

31 Quoted in Ibid, 401.
32 Interview with Julian Anderson.
33 Cagney, "Synthesis and Deviation," 401.
34 Interview with Dufourt.

On a personal level, Grisey and Murail *were* affected by the question of who composed what when, each seeing in himself the authentic originator and practitioner of spectral music. Their personalities were very different, their egos very similar. The friendship they formed in Rome could not last.

🙞 🙞 🙞

During Grisey's stay in Rome, his interest in Catholicism began to wane. This happened not despite but rather because of the bombastic omnipresence of religion in the city of the Vatican. According to Jocelyne, the composer also "suffered from the poverty of the Catholic ritual," a suffering that had already revealed itself in Grisey's earlier letters. As a conservatory student in Paris, he had frequented the Cathédrale Saint-Alexandre-Nevsky in the eighth arrondissement, a Russian Orthodox church which was the first of its kind in France.[35] Presumably, Grisey found the austere chanting of that tradition more powerful than the amateurish singing of hymns and organ improvisations at less prestigious Catholic churches. He might also have been inspired by a powerful passage in Dostoevsky's *The Idiot* that praises the Russian church and derides Catholicism.[36] Besides, the rift between sexual desire and the ascetic dictates of strict religion that had opened so early in Grisey's teenage years seems to have grown to an irreconcilable chasm. Grisey had a mistress during his time at the Villa Médicis, a circumstance that was painful for Jocelyne. As one friend said later, "I believe it was *women* who made him lose his faith."[37] Grisey's sexuality could not fit in the church-sanctioned institution of marital monogamy.

This doesn't mean that Grisey had abandoned religion completely; he remained spiritual. But he stopped attending Catholic services, looking more to Eastern religion and art in all its forms to nourish his soul. As the musicologist Pierre Rigaudière writes, Grisey immersed himself in art both religious and secular, finding meaning in both: "This cohabitation of two spiritual attitudes seems to me to be articulated according to the progressive evolution of the most fervent mysticism ... it is not a question here of making Grisey a layman, but of interpreting his insatiable appetite for reading, his need to cultivate himself unceasingly, as an opening on the infinite." Can Grisey's mature, spectral compositions be understood as spiritual music (besides the explicitly religious pieces of his youth, such as the Magnificat and *Deux Madrigaux*)? For Rigaudière, "There is no musical marker of the spiritual that can be highlighted by analysis. The spiritual in music can be the

---

35 Rigaudière, "De l'Esprit au spectre," 40–41.
36 He read *The Idiot* in August 1969. Lelong, *Écrits*, 314.
37 Interview with Lelong.

fundamental motivation of the work, can, like a catalyst, trigger the writing, even irrigate it, but it dissolves in it, present everywhere, visible nowhere."[38] There are markers of the *religious* that can be highlighted by musical analysis: Many of Messiaen's pieces have symbols of the Holy Trinity in them,[39] for example, as does Grisey's *Perichoresis*. Later Grisey works such as *Jour, contre-jour, Sortie vers la lumière du jour*, and *Quatre chants pour franchir le seuil* also deal with explicitly religious—largely ancient Egyptian—rituals. In Rome, he read the Egyptian and Tibetan *Books of the Dead* and continued to read widely on worship and religion for the rest of his life.

Rigaudière is right that the *spiritual* is difficult to pin down in musical analysis. In Grisey's music, spirituality manifests itself in a pervasive sense of wonder at the physical phenomenon of sound. His pieces are suffused with an admiring astonishment at the complexity and scale of life and time, on earth and in the cosmos.

There is still something unsatisfying about these explanations of Grisey's loss of faith. How could his deeply felt belief in Christ have dissipated so quickly? It seems the process was like those of his pieces, where things change slowly and subtly, then all at once.

An almost obsessive dedication to the arts replaced the intensive religious practice of Grisey's youth. The arts were the vector through which he connected with the ineffable in a way that the Catholic ritual could no longer provide for him. On January 15, 1973, he wrote in his diary, "Long night of ink, without hope, without expectation. I listen to Mozart's *Idomeneo* and I am suddenly taken by a crazy desire to plunge back into prayer and silence. God through Mozart."[40]

In November 1972, a representative of the storied Italian music publishing house Casa Ricordi had attended the premiere of *D'eau et de pierre* at the festival in Metz and became interested in Grisey's music. In the summer of 1974, during his stay at the Villa Médicis, Grisey signed a contract with the company, based in Milan. Ricordi has works by such household names as Guiseppe Verdi and Giacomo Puccini, and contemporary music legends like Nono, Varèse, and Berio in its catalogue. The first works of Grisey's to be published with Ricordi were *Périodes, Charme*, and *Dérives*. Besides *Charme*, which Cagney notes was "up to this point his most performed

---

38   Rigaudière, "De l'Esprit au spectre," 44.
39   See for example Griffiths, *Olivier Messiaen and the Music of Time*.
40   Paul Sacher archive.

work,"[41] Ricordi got into business with Grisey just as he was discovering his mature aesthetic. Though it was common for the composition talents of the Conservatoire National Supérieur to find publishers early in their careers, being accepted to Casa Ricordi at Grisey's young age was an unusual honor.

Grisey was one of the first composers signed by Mimma Guastoni, who joined Ricordi in March 1974 as editorial director. Born in 1940 in Milan, Guastoni was hired by the publishing house after finishing university, where she had studied literature and philosophy. She ended up remaining there for thirty years, building an important contemporary music portfolio.[42] A consummate businesswoman, Guastoni became the primary figure through whom Grisey experienced this side of the music industry. Their lengthy correspondence shows an artist and an editorial director grappling with their responsibilities toward each other and with the place of contemporary classical music in a changing society.[43]

One of those changes was represented by the initial terms of Grisey's contract with the publisher, which, according to Jocelyne, agreed to pay the largely unproven composer a monthly fee for his work over a period of three or four years.[44] Such an arrangement was exceedingly generous even for its time and is more or less unheard-of today. But Grisey was never the kind of composer to churn out pragmatic works, and by the late 1970s the publisher decided to void this agreement.

In 1973, in another sign that Grisey's career was progressing through the official channels, he was awarded the Prix Hervé Dugardin, from the Société des auteurs, compositeurs et éditeurs de musique, or Sacem (the French royalties society).[45] Named after the former director of the Théâtre National de l'Opéra Comique, the award was given to a young composer of "symphonic music," a large-scale genre in which Grisey had already begun to make his mark.

※ ※ ※

The Villa Médicis scholarship came with a final benefit: funding for a trip of the artist's choice. The assistant Grisey had hired for *Dérives*, Alexandre Rabinovitch-Barakovsky, had told Grisey about the aesthetic and moral dilemmas of Russian composers under the Soviet government, a topic Grisey found fascinating. He decided on Russia for his funded trip. He

---

41 Cagney, "Synthesis and Deviation," 362.
42 See Guastoni, "LinkedIn." Guastoni didn't respond to an interview request.
43 Paul Sacher archive.
44 Interview with Jocelyne Grisey.
45 Paul Sacher archive.

got the names of several composers he could meet with from Rabinovitch-Barakovsky and, in the fall of 1974, put together an application for a visa. But the Soviet government declined his request, saying, implausibly, that all the hotels in the country were fully booked.

Grisey didn't want the funding to go to waste. He and Jocelyne decided to go to Egypt instead, a country that had fascinated the composer since at least his late teens. In October 1974, they left for a two-week trip. They arrived in Cairo. And though they had planned to stay in the capital for a couple of days before moving on to the Valley of Kings, they met a young Egyptian who overheard them speaking French and offered to be their guide. This guide was a mixed blessing: he took the young couple to parts of Cairo they would never have dared to go to on their own, and introduced them to interesting young people, with whom they discussed the relationship between the sexes in Islamic culture. The guide took them to the carpet bazaar, but, when they tried to exchange some money, he made off with the equivalent of a couple of hundred dollars of their cash. For Jocelyne, at least, this exchange was worth it. "We saw things we would never have seen otherwise," she said.

In Cairo, the Griseys spent time at the museums of Egyptian history, where Grisey examined the sarcophagi for hours. "Gérard was very moved to see that the deceased was [depicted being held] in the arms of a woman," the goddess Nut, Jocelyne said. He was captivated by the idea that death had a sensual embrace.

Finally, they went to see the pyramids in Saqqara. Getting there was an adventure:

> We said to ourselves that we were going to get there by the local means of transportation. We took a bus at 7 a.m. and by 11 a.m. we had traveled five kilometers. It stopped everywhere, picking up people with live chickens. At 11 a.m. we took a cab. We arrived in Saqqara, and the guard told us that [the pyramids] were closed. We talked a little, he offered us tea and said that we could go inside, so we visited the site, the frescoes, without other people or tourists—it was fabulous![46]

Jocelyne recalls that the pilgrimage made a lasting aesthetic impression on Grisey, inspiring his later works *Sortie vers la lumière du jour, Jour, contre-jour, Anubis et Nout,* and the second movement of *Quatre chants pour franchir le seuil.* "He had very strong emotions in Egypt," she said. "And the idea for a score often came from a very strong emotion."

---

46   Interview with Jocelyne Grisey.

Chapter Seven

Ultimate Fusion (1974–78)

On his return from Rome, Grisey was confronted with a harsh though not entirely unexpected reality. Composition didn't provide enough income for him to support Jocelyne and himself; he would have to work. Between the fall of 1974 and the spring of 1980, the composer taught at a variety of music schools in the Paris area. This was a temporary fix which lasted too long and had inherent frustrations. Although Jocelyne earned more money than Grisey in her new position as a social worker, the two incomes still didn't add up to much: "The financial situation was very difficult," she said. Grisey's degree from the Conservatoire National Supérieur didn't qualify him to teach composition at the university level, which meant he was stuck working at *conservatoires d'arrondissement*.[1]

Back in France, Grisey took a post teaching musical analysis at the Centre Musical Edgar Varèse, in Gennevilliers, outside Paris. In 1975, he began giving courses in analysis and harmony at the Conservatoire Municipal de Romainville, in another suburb. Between 1978 and 1979, he also returned to the Sorbonne to teach as an adjunct, but his contract was not renewed (it's unclear why not). This precarious work neither alleviated Grisey's financial worries nor allowed him sufficient time and calm to compose. At one point, Grisey was up for a promotion at a local music school but declined because it would have involved twenty hours of work a week. "I was trying to protect him," Jocelyne said. "He needed so much time to compose."[2]

In 1972, before the couple had left for Rome, Grisey's parents had given them a sum of money for a down payment on an apartment in Paris. But the recession of 1973–74 hit the franc hard, and when they returned from Rome, they found the gift from Grisey's parents was worth far less than it had been. Back in France, Grisey and Jocelyne spent six months living with a

---

1   Interview with Jocelyne Grisey.
2   Ibid.

friend, an architect named Claude Leclerc, a situation which could only have contributed to the overall feeling of precarity.

Meanwhile, Grisey continued his post-Conservatoire education. On October 26, 1974, he began an acoustics course at the Sorbonne's Laboratory of Musical Acoustics at the Place Jussieu, a hulking modern tower in stark contrast to the nearby Latin Quarter. His professor was the acoustician Émile Leipp, whose book Grisey had read in 1972. The timing of Grisey's decision to take this course is striking: he had already finished *Dérives* and *Périodes*. But he clearly felt that his knowledge of the field was insufficient. This was part of his character: "Throughout his training, from his studying harmony in Belfort to his studying electroacoustics and mathematics with [Jean-Étienne] Marie, Grisey, having identified a shortcoming in his training or knowledge, took action to remedy that shortcoming," Cagney writes.[3]

Leipp had founded the Laboratory of Musical Acoustics at the Sorbonne in 1963. He was an essential figure in musical acoustics, with a particular interest in the use of spectrograms, illustrations of the frequency content of a sound, to analyze the overtone makeups of musical instruments. Leipp was also keenly interested in spectral music, as Cagney points out. The exchange went both ways.[4]

An exact record of the topics of Leipp's Sorbonne course has not been preserved. However, it seems likely that the course followed Leipp's book, *Acoustique et Musique*. As Cagney notes, the text fit remarkably well with Grisey's interests. It was

> written with an ideal future reader of Grisey's cast in mind; and in this regard it is little wonder [it] should have had such an influence on him; since, being one of the most talented composers of his generation, Grisey was perfectly disposed for the creative application of these acoustical notions as found in the books towards the coining of a new style of music taking better stock of contemporary acoustics and psychoacoustics.[5]

Grisey finished Leipp's course on May 24, 1975, and received a certificate confirming his participation from the Groupement des acousticiens de langue française.[6]

---

3   Cagney, "Synthesis and Deviation," 350.
4   Ibid, 352.
5   Ibid, 353.
6   Paul Sacher archive.

In the spring of 1975, Grisey's father, Jules Henri, became sick with a lung problem. The illness was possibly caused by exposure to toxic fumes from the car batteries in his garage.[7] He went to a hospital in Paris for treatment, where Grisey and Jocelyne visited him regularly. Though Grisey's father was stern, even violent, during the composer's childhood, they had become closer as adults. "After he retired, we had more contact with his father than with his mother," Jocelyne recalled. "He was more open, while she was rigid and not very emotional."[8] In a letter, Jules Henri referred to the couple as "my very dear children."[9]

One day at the hospital, Jules Henri lost consciousness. He was surrounded by doctors and quickly revived with an injection. When Jules Henri came to, he told Grisey, "Why did you do that? I felt like I was leaving. I was in a long hallway. It was easy, it was fine. Why did you make me come back?"[10] Jules Henri died eight days later.

※ ※ ※

In the summers of 1975 and 1976, Grisey and Jocelyne spent their vacations near the town of Remiremont, in the Vosges mountains. The region, where Grisey had already spent time as a child, is pretty and quaint, its peaks green and gentle. The Griseys stayed in a rustic hunting lodge belonging to a friend—without electricity or running water. Grisey would wake up at five a.m., drink coffee, and compose until ten. Then Jocelyne would make breakfast. After they ate together, Grisey would return to composing until the afternoon. Then the couple went on walks in the mountains. "Our only contact was with the farmers, who knew a lot about nature and animals, and told us about mushrooms," Jocelyne said. She spent her time cooking and reading while Grisey dedicated himself to his music. "It was so precious for him to have his time and especially his mind free, to not be disturbed by the daily routine and the need to go and give lessons—to be completely in his music," Jocelyne said.

Grisey was not an expert hiker. During a later summer, Jocelyne, who had spent time as a teenager in the Chamonix-Mont-Blanc valley in the French Alps, suggested that they go there for their vacation. She was surprised to find that Grisey was put out by the difficulty of the trails. She realized that, while walking, the composer was also thinking about his music, planning

---

7   According to Jocelyne Grisey, Detry, and Deguy. At least, it seems clear this is what Grisey himself believed.
8   Interview with Jocelyne Grisey.
9   Private archive of Jocelyne Grisey.
10 Interview with Jocelyne Grisey.

his forms in his head, and that a difficult trail was a distraction for him. On one walk, he gave up completely, and Jocelyne went on by herself to see the mountain lakes. After that, they decided to spend their summers elsewhere in the French countryside, where there were no mountains and Grisey could devote himself completely to his work.[11]

In 1975, after the completion of *Périodes*, the form for a large-scale musical cycle on acoustic phenomena began taking shape in Grisey's mind. "When I composed *Périodes*, I realized that the end was not an ending, that a sequel was needed, and I imagined *Partiels*, which was composed immediately afterward," he wrote.[12] The new work is so intertwined with its predecessor that the ending of *Périodes* is identical to the beginning of *Partiels*. The title has a dual meaning: partial in the sense of a fragment of a whole (the newly conceived cycle); partials in the sense of the components of an overtone spectrum. *Partiels* is scored for eighteen instruments: two flutes, oboe, two clarinets in B♭, bass clarinet, two horns, trombone, accordion, two percussionists, and a string sextet with two violas and a bass. Grisey completed the work in 1975 and received a commission fee of 9,000 francs from the French Ministry of Culture in January 1977.

As mentioned, the overlapping passage that ends *Périodes* and begins *Partiels* contains probably the most famous music Grisey ever wrote. As the musicologist Yves Krier writes, the piece "is the work of Grisey most frequently cited in articles or commentaries dealing with the specificities of spectral composition. Rightly or wrongly, it has often been considered, if not as the manifesto of the spectral tendency ... at least as its clearest manifestation."[13] The composer Frédéric Durieux adds, "The famous first part of this score, which gradually shifts from a harmonic trombone spectrum on the note E to an inharmonic spectrum, struck everyone. You've only had to have participated in any composition jury to realize this! What a lot of E spectra we have had to endure since then!"[14]

At the start of the work, three low Es, marked loud and accented, ring out in the bass. The pitches of the harmonic spectrum rise softly in the other instruments, resulting in an aural impression that is uncannily familiar, like a déjà vu. The overtone series is a sound that everyone has heard at some point. But Grisey's treatment of the phenomenon was attuned to acoustic realities in a radically new way. Grisey achieved the striking effect of the work not only by imitating the components of sound, but also their development

---

11 Ibid.
12 Lelong, *Écrits*, 139.
13 Krier, "Partiels, de Gérard Grisey, manifestation d'une nouvelle esthétique," 146.
14 Cohen-Levinas, *Le Temps de l'Écoute*, "Les Temps Traversés," 92–93.

in time. Every sound has onset transients, components of the overtone spectrum which are produced during the initial excitement of the instrument; a "stable" overtone series that occurs while it is held; and decay transients, which determine its changing quality as it dies away. The onset transients are particularly important: the acoustician Fritz Winckel explains that "an instrumental sound of constant pitch and intensity loses its character to a certain extent if one 'cuts off,' that is, renders inaudible, the typical attack."[15] But all three elements combine to give the sound its perceptual character—its birth, life, and death, in Grisey's phrase.

This holistic approach to the sound gives the opening of *Partiels* its striking quality. As Féron writes, the overtone spectrum on the note E is "constructed progressively, component by component, and aims to trace the temporal nature of most musical sounds: onset, sustain, and decay." The pitch material is concentrated on the odd-numbered partials which give the overtone spectrum its characteristic sound. The orchestration, too, is essential to the overall effect: "The modes of instrumental playing (as neutral as possible, without vibrato) and the dynamics employed (fading from *dal niente* to erase individual attacks as much as possible) all contribute to the annihilation of instrumental identities in favor of an ensemble sonority."[16] Ironically, Grisey hid the onset and decay transients of the individual instruments as much as possible in order to reproduce them in the macro ensemble sound.

Partiels is structured similarly to *Périodes*, while also building on ideas present in *Dérives*. Once again, the model is the stages of human breath, with areas of inhalation, exhalation, and repose. As the musicologist Chris Arrell describes it:

> Repose sections are primarily harmonic and rhythmically periodic. Inhalations [are musical processes which] move toward inharmonicity and rhythmic irregularity, or aperiodicity. Conversely, exhalations move toward harmonicity or periodicity. These large-scale oscillations between harmonicity/inharmonicity and periodicity/aperiodicity draw a tension graph that mirrors the compressions and rarefactions of a sound wave.[17]

Partiels represents the most sophisticated implementation of the breath metaphor in Grisey's music so far. In contrast to *Périodes*, the inhalation and exhalation sections in *Partiels* are in close relation to one another, while steadily decreasing in length throughout the work—from a pair lasting 180 and 136.5 seconds at the beginning to a pair lasting 78.5 and 72.9 seconds

---

15   Winckel, *Music, Sound, and Sensation*, 33.
16   Féron, "Gérard Grisey: première section de *Partiels* (1975)," 13.
17   Arrell, "The Music of Sound," 320.

toward the climax. According to Krier, "This can evoke a certain stress, a cause of a shorter, more oppressed breathing."[18] Another possible interpretation is that the structure evokes the quicker, shallower breaths which occur naturally during physical exertion or on the path to sexual climax. As mentioned, Grisey had remarked to Jocelyne that "physical desire, the breath, the beating heart" were important for his music. The global structure of *Partiels* confirms the pride of place of sensuality in the composer's musical thought: The entire work is a tribute to the subtle miracle of breath.

The first "inhalation" of the piece is a sort of zooming-in effect on its main overtone chord. This chord is repeated eleven times, with instruments added and the number of partials expanded higher up the overtone series. Each time we hear the sound we notice more of its details, as if we were examining an organism at progressively more magnified microscope settings. At the same time, Arrell writes, "the process of octave transfer [the downward transposition of high partials by octaves] steadily increases inharmonicity, the envelopes [the three stages of the sound: attack, sustain, and decay] mutate, and partials begin to enter out of sequence."[19] Increasing the overall tension, Grisey introduces various noise effects, such as irregular breathing and vibrato (in the winds) and irregular bow strokes (in the strings). The first exhalation is composed using difference tones, but most striking is Grisey's conversion of the resulting notes, which are below human hearing, into rhythm. This is the kind of moment that led to the reception of the piece as a "manifesto": the composer is showing that pitch and rhythm are not separate categories, but one and the same thing.

The second zone of rest in *Partiels* is not a full spectrum on an E, but a high, open fifth, dirtied slightly by flute glissandi. This crystalline timbre gains its periodicity from the repetitions, which are based on "quasi periodic" signals from the conductor. Grisey is not aiming for the precise periodicity a computer can produce, but rather the "supple" kind that issues forth from the musician's body.

The second inhalation takes a series of almost romantic melodic lines and entangles them increasingly throughout the process of increasing tension; the effect for the listener is of pushing a path through the ever-thicker greenery of an untamed jungle. The pitch material is again based on the sum- and difference-tone processes Grisey studied with Jean-Étienne Marie and builds up to an aggregate of beatings and trills which form the beginning of the second exhalation. In this section, Grisey makes another powerful psychoacoustic discovery, that periodicity and harmonicity outweigh the effects of

---

18   Krier, "Partiels, de Gérard Grisey, manifestation d'une nouvelle esthétique," 156.
19   Arrell, "The Music of Sound," 323.

speed. This exhalation builds into a section of extremely fast, high scales in the winds, but as listeners, we feel relaxation, because these scales occur on the harmonic spectrum and at increasingly regular intervals. They lead us to the third zone of rest: a beautiful canon.

The third inhalation builds organically from this canon, with the motives of the flute filled in and the other instruments placed at increasing closeness to one another, culminating in another dense texture. This time, the progress to the exhalation is broken up by what multiple musicologists call the "rupture," a series of five tightly dissonant scales in the whole ensemble. According to Arrell, this moment is a conscious attempt on Grisey's part to break up the neat processes that govern *Partiels*, adding a human, subjective component to the work.[20]

The beginning of the third and final exhalation is dominated by the sound of the accordion, the instrument of Grisey's youth, and an ominously thrilling descending scale. This last exhalation is followed by a relatively inharmonic zone of rest. In context, the formal ambiguity of the final sections of the work are effective: having established clear expectations in the main body of *Partiels*, Grisey gives himself the freedom to compose music of mysterious intensity, knowing that by now he can count on our concentration.

Like *Périodes*, *Partiels* closes with a section of music theater. The performers begin packing up their instruments and making post-rehearsal chitchat in four languages. As in the previous work in the cycle, there is satire at the grumpiness displayed by musicians when they have to perform a contemporary work: one German line is *"Das ist doch nicht möglich,"* or "That's impossible!" The composer Joshua Fineberg said, "It's like the Orchestre Philharmonique closing up their instruments and refusing to rehearse five minutes past [the scheduled end]. That is what it is. These terrible experiences with musicians packing up before the rehearsal was done. It was, 'Fuck you—I'll turn that into part of the piece.' [In *Périodes*] he has them giving [each other] funny looks over the tuning. That happened to him innumerable times in rehearsals."[21] The end of *Partiels* is even funnier: a percussionist opens his cymbals wide—and holds them there. It's a technique reminiscent of horror movies, when you know a jump scare is coming, but you can't say exactly when. Grisey makes us wait; *Partiels* ends with the percussionist in this position.

Partiels is a masterpiece and even an improvement over *Périodes*: while the two pieces share a structural and sonic sophistication, *Partiels* has a more effective dramaturgy, with its finely calibrated balance between inhalation, exhalation, and repose. In his article, Krier notes that the form of *Partiels*

---

20 Ibid, 330.
21 Interview with Fineberg.

has been subject to criticism: "Some interpreters consider the structure of *Partiels* too simplistic in its principles (too militant?) ... Let us recognize that this work was only the first state of a new conception that the composer, as well as his colleagues, knew how to make bear fruit, to develop, to transcend."[22]

But Grisey's artistic development can't be described as a progression from "too simplistic" to complex; *Dérives* was structurally more complex than *Partiels*, but the latter work has the more effective dramaturgy. Krier is correct to say that later Grisey pieces worked more subtly with acoustic and psychoacoustic phenomena; if there is a criticism of *Partiels*, it could be a slight didacticism in the treatment of the spectral material. In that sense, the piece *is* a musical manifesto. Besides that, the structural simplicity is a sign of aesthetic progress for Grisey: the clear perceptual framework allows the innovation and sonic expertise of *Partiels* to shine through and gives the composition its staying power.

On March 4, 1976, *Partiels* was premiered by Ensemble L'Itinéraire to a full house at the Nouveau Carré in the fifteenth arrondissement of Paris. The program began with a work by Monic Cecconi-Botella and Stockhausen's *Adieu für Wolfgang Sebastian Meyer* for wind quintet. Jacques Lonchampt, the critic for *Le Monde*, was enthusiastic about all the pieces, but was particularly avid in his praise for *Partiels*:

> [*Partiels*], excellently conducted by Boris de Vinogradov, [was] a very poetic score with wonderful orchestral writing. From a triple rasp of double bass, still blackened by the trombone (a formula that returns many times at the beginning of the work), light sounds escaped, an instrumental breeze, later more charged sounds, very diverse, often in harmonics, and also harmonious explosions, sequences of subtle timbres releasing enclosed dreams. A monster wakes up with frightful cries, the brass roams in phosphorescent lights, the woodwinds rustle like seagulls, the horns clatter, the percussion shivers. A real mystery lies behind these very pure episodes ...[23]

Grisey had found his voice, and the world was taking notice.

Grisey continued to compose with furious intensity. He finished his next work, *Prologue* for solo viola, quickly by his own standards, writing it between April and July 1976 and dedicating it to the violist Gérard Causé. From *Périodes*, the first piece in what was to become the cycle *Les espaces*

---

22 Krier, "Partiels, de Gérard Grisey, manifestation d'une nouvelle esthétique," 171.
23 Lonchampt, "'Partiels', de Gérard Grisey à L'Itinéraire."

acoustiques, Grisey worked forward to the engulfing harmonic spectra of *Partiels*; now he was working backward, to *Prologue*, the work for solo viola that became the introduction to the cycle. *Prologue* was the composer's first attempt to adapt the principles of spectral music to a solo instrument. Unable to compose ensemble textures, Grisey used ideas from the preceding pieces of his cycle to create a purely melodic work.

Like *Périodes* and *Partiels*, the two structural poles of *Prologue* are a harmonic spectrum on the note E and white noise. The fourth string of the viola, normally tuned to a C, is tuned instead to a B♮, allowing the player to realize the third partial of the very low fundamental. The first section of *Prologue* explores the spectrum in a series of melodic variations. This music becomes increasingly inharmonic, giving way to the second section, where glissandi overtake the discrete individual pitches of the spectrum, eventually climaxing in a section of pure noise. In the final, third section, the tonal center of *Prologue* "modulates" to a D, the third open string on the viola, as harmonic elements are reintroduced to the work in a more ambiguous form. Like its predecessors, the work moves from repose to tension and back to an uneasy peace.

In *Prologue*, Grisey expands his fascination with the processes of the body, applying it not just to the work's overall form, but also to its individual motives. The piece contains two cells that function as "inserts" in the large processes of the work: a short-long rhythm and an echo.[24] Grisey defined the first as a heartbeat. The second consists of a series of oscillating pitches decreasing in volume. As Baillet writes, both motives were "chosen here for their universal and naturalistic characters."[25] They function as aural tags, immediately recognizable bits of musical material which orient our ears and guide our brains as we follow *Prologue* through its musical development.

For his treatment of the main melodic material in the first section of *Prologue*, Grisey turned to a technique that Messiaen had introduced him to: melodic neumes, a compositional process taken from the Middle Ages, defined as "small melodic formulas applied to a syllable." Maybe the seeds of those lessons from several years earlier were beginning to flower; or maybe Grisey, faced with the uncertain prospect of composing one line for a single instrument again, was looking to attach himself to a tried-and-true method.

For this technique of cellular variation to be perceptible, it was imperative for the composer to start with an extremely simple melodic fragment. "We can perceive and memorize a melody in two ways," Grisey wrote in his program note to *Prologue*. "By the notes of which it consists, or by the *Gestalt* (the shape) of the melodic curve. *Prologue* is constructed entirely based on

---

24 Lelong, *Écrits*, 144.
25 Baillet, *Fondements d'une écriture*, 99.

this second type of perception."[26] In his 1886 book *Beiträge zur Analyse der Empfindungen* (*The Analysis of Sensations*), Ernst Mach pioneered this idea in terms of music. Mach pointed out that "when we begin with two groups of notes which begin on different notes but continue in the same proportion to one another, we recognize in both the same melody as viscerally as we recognize in two geometrically similar forms the same *Gestalt*."[27] In his 1932 essay *Über Gestaltqualitäten* (*On the Qualities of Form*), Christian von Ehrenfels adds the nuance that this visceral recognition is only possible when we can remember the entire shape of the melody.[28] As Baillet shows, Grisey's *Prologue* is based on an extremely simple cell with three notes, moving downward then upward. This cell allows us to pick out the individual neumes as their complexity increases, in odd numbers of notes from three to thirteen. These lengths align with the first odd partials of the harmonic spectrum, an example of the cohesion between macro and micro form in *Prologue*.[29]

While studying the sketches for the solo viola work, Féron noticed that Grisey identified specific archetypes of neumes from the Middle Ages while generating his melodic material.[30] Baillet concentrates instead on the variations of the six original melodic neumes, identifying the Messiaen-style process of "limited permutation," whereby "the pitches of the cells are always inverted in the same order." Both musicologists agree on the importance of the seventh neume. For Féron, the medieval melodic archetype that makes up this cell again form a mirror of the respiratory cycle. Grisey created structures of inhalation and exhalation within each individual neume while also setting in motion a global process of increasing tension. As Baillet says in his analysis, "It is the internal agitation of the neumes that increases over time."[31]

Despite Grisey's use of structural principles from Messiaen, however, the sounding result of *Prologue* is entirely his own. Grisey's periodic and echo motives, interspersed throughout the process of the work, are an important part of this. They function as easily identifiable signposts for our perception but are also subject to a process of change. Increasingly, the heartbeat and echo become one with the rest of the music.

The musicologist Jeffrey J. Hennessy picks up on a striking aspect of *Prologue*, the evocation of the Doppler effect in the variations on the echo

---

26 Lelong, *Écrits*, 143.
27 Quoted in von Ehrenfels, "Über Gestaltqualitäten," 2.
28 Ibid, 3.
29 Baillet, *Fondements d'une écriture*, 112.
30 Féron, "Gérard Grisey – *Prologue*."
31 Baillet, *Fondements d'une écriture*, 106.

motive. The oscillations between two pitches are slowly shifted down in frequency by microtonal degrees, in a way that clearly recalls the change in pitch of an ambulance passing by (at a less than frantic speed). Meanwhile, in the neumes that make up the main body of the work, the tension increases linearly, with the volume rising, the number of the notes accented expanding, and the spectrum moving toward inharmonicity, while remaining based on the fundamental E. Grisey achieves this effect by interpolating glissandi in his discrete melodic fragments. The glissandi take over until the individual pitches of the neumes are gone, and we are left with *fortississimo* tremolo glissandi at the climax of *Prologue*. Grisey marks this new section "extremely violent and grating, exaggerated bow pressure," and the effect is almost painfully tactile, like rubbing a finger vigorously against a piece of sandpaper. For Hennessy, this moment represents the "ultimate fusion" of the neumes and the cardiac gestures.[32] Two disparate things have become one. This climax ends, according to Grisey's performance instructions, in a state of "extreme calm."

The final section of *Prologue* represents an ambiguous return to harmonicity. There is a sort of drone on the open D string, with the neumes replaced by more ethereal grace notes and trills on the harmonic spectrum. The violist plays with their regular vibrato, reducing bowing pressure, ending the piece with "quasi periodic" repetitions of a D. While we have returned to a similar state as the beginning of *Prologue*, we have not landed on the original tonal center. Maybe we have ended on the seventh partial, with the fundamental E transposed downward past the limits of our pitched hearing and into the rhythmic underworld.

In 1978, after the completion of the original version of *Prologue*, Grisey expanded the solo part to include a series of instrumental resonators which add their sympathetic resonances to certain notes in the viola. Sympathetic resonance is an acoustic phenomenon in which one body stimulates another to vibration through common frequencies in their overtone makeups. This phenomenon occurs in string instruments such as the viola itself, due to the harmonic relationships between the strings. Grisey was using one of his favorite conceptual ideas in the sympathetic resonator version of *Prologue*: emphasizing and exaggerating—turning a microscope on—a subtle effect of musical acoustics. These instruments serve as a sort of Greek chorus for the work, providing a sparse commentary on the viola's monologue. As Grisey wrote in his program note on this aspect of the piece: "I really like this idea of ghostly instruments that sound by themselves without human intervention: a voice alone, the ghostly responses of uninhabited instruments, in an abstract and uncompromising structure. I hope to have succeeded here in

---

32 Hennessy, "Beneath the Skin of Time," 56.

stammering out what I believe to be music: a dialectic between delirium and form."³³ This aspect recalls the 1972 sketch for a work on sounding sculptures, as well as looking forward to the vast 1989 composition *Le noir de l'étoile*: it situates the composer's musical voice within a cosmos that rarely deigns to listen.

Despite the strength of the idea in the abstract, sympathetic resonance is finnicky, and it took Grisey time to land on a version of his idea that would be reliable and perceptible in performance. Especially difficult was the process of finding resonators that would produce an increasingly inharmonic effect throughout the work, since simple harmonic resonances produce the clearest results. Féron has reconstructed this process, which began with acoustic investigations in the studio, beginning in the late 1970s and continuing through the 1980s.³⁴ The first "resonator version" of *Prologue*, premiered in August 1978 at Darmstadt, used a sitar, a harp, a piano, a tam-tam, and a snare drum as the sympathetic-vibration ensemble. That premiere was plagued by problems—the sympathetic resonances were barely audible—and subsequent versions of the work replaced the sitar and the harp with an ondes martenot. Rarely content to let an imperfect version of a work stand, and hoping that the sympathetic resonator version of *Prologue* would be performed more often, Grisey continued to search for another way of rendering his idea perceptible. In 1996, the acoustician Éric Daubresse decided to use software to simulate the resonances of instruments. In 2001, three years after Grisey's death, Daubresse was able to secure the cooperation of the Parisian Institut de recherche et coordination acoustique/musique (IRCAM) to realize the project. This electronic version of *Prologue* has now been recorded several times and gives the work a cosmic loneliness that adds to its impact.³⁵

The musicologist Joseph R. Jakubowski analyzes *Prologue* in terms of its relationship with the human body. While Jakubowski never makes the explicit connection between the embodiment of *Prologue* and the role of sexuality in Grisey's artistic project, his study is valuable for illustrating the intertwinement of these two aspects of the composer's aesthetic. For Jakubowski, the heartbeat motive acts as a symbol of the physical aspects of *Prologue*. In the quiet moments after sex, or "sleeping side by side" as Grisey and Jocelyne did as young adults, we are more likely than usual to perceive this heartbeat, or any of the bodily rhythms of another person. More broadly, the violist, while performing Grisey's work, illustrates through the physical act

---

33   Lelong, *Écrits*, 144.
34   Féron writes a detailed description of this process. See Féron, "Gérard Grisey – *Prologue*."
35   Listen for example to Garth Knox's recording on his 2002 album *Spectral Viola*.

of playing the process of tension and release that animates the composition: "The violist's more effortful movements move at more rapid tempi and navigate more extreme arcs of acceleration," Jakubowski writes. "The shape of the respiration is thus amplified with a sense of urgency, purpose, and perhaps even abandon as the piece drives on toward its formal climax." Citing the musicologist Mariusz Kozak, Jakubowski adds that "the listener enacts or 'secretes' musical time in the embodied encounter with the unfolding music."[36]

Grisey was keen to make his work on *Prologue* count financially. In 1977, Grisey and Jocelyne bought a small, attic apartment at 40 Boulevard de la Bastille, in the twelfth arrondissement of Paris.[37] But, as mentioned, the 1970s were a decade of economic turmoil globally, with oil shortages and political upheaval contributing to high inflation in many wealthy countries. Besides the shrinking of Grisey and Jocelyne's nest egg after their return from Rome, the effects of this inflation were felt acutely in Italy, where economic crisis and political terrorism led to a period known as the *Anni di piombo*, or the Years of Lead. The value of the lira dropped precipitously, and in 1977, statistics showed one million unemployed people under the age of twenty-four. The always-vulnerable cultural sector immediately felt the sting of the contracting economy.

On April 5, 1977, Mimma Guastoni from Ricordi wrote to Grisey to tell him the publisher had declined to pick up *Prologue* as a result of his requested fee of 3,000 francs, apparently higher than the going rate. "It is certainly not a question of the amount, but purely a question of principle and fairness in the kind of relationship we have with our other authors," Guastoni told him. "We will be very happy to publish your piece if you can decide to submit it under the normal conditions." She also offered Grisey copyist's reimbursement for his work in preparing the score for publication. Grisey seems to have eventually relented. In May 1977, Guastoni pointed out that the fees Ricordi had earned through Grisey's compositions had not yet matched their expenditures in publishing his work.[38]

Grisey felt that *Prologue* was not being treated with the respect it was due, and that Ricordi didn't appreciate the interest that his compositions were attracting.[39] The composer saw himself as an already established talent; Ricordi, not unreasonably, perceived Grisey as one young composer among many on its roster. Grisey's idealistic notion of the profession of the

---

36 Jakubowski, "Embodied Form in Grisey's *Prologue*."
37 Interview with Jocelyne Grisey.
38 Paul Sacher archive.
39 Ibid.

composer, possibly shaped by the great public importance of figures such as Boulez, Stockhausen, Messiaen, and Ligeti, was tempered by reality.

The musical future of *Prologue*, too, remained unsure: the work would not be premiered until the summer of 1978, at the Darmstädter Ferienkurse für Neue Musik, in the version for solo viola and live instrumental resonators.

In 1976, Boulez had founded a new music ensemble, Ensemble Intercontemporain, with the support of French Culture Minister Michel Guy. One of his earliest commissions was to Grisey, who began composing *Modulations* for thirty-three players the same year.[40] Grisey finished the piece in 1977, dedicating it to Messiaen for his seventieth birthday in December 1978.

Modulations is scored for a small chamber orchestra, with doubling winds and brass; five violins, three violas, two cellos, and two basses; two percussionists with complex setups; harp; and keyboards, with an emphasis on the Hammond organ. The work marks a new stage in *Les espaces acoustiques*, with a more abstract approach to the structure than in the previous three pieces. Though the harmonic spectrum on the note E remains at the core of the composition, and Grisey retains the harmonic spectrum and white noise as the outer poles of the work, the processes are significantly more complex than in *Périodes*, *Partiels*, and *Prologue*. As Grisey wrote, "The Material no longer exists in itself, it is sublimated into a pure becoming of sound which is constantly changing and elusive in the moment: everything is in motion."[41]

Modulations is a less theatrical work than its predecessors, but it begins where *Partiels* left off, with the percussionist performing a pantomime of a massive cymbal crash. This is both a joke and a demonstration of the psychoacoustical phenomenon that Jakubowski pointed out in his essay on *Prologue*: volume and tension are physical, not just musical, impressions. In this moment, Grisey asks the percussionist to create "muscular" and psychological tension. Later in the piece, he requires complete immobility during a grand pause, a technique he had used in student pieces to maintain tension.

Baillet describes the structure of *Modulations* in terms of five large-scale processes which take place one after another, moving between inharmonicity and harmonicity and vice versa.[42] Grisey sets up two sonic objects which he modifies gradually and simultaneously. The first is a chord on the harmonic spectrum of E, the other a "shadow" of this sound, created using sum and

---

40 Ibid.
41 Lelong, *Écrits*, 146.
42 Baillet, *Fondements d'une écriture*, 116–135.

difference tones. The first process is one of convergence between these two objects. The alternations between them take place in different parts of the orchestra, first with skittering, then tenuto strings, creating a stereo effect that has a calm beauty—Grisey marks the last section of the first process to be played like a "lullaby." The composer Alex Vaughan explains Grisey's use of silence to separate the two sonic objects from one another. He remarks that they

> never appear simultaneously, overlap or hang directly onto one another. The result of this is a certain degree of silence or whitespace between each chord: this whitespace is critical to the overall character of the music, giving it an element of dryness which then adds further to the sensation of inharmonicity and aperiodicity. In one sense we could say that the score has 3 objects; sustained chords, tremolo chords and silence. The varying duration of these 3 objects thus creates unpredictable and incomprehensible periodicity.[43]

John Cage famously composed *4'33"* to illustrate the aural ephemera which make up the "silences" that our brains usually ignore. Vaughan notices Grisey's dramaturgical use of silence, which creates points of relaxation in the music while evading the predictability we seek to impose on it.

Using Grisey's sketches, Féron discovers an elaborate rhythmic structure of diminution in *Modulations*. (He calls this structure a "pseudo-pyramid," hinting at the Egyptian influences which became explicit in Grisey's next works.) For the musicologist, these structures are "comparable to those that we encounter in serial music. For the first time, Grisey is controlling the fundamental rhythmic material on the basis of the spectrum."[44] It is fitting, Féron believes, that Grisey did this in a work dedicated to the "rhythm-matician" Olivier Messiaen. But this is no one-off tribute; Grisey would continue to devote equal attention to his rhythmic material in future works. The complex series of proportional calculations based on the ratios of the harmonic spectrum at the beginning of *Modulations* give this music its engagingly varied periodicity. We know roughly—but never pedantically—when the next variation is coming.

The second section of *Modulations* is wave-like, with staggered swells traded between winds and bowed and plucked strings. The composer's idea from the *Vagues* section of *Vagues, Chemins, le Souffle* has resurfaced, this time in more refined form, moving from inharmonicity to the harmonic spectrum and back again. The third part, a brief section lasting two minutes,

---

43 Vaughan, "Variation, Transformation and Development in Gérard Grisey's *Les espaces acoustiques*," 27.

44 Féron, "L'organisation rythmique dans la première section de *Modulations* (1976–77) de Gérard Grisey," 47.

has a restful character, subtly orchestrated but moving quickly and perceptibly from inharmonicity to the harmonic spectrum. Structurally, this section uses generator tones and gestural shapes taken from *Prologue*. Grisey also explicitly composes the beatings created by the Hammond organ, quantifying the sort of pulsations used so often in the early bars of works by Scelsi.

The larger fourth section is the most structurally complex of *Modulations*, with three subprocesses and the orchestra divided into four groups. It builds on melodic cells from *Prologue*, using a variety of techniques, such as canon, shortening of note lengths, and noisy special effects, to increase tension, accelerate the pace, and thicken the texture of the music; the complete chromatic scale is present in the orchestra. It's important to note that Grisey composes a *metaphor* for white noise here: real white noise contains all possible frequencies, not just the twelve that happen to make up the Western tonal system. The fully chromatic saturation of this section makes it sound like certain works by Ligeti and Friedrich Cerha; it is the constant pendulum-like motion between sonic poles that makes *Modulations* unique.

This section climaxes in what is always one of the highlights of *Les espaces acoustiques*: six inharmonic block chords that somehow always sound highly melodic—maybe because, since *Prologue*, it has been a good thirty minutes since there has been anything much like melody. Baillet describes this moment as the result of a complex process using the transposition of neumes and the realization of the spectra of muted brass.[45] Despite the intricacy of this process, though, in context it still sounds almost tonal.

The final section of *Modulations* begins on a unison E. This part is divided into ten increments of deterioration, again taking their durational proportions from the harmonic spectrum. During this softly tense end to the piece, as Baillet shows, the fundamental note of the chords moves down by half-steps, a "unique phenomenon in *Les espaces acoustiques*."[46] The music progresses from the unison back to an atmosphere of inharmonicity, preparing the way for the next piece in the cycle, the climactic *Transitoires* for full orchestra.

The aural differences between *Modulations* and the previous works in the cycle are pronounced enough that Vaughan calls the work "outstandingly different in character to its brothers."[47] His main argument for this judgment is the openings, which do sound different, though broadly they represent different points on the same spectrum between harmonicity and inharmonicity that undergirds the entire cycle. In that sense, *Modulations* is less an outlier than it is a step up in structural sophistication and dramaturgical

---

45 Baillet, *Fondements d'une écriture*, 131.
46 Ibid, 132.
47 Vaughan, "Variation, Transformation, and Development," 22.

finesse from its predecessors. As Vaughan writes, the composition "engages the listener with enough repetition with which to comprehend the composition's material and yet avoids becoming monotonous or dull. The transitions and changes which take place are so delicately gentle and smooth, that the audience is almost completely distracted from perception of the work's larger structural concepts."[48]

Modulations was premiered in March 1978 at the Théâtre de la Ville by Ensemble Intercontemporain under the direction of Michel Tabachnik. *Le Monde* ran a preview piece, in which Grisey reflected on the difficulties of the rehearsal process. He told Gérard Condé:

> I have the reputation of being difficult at rehearsals, demanding; rather it is that instrumentalists or certain conductors, on seeing such simple things, relax their attention, whereas this should encourage them to listen to themselves more. My scores require absolute accuracy of intonation. However, most often, for contemporary music, we don't even tune anymore ... probably because we implicitly equate [new music] with dissonance, and therefore with wrong notes. [49]

Despite these difficulties, *Modulations* became known as one of Grisey's most powerful works. Reviewing a later concert, the critic Jacques Lonchampt wrote that it was "one of the classics of the Ensemble Intercontemporain, with many things that engage the imagination as much as the ear."[50] With *Modulations*, Grisey created a musical world where spine-tingling beauty and tension coexist as they do in our own.

---

48   Ibid, 31.
49   Condé, "Retour à l'évidence musicale."
50   Lonchampt, "Dufourt, Boulez, Grisey, Messiaen."

Chapter Eight

Astarte (1978–79)

On October 10, 1978, the Ministère de la Culture announced to Grisey that its Commission de Commandes Pédagogiques had awarded him a commission for a youth or amateur orchestra, for a fee of 5,000 francs.[1] The piece that resulted from the commission was titled *Manifestations*.

Grisey's original concept was for a twelve-minute piece in four movements. He only completed the first movement, a study on the harmonic spectrum called *Manifestations: ... pour trouver le silence* (*Manifestations: ... to find the silence*), and the fourth, a musical joke named *Manifestations: pour échapper à la television* (*Manifestations: to escape the television*). He never finished the inner movements, though he did give them names and make notes on potential forms. The second, on the theme of acoustic beatings, was to be titled *... pour avoir un air de joie* (*... to have a sense of joy*); the third, on white noise, was tentatively named *pour que les arbres... .* (*... in order for the trees*). Several detailed sketches for *... pour avoir un air de joie* exist but were never composed through.[2] They suggest that the finished piece would have included a significant spatialization component.

The two completed movements of *Manifestations* (initially called *Incantations*) add up to a minor work, meant to be easy to perform. But they still show the extent to which Grisey's spectral ideas of structure had become anchored in his thinking. This was not a hasty commission that he could just toss off; he made detailed and intricate sketches for the piece. The improvisatory compositions of his youth and the aleatoric or installation-like pieces of his student days were now permanently banished from his compositional method, even when the stakes were low.[3]

---

1 Paul Sacher archive.
2 An alternative title was *... pour trouver un air de joie*.
3 To my knowledge, no musicologists have analyzed this piece, so the following analysis is my own, based on the sketches in the Paul Sacher archive.

In the first movement of *Manifestations*, the two flutes, each assigned to an orchestral group, have the most difficult parts. Grisey noted this in his sketches, suggesting that the piece was composed for a particular youth orchestra. Grisey assigns each flute pitches from a harmonic spectrum on C. Flute one gets the odd partials, flute two the evens.[4] Each flute performs a series of durations which are varied but tend to decrease in length toward the middle of the piece before tending to increase again; the number of available pitches grows at the same time, meaning that each flute has a rigorously structured and clearly audible "intensity crescendo" toward the center of the movement.

The orchestra accompanies the flute soloists in an extremely simple, half-note rhythm; most instruments change notes only occasionally, making the individual parts easy. (Still, some instrumentalists are required to play quarter-tones.) Like the solo flute parts, the orchestral harmonies in the piece are rigorously structured. In the first orchestral group, Grisey gradually modifies an odd-numbered harmonic spectrum on C. He increases the width of the intervals in the harmonic spectrum, first at its upper end, then moving progressively downwards to the wider and more decisive lower formants and fundamental. This technique recalls the octave transfer process in *Partiels*. In the second group, *even*-numbered partials are also gradually modified; this time the width of the intervals *decreases* as the process goes on, but the "zone of change" also moves downward from the upper to the lower partials. At the middle of the piece, this process flips around its axis. The two orchestral groups switch places, with group one ending on a chord of the even partials and group two on the odd partials of C. As in the flutes, the durations of these harmonic blocks tend to decrease toward the middle of the piece and tend to increase again toward the end of it.

These macro processes are mirrored in miniature in two *ad libitum* instruments, one in each group: Grisey offers the choice of accordion, electric organ, harmonium, muted horn, or other low instruments. These groups play constant, overlapping swells, achieving in half a bar what the entire work does in six minutes.

Rather than an aesthetic progression, ... *pour trouver le silence* solidified Grisey's mature spectral thinking, as he adapted his ideas into a score easily digestible for non-professional musicians. Still, the piece is remarkable for the way it distills Grisey's sophisticated structural ideas from a vast work like *Dérives* to a simple, approachable form. Grisey's music, and spectral music in general, is often associated with forbidding difficulty for the performers. *Manifestations: ... pour trouver le silence* shows that it doesn't have to be that way.

---

4   With a few exceptions: Grisey added to this material the seventeenth, nineteenth, and twenty-fifth partials, transposed down into the flute's middle range. This was probably to get more notes than the repetitive even partials.

The second completed movement, ... *pour échapper à la télévision*, is a musical gag that is just over a minute long. Two percussionists play polystyrene and sandpaper while another four performers inflate balloons until they pop, beginning the movement proper. Three orchestral groups—woodwind, xylophone, and woodblock; piano and bongos; and strings—play dissonant clusters.

Even in this brief and silly piece, the structure is rigorously controlled. The number of notes in each group's clusters tends to decrease as the piece progresses, as does the "rhythmic density." The number of notes *in common* between each group increases. No recording of *Manifestations* is currently available.

As mentioned, Grisey's fascination with ancient Egyptian civilization dates back at least to his late adolescence and was heightened by his trip to the country with Jocelyne. When the composer was seventeen years old, he had made an entry in his diary that described a vivid dream. He was going to marry an Egyptian woman:

> I had a strange dream last night ... I was madly in love with a girl who looked like an Egyptian princess. I was driving with my parents for our upcoming wedding, when I pointed out to my mother the girl who was to become my wife. My mother told me that her appearance, her way of dressing (she was an Egyptian!), everything told her that this girl was not for me and that our union was out of the question. We kissed then, a first, a last and a single time ... [5]

This dream shows an association in Grisey's mind between sensuality and Egyptian civilization, an idea which is culturally pervasive—in popular depictions of Cleopatra, for example—and which may have contrasted for him with the more rigid sexual morality of his Catholic youth. Given the connection between this sensuality and Grisey's musical aesthetic, it's not surprising that the composer attempted to integrate elements of Egyptian thought into his compositions.

Grisey's first works to be explicitly inspired by ideas from ancient Egypt were a pair of pieces, *Sortie vers la lumière du jour* and *Jour, contre-jour*. Written in between the two major works of *Les espaces acoustiques*, *Modulations* and the later *Transitoires*, Grisey saw these twin compositions both as "a parenthesis in my work and a synthesis of my current research." Both titles reference the sun god Ra, responsible for the star completing its cycle around the earth.[6] The first work, commissioned by Radio France,

---

5   Paul Sacher archive.
6   Ikram, *Ancient Egypt*, 118.

which Grisey composed between January and July 1977, is a slight adaption of the title of *The Egyptian Book of the Dead*: in French *Livre pour sortir au jour* (*Book for Coming Forth by Day*). This text originates from the French Egyptologist Jean-François Champollion, who deciphered the meaning of hieroglyphs using the Rosetta Stone in 1820. In 1842, a German scholar named Dr. Carl Richard Lepsius compiled a thorough version of these funerary scrolls, subsequently translated by scholars across Europe. As John Romer notes in an introduction to a modern edition of *The Book of the Dead*, the text "is a scholarly illusion conjured from the randomly surviving relics of a distant past," but adds that these elusive fragments leave us with "kaleidoscopic hints of meaning, and prose that shimmers off the page."[7] This aligns well with the listener's impression of the composition, where the overlap between the Egyptian imagery and the music is elusive and metaphorical. However, there is some evidence that Grisey took his idea quite literally: the musicologists José L. Besada and Cristóbal Pagán Cánovas discovered a sketch among the composer's archives where pitch information was plotted along a timeline containing the twenty-four hours of the day.[8]

In his program note, the composer makes an analogy between the "very simple and obvious curve" of the work's musical structure and the motion of Ra's boat in the sky. Grisey cites a passage from *The Egyptian Book of the Dead* that functions less as an analytical guide than it does as a sort of poetic epigraph. The passage is from the Papyrus of Nu: "The heavens are opened, the earth is opened, the West is opened, the East is opened, the southern half of heaven is opened, the northern half of heaven is opened, the doors are opened, and the gates are thrown wide open to Ra [as] he cometh forth from the horizon."[9] This triumphal language appears to align with the moment in the music where midday is reached, a passage of complete harmonicity.

The title of the second piece, *Jour, contre-jour*, which Grisey composed between 1978 and 1979, translates both to *Day, Against the Day* and to *Light, Shadows*. It refers to the motion of the sun around a fixed architectural object in Egyptian civilization such as a pyramid or obelisk, a process the ancient Egyptians associated with "rebirth and resurrection": the path of Ra's barque started in the west, where the sun sets, and ended in the east, where it rises.[10] Though these concepts reflect an external source of inspiration for the composer, they are not quite as far

---

7 Romer's introduction to *The Egyptian Book of the Dead*, trans. Budge, xxvi–xl.
8 Besada and Cánovas, "Timelines in Spectral Composition."
9 Budge, *The Egyptian Book of the Dead*, 390.
10 Ikram, *Ancient Egypt*, 155.

removed from the stuff of sound that fascinated Grisey as they seem on first analysis. For him, after all, sounds had births, lives, and deaths. They were like any other organic creature, and took part in the cyclical processes of existence which the Egyptians perceived in the motion of their sun god around the earth.

Sortie vers la lumière du jour opens with the high sound of the Hammond organ, building on Grisey's use of the instrument in *Modulations*. Its timbre lends the entire work an otherworldly color. Some six minutes of music centered around the sleek sound of its single pitches follow. Like so many of the composer's pieces, *Sortie vers la lumière du jour* is built around a structural duality. Baillet finds a symmetrical form constructed around contrasting sections of harmonicity and inharmonicity.[11] In the first half of the piece, long harmonic sections, their chord progressions developed using sum and difference tones, expand in range and move downward toward the lower registers, while progressively decreasing in duration. The short inharmonic sections remain constant. The target of the harmonic section's chord progression is a "dilated" version of the harmonic spectrum on G (a harmonic process analogous to the temporal one).[12] This dilated chord, in turn, prepares our ears for the pure harmonic spectrum, which arrives at the exact center of the composition—the zenith of Ra. "There are no shadows here, it is a pure sound at the height of its brightness. It is the noontime of sound," as Grisey wrote in his program note to the work.[13] At this moment, the harmonic and inharmonic building blocks of the piece are of exactly equal length. Then the piece turns around on itself: the length of the harmonic music remains (now roughly) constant, its harmonies turned on their axis and thinning out while moving ever further downwards, while the noisy inharmonic section increases in length.

Sortie vers la lumière du jour is an effective work of refined color and orchestration. Criticisms can be made, however, of its schematic structure, which makes it a bit predictable; the brevity of the climactic moment on the harmonic spectrum of G means that the passage fails to achieve quite the transcendence the composer associates with it in his writings. As Baillet points out, because "the second part now corresponds to the decrease in

---

11   Baillet, *Fondements d'une écriture*, 160. Baillet's diagrams are elegant demonstrations of the work's form.
12   The notes of the harmonic spectrum are modified by progressively larger intervals: fundamental; first overtone plus a minor second; second overtone plus a major second, etc. Baillet, *Fondements d'une écriture*, 162.
13   Lelong, *Écrits*, 152.

tension," it "must be shortened to avoid boredom."[14] This is a weakness in the theoretical elegance of *Sortie vers la lumière du jour*.

Baillet describes the second work, *Jour, contre-jour*, as the "more definitive version" of its predecessor, with a tweaked instrumentation and a tape part, and the effect of listening to both pieces in succession confirms this impression. The most obvious addition in *Jour, contre-jour* is this tape part, which creates a more sharply cut distinction between the harmonic and inharmonic sections. Formally, Grisey adjusts the length of these sections to reflect seconds, rather than pulsations, and varies their lengths more. The tape part, as well as some refinements in the scoring of the inharmonic sections, means the lack of momentum in the second half of the work is alleviated, leading to what Baillet describes as "a true fascination in the torpor of the noise zones."[15] On the microscopic level, Grisey also added additional touches to *Jour, contre-jour* that make the work more obviously his own: the tape introduction includes heartbeat rhythms, one of his favorite techniques; there are theatrical instructions, such as a spotlight and a gradual brightening of the hall lights at the opening; and the zenith moment, though the same length, is scored with more confidence.

For the musicologist Ben Taylor, the tape part has conceptual resonance as well. "Grisey's engagement with electronic music goes further than including fixed media," he writes, adding that *Jour, contre-jour* displays "an unapologetically electronic and sometimes mechanized approach to his ensemble."[16] For Taylor, the electronic conception of *Jour, contre-jour* does nothing to dampen its resonance on the human scale. "The moment of transformation and integration of life and death, humanity and disembodied electrical energy, is at the heart of the work," he writes.[17]

Sortie vers la lumière du jour was premiered on October 28, 1978, by Ensemble Musica Negativa under Rainer Riehn, at the prestigious Donausechinger Musiktage in southwestern Germany. The *Le Monde* critic Gérard Condé found the piece convincing in its second reading, with Intercontemporain under Boris de Vinogradov, because it "breathed unsuspected life into these sudden crescendos and decrescendos that illuminate the main theme."[18]

On March 9, 1979, Ensemble L'Itinéraire premiered *Jour, contre-jour* at Radio France's concert hall, the Maison de Radio. In a *Le Journal* review of

---

14   Baillet, *Fondements d'une écriture*, 157–160.
15   Ibid, 160.
16   Taylor, "The Acoustic Ensemble as Spectral Synthesizer," 2.
17   Ibid, 13.
18   Condé, "Stockhausen, Michaël et les autres."

the piece a year later, the critic Philippe Andriot pointed out that the audience should not read the program note, as it gives away the form of the piece.[19]

Meanwhile, Grisey began planning for a possible return to the Darmstädter Ferienkurse, his first visit since 1972. He arranged for scores for *Périodes*, *Partiels*, and *Prologue* to be sent to Ernst Thomas, the former *Frankfurter Allgemeine Zeitung* critic and festival director. Grisey also signaled his willingness to discuss his instrumental techniques and "aesthetic direction" with the participants of the course. Thomas was enthusiastic and offered the composer the opportunity to present his works in an analysis seminar on a full scholarship of 750 Deutsche Mark. He also said he'd try to arrange for a performance of one of Grisey's pieces. Thomas noted that the themes of the twenty-ninth edition of Ferienkurse would be twofold: the "simple" and the "beautiful."[20]

Grisey responded gratefully, writing, "In my opinion, explanations are extremely important for our generation, since they don't connect directly to the so-called Darmstadt aesthetic, but are slowly building to a new and important way of composing music." For performance, he suggested *Partiels* and the recently completed *Modulations*. He also recommended a "public rehearsal with explanations," saying it was important for him that the students receive "a concrete impression of the sounds." This idea represented a core belief of his: that music always preceded theory, even (or especially) at Darmstadt, a festival closely associated with abstract approaches to composition.

Thomas decided to have *Prologue* performed because the radio orchestras in the region were on vacation. Grisey was dissatisfied: "*Prologue* seems to me to be a short and not particularly representative example of my music," he wrote. The two continued to negotiate details such as rehearsal timing until June 1978, shortly before the festival was scheduled to begin, with Grisey adding a final wish that *Prologue* be played in a small or medium-sized venue. A large hall "is very unfavorable for the piece; the resonators become inaudible," he wrote.

The composers teaching the prestigious studio courses were the British polymath Brian Ferneyhough, who writes music of staggering complexity; Helmut Lachenmann, the German pioneer of *musique concrète instrumentale*, a style which deconstructs the possibilities of classical instruments; and Cristóbal Halffter, a Spanish composer of kinetic atonal music. The artists

---

19   Cohen-Levinas, *L'Itinéraire en temps réell*, 417.
20   Archives of the Internationales Musikinstitut Darmstadt.

who joined Grisey in presenting analysis classes were associated with an interest in simplicity and the combination of musical styles from various periods: Wolfgang Rihm, Jolyon Brettingham Smith, and Hans-Jürgen von Bose. The musicologist Carl Dahlhaus gave a lecture on "the simple, the beautiful, and the simply beautiful." While this theme was meant as a polemical rebuke to the proceedings of past Darmstadt festivals, Grisey explicitly positioned spectralist music as a third way outside the presumptive binary between complex and ugly and simple and beautiful.

Grisey gave his Darmstadt analysis lecture on August 6, 1978, at the historic Georg Büchner Schule, speaking in French and excellent German. He announced his intention to only discuss music that the students would have the opportunity to hear. Grisey played the students a recording of *Partiels* (in the version by Ensemble Ars Nova under the direction of Boris de Vinogradov), adding that he didn't "feel like" discussing *Prologue*—it would be pointless to discuss the piece since the students hadn't heard it. The presentation of *Partiels* received enthusiastic applause from the students. It seems that Grisey's foregrounding of human perception appealed to them. The same applied to his case for consciously imperfect compositional processes, which he made using the examples of the human heart and the ceilings of the Greek temples of Paestum, in southern Italy, where symmetrical motives were varied just enough to give the eye a pleasant, rather than mechanical, sense of symmetry. (Grisey learned of this detail from a dig led by the archeologist Paolo Matthiae, which he read about during his stay in Rome.) As Gilles Deleuze writes, "God makes the world by calculating, but his calculations never work out exactly."[21]

Grisey criticized the mathematical rhythmic structures present in works by composers such as his teacher Messiaen and Boulez, arguing that there was no way their intricacies could be perceived by the human ear. He then briefly analyzed aspects of *Dérives*, such as the conversion of very low difference tones—too low to be perceived by the human ear as pitch—to rhythms in the percussion. He also related an anecdote from the premiere of the piece which referred to the sum- and difference-tone technique, which he had dubbed the shadows of sounds. "The musicians that premiered the piece came up to me and said, 'What happens at that point? When I'm playing, I have the impression that I'm walking on clouds, that I'm floating,'" Grisey said. "That makes sense, because the sound that you start to play is already in the air. Its aura is there."[22]

---

21 Deleuze, *Difference and Repetition*, 293.
22 These quotations are from the audio archives of the Internationales Musikinstitut Darmstadt, where Grisey can be heard presenting in French and German in a clear tenor voice.

Throughout the lecture, Grisey read what he called "flashes," brief statements or questions. One was a satire of an overlong Oscar speech, where Grisey thanked composers from Stockhausen and Xenakis going back to Ockeghem and pygmy music—to widespread hilarity from the students. "Any similarity between my sounds and those of the composers named is knowingly and willingly subconscious," Grisey said. This lecture later became the essay "Devenir du Son," or "The Becoming of Sound."

Grisey ended the lecture with shoutouts to his colleagues Tristan Murail, Hugues Dufourt, Jens-Peter Ostendorf, and Mesías Maiguashca. Punning on the latter's first name, he said, "*Ich bin kein Messias*" ("I am no Messiah"), to further appreciation from the attendees.

While Grisey's first lecture at Darmstadt seemed broadly successful, the performance of his *Prologue* on the following evening of August 7, by the violist Gérard Caussé, met with a mixed reception. The venue, the Städtische Sporthalle—a large gymnasium—did not fit with Grisey's request for a smaller venue. In the *Darmstädter Tagblatt*, a critic bemoaned the event's technical difficulties, complaining that, like Ferneyhough's electronics, Grisey's resonators refused to work "even after almost half an hour of 'repairs.'" The review continued, "The impression remained of a rather conventional viola solo, gradually made unrecognizable by overmodulation. It, too, begs the question of whether the vast technical possibilities were not played with too frivolously and too credulously, instead of aiming for clean craftsmanship."[23]

Norbert Ely, writing for the *Darmstädter Echo*, agreed, saying that the effect of the resonators was hardly perceptible. But he enjoyed the solo in and of itself, saying that it "contained enough interesting aspects," and that he could feel Grisey's talent for composition. The most sympathy for Grisey's aesthetic project came from Gérard Condé, who wrote:

> Someone like Gérard Grisey (born in 1946), also in charge of an analysis course in Darmstadt ... seeks to explore phenomena whose urgency and complexity had been minimized until now, to analyze them in order to try to identify the laws that govern them, to consider harmony from an essentially acoustic point of view and no longer only in terms of aesthetics or syntactic coherence.
>
> It would therefore be wrong to believe that nothing happens any more in Darmstadt because the buzzwords have ceased to spring up like fireworks from a great international festival. The future will tell whether revolutions are still being formed there.[24]

---

23 Press clippings in the archive of the Internationales Musikinstitut Darmstadt.
24 Condé, "Recherches de musique contemporaine."

With time, the reputation of *Prologue* grew. In 1986, Condé published a review of an Ensemble L'Itinéraire performance featuring Grisey's solo work alongside compositions by Levinas and Philippe Manoury. The text was unusual for describing a critic's evolving relationship with a piece:

> Several performances have not altered the singular power of this music, which asserts itself from the outset with the periodic double repetition of a low C [the note is actually a B], then evolves toward ever more unpredictable horizons: melodic purity is followed by more troubled sonorities until the initial purpose is erased, absorbed by its developments. In ten years, this score has matured to the point of being able to detach itself from the idea that gave rise to it, of making various instruments resonate sympathetically. Deprived of what seemed to make it unique at the time, it has lost none of its eloquence.[25]

Condé adopts Grisey's own way of talking about sound when he mentions the "periodic" low B. Smuggled in through Grisey's compositions, people were thinking about music in a different way.

❦ ❦ ❦

In the late summer of 1978, Jocelyne got pregnant. The first order of business was to improve their living situation so that Grisey could continue to compose despite the inevitable racket of a newborn. The small apartment in the Boulevard de Bastille they had bought in 1977 was less than ideal for a family. The neighborhood was a little rough, the space was cramped for three people, with limited privacy, and the apartment had skylights, but no windows. It was also a fifth-floor walkup. Grisey didn't have a studio to work in, and he needed extreme quiet to compose. Jocelyne learned that a modest apartment on the third floor of the same building was on sale, and it was going cheap.

"We have to buy it on credit," Jocelyne told her husband.

"It's too dangerous," Grisey answered, maybe worried about his inability to make enough of a contribution to the family's finances.

Jocelyne insisted.

"Finally, we bought it," she recalled. "Gérard could work on the fifth floor." She would spend her days on the third floor with the baby, and the family could sleep on the top floor again at night.

During the pregnancy, Grisey had been certain that this child would be a girl. He wanted to name the child Astarte, after the Mesopotamian goddess of "sexual love and fertility,"[26] a choice that reflected his 1970s fascination

---

25   Condé, "Sympathies."
26   Susan Ackerman, "Astarte: Bible."

with world religions. Jocelyne convinced him to go with the less unusual Esther instead.

On May 6, 1979, Jocelyne gave birth to the couple's child. It was a boy. They called him Raphaël.

The Griseys spent their first months as a family in nature: in the Vosges mountains, then at a friend's house in Provence. Grisey continued to compose while Jocelyne occupied herself with the newborn Raphaël. Jocelyne had wanted a child, and Grisey's love for his Raphaël was always profound. But it's not entirely clear whether Grisey wanted to have children as much as his wife did. Parenthood "was not always obvious" for the composer, Jocelyne said. In Grisey's childhood, Jules Henri was a strict and distant figure, and Grisey hadn't had a model for a cozily intimate fatherhood. Jocelyne thinks that Grisey may have hoped for a girl because he saw a son as a rival for her affection.[27]

At the same time, Grisey was straining against the boundaries of monogamous marriage. He still had mistresses. Jocelyne knew this and suffered from it, but the real pain came from the fact that he wanted her to know about them, and even console him when things became complicated with these other women. "He wanted me to be his confidant," Jocelyne said. "I told him, 'It's your life, if you need to talk about it, do that with his someone else. We have our life as a couple. What matters to me is that we continue to have a couple's life that satisfies us, that we both feel good in. Your private life is your secret.' These were very difficult moments for me."[28]

The term "spectral music" was born the same year as Raphaël Grisey, in an article titled "La musique spectrale," by Hugues Dufourt, who also enjoyed an education in philosophy. It was one of the earliest pieces of writing to verbalize the aesthetic developments in Grisey's pieces of the 1970s (and in Murail and Dufourt's own works). The article is polemical and powerful; it defines spectral music explicitly against serialism. Dufourt writes, "Spectral music is based on a theory of functional fields and on an aesthetic of unstable forms. It marks, on the way traced by serialism, new progress towards immanence and transparency."[29]

Though Dufourt's article accurately described Grisey's music, he never warmed to the term "spectral," feeling it evoked the harmonic series too

---

27 Interview with Jocelyne Grisey.
28 Ibid.
29 Dufourt, *Musique, Pouvoir, Écriture*, 294.

concretely. More importantly, he thought the label lumped him in with his fellow composers, eliding their aesthetic differences. In one undated fragment about dealing with musicologists, Grisey wrote, "They make me feel like an insect that they take a moment to observe before sending me to join my labeled, indexed fellow species. No one wants to become a number in a collection, no matter how prestigious it may be. Especially since our intimate life is at stake, our being in the world, that delicate organism with fragile wings."[30] This is an understandable reaction. Still, at the close of the 1970s, no matter how unique Grisey felt, he was considered part of a musical movement. This movement now had a name.

To close out a productive decade, Grisey composed *Tempus ex Machina*, a percussion sextet for the virtuosic ensemble Les Percussions de Strasbourg, between March and August 1979. The piece was Grisey's first to forgo pitched sounds completely and zoom in exclusively on the phenomena of rhythm and time. It's an attempt to further abstract the aesthetic principles of spectralism into a structural scaffolding: as Grisey wrote in his program note, the limited timbral palate "allows for an acute concentration on the temporal structure. It is a purification, through which the color is reduced to what is strictly necessary: only the form emerges, and the slightest error is fatal!"[31] It seems possible that the fervor of his conception ("purification") was a reaction to those critics who saw Grisey as a superficial colorist. The title *Tempus ex Machina* is a play on the literary device of *Deus ex machina*, with the Latin for "time" replacing "god": *Time in the machine.*

The six performers may be either set up in a row facing the audience, or preferably placed in a circle around it. For Baillet, *Tempus ex Machina* is "undoubtedly the work of Grisey's where his taste for numerical structures is pushed the furthest," and the musicologist explains the basic mathematical processes from which all the durations in the piece derive. First, Grisey took a duration of 168 beats as the temporal "fundamental" of the composition. Then, he divided this fundamental by a series of whole numbers between three and eight, analogous to low partials in the harmonic series. Finally, he divided each of the resulting durations by half repeatedly, leading to a series of ever-shorter lengths that nonetheless will never reach zero.[32] This recalls the process of radioactive decay known as half-life, a process Grisey doesn't mention specifically in the context of *Tempus ex Machina*, but which fits neatly with his interest in biological time.

The first section of *Tempus ex Machina* is a sophisticated process of acceleration which lasts about six minutes. Each percussionist plays simple

---

30 Lelong, *Écrits*, 202.
31 Ibid, 153.
32 Baillet, *Fondements d'une écriture*, 168.

bass-drum pulsations, but in different tempi; as the section progresses, they each accelerate by the same proportions, but still in different speeds. The music is difficult, made realistic because of the simplicity of the rhythms which are being played in different tempi. Baillet notes that loud, short interjections on woodblocks of various sizes mark aurally the successive notching-ups of speed, and it is through this technique that the music gains so much of its momentum.[33] Meaningful signifiers reach a density where they become pure texture; there is a pleasurable feeling of being overwhelmed.

The second section of *Tempus ex Machina* begins with a roughly opposite process: as the rhythms produced by the woodblocks become impossible to separate aurally, Grisey adds new durations that cause the music to slow down gradually again. To this more rhythmically sedate music, Grisey composes new, more complex percussion timbres to keep the attention of the ear. As this section transitions into the next part, the music increases its density again, sounding like pattering rainfall.

The third section of *Tempus ex Machina* consists of another complex process, making use of the spatial potential of the ensemble (though the effect is more powerful if the percussionists are set up in a circle). Baillet describes its structure: "To each phase corresponds a similar evolution: decrease of the tempo, of the number of pulsations, of the dynamics; then an inverse increase. From one phase to another, we observe a maximal and minimal decrease of pulsations. A change in the direction of rotation corresponds with the minimum tempo in each phase."[34] This process creates exciting, immersive music, but the intricacies of its development aren't clearly audible.

The final section of *Tempus ex Machina* functions analogously to the opening of *Partiels*: a sonogram of a low bass drum is presented in a series of dilations, and scored with aperiodic, primal—even whale-song-like—gestures in tam-tams, gongs, and bass drums. The work closes with a surprising, disruptive return to the high woodblocks that delineated the opening of the piece, a concession to formal intuition in such a mathematically composed work.

Still, the abstraction in *Tempus ex Machina* makes itself felt: not necessarily in the perception of the processes, except for the clear first one, but in a sort of austere continuity that gives the piece a special place in Grisey's mature spectralist period. For the composer, the piece was "a vehicle of time" leading to the interior of the sound of the bass drum which concludes the work, a sound he conceived of physically, as having a body.

---

33 Ibid, 170.
34 Ibid, 170.

Grisey ends his program note with a reference to Lewis Carroll's *Alice in Wonderland*: "After many twists and turns, we have reached our goal: the other side of the mirror." Before she passes through the looking glass, Alice says, "Let's pretend the glass has got all soft like gauze, so that we can get through."[35] In *Tempus ex Machina*, the permeable, soft glass is time.

---

35 Carroll, *Through the Looking Glass*, 13.

Figure 1. Grisey with his first Hohner accordion.

Figure 2. Grisey as an altar boy.

Figure 3. Grisey in his accordion-soloist days.

Figure 4. Grisey in his room at Sainte-Marie de Monceau in Paris, ca. 1965.

Figure 5. Grisey and Jocelyne Simon at their wedding on June 26, 1970, at the Institution Sainte-Marie in Anthony, a suburb of Paris.

Figure 6. Grisey and France Detry with Raphaël and Detry's son Renaud in Brittany, ca. 1989.

Figure 7. Grisey (on vacation in Italy with France Detry), ca. 1990.

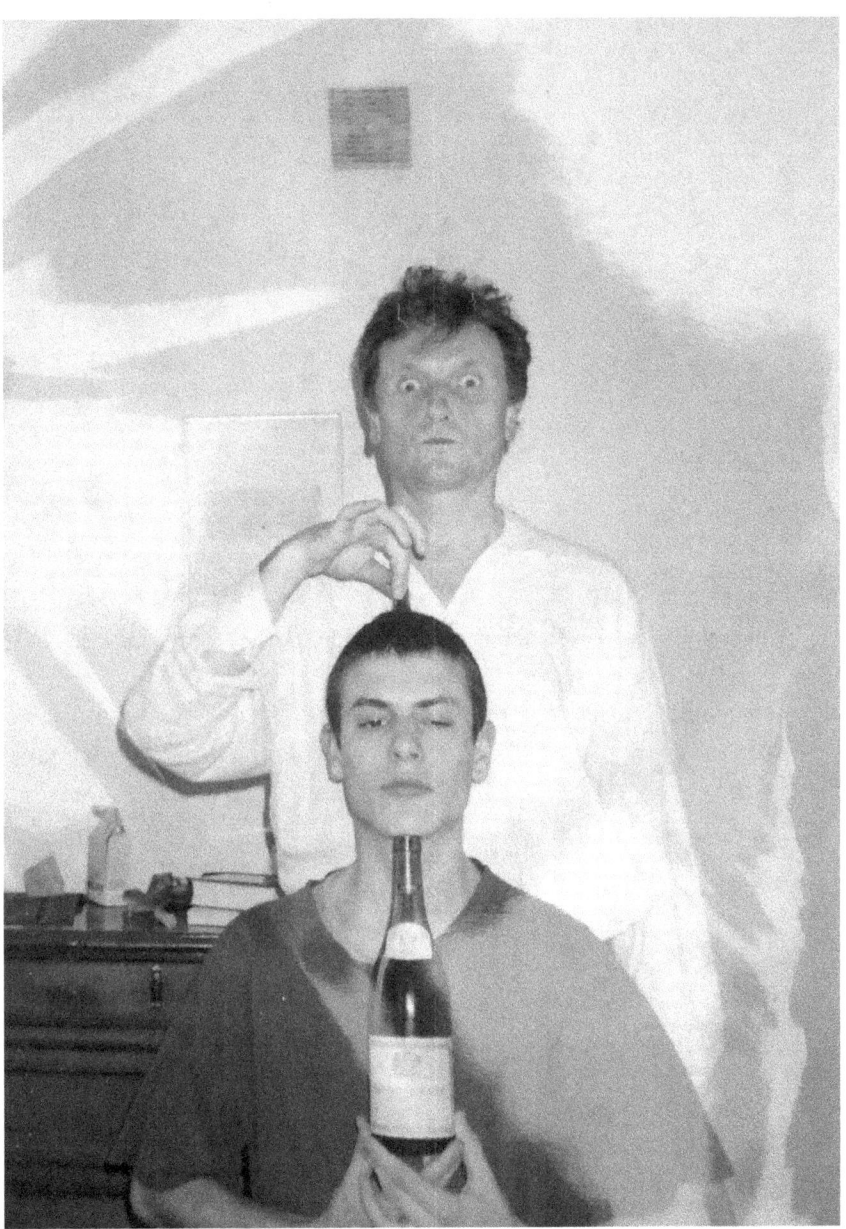

Figure 8. Sommeliers Gérard and Raphäel Grisey uncorking a rare vintage.

Figure 9. Grisey (on vacation in Morocco with Mireille Deguy), ca. 1992.

Figure 10. Gérards Grisey and Zinsstag at the thermal baths in Vals, Switzerland, ca. 1996.

Chapter Nine

Extreme Pleasure, Extreme Pain (1980–82)

From January 3 to March 31, 1980, Grisey participated in a course for composers at IRCAM, the musical research institute founded by Pierre Boulez at the Centre Pompidou in Paris. In these early days of the institute, the technology was clunky, with even simple acoustic procedures requiring hours of labor. But the participants' enthusiasm was palpable; the atmosphere was one of chaos, excitement, and fruitful exchange between science and art.

Grisey's teacher during the course was the eminent American psychoacoustician David Wessel, whom Boulez had brought to Paris in 1976.[1] In the summer of 1980, Wessel was joined on the IRCAM faculty by Stephen McAdams, a Canadian researcher who specializes in music cognition and perception, topics of acute interest to Grisey. Wessel introduced Grisey to McAdams.

Grisey's interest was moving from the abstract concepts of traditional acoustics, explored in pieces such as *Périodes* and *Partiels*, to the messier realities of the human processing of sound. Grisey had wide-ranging conversations with McAdams throughout the early 1980s. They organized some "mini informal experiments" on the composer's idea of instrumental synthesis, where a spectral harmony strikes the ear as somewhere between a chord with distinct pitches and a single sound. This state of fragile fusion was of profound interest to Grisey at this point in his aesthetic development. "I remember hearing a rehearsal. Boulez was conducting a piece of Grisey's," McAdams recalled. "Boulez had a very analytical ear and he could hear anything out of anything, regardless of how complex it was. He was trying to make it so that he could hear everything. Grisey was like, 'No, no, no, no. It's supposed to all melt together.'"[2]

Grisey and McAdams tried to find the point where this state of fusion would disintegrate: when did certain pitches or overtones emerge to the extent that our brains would process them separately? How could the Western tuning of

---

1 Andrews, Maclay, Devaney: "David Wessel in Memoriam."
2 Interview with McAdams. The piece was probably *Modulations*.

equal temperament be tweaked to achieve this spectral fusion without recourse to complex microtonal notation? The ultimate judge for the integration of these scientific experiments on instrumental synthesis in Grisey's music was a non-scientific one, namely Grisey and McAdams's "collective ears."

McAdams was struck by the lack of boundaries in Grisey's thinking. While other composers at IRCAM wanted to keep their musical thought separate from science, for Grisey, research, as well as art and literature, "all fed in, and then it went through the dog breeder of his mind and came out as a compositional idea," McAdams said. "In his wild, open mind, everything fed into his secretive thought processes."[3]

They remained in touch, and Grisey made extensive use of the insights he gained in their work together. (Grisey consulted McAdams for his Darmstadt presentation "Tempus ex Machina.") Beginning in the early 1980s, Grisey's pieces show the imprint of the more sophisticated psychoacoustical thinking to which McAdams introduced him.

On April 3, 1979, Grisey had received a letter of acceptance from Dr. Wieland Schmied, an Austrian art history and critic, for a scholarship from the Deutscher Akademischer Austauschdienst (DAAD), which brings artists to Germany for working stays. Grisey's stated goal during the period of the scholarship in Berlin was to complete the cycle *Les espaces acoustiques*. He was to receive a monthly stipend of 2,600 Deutsche Mark for a year, along with travel costs for him, Jocelyne, and Raphaël from Paris to Berlin.[4]

By early 1980, Grisey had decided to come to West Berlin that April. His requirements for the apartment were specific:

> An apartment with four rooms, large enough that I can isolate myself (my son is eight months old!). If not, then an apartment and a studio that is as close to the apartment as possible. While composing, I'm extremely sensitive to noise (music from the neighbor's, street noise!!!) I would also prefer an apartment close to a park, but not too far from the city center.[5]

The DAAD offered Grisey a "relatively quiet" three-room flat located at Am Storkwinckel 12, in the well-to-do neighborhood of Charlottenburg, near the Grünewald forest. They also offered him the option to move in the middle of his stay if something larger became available. But Grisey, stressed by the difficulty of maintaining enough concentration to compose with a small

---

3   Interview with McAdams.
4   Letters in the archive of the DAAD, Berlin.
5   Ibid.

child at home, remained a stickler: "I would like to work in Berlin as much as possible and not move around. When you write 'relatively quiet' I get very nervous, because I would like a *very quiet* apartment! ... Therefore, I'd be very thankful if you could find a larger and quieter apartment that is also available for the duration of my stay."

Grisey eventually relented and accepted the apartment in Charlottenburg. He arrived in Berlin on April 21, 1980, alone at first, and stayed at the Hotel Steiner for a few days. Grisey signed up for German classes and settled down to compose, with DAAD staff handling publicity, connecting him to other artists, and organizing concerts. Grisey did end up moving, in the summer, to a new address on Giesebrechtstrasse, which was more centrally located—and presumably quieter—than Am Storkwinckel.

Later that year, Grisey met Folkmar Hein, a sound technician who collaborated frequently with DAAD composers in his capacity as a sound engineer and lecturer at the Technische Universität.[6] Grisey came to Hein with a specific request: he was dissatisfied with the realization of the tape part of *Jour, contre-jour* and wanted to know if Hein could help. Electronic technology was on the cusp of its digitalization phase, so Grisey brought Hein the score and a carton of tapes; Hein organized and improved the electronic material. He created a score for the mixer part, including markings on the physical tape which allowed the engineer to sync up the electronics, especially its dynamics, with the instrumental ensemble.

The new version of *Jour, contre-jour* was premiered on April 29, 1982, at the Centre Pompidou by Ensemble l'Itinéraire. Hein could not attend the performance but remembers that Grisey was much more satisfied with this new realization. Their cooperation was also pleasant, which suggests that Grisey was working without quotidian worries for the first time since his stay in Rome. "Grisey was extremely nice. He was happy, funny, in a good mood," Hein said. "He was always punctual. I only have good memories of that time and am so thankful to have known such a person."[7] Importantly for Hein—sound engineers in Germany get rigorous training and are often extraordinarily musical—Grisey didn't treat him as an employee with a menial, technical task, but as an artistic peer.

Ernst Thomas, the director of the Darmstädter Ferienkurse, wanted Grisey to come back to the 1980 edition of the festival, and Grisey accepted the invitation, noting his "very good memories" of the 1978 course. This time,

---

6   Interview with Hein.
7   Ibid.

Grisey suggested that Thomas invite the other members of the spectral cohort: "As you know, the object of my musical research is a common one with other composers of my generation. Therefore, it seems important to me to organize the days in the form of a seminar, rather than a composition course." In addition to analyses of his works *Modulations* and *Sortie vers la lumière du jour*, Grisey recommended that Thomas schedule discussions of Murail's *Territoires de l'oubli*, *Ethers*, and *Mémoire-Erosion*—Murail was already invited to the festival—and of compositions by Hugues Dufourt and Jens-Peter Ostendorf. "Since this is more of an artistic presentation than a real composition course, the opportunities for the presentation of student compositions would be reduced," Grisey wrote. "It seems important to warn the students of this." Grisey asked if the festival could perform *Modulations* this time. Thomas agreed readily. He offered full scholarships to Dufourt and Ostendorf and arranged for a performance of *Modulations* with the Krakow Radio Symphony Orchestra under the direction of the Polish conductor Antoni Wit.[8]

As the summer of 1980 approached, Grisey consulted Murail and Dufourt about the content of his lecture, "Tempus Ex Machina: Reflections on Human Time." In a letter to Dufourt dated July 5, 1980, Grisey worried about the "derisive adjectives" that could be applied to the group at Darmstadt, a place where composers and critics were quick to categorize. He'd already heard two, "the art of the transition," and "the young French school," both of which he detested, and Dufourt's "spectral." Instead, he proposed "liminal," a term that originated from the Latin word *limen*, meaning a threshold or sill. In a letter, Grisey made his case to Dufourt:

> The threshold unites all of us. It's our common denominator. It can have a dynamic sense (only an idiot remains on the threshold!!!). It supposes at least two fields and invites movement. We play with thresholds as others play with the [twelve-tone] series. Spectral: too static, too vague (*Stimmung* and Tibetan music are spectral music).[9]

Grisey lost this battle over terminology. But he had a point. One of the most frequent critiques of the spectral school at Darmstadt was that the focus on the harmonic series was an unnecessary limitation. But neither Grisey nor his colleagues wanted to compose only with the notes of the spectrum. Grisey's complaint was that "spectral music" *implied* they did.

Grisey sent Thomas a draft of his lecture, asking him to arrange for professional translations of the French text. From July 9 to July 13, 1980,

---

8   Internationales Musikinstitut Darmstadt archives.
9   Lelong, *Écrits*, 317–18.

Grisey went to Krakow, Poland, where he attended Wit's orchestra rehearsals of *Modulations*. "As I remember, the composer was very satisfied especially that the orchestra showed a positive approach to him, which is not always the case with orchestras playing modern music," Wit said.[10]

Grisey arrived in Darmstadt on July 20, 1980. (Ultimately, Dufourt and Ostendorf were unable to attend the festival that year.) Local critics were not enthusiastic in advance of the event. "The number 30 appears a dangerous one, in any case the thirtieth edition of the International Ferienkurse für Neue Musik seems markedly tired and aged," wrote Wolf-Eberhard von Lewinski in the *Süddeutsche Zeitung*. "Its form is unchanged, its content—at least considering the concerts in the first few days—paltry. However, the composition, analysis, and interpretation courses do seem to be attracting significant interest and promise to operate at a high level." The critic Petra Stadler claimed that "the broad path of the avant-garde has obviously reached a sort of dead end."[11] As the new music scene splintered and the former titans of Darmstadt occupied themselves elsewhere, the relevance of the festival was increasingly in doubt.

Grisey's four-day course began on the afternoon of July 21, 1980.[12] He started with the in-progress cycle *Les espaces acoustiques*, translating the title poetically into German as *Akustische Spielräume* (*Acoustic Play-Spaces*). Grisey joked about the small number of available scores for students: "I have a good publisher, but an *Italian* publisher," to laughter, and played an excerpt from *Modulations*. When a student asked Grisey how musicians were able to *hear* the microtonal intervals in these pieces, the composer gave a revealing answer:

> I have to be perfectly honest, that's a huge problem, especially in modern music. For several years, musicians have gotten use to: "It's modern music, *pugh pugh*, you don't hear anything anyway. Major second, minor second, wrong octaves, it all sounds the same. It's just a big mass [of sound], it doesn't matter how I play." And they are astounded when you say, "You, please play a little higher or a little lower, the fifth is wrong, there are vibrations." It happens often: you ask for an octave, and it's wrong. They can't play an octave. Well, they can play an octave, but it's become a habit in modern music that you don't pay attention to it. That's the first issue. And the second thing is, there are some musicians who hear extremely well, and others who don't hear at all.

The composer also recalled his trouble convincing orchestral musicians to perform the theatrical elements in between *Partiels* and *Modulations*:

---

10 Interview with Wit.
11 These press clippings are in the IMD archives.
12 Audio recordings of these lectures are also in the IMD archives.

A trombonist was very mad at me. He said, "What is this shit, this theater, you are mocking the musicians. We're not like that, we don't talk during our rehearsals." I said, "No, I'm asking you to do something I couldn't ask of a large orchestra. With a small group I can require a bit of humor." He calmed down a little. And then I noticed that he had done what I required of him [just earlier]: he had packed up his instrument during the rests so that he would be able to leave more quickly. He couldn't do the packing up [in the score], he had already. He had to unpack his trombone again. That's why he was mad![13]

Despite the charm of these anecdotes, there remained an obvious gulf between Grisey's musical aesthetic and the students. The young German composers, in particular, often seemed as if they were searching for explanations: *why* had Grisey chosen the Hammond organ for *Modulations*? (Unlike a regular organ, it's possible to transport.) *Why* the central importance of the note E? (There was no symbolic meaning.) *How* did he choose the order of the varying processes he used? "*C'est mon imagination*," Grisey answered, insisting, finally, on the predominance of the composer's intuition. "My theory is, you try to do as precisely as possible what you've dreamed, but it never works completely ... And that's why you continue to compose."

One student asked Grisey what he had learned in the process of composing *Modulations*. Grisey mentioned his satisfaction with the instrumental synthesis effect.

"Yes, but there must be something negative?" the student pressed.

"I'm sorry, truly, but there's nothing in the piece I'm dissatisfied with," Grisey responded. "But I have to be clear: when I write music, I don't compose a piece in one, two, or three weeks. I worked on [*Modulations*] for a year and a half, every day. And when I'm finished, I'm certain of how it sounds."

After lunch, Grisey read the class a quotation given to *Le Monde* by Pierre Boulez: "I'd really like for the young to violently attack us, but there are just one or two dog-barks, and nothing more. I told the Darmstadt presenters they should invite the students as teachers, and I would attend as a student. But they are unable to find anyone." Grisey let the quote resonate while outlining his approach to music.

Next, Grisey introduced the students to his concept of the "skeleton of time," meaning the underlying pulse of a piece determined by the composer. This could be a metronome value or chronological time, measured by the second. For him, this unit had little relationship to the time of musical perception. Grisey criticized rhythmic structures in which the lack of audible meter allows the listener's perception to grasp only relative durations, rather

---

13   Audio from the IMD archives.

than *rhythms* per se. "A micro-pulsation allows the interpreter or the conductor to count and realize these durations, but it exists only as a mode of operation, without any perceptual reality," Grisey said. His targets included Messiaen (prime numbers); Bartók (the golden ratio); Stockhausen (the Fibonacci sequence); and others. He singled out Boulez's rhythmic structures as "the invention of a conductor, denuded of sense," and the imperceptibility of similar structures in Stockhausen's *Gruppen* and Ligeti's *Lontano*.

This presentation marks the first sustained public attack by Grisey on Boulez's musical ideas. As Jonathan Goldman points out, much of this acrimony was based on a hardcore serialist statement Boulez made in 1963. Boulez's serialism became less doctrinaire in the 1970s, but because he was too busy conducting to write music-theoretical texts, other composers continued to see him as an avatar for "serial music in its most exacting form."[14] On a more emotional level, Boulez was such a towering establishment musical figure in France and abroad that it was easy for Grisey to blame him for everything he felt was wrong with contemporary music. (In 1986, Boulez dismissed spectral music as consisting essentially of tonal seventh and ninth chords; he claimed it was unable to do anything else. Goldman believes this statement was aimed at *Partiels*.[15])

For Grisey, a positive example of perceptible rhythmic structures was Stockhausen's *Stimmung*, the work that had so impressed Grisey, Vivier, and Boudreau in 1972. The piece "shows us that only certain elementary—even primary—rhythms give us enough transparency to divine the *tempo* of those rhythms," he explained. The other works seemed to require a super-listener for their structures to be perceived. (Speaking German, Grisey used the Nietzschean term *Übermensch*.)

A student posed a question: what if Messiaen and Boulez's *intention* was not to make their rhythmic structures perceptible? Grisey conceded that the point was probably correct, but continued:

> I still think it has to be said, because these [rhythmic] differences became so important analytically, that they mistook the map for the territory. They didn't know anymore what was perceived. And that's what we—I say we, but not in the Charles de Gaulle sense, please [laughter], just because I'm not the only one who thinks this way—Murail and other composers share my opinion. We believe there must be confluence between structure and phenomenology, what we perceive. We don't want to work [outside] time.

Grisey's remark about mistaking the map for the territory was a slight misquotation of a famous aphorism by the philosopher Alfred Korzbski, who remarked that "a map is not the territory": an abstraction of a real-life

---

14 Goldman, "Boulez and the Spectralists between Descartes and Rameau," 214.
15 Ibid, 220.

phenomenon should never be confused for the phenomenon itself.[16] The reminder was extremely important in the context of the contemporary music of this time: *the score is not the music*. Grisey went on, "I'm interested in the totality of what's heard, and I use all the means available to realize that. Not the other way around."

At this point, Grisey introduced a theoretical concept that became one of his most important innovations: a table of categories of musical events, grouped from "order" to "disorder." The idea, along with many others in this lecture, is from Abraham Moles's 1958 book *Information Theory and Aesthetic Perception*. Moles's book used the mathematical concepts of information theory developed by scientists such as Claude Shannon and applied their insights to aesthetic perception. For Moles, an elementary aspect of form in its broadest sense was predictability or "redundancy": "A *degree of predictability* exists, which is nothing less than the *degree of continuity* of a phenomenon, a measure of its regularity."[17] Building on this idea, Grisey's table grouped musical phenomena from maximum predictability (periodicity) to zero predictability (statistic distribution). He classified intervals by their degree of roughness—the acoustical term for the musical word dissonance—and timbres by their degree of inharmonicity. When a student asked what concrete musical elements could be grouped in this table, Grisey brightened up: "A good question," he answered. "Everything."

Periodicity, Grisey went on, was important as "the simplest, the most probable phenomenon." He noted that perfect periodicity of the kind created by a computer "provokes nothing but boredom and disinterest," drawing a connection between extremely predictable rhythms and neuroses (using, as an example, a repetitive aria from Mozart's *Die Entführung aus dem Serail*). Grisey also pointed out the tenacious pattern-forming capacity of human perception: if we hear three events which are relatively periodic to one another, we expect a fourth, despite the statistically irrelevant sample size; this constitutes another insight from *Information Theory and Aesthetic Perception*.

A student asked an important clarifying question: why did Grisey call disorder "static"? Wasn't disorder always in motion? Grisey answered that "static" music was music that didn't seem to be *moving perceptibly* from one point to another. Precisely because the leaping, skittering sounds of many serialist pieces were constantly in motion, the music never seemed to be *going* anywhere.

---

16 Korzbski made this remark at a 1931 lecture. https://fs.blog/map-and-territory/.
17 Moles, *Information Theory and Aesthetic Perception*, 99.

Tristan Murail joined Grisey for the next part of the presentation. Grisey continued with his idea of dynamism and continuity, the concept of perceptible musical processes. Gradual increases and decreases in the number of musical events in a given period of time—building on Moles's notion of the "thickness of time"—could be generated using arithmetic or geometric progressions. (As if reminding himself, Grisey cautioned against overusing this technique: "Our spirit quickly tires of this game.") In an example of a thought process typical of Grisey, he quickly linked these mathematical insights to aesthetic ones, in this case to Werner Herzog's film *Aguirre: The Wrath of God*. The work dramatizes a doomed Spanish expedition to El Dorado; the pace of the action slows gradually but perceptibly as the colonists die and the futility of their mission becomes apparent. As a musical illustration of this idea, Grisey played an excerpt from *Partiels*, where dissonant horn trills and string ricochets give way to an increasingly dense string texture with notes from the harmonic spectrum—from "gray to light."

These insights represented an important way of thinking about composition in relation to the listener. But the students in the course—maybe put off by Grisey's dutiful reading from his notes, the lack of focus on their own work, or hunger—seemed bored. "My patience is being sorely tested," one said. They broke for lunch.

The lecture continued with the "flesh of time," meaning the phenomenological and psychological aspects of music, or "the unsaid of musical composition," as Grisey put it. The listener plays an essential part in constructing the perception of the piece; he needs little aesthetic information to begin. Grisey cited Messiaen's phrase that "all you need to make music is at least two sounds, or one sound and silence,"[18] and referred to a passage from the end of Vladimir Nabokov's hypersexual and sensual novel *Ada or Ardor*—scientific works by writers such as Moles and poetic explorations by authors like Nabokov flowed together in one current in Grisey's mind. In the section quoted in Grisey's lecture, Nabokov's protagonist is driving to see his half-sister after a long time apart; they had a searing sexual relationship when they were both children. Throughout this internal monologue, Nabokov makes it clear that his narrator is so absorbed in his thoughts that he frequently comes close to causing serious car accidents:

> Maybe the only thing that hints at a sense of Time is rhythm; not the recurrent beats of the rhythm but the gap between two such beats, the gray gap between black beats: the Tender Interval. The regular throb itself merely brings back the miserable idea of measurement, but in between, something like true Time lurks. How can I extract it from its soft hollow?[19]

---

18 Lelong, *Écrits*, 80.
19 Nabokov, *Ada or Ardor*, 421.

In this passage, Nabokov describes the essence of time as existing in between the "regular throb" of sex. This prefigures a striking remark Grisey made about his later piece *Les chants de l'amour*: "Music has at least this in common with Love: through it, the human being discovers and understands Time." Intimacy is a mirror that reflects the finite nature of our biological rhythms.

Relying on further insights from Moles, Grisey noted that when the musical events within a certain amount of time are difficult to predict, our perception "contracts." We are less able to process the full scope of these events: these passages "leave a violent trace in our musical memory, which makes us less capable of capturing the form of the musical discourse," Grisey explained. When the events in the same amount of time are highly predictable, our perception is free to examine these events in detail; time is "dilated." Grisey liked to compare dilated listening to the examination of tiny organisms under a microscope. Like Pascal, he envisioned the universe as both infinitely small and infinitely large; as he told the Darmstadt students, the value of the electronic studio was that it could serve as a sort of microscope for composers.

To demonstrate dilated musical time, Grisey used examples from the classical canon: in the first movement of Mozart's Symphony no. 40 in G Minor, a repetitive four-bar alternation between an E-flat dominant seventh chord and A-flat major chord; in the first movement of Brahms's Piano Concerto no. 2 op. 83, a gently alternating, static diminuendo in F-sharp major; in the first movement of Bruckner's Symphony No. 9, a motivic canon between the first and second violins. Grisey also cited the famous prelude to Wagner's *Ring* cycle, where the orchestra plays a three-minute overture on a single E-flat major chord, like a titanic upbeat to the three-and-a-half-day work.

Grisey also elaborated on the violent essence of music, an idea that fascinated him for the rest of his life. As the philosopher Georges Bataille wrote in his book *Eroticism*, which Grisey cited in the bibliography of "Tempus ex Machina," existence enfolds "the oneness of extreme pleasure and extreme pain, the oneness of being and dying, of knowledge finishing with this dazzling prospect and final darkness."[20] Bataille insisted on the inseparability of violence and transcendence, adding that "we can only reach a state of ecstasy when we are conscious of death or annihilation."[21] Grisey applied this insight to music, recognizing the violent essence of sound and interrupting his gradual processes with sudden ruptures.

Grisey concluded his lecture with a short note on the "skin of time," or the flawed and halting communication between the aesthetic idea of the

---

20   Bataille, *Eroticism*, 257.
21   Ibid, 267.

composer and the listener's private construction of a work. Citing Moles again, Grisey described memory as an active force at odds with the artist's intention, selecting some aspects from a piece for storage while discarding others. "It does not follow at all automatically that the composer's intention will be perceived in one manner or another," he explained. Techniques such as repetition and violent interruption of a musical process were not guaranteed to be perceived that way. The listener "remodeled, completed, sometimes destroyed" the form of a work as dreamed up by its author.

The bibliography associated with "Tempus ex Machina" included musical treatises and polemic (Stravinsky, Messiaen, Stockhausen, Boulez); philosophy (Bataille and Gilles Deleuze's *Difference and Repetition*); science (Moles); fiction (Nabokov); and, most difficult to categorize, Carlos Castaneda's 1974 *Tales of Power*. The book describes a spiritual journey among the shamans of the Yaqui Indian tribe in Mexico. It was originally marketed as non-fiction anthropology but later revealed to be pure fiction.[22] Still, in many ways Castaneda's book reaffirms the central thesis of Moles's experimental approach, but in new-age terms. Castaneda's main character, don Juan, makes an observation that fits well with Grisey's idea of the skin of time: "We are always one step removed and our experience of the world is always a recollection of the experience."[23]

As Grisey concluded, he made it clear that his ideas were not meant to be prescriptive. Maybe it was obvious, but Grisey repeated that he did not wish to remove the intuitive, subjective element from composition; rather, he took the knowledge of the imperfect listener as emboldening. Quoting Edgard Varèse, he said, "The last word is the imagination."

On June 23, 1980, Grisey began looking at student compositions, a process that yielded a few revealing moments. The Romanian composer Călin Ioachimescu was presenting one of his works.

"How long is the piece?" another student asked Ioachimescu.

"Don't tell him," Grisey said. "I'm interested in the subjective feeling of time. I mean, sometimes it's astounding: [you think] what a long piece! And then you learn it only lasted fifteen minutes. Or vice versa. That is interesting—so, please. I never listen to a piece for the first time with the score. It's a personal thing."

The following morning, during the lecture, Grisey returned to his spectral ideas, discussing the idea of instrumental synthesis with Murail. When orchestrating the harmonic spectrum of a given instrument, Grisey recognized he was doing so with other instruments—each of which has its own unique harmonic spectrum. The result doesn't model the original sound, but

---

22 Marshall, "The Dark Legacy of Carlos Castaneda."
23 Castaneda, *Tales of Power*, 47.

results in something *other*. That is a key poetic paradox in Grisey's technique: he sacrificed logical rigor for the depth and intricacy of sound. (Boulez criticized this exact aspect of Grisey's work, but, as Jonathan Goldman writes, "Boulez acted as if Grisey didn't know about the paradox."[24]) The harmonic power of Grisey's music arises *because* instruments tend to resist synthesis; the paradox at the heart of it is enriching, not destructive.

When Grisey's students presented their work again, the German composer Stephan Wunderlich opened with a John Cage-style performance-lecture during which he criticized Grisey's presentation. "I would say that the most basic thing hasn't changed," Wunderlich said. "The object remains. The parameters of the note have just changed to other parameters. But it's still about objects, there is no connection between the micro- and the macro-cosmos." Stockhausen's ideas were clear in this objection; the German composer valued formal rigor above all else. An argument ensued, with Grisey translating between French and German but not revealing his own thoughts. Murail, coming to Grisey's defense, said, "There's a problem, nobody understands. Can you be a little clearer?" The tenor of the discussion was heated, but—as often in confrontational composition lectures—the content of the disagreement was not entirely obvious.

After the conclusion of Grisey's lectures, his *Modulations* was performed on July 30, alongside *Windrose* by the Polish composer Włodzimierz Kotoński; Murail's gorgeously disintegrating *Gondwana* and richly dynamic *Treize couleurs du soleil couchant*; and Wolfgang Rihm's *Cuts and Dissolves*, a piece inspired by techniques from film. As at the previous festival, the critics were frequently dismissive of the spectralists. For Wolf-Eberhard von Lewinski, *Modulations* was "a disconnected collection of sonic effects, presented in the manner of a dull meditation." In the *Darmstädter Tagblatt*, an anonymous critic wrote that Murail and Grisey's pieces were "astonishingly similar, in the actually long-since obsolete mode of meditation exercises with wave-like sonic movements to more or less suggest that the listener fall asleep." Another critic called the two composers Siamese twins. For Heins Ziegert, the works were purely "decorative." The only positive response came from the critic Petra Stadler, who called the spectral works "appealing," noting that they were greeted with much applause.[25]

* * *

In early 1981, the Swiss composer Gérard Zinsstag came to Berlin on a DAAD scholarship. Grisey and Zinsstag became fast friends. "We spent a lot

---

24   Goldman, "Boulez and the Spectralists between Descartes and Rameau," 221.
25   Press clippings in the IMD archives.

of time together," Zinsstag said. "Not a week passed when we didn't meet or at least talk on the phone."[26]

In April 1981, after the first year of his scholarship was up, Grisey requested additional time in order to finish his composition *Transitoires*, a request the DAAD granted until the end of August with a reduced scholarship of 1,581 marks per month.[27] In the warm summer of 1981, Grisey and Zinsstag met frequently to ride bikes in the Tiergarten or bathe at Wannsee. Zinsstag said, "We went swimming, heard lots of music, exchanged scores."[28] Besides the need to finish the orchestral score, the extension reflected both Grisey's friendship with Zinsstag and the satisfaction Jocelyne felt while in Berlin, where she had time to focus on raising Raphaël. Their son made his first steps there.[29] (Raphaël now lives in Berlin.)

For all appearances, Grisey's stay in Berlin was his most carefree period in a long time, though his infrequent diary entries from this period hint at amorous and even existential worries beneath the surface. In July 1981, he wrote to an unnamed "friend," probably a mistress: "You left me with a wound that I can't close. The space into which we have expanded together in such a short time is now suffocating me ... . I haven't had time to discover the slightest flaw in you. It is unbearable! I'm begging you, give me something to make me stop thinking of you from morning till night." A month later, he wrote enigmatically:

> I'm afraid ... not of falling, or of disappointment, but that we won't be able to withstand the sound that the wind makes on these strings, since they are attached to the tautest and most fragile fibers of our being.
>
> ... Dilation, an intermediate state between pleasure and pain. I listen to this dilated space, it moves with me, but I worry about frightening this superb bird ...
>
> I hold my breath: let's try to perceive the slightest movement, the most subtle colored reflections. The moment in all its silent beauty.[30]

The same month, Grisey wrote another diary entry, this time in the form of a poem:

> My old defenses are falling, one by one, like an onion peel. Then, one evening, I threw myself, arms and legs spread, into the emptiness of a glance.
> I almost reached the bottom.

---

26   Interview with Zinsstag.
27   DAAD archive.
28   Interview with Zinsstag.
29   Interview with Jocelyne Grisey.
30   Paul Sacher archive.

It's not much bigger than the head of a pin. When the thought sweeps the night with its thin beam, sometimes it briefly illuminates this tiny, brilliant thing.
... Fear.
That barely visible tear bleeds with such light!
The Unknown rapes me.
Then the beautiful, indifferent eyes lowered their eyelids.
I remained at the bottom.
... To see.[31]

These lyrical diary entries show the proximity for Grisey of the "extreme pleasure and extreme pain" that Bataille describes, extremes that connect his understanding of music with his experience of erotic and romantic love. On August 20, 1981, Grisey noted a bit of more practical wisdom from Jocelyne: "What we call our strengths," she had told him, "are perhaps just the expressions of our limits."

Grisey's Berlin residency concluded at the end of August. The DAAD secured a performance of *Modulations* on April 25, 1982, alongside works by Sukhi Kang and Maurice Weddington, performed by the Berlin Radio Symphony Orchestra under the direction of Jacques Mercier. The critic Gottfried Eberle praised the "fascinatingly changing ethereal sounds which at times remind one of Schoenberg's *Klangfarbenmelodie* in his Pieces for Orchestra op. 16."[32] For another writer, however, the piece was a "dignified, not especially important work by a representative of young France."[33]

Grisey composed his *Solo pour deux* (*Solo for Two*) between April and June 1981, during his stay in Berlin, with revisions made the following year. Scored for B♭ clarinet and trombone, the piece was commissioned by the Centre Pompidou and dedicated to the clarinetist Michel Arrignon and the Israeli trombonist Benny Sluchin, both of whom were members of Ensemble Intercontemporain at the time. Despite the arms-length relationship between these Boulez-dominated institutions and the spectral school of composers, Grisey had once again managed to finagle his way into a small but prestigious commission.

The imprint of Grisey's work at IRCAM in early 1980 is unmistakable in this work, which, like *Sortie vers la lumière du jour* and *Jour, contre-jour*, uses acoustic instruments to produce music that *sounds* decidedly electronic.

---

31 Ibid.
32 DAAD archive, Eberle, "Ohne Werbetrommel kein Echo."
33 DAAD archive, W. Sch., "Der Jazz lässt freundlich grüßen."

Grisey's approach to the composition of the work had a scientific character. "In 1980, a lecture by [the acoustician] Michèle Castellengo on the multiphonic sounds of the clarinet posited that a large proportion of these sounds resulted, in fact, from simple harmonic relationships, the fundamental being absent," Grisey wrote. "Almost immediately I had the idea of a duo playing on spectral fusions."[34] Many of Grisey's works from this period explore acoustical phenomena, but this small piece is the first where the composer is inspired by a scientific hypothesis.

Grisey described *Solo pour deux* as consisting of a "single process," though separate sections are distinguishable. The work begins with a through-composed exploration of beatings around the microtonal variations of a D♮; the intervals between the two voices gradually increase. To enrich this trajectory Grisey adds a series of grace notes that fill in—even saturate—the harmonic spectrum and increase the density of the overall texture. Both instruments alternate between pitch and noise, the poles of harmonicity and inharmonicity. Eventually, the steadily rising motion of the work is reversed (at one point, the trombone even plays above the clarinet), with both instruments moving back downwards in close intervals, and the harmonics moving back to the original fundamental. At that point, Grisey composes a series of periodic pulsations using the numbers of the Fibonacci sequence—an interesting choice, considering he explicitly criticized the use of those values in Stockhausen's compositions.[35]

Grisey's instrumental synthesis is successful in *Solo pour deux*, with the clarinet and trombone often sounding like a third, nonexistent instrument, born in a mad scientist's acoustic laboratory. For the critic Wolfgang Hofer, the effect is like "a new kind of archeology."[36] Hofer also compares the work to the medieval motets of Guillaume de Machaut. This is due to the overlap in overtones between the two instruments: when the clarinet plays a note already present in the trombone spectrum, it melds within our brains, on the cusp between one sound and two.

With this piece, Grisey returned to a favorite theme: the possibility or impossibility of the total fusion between two beings. The title *Solo pour deux* implies oneness and interpenetration, between instruments—in overtone correspondences—and between people, in the physical intimacy of sex. Grisey himself seemed keen to undercut the scientific origin of the work. After describing these aspects of the composition, he concluded his program note with the laconic reminder that "the previous boring words to not make

---

34   Lelong, *Écrits*, 154.
35   Ibid, 62.
36   Hofer, "Gérard Grisey: Aufbrüche: Ins Unbekannte," KAIROS liner notes.

us forget the initial eroticism of this piece." *Solo pour deux* was premiered on October 1, 1982, at the Venice Biennale.

Grisey also composed *Transitoires* for large orchestra during his stay in Berlin. As the penultimate work of *Les espaces acoustiques*, the piece represents the apotheosis of the composer's musical thinking in this period. It's also a return to the large scale of *Dérives*, but with a decade's worth of aesthetic lessons learned.

The title refers to the term "transients" from acoustics. As mentioned, transients are the unique partials created by the construction of the sounding body at the beginning and the end of a sound, which Grisey liked to describe as their births and deaths. Transients are of utmost importance to the human perception of timbre. As Émile Leipp explains:

> The auditory role of the attack transients can be easily highlighted thanks to the appearance of the tape recorder. One records a violin note, an oboe note, etc. Then, with scissors, we cut the [beginning] of the sound, which we can easily locate. The sound is played to subjects who have not seen the operation: in many cases, the instrument is no longer recognized![37]

Transitoires works explicitly with structural elements reprised from earlier pieces in *Les espaces acoustiques*. The piece opens with an optional introduction, around five minutes in length, which alludes to music of the previous pieces with a sort of heightened ominousness; even if it doesn't have to be included, it has primal power, and prepares the ear for the allusions that follow. The first *obbligato* section of the work opens with bass pulsations that immediately recall *Partiels*. As Baillet has shown, this section is also structurally similar to the earlier composition.[38] Its development closely tracks the thirteen repetitions of the trombone spectrum (though the science-fiction sound of the Hammond organ also ensures that *Modulations* remains in our ears). But now the composer works with actual spectrograms, rather than a theoretical harmonic spectrum. This material is slowed down more extremely than in *Partiels*, allowing the listener to perceive its grains in greater detail. The most important difference in this piece, however, can be heard in the bass motive, which no longer just plays *arco*, but also *pizzicato* and *spiccato*. Grisey had spectrograms of these sounds made—their transients are different, creating the different timbres we perceive—and orchestrated them. Less perceptible are complex processes of rhythmic motive development and the

---

37 Leipp, *Acoustique et Musique*, 154.
38 Baillet, *Fondement d'une écriture*, 136.

overlapping of different temporal dilations which Grisey associated with "an intermediate state between pleasure and pain," again recalling Bataille's phrase. The musicologist notes that the temporal dilations can only be heard in "utopian" terms, though they demonstrate the sophistication of the composer's musical thought processes in this work.[39] Also noteworthy is the lack of progression between harmonic and inharmonic poles in this section, which could have become a crutch. This music, thanks to the masterful orchestration of the new transient spectrograms, carries the listener along in its powerful current.

The next, shorter section shimmers like a weak sun on a foggy day, its rays of light refracted irregularly through the molecules of clouds. It follows an analogous structure to *Partiels*. The harmonic progression is generated through a sum- and difference-tone process, with solo parts representing periodic and aperiodic rhythms. As these parts fall steadily in range, Baillet notes, they become a metaphorical representation of the low frequencies, which we perceive as rhythm instead of pitch. Baillet also discovers that neumes from *Prologue* control these rhythmic variations. The more distinct poles of earlier pieces reappear in this section as well: the texture rises from low to high ranges, moves from inharmonic sounds to harmonic ones, and progresses from aperiodic to periodic rhythms.[40] The sun is getting stronger and cuts through the disappearing mist.

The third section of *Transitoires*, music of delicate, interwoven pulsations, divides the large orchestra into five independent groups of similar instrumentations. It combines a rhythmic process from *Partiels*, as Baillet shows, with a polyphony between instrumental groups from *Modulations*.[41] The brass instruments lead the process: their melodic lines "contain more and more notes, the frequency and dynamic range widens, the durations between each sound move from the periodic to the aperiodic, and the pitches, at first part of a harmonic spectrum on B, move away from it gradually," Baillet writes.[42] Eventually, five chords based on different fundamentals sound at the same time. This results in a strongly inharmonic, rich chord.

The penultimate section of the work consists of an alternation between two complex sounds. The first is the contraction of very high partials into a dissonant cluster; the second, a harmonic series modified by filtration. For Baillet, these two chords, with their many common notes (they are both based on an A♭ harmonic series), are "perceived as the variously colored

---

39   Ibid, 142.
40   Ibid, 149.
41   Ibid, 148.
42   Ibid.

repetition" of the same note.⁴³ The effect is like looking at an outdoor sculpture alternately between dawn and dusk.

Throughout *Transitoires*, Grisey plays with structural elements of the preceding works in *Les espaces acoustiques*; in the final section, he makes the connection explicit. The alternating chords are gradually reduced to their highest and lowest pitches and fade out. We are left with a downward fifth in the viola, E♭–A♭, which, if *Transitoires* has been performed as part of the cycle, immediately brings the ear back to *Prologue*. It also guides us into the final work, *Épilogue*. Though *Transitoires* is a work of extraordinary power, and arguably the culmination of the entire cycle, it is laced through with references and plays on the pieces preceding it—both sublimated in its structure and audible on the first listening. Without the rest of the cycle, Baillet finds its global form of decreasing tension "curious."⁴⁴ And without *Prologue*, the conclusion loses its touching return to intimacy. Grisey seems to admit as much in his program note for the piece. "Memory, resurgence, and bursting: *Transitoires* reveals the unsuspected aspects of the material and ends in a primal melody, a kind of lullaby where the viola quotes many snippets of the *Prologue*," he wrote. "From this Pandora's box *Épilogue* will emerge."⁴⁵

On October 5, 1981, a preliminary version of *Les espaces acoustiques* was premiered at the Venice Biennale. Gérard Caussé reprised his performance of the solo part, with the larger works performed by the Orchestra Sinfonica Siciliana under the direction of the Italian conductor Gabriele Ferro. This version included the new *Transitoires*. The performance gave a sense of the larger shape of this massive composition, a work that had previously been heard in bits and pieces.

Writing in *Le Monde* on October 20, Gérard Condé set the scene for Grisey's performance at the prestigious festival. The theme of the 1981 Biennale was "After the Avant-Garde," and by this time the critic was able to pick up on a sea change in the aesthetic atmosphere. "What one notices today in almost all the composers is a concern, if not to flatter the lazy curiosity of the listener, at least to not put him off systematically," Condé wrote. "Twenty or thirty years ago, one could say without blushing that the public's pleasure was not important … The public, for its part, has evolved; it is no longer entirely convinced of the need to make an effort to deserve its pleasure."⁴⁶

---

43 Ibid, 149.
44 Ibid, 151.
45 Lelong, *Écrits*, 148.
46 Condé, "Oeuvres contemporaines à la Biennale de Venise."

This change, which dovetails neatly with the early preoccupations of the spectralists, was not entirely due to them: composers whose work represented a renewed interest in the audience's pleasure, and whose pieces were performed at the 1981 Venice Biennale, included Terry Riley, Wolfgang Rihm, and Hans Werner Henze. For Condé, even the works of the avant-garde masters Boulez, Stockhausen, and Xenakis showed an increased willingness not just to challenge, but also to please their audiences. As the young firebrand Boulez had once influenced Messiaen, the newer generation of composers left a mark on their own elders.

Grisey's musical-aesthetic thinking went beyond the idea of accessibility; the complex idea of perception formed the basis of his work. Grisey was often dismissive of his neo-Romantic and minimalist counterparts. (Condé was skeptical too, at one point claiming that Terry Riley's *G-song* for string quartet "could be mistaken for Pachelbel's Canon.") In contrast, the preliminary performance of *Les espaces acoustiques* stood out for the critic:

> The event of this Biennale for the French was naturally the almost complete performance of Gérard Grisey's cycle *Les espaces acoustiques*, five pieces for one to eighty-four instruments (the sixth is not yet written) which cannot be analyzed here, but which one can affirm, after this first attempt and in spite of certain weaknesses in the performance of *Périodes* and *Partiels*, can legitimately occupy an evening. The initiative of the Biennale will thus have been precious, and one cannot doubt that there will soon be an opportunity in France to reveal a work which, by the power of its breadth and its unusual dimensions, will undoubtedly be a landmark.[47]

A version of *Les espaces acoustiques* shorn of the *Épilogue* contains much beautiful music, but without the descending viola fifths at the end, the piece is missing a moment that would define it as a cycle. It would be another four years before this cycle, undoubtedly one of the most important works in Grisey's oeuvre—and one of the most important in the second half of the twentieth century—would receive its strange and fitting culmination.

In the fall of 1981, after the Griseys returned to their Belleville apartment in Paris from Berlin, the composer was invited by the Alliance Française to the United States to give lectures on his music for a month or two. Jocelyne looked after Raphaël and worked part time as a social worker while Grisey traveled around the U.S. Jocelyne remembers that Grisey wrote to her from San Francisco saying that he'd be more than happy to take a job there. After he returned to Paris, Grisey saw a job advertisement for an Assistant Professor of Composition at the University of California at Berkeley and applied. He went back to California for his interview.

---

47 Ibid.

Grisey got the job. It was a prestigious position with the possibility of advancement, but—as is common in artistic and academic careers—it forced him to uproot his family once more. "I was not at all happy," Jocelyne said. "Berlin had been very good, but after returning to Paris I had to reorganize my life and my work. And then I had to leave again."[48]

Grisey's friend Gérard Zinsstag had been renting a house in the Swiss Alps in a tiny village called Schlans, in the canton of Graubünden, and after the two composers became close in Berlin, he began inviting Grisey there. The village is located at about 4,000 feet, with a view that stretches over the valley and into some of Switzerland's highest mountains. It seems that Grisey first visited Schlans the Easter before he moved to California.[49]

The house had ten small rooms and a brick oven. Initially, Grisey only came earlier in the year because he had strong allergies, but he eventually discovered the wonders of antihistamines and started coming in spring and summer too. They spent their time composing, sitting outside talking, and hiking (though Grisey was afraid of heights).[50]

For Grisey, Schlans was a place of calm, repose, and natural beauty where he was free to dedicate himself to his art. The musicologist Theo Hirsbrunner recalled, "I have always wondered about this predilection for solitude in the mountains from a composer who was, after all, a long-time Parisian. But Grisey spoke to me several times about the discomfort of living in such a big city with its continual agitation. Facing the highest peaks of the Alps, Grisey found peace to compose his works."[51]

In the summer of 1982, Grisey attended the thirty-first edition of the Darmstädter Ferienkurse. This time, the spectral contingent was well-represented, with Michaël Levinas, Hugues Dufourt, and other composers joining Darmstadt veterans Grisey and Murail. The spectralists were going to the citadel of rigorous, structural, German musical thought. Grisey quipped, "*L'Itinéraire à Darmstadt, c'est Tintin en Amerique!*"[52]

---

48 Interview with Jocelyne Grisey.
49 Zinsstag isn't sure of the exact year.
50 Interview with Zinsstag.
51 Hirsbrunner, *Le Temps de l'Écoute*, 225.
52 Grisey, "Autoportrait avec l'Itinéraire," cited in Lelong, *Écrits*, 209.

On July 13, 1982, Grisey gave a lecture called "La Musique: Le Devenir des Sons" ("Music: The Becoming of Sound"), published as an article later that year.[53] The talk was briefer than "Tempus Ex Machina" from 1980, but summarized Grisey's previous thinking and opened a window on his new preoccupations. (The Belgian musicologist Harry Halbreich did a live translation of Grisey's presentation into English, with a posh British accent.) It showed that the 1979 debate on the best term to describe the "spectralists" with Dufourt was not settled—at least not in Grisey's mind. Grisey told the students at Darmstadt that he hoped to preempt the "wise musicologists giving us a reductive and approximate name." Besides "liminal," he proposed "differential"—difference is the prerequisite for tension and allows composers to avoid both hierarchization and the complete leveling of parameters—and "transitory," because of its sense of the movement of forces—the *life*—in sound.

None of these three terms caught on, but they did provide Grisey with a structure for his lecture. Under the heading *Différentiel*, he began with a closer look at the concepts of consonance and dissonance. More neutral, he said, was the acoustical concept of roughness (as previously mentioned); dissonance is a cultural term, he pointed out. Without assigning hierarchies to these concepts, Grisey emphasized that the difference in the roughness of two sounds was a compositional phenomenon he was interested in "playing with." He continued, "I say play, and not dominate, not with notes but with the nature of sound, in a way that recognizes their different 'races and ethnicities' and respects their culture." In tonal music, dissonance was to be properly resolved; in atonal music, consonance was received with an "embarrassed smile." For Grisey, this continuum was an aspect of the human perception of sound to be explored, like the continuum between the harmonic spectrum and white noise and the continuum between periodic and aperiodic rhythms. The term "differential" summarized Grisey's idea. "What happens between a sound A and a sound B?" he asked. "The essential. 'Tempus ex Machina,' not chronological but phenomenological and musical time, is located at the intersection of this difference, or absence of difference. It is this monster [the scale between difference and the absence of difference] that musicians discover, trembling a little, by dint of patience, intuition, and naivety."[54]

While the term "liminal" represented a broad aesthetic, even philosophical point of view for Grisey, it also had a concrete musical meaning: mainly, Grisey emphasized again, that the serialist way of describing music in discrete parameters was "inapt." In acoustics, these parameters are all connected with

---

53 IMD archives.
54 Lelong, *Écrits*, 57.

one another, timbre and intensity bleeding inexorably into pitch and duration: each parameter affects our perception of the others. To demonstrate, Grisey played the Darmstadt students excerpts from *Partiels* and *Modulations* and cited similar examples from his colleagues Dufourt and Levinas.

This idea had implications for Grisey's conception of musical form which, he said, "becomes revelation on a human scale," a perceptual mirror that "deforms, focuses, multiplies, selects, 'corrodes.'" Inspired, maybe, by Georges Bataille's *Eroticism*, which he already cited in "Tempus ex Machina" from 1980, Grisey claimed that "musical form has something terrifying: it is related to voyeurism and rape, but also to vivisection and genetic manipulation." For him, music was part of Bataille's "sacred time," enabling transcendence but stalked by violence, unifying "extreme pleasure and extreme pain."

Grisey then arrived at the polemical quote that became one of his most famous sayings. "We are musicians and our model is sound and not literature, sound and not mathematics, sound and not theater, visual arts, quantum physics, geology, astrology or acupuncture!" he said. The line elicited guffaws from the Darmstadt students. It also opened him up to later accusations of hypocrisy. As his friend, the American spectralist composer Joshua Fineberg, has written:

> This is a funny quote coming from Grisey. Here is a composer who wrote a piece called *Le noir de l'étoile*, which is built around the sound of a pulsar; and a piece called *L'Icône paradoxale*, that's based on a De La Francesca painting. The whole *Les espaces acoustiques* cycle has a very large theatrical component; and had he lived longer, he might well have made it around to geology and acupuncture as well. While one might simply decide that he changed his mind in the years after he wrote those words—since most of those pieces are from somewhat later—I don't think that is the case. I believe that right up until the end of his life this conviction had not changed. I do not think he ever believed that composers should not be nourished by extra-musical ideas from unrelated fields. Rather, he thought that in the end, whatever ideas helped get you there, what matters, what music ultimately is about, is the transformation of sound and its effect on a listener. Whatever extra-musical ideas might have led you to create your sonic objects, they in no way validate them.[55]

An orchestral concert of works by the spectralist group took place on July 14, 1982, with the Symphony Orchestra of the Westdeutscher Rundfunk under the direction of the Hungarian conductor and composer Péter Eötvös. It featured Levinas's shuddering *Les rires du Gilles* for five instruments and tape and *Appels* for seven instruments (with the same title as the

---

55 Brown, "A Gérard Grisey Playlist."

unfinished Grisey sketch), a noisy spectral work based on a rising motive; Tristan Murail's subtle concerto for ondes martenot and ensemble, *Les courants de l'espace*; and Dufourt's *La Tempesta d'après Giorgione*. Grisey's contribution was *Jour, contre-jour*.

Once again, German critics were dismissive. On the public radio station Hessischer Rundfunk, one journalist said of the spectralists' evening, "No point needles the audience, no aspirations keep it tense and make it hold its breath, rather the opposite: There are pleasant aspirations, which recall a carefully planned, luxurious seance, and a typical genteelness." He complained that *Jour, contre-jour*, "with its heartbeat, noise, and spherical sounds, implies the musical idiom of a science fiction film." In the *Süddeutsche Zeitung*, Wolf-Eberhard von Lewinski wrote that the music of the young French composers at Darmstadt "was already out of date," and that Murail's *Territoires de l'oubli*, performed in a chamber music concert on July 15 by Ensemble L'Itinéraire, "induced partially dismissive, partially indifferent reactions" from the audience. Detlef Gojowy called the music "concrete, technically perhaps a bit dilettante … not shying away from film scores and middlebrow entertainment."[56]

On July 16, the entire spectralist group—Grisey, Murail, Dufourt, Levinas, and the Romanian-French composer Costin Miereanu—joined Halbreich for a tumultuous panel discussion. The questions began cordially: a first student wondered whether the group's interest in the harmonic spectrum was an artificial limitation, a substitution for the loss of tonality, melody, and modes. Murail pointed out that the harmonic spectrum was just one small element of the spectralists' work, despite their label. Grisey added, "We shouldn't be afraid of limitations." For him, they could paradoxically be freeing, ways of "renewing" composition.

The panel offered clues to the interpersonal dynamic among the spectralist composers. Grisey and Murail were the most known, representative composers of the aesthetic; Dufourt was the philosopher; Levinas, according to Dufourt, the one who "throws dynamite in the whole process." Levinas, for his part, said that music *was* more than just sound—it also contained theater. Dufourt, hoping to counter the perception of the spectralists as a closed unit, noted that their aesthetic discussions sometimes became so heated that they "turned their backs to each other."

One student told the group that while "it's obvious to me that there's a wall of talent here," he was "concerned that the [spectralist] direction is a bit of a dead end aesthetically. We've already heard a lot of the sounds here." A German composer added that he thought the spectralists had invented nothing new: questions of predictability and memory in music were discussed by

---

56 Press clippings in the IMD archives.

Ligeti, Adorno, and Stockhausen in the late 1950s at Darmstadt, he noted correctly. Listening to the music, he added, he was unable to perceive a sense of form on a grand scale, meaning that Grisey's concept of "*preaudibilité* did not work." For the student, the work of Giacinto Scelsi was proof that what the spectralists were striving for—and, in his opinion, failed to achieve—was possible without theoretical justifications.

This led to a lengthy back-and-forth between Dufourt and the student. Grisey's counter to the student was simpler, but more effective: "I have the impression that all these ideas were always present in music theory, but were never put into practice," Grisey said. Stockhausen's concept of "*Erlebniszeit* [how the listener experiences time] is very interesting, but the music still seems far away from it." In fact, Stockhausen *had* immersed himself in many of the same questions in the late 1950s to early 1960s. Their musical answers, both valuable, were profoundly different.

Another German student chimed in to say that she found the spectralists' theoretical lectures boring, and was horrified to hear music, "a vital, sensual art," being spoken of in such an abstract way. By now, the French composers were audibly losing their patience with the critiques. (Besides the "wall of talent" comment, nothing positive had been said about their music.) The student said that she found all the pieces too long: "Unless I wasn't listening correctly."

"I think that is the case," Grisey snapped back, in German.

Then he collected himself. He explained that, for him, music always came first. The theories came after and weren't particularly important to him. But the French composers were discussing them because they were at Darmstadt, a gathering of experts. "We talked about music like surgeons," Grisey said, "and that is terrible. But it's Darmstadt, so that's the way it should be." It would be Grisey's last visit to the summer courses.

Chapter Ten

The Grains of Sound (1982–86)

In the fall of 1982, Grisey officially began his teaching duties as Assistant Professor of Composition at the University of California at Berkeley.[1] He moved into a house at 1934 San Antonio Avenue, in the Berkeley Hills, that had a view of the Pacific Ocean. He went by himself first to get set up. Jocelyne and Raphaël joined him later.

Behind the prestigious composition department at the University of California at Berkeley towered American neoclassical composer Roger Sessions. In 1928, Sessions had helped Aaron Copland, the artist whose name became the byword for musical Americana, organize a series of concerts. Sessions's music was vital, melodic, and rhetorical, rather than textural; he drew inspiration from twentieth-century composers such as Rachmaninoff, Bartók, and Hindemith. This style was a continent apart from the work that inspired Grisey as a young man: the more experimental pieces of Messiaen, Ligeti, and Stockhausen. Sessions taught in Berkeley between 1945 and 1950, and he served as a visiting professor in the 1966–67 academic year, when he was awarded an honorary degree.[2]

Sessions died in 1985 at almost ninety. His legacy at Berkeley lived on most clearly in the person of Andrew Imbrie, a gifted child prodigy and somewhat conventional modernist composer who taught in the composition department from 1949 to 1991. That long tenure meant Imbrie had already been at Berkeley for over three decades before Grisey arrived at the university. Imbrie was the "old master of the department" by that time, and, despite a certain kindness, was not known for his social graces.[3]

Imbrie was not thrilled by Grisey the interloper. One evening, Imbrie, who had the prim manner of a patrician Princetonian (his alma mater), went to a composers' concert at the university at which excerpts of *Les espaces*

---

1 Paul Sacher archive.
2 Cyr, "Roger Sessions at Berkeley: A Personal Reminiscence."
3 Interview with Fishman-Johnson.

acoustiques were performed. Like some German critics at Darmstadt, Imbrie heard something offensively countercultural in the music. One student of Imbrie's, who came to a lesson gushing about Grisey, recalled Imbrie's response: "You know, I don't smoke marijuana."[4] The composer Evan Ziporyn, who began studying with Grisey in 1984, heard Imbrie react in a similar way:

> He was carrying on for days about the piece. Going on about, "I don't do drugs, I don't need to *space out*." This ridiculous idea that this was somehow music to space out to, and that it was related to drug culture, which was by then certainly anachronistic. But he had these strong aesthetic, ideological objections to the music, which basically came down to, he found it boring.[5]

Another, less overtly hostile colleague of Grisey's was Olly Wilson, a pioneering Black classical composer (who also had expertise in jazz and West African music) nine years older than the Frenchman. The two men shared a working-class background—Wilson's father was a butler, his mother a seamstress—but grew up in vastly different cultures.[6] Wilson wrote music that combined modernist rigor with melodic and rhythmic vitality. Despite its quality, it is not hard to imagine Grisey finding it too close to film music, and not seeing Wilson as an aesthetic ally. Like Imbrie, Wilson was a career academic. He served as a professor at Berkeley—with just one short break—between 1970 and 2002.

The colleague that came closest to sharing Grisey's interests was Richard Felciano, a Californian who had studied at the Conservatoire National Supérieur in the 1950s.[7] Like Grisey, Felciano combined a rigorous conservatory education with an interest in the counterculture and experimental music: in the early 1960s, Felciano explored the intersections between acoustics (particularly the Doppler effect), architecture, television, and music, working in San Francisco with composers such as Morton Subotnick and Pauline Oliveros.[8] Felciano later collaborated with the psychoacoustician David Wessel, whom Grisey had met at IRCAM, and, in 1986, Felciano created the Center for New Music and Audio Technologies at Berkeley, on the model of the French institution. But Felciano had already joined the Berkeley faculty in 1967,[9] meaning that he was used to the vagaries of the

---

4   The student asked that this memory remain anonymous.
5   Interview with Ziporyn.
6   "Olly Wilson."
7   From Felciano's website.
8   "Richard Felciano."
9   "Felciano, Richard | Encyclopedia.com."

American academic system by the time the younger French composer arrived in California. Their compositions are also very different. Where Grisey used acoustics in justification of sustained, wavelike, ecstatic sounds, Felciano favored more disparate, disjunct structures. Nevertheless, in a "polarized" music department, these two found themselves on the same team.[10] Edward Jacobs, who studied composition with Grisey in 1984, said, "Felciano was probably the only one who would have had a real appreciation for what Grisey was doing."[11]

It's no surprise that Grisey and his veteran academic American colleagues struggled to connect. They came from vastly different worlds. They had different backgrounds, different aesthetics, different kinds of careers, different ideas about what it meant to teach composition. A typical example of this cultural and musical gulf was Schenkerian analysis, a musicological technique invented by Heinrich Schenker, an eminent German-Jewish music theorist. Considered gospel in the context of American academia, Schenker is not taught at all in Europe.[12] In 1985, Grisey remarked, "I'm reading about Schenker's analysis, unknown in France, since everybody in the U.S. seems to swear by Schenker's holy name!"[13] Grisey's casual irreverence toward American academic sacred cows could not have helped him fit in.

These differences were apparent even to the students. Ziporyn recalled:

> By the time I got there, he did not have much to do with the rest of the faculty, and they did not have much to do with him. There was a real tension between him and the composition faculty there ... [In this period] there were really the modernist culture wars going on in academia. It sounds absurd now, but they were really vicious.[14]

The inevitable tensions of this arrangement were exacerbated by the fact that Grisey was broadly skeptical of American classical music. "I just don't imagine there were a lot of people who he felt were on the same wavelength as him," a student, the composer Ellen Fishman-Johnson, said.[15] "He really detested that American style of composition." Jacobs noted that Grisey was "the odd man out in the American system."[16]

More prosaically, the bureaucratic duties of an American professor took Grisey by surprise. He had understood his responsibilities as being set at

---

10   Interview with Fishman-Johnson.
11   Felciano is ill and couldn't speak with me at the time of this writing.
12   At least until recently. For a summary of the contemporary debate on Schenker, see Brown and Giovetti, "Music, In Theory."
13   Paul Sacher archive.
14   Interview with Ziporyn.
15   Interview with Fishman-Johnson.
16   Interview with Jacobs.

seven hours per week. That was theoretically true. But Grisey was also expected to attend faculty meetings, commitments which often doubled the length of his working week. "He was very disappointed, because he had to go to the university basically every day, an hour here, three hours there," Jocelyne said. "It was not in his contract, but he had to do it anyway."[17] For the composer Joshua Fineberg, there was a lack of communication on both sides about what they expected from one another. Grisey

> took the Messiaen style: he would do a whole day with everybody. He tried to do that at Berkeley, which they hated. I really think it wasn't that he wasn't respecting the position. No one was ever clear with each other. They thought they were giving this guy with no doctorate a tenure-track junior professorship. He thought they were hiring a senior composer. The idea that you could go every week, two or three days a week, to meet with students who hadn't done any work half the time, it just made no sense to him.[18]

Once again, Grisey would have to jealously guard his time and silence to compose.

❦ ❦ ❦

South Korean composer Hi Kyung Kim remembered that Grisey's English was limited at first. But Grisey's analysis class was useful, featuring insightful introductions to composers such as Debussy, Messiaen, and Boulez. The lessons would last for about three hours, with a break for coffee at Espresso Roma.[19]

The music of Edgard Varèse was a particular area of interest for Grisey at this time. He and his students analyzed the orchestral piece *Arcana*, focusing on the first five pages, where a tightly coiled melody in the low strings and bassoons gives way to a dissonant chord, built from the bottom, that in its shape—if not its individual pitches—resembles the harmonic spectrum. There is a marked similarity between this music and the first section of *Partiels*. In his teaching, Grisey had begun highlighting historical models for spectral music.

The seminar formed the core of Grisey's teaching activities at the university, the model being Messiaen's classes. Fishman-Johnson was struck by Grisey's musical catholicism. While her previous studies had focused on serialist techniques, Grisey discussed everything from pygmy and gamelan music to the latest compositions by Murail, Xenakis, Scelsi, and others. Grisey

---

17   Interview with Jocelyne Grisey.
18   Interview with Fineberg.
19   Interview with Kim.

"would say that ... there are ways that you can get from point A to point B in an organized manner," Fishman-Johnson said. "He always got to the core of everything he was talking about, in terms of being able to think more broadly about music, not just pigeon-holing yourself into something."[20]

As Fineberg implies, Grisey had high expectations of his students. Several students in his class said that he kicked out a female composer from his seminar because he thought she wasn't at a high enough level musically. According to Kim, he "tossed her to the [other] faculty," an action which did not endear him to his colleagues. (Grisey was supposed to be as responsible for beginning undergraduates as he was for the more advanced graduate students.) As Fishman-Johnson noted, this decision may have involved an element of misogyny: "That happened to women a lot during those times."[21] It was part of the larger culture clash that began with his aesthetic and permeated all aspects of his approach to the job. Edmund Campion, who studied with Grisey at this time, said:

> The cultural contrast between France and Berkeley was just too great. He was a very strong-willed person. He basically insisted on living as if he was still in Paris, and it just didn't work. Particularly with regard to how Berkeley is so sensitive to diversity and interaction with students. He was an artist; he would just interact with everyone in his full persona. And this didn't quite translate to the professorship at Berkeley. He ran into conflicts of expectations.[22]

These issues carried over into Grisey's time management. "He was happy to have interesting students, but it was his first time teaching and he had to prepare, and he was disappointed that he didn't have more time to write music," Jocelyne said. "It was very difficult ... He became depressed. He wanted to teach his seven hours, and then write and live."[23]

Accordingly, Grisey appeared uninterested in giving private lessons, the one-on-one interactions that form the basis of so much American composition teaching. Ziporyn remembers having a grand total of two private lessons with Grisey; they lasted just ten minutes each. Jacobs recalls the anxiety (and occasional triumph) of being plucked out of Grisey's potluck dinners to examine his latest music at the piano with the composer:

> We all met over at his house for three-plus hours. He took us one by one over to his piano, and looked at whatever we were working on. If somebody did something interesting, then he would call everybody over to look

---

20   Interview with Fishman-Johnson.
21   Ibid.
22   Interview with Campion.
23   Interview with Jocelyne Grisey.

at it. In all honesty, I only remember one moment when he called everybody over to look at something … Probably the reason I remember it is because it happened to have been one of my ideas. I have no idea what he found interesting about it. He didn't really articulate what he found interesting. Everybody looked at me because after a few months, it was like the only compliment that had emerged. He was short on compliments. He did like some of the food some of the people made. There were some good freewheeling conversations, lots of wine, and so on.

It became pretty clear after the first week that wine was perfectly fine. In fact, it was probably a really good idea, especially if you had to wait two and a half hours until he got to your music. It was better to be a little toasted.[24]

Jacobs found that it wasn't until he told Grisey about his background in jazz that the teacher began showing him some deference. "Jazz players are the best musicians in the world," Grisey told him.

Grisey having students over to his house may have had a method behind it. Fishman-Johnson was struck by the variety of literature on display. She noticed that he always had a coffee-table book on architecture open. This was not for show; every time she visited, the book was opened to a different page. These visits also included peeks behind the scenes of Grisey's compositional process. Fishman-Johnson said:

> I remember going into his studio once. It was a big room, full of light. The way he composed, he had a large piece of paper [where] he was figuring out everything, large manuscript paper. And you could see there were also very large charts about how everything was working spectrally. I remember commenting, "You could compose like this for a lifetime, and you'd never run out of material." And he said, "Yup."[25]

Ziporyn, already an advanced musician with a personal aesthetic, was grateful that Grisey introduced him to new types of music without trying to over-structure his development. Though Grisey had weaknesses as a teacher, he grasped something slippery and essential about his job in his first years practicing it: teaching composition was about, Campion said, "giving [students] permission to do their project."[26]

Despite Grisey's apparent lack of interest in private lessons, many of his students remember one or two remarks he made to them which came to have a remarkable influence on their later work. These remarks were often brief, even mysterious, in the guru mode of Dutilleux and Messiaen. For

---

24 Interview with Jacobs.
25 Interview with Fishman-Johnson.
26 Interview with Campion.

Kim, the influential comment Grisey made was that she should "try to get rid of melody." For Fishman-Johnson, it was when he told her, "You're too old to be so conservative." Grisey once said to Ziporyn that "there are things that are interesting in your music, but they are not the things that you think are interesting in your music." For Ziporyn, these gnomic pronouncements "gave me quite a lot to chew on. That's more than I've gotten from some composition teachers who were going over every note!" Maybe it was the very vagueness of these lessons which allowed Grisey's students to apply them as they saw fit, like the customers of a fortune teller.

Besides his complicated presence as a teacher, Grisey's music itself was an essential model to his students—not as something to imitate, but for its consummate sense of completeness. "I go back to his work just to get grounded," Fishman-Johnson said. "Even though he would say sometimes, 'No one cares about your emotions, so don't over-emote,' I think his pieces always get to a wonderful place of emotion. There's a place, usually at the golden section, where things come together." At these moments, she added, "the world starts to make sense."[27]

When he began his duties as an assistant professor at Berkeley, Grisey was thirty-six years old. He was closer in age to his graduate students than to the other professors and looked to these students for companionship. Ziporyn and Michael Tenzer, a composer who joined the class in the winter of 1983, both socialized with Grisey outside the framework of the university. Grisey seemed lonely, and they were flattered and a little bemused that he was willing to spend time with them. Ziporyn recalled:

> I liked the guy. I liked hanging out with him ... I felt sorry for him, because he was isolated. He clearly wanted to be in Paris. He clearly felt like he had ended up almost on this desert island or something. He wasn't really connected to what was going on in the Bay Area. He [must have] needed friends, because he was very happy to hang out with us. We were graduate students who were ten years younger than him.[28]

In this period, there was a certain sadness to Grisey. "I found there was a vulnerable side to him which I really liked," Tenzer said.[29]

But Grisey's insouciance with women was also obvious to his composition students at Berkeley. "Being a woman composer, there was certainly enough talk that I knew not to get too close," Fishman-Johnson said. "Truthfully,

---

27 Interview with Fishman-Johnson.
28 Interview with Ziporyn.
29 Interview with Tenzer.

he never was inappropriate to me … I saw him as the master. I didn't want to go further in terms of trying to be friendly."[30]

Ziporyn was aware of this dynamic, too. "I do remember some of my female peers feeling like … he would have had trouble today," he said. "He would definitely [walk past] female graduate students and look behind his head. He was a flirt. But that was an era, nobody found it outrageously objectionable as they might now. They were amused by it."[31]

❦ ❦ ❦

Grisey had met the Canadian maverick composer Claude Vivier at Darmstadt in 1972. They stayed in touch, meeting in Montreal in 1978, when *Partiels* was performed there. In 1982, after a period of intense study with Stockhausen, Vivier moved to Paris.

On March 7, 1983, Vivier was in the process of composing a powerful and enigmatic new work titled *Glaubst du an die Unsterblichkeit der Seele* (*Do You Believe in the Immortality of the Soul*). As with Grisey, frequent sexual encounters were a necessary balance to the process of musical composition for Vivier, and that evening, he went to a bar in the city. He picked up a young man named Pascal Dolzan for sex. They went back to Vivier's apartment. Had Dolzan taken the time to look around, he could have read the following words on the final pages of Vivier's score:

> I couldn't tear my eyes off the young man it seemed as if he had been sitting across from me for all eternity and it was then that he addressed me, he said: "quite boring this metro, huh!" I didn't know how I should respond and said, somewhat disoriented at having my gaze returned "yes, quite" then perfectly naturally the young man came to sit down next to me and said: "my name is Harry." I answered him that my name was Claude and then without further introductions he took out of his dark black vest that he probably bought in Paris a knife and stabbed me right in the heart.[32]

In Vivier's apartment, Dolzan stabbed the composer to death. Vivier, who was thirty-four years old, lay in his apartment for three days before he was discovered. Dolzan was later arrested for the murder of Vivier and two other gay men who had also picked him up for sex. It was as if Vivier had predicted the circumstances of his own murder.[33]

---

30   Interview with Fishman-Johnson.
31   Interview with Ziporyn.
32   Claude Vivier, *Glaubst du an die Unsterblichkeit der Seele*.
33   Gilmore, *Claude Vivier*. Gilmore argues persuasively that the murder was no more than an eerie coincidence.

Little is known about Grisey's immediate emotional reaction to the tragedy. Instead, we have his composition *Anubis et Nout* for solo contrabass clarinet, which Grisey dedicated to "the memory of my friend Claude Vivier, murdered in March 1983." It was an unusual choice for him to name the cause of Vivier's death directly on the score, a choice that seems like a protest at the unjust workings of fate.

Grisey composed *Anubis et Nout* between July and August 1983. It was commissioned by the Dutch clarinetist Harry Sparnaay and the Festival Pontino di Musica and was his first completed solo piece for a wind instrument since *Charme* for B♭ clarinet from 1969. There are worlds between the early work and the mature one, both in the simplicity of the conception and the refinement of the execution of *Anubis et Nout*.

The piece returns to the Egyptian theme of *Sortie vers la lumière du jour* and *Jour, contre-jour*; this time, the inspiration is not a text, but the Egyptian pantheon itself. The god Anubis is a god of the dead and the inventor of mummification in the Egyptian creation myth, represented in Egyptian art by the head of a jackal. Nut (Nout in French) is the goddess of the sky, drawn often in the sensual form of a naked woman embracing the entire earth with her body. As Grisey wrote in his program note, Nut is "the celestial vault, the Egyptian night and the mother of the sun. She is sometimes depicted inside sarcophagi, where she covers and protects mummified bodies."[34] The dualistic conception of Grisey's *Anubis et Nout* follows the death myth of Egyptian religion, where souls are judged during the night before coming forth by day to a form of heaven that is exceedingly close to life on earth. Egyptian burial items were frequently inscribed with instructions or prayers for this passage, and in this work, it was as if Grisey were composing a similar guide for his murdered friend.

Though Sparnaay was the dedicatee of *Anubis et Nout*, Grisey did most of his initial sonic research with Jean-Noël Crocq, a French clarinetist who was a member of the Ensemble L'Itinéraire. Crocq told the saxophonist Rhonda Janette Taylor that he met Grisey in Paris to try out ideas—probably during one of Grisey's vacations from Berkeley.[35] Grisey brought "the idea of indexing the changes of timbres and of pitches obtained by the addition of fingers in the low part" of the instrument. They also explored the tendency of the bass clarinet's harmonic spectrum to skip the second overtone, the octave; its formant sound is based strongly on the fundamental and the third overtone, the fifth. Grisey took careful notes on the resulting effects.[36]

---

34 Lelong, *Écrits*, 160.
35 Taylor, "Gérard Grisey's Anubis et Nout," 98.
36 Ibid, 99.

The first movement of the work, *Anubis*, uses the undertone or subharmonic series, an inversion of the intervals of the harmonic series. Compared to the very real implications of the harmonic series on instrumental performance, the subharmonic series is largely a theoretical grouping of pitches, an idea that fits neatly with the movement's thematic focus on the god of death. Below the spectrum—below the earth—lies the imperfectly understood.

Taylor describes *Anubis* as having four sections with two main types of material. The first section consists of arching melodic lines, or "pitch pendulums," based on intertwined subharmonic and harmonic series, whose fundamental tones also rise chromatically. At the same time, Grisey "is also playing an additive/subtractive game with duration," Taylor explains.[37] This rhythmic technique uses the whole-number proportions of the harmonic series, returning to a simpler structural method than some of the complex plans Grisey used in *Modulations* and *Transitoires*.

The second and longest section of *Anubis* begins in the mysterious depths of a low, growling E♭. We hear Grisey's work with Crocq in the alternate fingerings that shift the timbre and pitch of this E♭; a series of rhythmic motives are introduced on top of the drone, a polyphonic effect that recalls a soul trying and failing to escape the underworld. As Taylor observes, Grisey introduces a cantus firmus in the low voice that continues into the next section, a modified recapitulation identifiable by its ascending-descending melody.

The final section of *Anubis* consists of a series of descending pitches, repeated rhythmically, which sound like slow, echoing footsteps. This music is embedded in a process of deceleration, creating "the perception of musical time slowing down," Taylor writes.[38] As in works from *Les espaces acoustiques*, the dynamics expand and then contract in range. The movement ends with a short, slap-tongued *pianississimo* D♭.

Nout is about half the length of *Anubis*, its texture clear and crystalline. In this piece, the composer explores multiphonics on the fundamental and third overtone; in a good performance, the bass clarinet can be heard playing two notes at once, rendering its formants plainly audible. *Nout* is still, even static, highly limited in pitch material; it conjures the image of an empty blue sky. But just as *Anubis* rises, *Nout* descends. Grisey undermines his Egyptian duality. Each movement has one predominant character, but both contain harmonic and subharmonic spectra. Life and death are inseparable.

Compared with Grisey's *Charme*, *Anubis et Nout* is the work of an artist whose aesthetic has matured into an unmistakable personal voice. (Because the instrumentation of the two pieces is so similar, they are easier to compare than *Prologue* and *Anubis et Nout*.) *Charme* was an effective, well

---

37   Ibid, 54.
38   Ibid, 80.

thought-through piece that nonetheless has an almost anonymous quality: the listener would be hard-pressed to identify Grisey from the music alone. *Anubis et Nout* doesn't include the explicit spectral statements of a work like *Partiels*. But in its directness of expression, structural sophistication, and bold simplicity, *Anubis et Nout* is identifiable as a mature Grisey composition. In contemporary music, solo pieces frequently pose a challenge, eliminating as they do the possibility of complex textures. In the fourteen years since his last solo piece, Grisey learned to complete this fraught task in a way that expressed his deepest artistic convictions.

On June 16, 1984, Sparnaay gave the world premiere performance of *Anubis et Nout* at the Festival Pontino di Musica. Sparnaay told Taylor that the audience reception to the work was positive. Raffaele Pozzi, an Italian critic, gave the piece a warm review in the *Nuova Rivista Musicale Italiana*, later writing in his liner notes for an early recording of *Anubis et Nout* that the piece "confirms [Grisey's] status as one of the most original and rigorous figures on the French musical scene today."[39]

In 1989 or 1990, Grisey approached Claude Delangle, the French saxophonist who performed with Ensemble Intercontemporain and taught at the Conservatoire de Paris, about adapting *Anubis et Nout* for low saxophones, eventually settling on bass saxophone in B♭ or baritone saxophone in E♭. Delangle told Taylor that Grisey liked the saxophone because the composer "was not bothered by the popular origins of the instrument; he had himself begun music by studying the accordion and didn't have a 'complex' that way."[40] The two men worked out the details of the transcription together, adjusting the range, adding sung pitches in the first movement, and tweaking the overtones in the second. Both versions of *Anubis et Nout* are effective, the original contrabass-clarinet version mysterious and cosmic, the saxophone arrangement visceral and gritty. The saxophone version premiered on May 22, 1991, at the Castello di Rivoli outside Turin. "The public was very receptive and was very impressed by this work," Delangle told Taylor. Today, the saxophone version of *Anubis et Nout* is performed more commonly than its contrabass-clarinet counterpart. Taylor writes that the piece is "on par with the most sophisticated and engaging modern solo saxophone repertoire."[41]

Despite Jocelyne's reluctance, the move to Berkeley agreed with her. She found herself with more time to herself than she was used to, since now she

---

39 Ibid, 28.
40 Ibid, 32.
41 Ibid, 95.

didn't need to work to support the family. She joined a cooking club and a book club and practiced her English. Raphaël, now a toddler, attended a Franco-American bilingual kindergarten.[42] But Grisey was starting to feel that his relationship with Jocelyne was in crisis for reasons that are not entirely clear. In November 1982, he wrote in his diary, "Against all evidence and strange as it may be, I love Jocelyne; I can't get enough of her soul. Is it not to escape this obsession that I do it so often?"[43] (By "do it so often," he clearly meant sleeping with other women.) He threw himself into a passionate affair with a Jewish-American woman from a wealthy background named Jane.[44]

By May 1983, toward the end of Grisey's first academic year as a professor, his doubts about their relationship became apparent to Jocelyne. At first, she "didn't understand how depressed Gérard was becoming," Jocelyne said. One day, Grisey went to San Diego for a music festival with a pretty female student. He called Jocelyne from there and said that he wanted a separation.

Grisey told Jocelyne he imagined living on his own, with his wife and child in a separate apartment in Berkeley. But they couldn't afford both, alongside Raphaël's school fees. Jocelyne considered applying for a green card and getting a job as a psychologist, but there were bureaucratic and linguistic obstacles. Since Jocelyne had moved to California to be with Grisey, and now he wasn't speaking with her or with Raphaël, she made a decision. "I had to do *something*," Jocelyne recalled. "I decided to go back to France, at least for a while. I hoped that Gérard would change his mind. But he didn't. And so, I came back to France with Raphaël." She was able to find a job in her field of social work in Paris, and she and Raphaël stayed there.

The problem wasn't exactly that Jocelyne was jealous. By the time they had arrived in California, she had become reconciled to Grisey's need to have additional lovers. She said:

> He had girlfriends, mistresses. That wasn't always easy for me. It was obvious. He told me, "You are my port of call. Even if I need to have other women, I need you too." That helped me. I helped him to write his music, I took care of his everyday life. I was convinced that he was a good musician, and so I thought, "Of course, another woman could do what I do, but I am here."[45]

---

42 Interview with Jocelyne and Raphaël Grisey.
43 Paul Sacher archive.
44 Some, but not all, of Grisey's students remember that she was a graduate student. No one could remember her last name, so I couldn't track her down for an interview.
45 Interview with Jocelyne Grisey.

But, as mentioned, she was discouraged by Grisey's need to *speak* of his lovers with her: to bring these women into their "life as a couple." In June 1983, after the end of the semester, Grisey and Jocelyne met in Paris. "I thought we were finally going to talk about us," she said, "but he just went on and on about his new girlfriend." She realized that they were not going to get back together.[46]

A handwritten fragment from Grisey's archive sheds some light on his thought process at this moment of great personal upheaval. It illustrates the depth of his love for Jocelyne, but also betrays a patriarchal—even, in places, condescending—view of her role in their family. Grisey admired Jocelyne's qualities as a mother, her spirituality, and her "deep love and understanding of music," but seemed to find her overly serious and overbearing at times.[47] The things he hoped to find in a partner had hardly changed since his teenage years: the utmost admiration for his musical creations; a common sense of purpose in spirituality; and the sensuality that could ground those abstract currents of the mind in the physical world.

In another fragment from his papers, undated but likely from around this time, Grisey drew a diagram containing the qualities of what appears to be an ideal woman. They included: "art and sensitivity"; "discriminating insight"; "discriminating awareness"; "intellect/culture"; "desire"; then, connected with arrows, "passion/sensual/compassion/spiritual." In another undated fragment, Grisey drew himself a diagram of a sort of ideal music. To achieve equilibrium, it needed "intelligence/calculation; spirituality, soul, and tenderness; beauty, and sensuality."[48] For Grisey, a perfect woman and a perfect composition were—however unattainable in reality—almost the same thing.

Both these fragments reflect Grisey's unshaken idealism toward relationships. In the meantime, the suffering caused by his breakup with Jocelyne was real. The pain that permeated Grisey and Jocelyne's separation made it difficult for the two to co-parent their son, at least at first. Raphaël told Jocelyne, "I want to kill my father, I want to kill you, and I want to kill myself."[49]

In this period, Grisey's twice-yearly visits to France were causes of great stress. He was busy composing and promoting his career and did not always

---

46 Ibid.
47 Paul Sacher archive. There's also an earlier "draft" of this note which is significantly more generous. Grisey might have been trying to convince himself that he made the right decision by leaving Jocelyne.
48 Ibid.
49 Interview with Raphaël and Jocelyne Grisey.

dedicate himself completely to his son. "When his father went back to America, Raphaël was not well," Jocelyne said. "It took a few weeks [after] for him to get better."[50] Grisey had a rather traditional, hands-off understanding of fatherhood, a quality that did not serve him well during this time of crisis.

Grisey loved his son deeply. While they were living on different continents, he would record heartfelt messages to Raphaël on cassette tapes and send them by mail. His son would be able to sit and listen to his father's voice, without the expense and pressure to make conversation of long-distance phone calls. Over time, they were able to repair their relationship.[51]

At first, Grisey didn't want to file for divorce with Jocelyne. He threw himself into his liaison with Jane, but turned to Jocelyne in the frequent moments when he felt overwhelmed by the intensity of the affair or beaten down by hurt and loneliness. Jocelyne encouraged Grisey to seek psychological treatment. She recalled:

> He continued to be depressed. He phoned me often, and I was very uneasy, because I had the sense that he was close to suicidal. He called at night. He was lost. I was in touch with a psychologist ... One morning, Grisey phoned me, it was about six in the morning in California. I asked him if he had already had breakfast. He said no. I told Gérard, "Have breakfast, and then, at eight, you can call this psychologist." And he did it. After he was better. He went in for treatment. Later I called the psychologist, who told me he had been having a delirious episode.[52]

Grisey's mental anguish came with a painful bodily sensation. During the episode, Jocelyne said Grisey "thought that his spine was splitting." It was as if, having broken up his family, the composer felt that his physical being was being torn apart. The psychologist recommended that Grisey stay in a closed institution for a time. He refused but did accept a Valium prescription. "Nothing was good, he was indifferent to everything," Jocelyne said.[53]

In late February 1984, Grisey returned to Berkeley from a stay in Paris. In a letter to a group of friends that included Zinsstag, Grisey described the painful consequences of his breakup with Jocelyne. To make matters worse, Jane had suddenly left him. The letter is mainly a cry for help. It also shows Grisey's primal association between music and his sensuality:

> You know I was having a difficult but passionate relationship with an American woman—more or less the cause of my separation from Jocelyne.

---

50 Interview with Jocelyne Grisey.
51 Interview with Raphaël and Jocelyne Grisey.
52 Interview with Jocelyne Grisey.
53 Ibid.

Several times [Jane and I] found ourselves on the verge of breaking up. During my stay in Paris, I took the time to write a very long letter in which I tried to analyze, to understand, to air and to open new perspectives.

In response, and only three days before my departure, I received a love letter [from Jane] so tender and moving that I arrived in Berkeley exhausted but with my arms open ... my tenderness offered and my suitcases full of gifts.

My friend came to see me that evening. She stayed for five minutes to tell me with a slight smile that everything was over. After a few sentences of barely imaginable sadism she left and I never saw her again. My few subsequent attempts to contact her were haunted by [her] sadism.

Then, I collapsed more and more every day, until the limits of madness, where words are not enough ... I am literally haunted by this gesture, by this psychological murder, this bullet shot between the two eyes, much more than the separation that could have happened in a thousand other ways even if it was inevitable. My emotional, moral and cultural solitude is impossible to describe.

It remains for me ... to understand why this wound was waiting for me in the shadows. Why this dagger in the back? Why did I rush to this woman so devoid of the most elementary compassion? Why did I desire this rock to smash myself into it?

The worst part is this: I miss Raphaël, and music betrays me. I am unable to compose any sound.

But, friends, if another man is not born from this rubble, I will be a poor, fragile, romantic fool lost in the twentieth century in a country where only strength and consumerism count!

Life and death are fighting in me ... for how much longer?

And then, as Debussy said, "One does not forget so easily the caresses of a body!"[54]

In this last line, Grisey made a link between himself and Debussy, one of history's most sensual composers. As the musicologist Julie McQuinn writes, "In the case of Debussy, every possible relationship seems to have carried with it an erotic tinge, and thus a web of relationships filled with erotic possibilities, all orbiting around a music that defied convention."[55]

In late August 1984, France Detry, a strikingly beautiful, dark-haired, French-speaking Belgian woman went on vacation to Club Med in Tunisia

---

54   Paul Sacher archive.
55   McQuinn, "Exploring the erotic in Debussy's music," 119.

with her two sons.[56] A painter by vocation, Detry was working a dead-end job at an American fertilizer company in Brussels; the firm was so sedate she suspected it of being a CIA front operation. She'd recently divorced her husband, who'd cut her off from his significant wealth. The vacation was a last-minute affair organized by Detry's mother. Club Med specialized in all-inclusive holidays, and the resorts were not the kinds of places a sophisticated person like Detry would normally have ended up.

On her second or third day at Club Med, Detry saw a man standing about fifty feet away, looking lost. He was wearing a beige jacket and white pants, and he was reading a brick of a book.

"What are you reading?" Detry asked Grisey. The answer: Robert Musil's 2,000-page, densely philosophical satire of life during the twilight of the Austrian empire, *The Man Without Qualities*. (Grisey hadn't gotten any better at relaxing on vacation.)

The two began to talk. Grisey was on a last-minute vacation too, with Raphaël. Detry didn't find him handsome, exactly: he seemed worn out. Raphaël was in a state as well, having come down with meningitis; adding insult to infection, he was being eaten alive by the local mosquitoes. But Detry and Grisey clicked immediately and became inseparable.

For Detry, the conversation that remains most memorable concerned the sounds of the children playing in the evenings. "Listen to this sound of the children shouting," Grisey told her. She said, "It really opened my ears to listen like that … going into the sound and perceiving all the grains of the sound. It was what he was doing all the time in his head."[57]

Grisey returned to Europe a few weeks before Detry. But Detry's flight back to Brussels was routed through Paris. It arrived late at night, and the connection was the next day. She didn't have a place to stay with her two sons or enough money to book a hotel. She called Grisey and asked him if he could put them up for a night. When Detry arrived with her sons, Grisey was at the airport waiting for her. He booked one room for Detry and himself and one for the children. "For me it was the most romantic place," Detry said. "The rooms were very small, but there were beautiful Russian paintings on the walls. I had the feeling of a kind of crystal joy." Grisey returned to Berkeley, and Detry went back to her home in Brussels. They began writing each other letters and seeing each other whenever possible. When Grisey came to Paris to visit Raphaël, the two would meet.[58]

When apart, the composer and Detry exchanged letters that spoke to the depth of their brief yet extraordinarily intense connection. Though Grisey

---

56   Probably, but Detry isn't sure of the exact year.
57   Interview with Detry.
58   Ibid.

had a new girlfriend in Berkeley at the same time, it was clear to Detry that she was the main object of the composer's passion.

In Berkeley, Grisey longed both for more time for composition and reflection, and for deeper and more meaningful human contact. His administrative duties at the university ate into his time for thinking, but his interactions with fellow faculty and the students didn't give him the kind of social intimacy he craved. "Right now, I feel surrounded," he wrote in one letter. "So many people love this kind of active life because it fills in all the gaps, it obstructs the moments of silence where one risks discovering the reality of things. For me, these moments in which I perceive my deepest rhythms, these hours devoted to musical creation, are so unavailable to me, and I feel like I will literally collapse if I don't get them."[59]

At the same time, the people who were most important to Grisey felt hopelessly far away. The artist had discovered a common truth: love and friendship make a place home; a place, no matter how wonderful, cannot be a home without those things. He wrote Detry, "I'm sending you lots of love, lots of this creative energy which devours me, a thousand kisses along your back and thighs, a thousand shivers near your earlobes, a million little hairs that stand up on your arms and a long and interminable kiss across the 12,000,000,000 centimeters from here to Brussels."

This longing for his loved ones could tip into an isolation of worrying intensity, of the kind that had made Jocelyne encourage Grisey to visit a psychoanalyst. In one letter, he told Detry he went out for a cappuccino simply to be around other people. He was unable to escape his thoughts:

> What a strange solitude! I withdraw, I'm afraid of everything; slightly misanthropic ... Alone.
>
> Here, I'm just an anonymous composer, crushed by the American system and its violence. I'm without family, without love, and almost without friends. I protect myself in this beautiful house where I ordered some flowers this morning and where your picture smiles at me from the dresser ... .
>
> I'm becoming hard on the outside and fragile on the inside, my penis is getting old, my desire for the wound of death [growing]. More years like this? No, better to die immediately. Fear.
>
> What I am afraid of is that I no longer dare to live.

Grisey told Detry he envied the moorings of her life: her children, her work, her mother, her friends, her meditation, and her painting.

The one constant during this period of isolation and soul-searching was Grisey's compositional work. His letters to Detry encompass references to *Les chants de l'amour*, *Épilogue*, and *Le noir de l'étoile*. The first piece is most present in the letters.

---

59 Letters in the private archives of France Detry.

Grisey began making the first formal sketches for *Les chants de l'amour* in the summer of 1981, collaborating with the researchers Xavier Rodet and Yves Potard at IRCAM, who developed a computer program called Chant to aid the composer in his process.[60] The impetus for the piece was baldly romantic: Grisey's passionate and unhappy affair with Jane. But by the time he met Detry, that inspiration had been sublimated into explorations of a new world of sonic possibilities. On October 22, 1984, he wrote to her:

> I'm still working like crazy, completely in love with this piece. Everything is in my head: I have to realize it. I have to face this rebellious and elusive matter: the sound. The copying exhausts me. It is good for me to think that I sacrifice everything to it. It is the best of me. Sometimes it is almost impossible for me to imagine the combinations of these sounds, so unheard of, produced by IRCAM's computers ... How to apprehend the inaudible? Yet I feel a confidence and serenity that increases my energy tenfold. This piece, so ambitious, so unattainable, so difficult, so crazy, but no less important for it. Impossible, insupportable, but what a thing!
>
> As you see, I don't think about anything else, I don't talk about anything else. The world does not matter: a child is being born. If everything goes well, maybe by the end of January. I have been carrying it inside me since the summer of 1981. I'm so heavy I could burst!

Even for Grisey, for whom each composition represented an unprecedented expenditure of energy, *Les chants de l'amour* required a supreme effort. In another letter, he wrote to Detry, "I work, I work, I work, always overwhelmed by this interminable composition. How long this music is! ... Every sound causes me so much pain that I'm often close to giving up." In the same letter, he compared the process of composing *Les chants de l'amour* with *Dérives*, another work that emerged from crisis and which bore "the seeds of a future music." Like *Dérives*, too, this work would have greater importance in Grisey's mind than in its critical reception—maybe a necessary result of treading on such unfamiliar terrain.

Despite the difficulty of the compositional process, the act of musical creation provided Grisey with great solace during this difficult time. Grisey told Detry that music "is the only justification for my existence, if there is any, and I believe more and more that my music will remain long after me, as if my soul were made up of sounds." In another letter, he described listening to the strange, plaintive Kyrie at the beginning of Beethoven's *Missa solemnis*

---

60 Lelong, *Écrits*, 156.

and bursting into tears. "Music is not my *thing*, my hobby," he wrote. "It is the meeting of delirium and the forms of drama and number."[61]

🍂 🍂 🍂

Les chants de l'amour occupies a peculiar place in Grisey's mature oeuvre. His first finished piece to work with the voice since the student composition *Initiation*, as well as his most in-depth electronic project to date, the piece shows the composer on unfamiliar terrain and unable to fall back on his skill with instrumental orchestration. And though many contemporaries consider *Les chants de l'amour* to be the greatest failure of his post-*Périodes* career, the composer himself considered it a turning point in his aesthetic development.

Maybe that's why Grisey wrote a program note for *Les chants de l'amour* that surpasses the usual purview of these texts, going into unusual analytic detail. Ironically, considering that the direct source for the piece was his obsessive, unhappy affair with Jane and the following relationship with France Detry, Grisey's text tried to skirt the topic of subjective inspiration:

> In a recent interview I was asked the question: "Why love songs?" I did not know how to answer, because if the love song, like the love poem, is a difficult genre, it is even more difficult to talk about. Besides: is it a genre? Are there still some common points between the excess of twelve human voices confronted with the synthetic voice of the computer, and the *Liebeslied* of a Schubert or a Schumann? Although neo-romanticism is fashionable, I will avoid exegesis and subjective, spicy anecdotes, and speak only about the formal concept of this piece.[62]

But Grisey couldn't quite help himself. He continued, "First and foremost, Music has at least this in common with Love: through it, the human being discovers and understands Time." This insight recalls the previously mentioned passage on rhythm in Nabokov's *Ada or Ardor*, which Grisey cited in his 1980 Darmstadt lecture. But Grisey went further: he recognized that music and love make time tangible. The supple periodic rhythms of certain music and of sex remind us of our own, omnipresent biological rhythms. Musical transformation gives the passage of time shape, as do the changes in a lover's body as the years go by. In a video documentary about the work produced at IRCAM, Grisey said, "Love in the piece is the relationships—all the possible forms of relationships, from best to worst. All these exist within the choir, that is, between the human voices themselves."[63] *Les chants de*

---

61 Letters in the private archive of Detry.
62 Lelong, *Écrits*, 155.
63 Quoted in "Les chants de l'amour de Gérard Grisey," Bruno Bossis, *Le Temps de l'Écoute*, 232.

l'amour is the composition in which the intertwinement between sexuality and music becomes most apparent in Grisey's entire output.

The array of musical and literary influences and techniques used in this work is wide, contributing at times to a lack of focus, which is one of its weaknesses. As sonic inspirations, Grisey cites his beloved medieval composers Johannes Ockeghem and Guillaume Dufay; the Ituri forest pygmies, whose gorgeously overlapping, textural songs are in fact clearly audible in the *Chants*; and the Dagar Brothers, singers of Indian dhrupad, an ancient vocal genre, whom Grisey got to know during his scholarship in Berlin.[64] His literary sources were also wide, and a bit new-age. The work opens with a dedication to "all the lovers of the world" in ten languages, adding the names of famous lovers; "litanies on the word 'love'" in French, English, German, and Hungarian; and three extracts from Julio Cortázar's avant-garde choose-your-own-adventure novel *Rayuela*, whispered in the original Spanish. Certain non-verbal sounds, Grisey writes, were chosen "mainly for their erotic character." The names of famous lovers, the mix of languages, and the non-verbal sounds are all prominent in Claude Vivier's 1977 work *Love Songs* for four female voices and three male voices. The two pieces also share textures based on the harmonic spectrum, an element which relates both works back to Stockhausen's *Stimmung*. In other ways the two pieces are as different as their respective composers. Vivier's work has the childlike naïveté and unmistakable, strange melodic invention typical of the Canadian composer's oeuvre, while Grisey's piece shows his ear for ensemble sound and dramaturgy.

The text that determines the form and much of the sound of *Les chants de l'amour* is the simple phrase "I love you," an expression whose Hollywood banality became fraught with deeper associations of loss through Grisey's break with Jocelyne and his search for meaning in relationships. For *Les chants de l'amour*, Grisey made an analysis of the formants of the phrase, then used this sonic information to determine "the form, the durations and the frequencies" of the entire work.[65]

Les chants de l'amour is divided into five "movements" and twenty-eight sections, with seven harmonics of an imperceptible "hyperfundamental" forming the harmonic scaffolding of the piece. As Grisey notes in his program text, each section follows the kind of respiratory shape so essential to his mature music since the completion of *Périodes*. This time, the model is pegged more specifically to the phrase "I love you," where "I" represents the inhalation, "love" the constant flow of the sound, and "you" its exhalation. Each section follows this shape, more or less closely, and also consists

---

64   Presumably the younger Dagar Brothers.
65   Lelong, *Écrits*, 156.

of a central vowel, two principal formant frequencies, and two "principal durations."[66] The ebb and flow of the sections of *Les chants de l'amour* can largely be traced by ear.

Les chants de l'amour opens with the spoken "dedication" and soloistic rising overtone scales in the voices, rising up from the third bass to the first soprano. (These scales sound a little awkward.) As the musicologist William Mason explains, this section, based on a G hyperfundamental, consists of "plainly stated arpeggiations of the harmonic series [that have] the feeling of emergence and even of nascence."[67] The next seven sections that make up the first movement have an almost minimalist character, with overlapping, upward patterns that rise further up the spectrum as the material progresses; the Ituri forest pygmy music is clearly audible. The text is chosen purely for its sonic properties here: isolated vowels and consonants. Typically, Grisey plays with the durations of the three constitutive elements of each section, giving each wave a unique shape. In the fifth section, the composer introduces a "quasi yodel" in the third soprano, adding a sensual rubbing dissonance to the purity of the harmonies.

The second movement responds to the first with a certain symmetry. The interlocking vocal patterns move largely downward, and where the synthetic voice was held in the first movement, it now pulses. Vowels are replaced by consonants. Sinuous lines enter the texture, elaborations of the soprano's independent yodeling. In the first movement, unpitched sounds were confined to the introduction; here, they become integrated into the complex texture. A contralto motive is marked "erotic panting" (contradicting the composer Bruno Bossis's interpretation that *Les chants de l'amour* is about love that "seems closer to tenderness and childish naïveté than to the adult world").[68] Throughout the movement, Grisey continues to play with the shape of his tripartite waves, and in its final section, he dedicates long measures to the exhalation, formed purely out of noise. The movement closes with six seconds of immobility, then loud laughter, reaching the structural middle point of *Les chants de l'amour*.

After the silence that marks this middle point, the third movement begins. The texture is remarkably sparse. The text for this section consists of "litanies on the word love." They begin with melodic interpolations of the word on a plaintive downward major sixth, but thicken in texture throughout the movement, later including such compounds as the English "lovelorn" and the German "*Liebesdurst*" (the sheer variety of German compounds including the word *Liebe* makes this section funny). This movement also includes

---

66   Ibid, 156.
67   Mason, "Feeling Machines," 144.
68   Bossis, "Les chants de l'amour de Gérard Grisey," in *Le temps de l'écoute*, 267.

the evocations of famous historical lovers. Structurally, it contains maybe the most obvious intertwinement of the macrocosmic and the microcosmic in the piece: in six units, it follows the respiratory pattern which is the guiding principle of *Les chants de l'amour*; at the same time, both the choir and the synthetic voice inhale and exhale, swelling to miniature climaxes before ebbing away. The overall form is inscribed in each passing moment.

In the fourth, penultimate movement of the piece, the sparseness of the preceding section is washed away by the climax. Soft vowels are replaced by harsh, loud consonants and noisy synthetic sounds. The "exhalations" become barely perceptible: we hear mostly high points of tension, followed by rest, with little transition. Nonetheless, the exhalation has its place in the overall form of the movement, as the climax slowly gives way to scattered, accented consonants and a section of processed dialogue that sounds like it was ripped from an old-fashioned Hollywood romance. The fourth movement concludes with probably the most beautiful music of the entire *Les chants de l'amour*. After the electronics play sliding chords consisting of high harmonics, and the male voices exclaim "più forte!"—a musical and sexual joke—the choir enters in an undulating overtone lullaby. The soprano reprises her sinuous minor-second "yodeling" from the beginning of the work. This movement contains the piece's two extremes, its wildest aggression and most gentle solace.

In the first half of the brief coda, Grisey repeats residual material from the rest of *Les chants de l'amour*. The work closes with a "love duet," marked "like a very tender, very naive game." In this language, there are echoes of Grisey's earliest understanding of sexuality, when he described the innocence and "search for pleasure" of his and Jocelyne's carnal relationship as young adults. A contralto and a bass speak to one another, stretching out the central phrase "I love you." They stop speaking, and then the residual sounds in the tape part melt away.

Les chants de l'amour was premiered on June 3, 1985, in the Espace de projection at IRCAM. The performance was led by the German conductor and composer Clytus Gottwald, whose Schola Cantorum Stuttgart specialized in early repertoire and vocal polyphony.[69] Gérard Condé's review for *Le Monde* was largely positive. While he noted the similarities between the beginning of *Les chants de l'amour* and Stockhausen's *Stimmung*, Condé found the newer piece to gain in richness as it progressed:

> First, there is the immense fortissimo laughter that we did not expect, then the polyphonies of whistling synthetic voices, prolonged by the sensual counterpoints of the men singing in falsetto. If the sighs and gasps seem more conventional, the (ironic?) introduction of the snoring, by its

---

69 Gottwald's performance of Ligeti's *Lux aeterna* was the one used in the film *2001: A Space Odyssey*.

incongruity and its raw realism, adds to certain naive elements that we had noticed until then.

But these naive elements, which at first appear to be weaknesses, soon reveal their power, as it is rare to see an artist dare to come so close to the ridiculous in order to reach a higher degree of sincerity. So, when the work ends—it lasts forty minutes—one feels the need to hear it again to appreciate the beginning in the light of what follows.[70]

These "naive elements" make *Les chants de l'amour* occupy an uncomfortable place in Grisey's oeuvre. In a review of a 1993 performance of the piece in Zurich, Sibylle Ehrismann wrote that "the polyphonic weavings of the voices couldn't cut through the dominant synthetic voice, so that a certain sameness resulted."[71] For his former student Ellen Fishman-Johnson, it was his worst piece. Julian Anderson, an almost constant admirer, didn't like it, and the Romanian spectralist Horatiu Radulescu found it too "Hollywood."[72] Joshua Fineberg said, "I've always thought, for him, [*Les chants de l'amour*] was this big failure that he could never wrap his head around why he didn't get it right ... He never said that outright, that's something he would never say. But he clearly was never satisfied with it, or at least with how it was done."[73] Gérard Zinsstag thought the work had beautiful moments but was generally "abstruse."[74]

It seems as if, by 1985, the composer was known more for his sleek, polished pieces than for his playful, experimental flights: a reputation that persists, with good reason. But, if we remember Grisey's anecdote about the theatrical section of *Périodes* and Murail's dismissal of it, the tension between Grisey's musical mastery and his interest in the absurd was long present. As a piece, *Les chants de l'amour* has real issues: it's too long; its textual curation is haphazard; its form and dramaturgy are less inexorable than other works; its electronics part now sounds dated. But at least part of the reason the work sits so uncomfortably within Grisey's output is because it clashes with the general perception of who he was as a composer.

At some point in the mid-1980s, Grisey encountered D.H. Lawrence's 1929 novella *The Man Who Died* (originally titled *The Escaped Cock*).[75] He made sketches for a project based on the text, either an opera or a ballet. Though

---

70   Condé, "Gérard Grisey voix et ordinateur."
71   Quoted in Cohen-Levinas, *L'Itinéraire en temps réel*, 529.
72   Interview with Julian Anderson.
73   Interview with Fineberg.
74   Interview with Zinsstag.
75   Sketches in the Paul Sacher archive. The musicologists there date it to around 1984.

the idea never progressed to anything concretely musical, Grisey's interest in the text is revealing, an illustration of his evolving thinking on spirituality and sensuality and a suggestion that he would have liked to compose a large-scale stage work.

The Man Who Died takes place in the immediate aftermath of Jesus's resurrection. In the first chapter, God's son walks out of the tomb, past the dozing Roman soldiers, and receives shelter from a poor peasant couple with an incongruously virile rooster. Jesus is pale, weak, barely alive; but as he watches the rooster's lusty vigor, he decides to renounce his mission as a prophet and savior of the world. He feels he has earned his portion of normal human life and the earthly pleasures that come along with it. "He was a virgin, in recoil from the little, greedy life of the body," Lawrence wrote. "But now he knew that virginity is a form of greed; and that the body rises again to give and to take, to take and give ungreedily."[76]

Jesus leaves the Holy Land and arrives at an Egyptian temple of the goddess Isis, also under Roman rule. Here Grisey's interest in the story becomes obvious: beyond the elevation of sex to a spiritual principle, Lawrence merges Christian and Egyptian myth with an even hand. The beautiful, virginal priestess of the temple falls in love with Jesus; the savior, blasphemously, does obeisance to Isis; the man and the woman are united in transcendent lovemaking. Eventually, Jesus renounces all erotic prohibitions. As the Messiah, he says, "I wanted them to love with dead bodies. If I had kissed Judas with life love, perhaps he would never have kissed me with death. Perhaps he loved me in the flesh, and I will that he should love me bodilessly, with the corpse of love ..."

The story has a happy ending. The Romans, aided by the Egyptian slaves, attempt to capture and punish Jesus again. This time, he sees them coming, and escapes on an Egyptian boat to wander the earth. Jesus's spiritual development in *The Man Who Died* closely mirrors Grisey's own. Both found a way of integrating sensuality into their spiritual thought, rejecting what they came to understand as pointless erotic prohibitions in favor of the worship of living sensation.

Unfortunately, Grisey's sketches give little sense of the sounds he might have imagined. He did consider some sort of synthesis between two distinct sound worlds, attached respectively to Jesus and to Isis. Besides that, he made quite beautiful sketches of various abstract symbols associated with the two worlds: Christianity (the Cross, the Fall, the Rape of the Temple) and Egyptian religion (the sun, the boat, the spiral). He also made drawings that showed the unnatural positions of Jesus on the cross, and the more flowing movements of the goddess Isis. Then he abandoned the project.

---

76 Lawrence, *The Man Who Died*.

Grisey's drawings recall the work of the American experimental stage director Robert Wilson. Grisey may have noted them down while inspired by the idea of working with Wilson. In May 1981, Grisey had written to him saying he hoped to write an opera. Grisey had also attracted interest from Bernard Lefort, the artistic director of the Opéra National de Paris, who offered Grisey the chance to compose a "Quarter-Hour Opera." Grisey told Lefort that he was interested and that he hoped to involve Wilson in a project.

It was not to be. "At this time from listening to your music I don't know how to begin a collaboration," Wilson wrote back.[77] According to Grisey's friend Guy Lelong, the composer encountered the director another time in Paris, but "Wilson ... practically sent Grisey packing."[78] Grisey, always sensitive to perceived slights toward his artistic worth, was hurt and stopped pursuing the collaboration.

※ ※ ※

In the mid-1980s, Grisey developed a fascination with the Czech composer Leoš Janáček. Janáček, who lived between 1854 and 1928, was largely unrecognized during his lifetime. At a moment of radical experimentation in European musical history, Janáček had dug deep into folk music and the rhythms of his native language for inspiration. There are important parallels between Grisey's and Janáček's music. Both were interested in the power of small melodic and rhythmic cells that morphed even as they repeated—their short-term predictability could be harnessed to play sophisticated musical games with perception and surprise. Both believed music had the power to illuminate the hidden processes of the human psyche, and both made sexuality an explicit theme in their compositions.

Grisey introduced the Canadian composer François Rose to Janáček's *Nursery Rhymes*.[79] In its use of small cells that come to life and develop on their own terms, the flute and clarinet writing in this work recalls the texture of Grisey's later composition *Vortex Temporum*. In Janáček's piece, these instruments seem to spiral around a minuscule axis, an image essential both to Grisey's work and to his understanding of his trajectory: in 1981, Grisey wrote, a little mysteriously, "Every psychic life has a specific form. Mine is a spiral."[80]

---

77 Paul Sacher archive.
78 Email from Lelong, December 23, 2021. Julian Anderson hinted at a similar interaction, though he didn't name Wilson.
79 Interview with Rose.
80 Paul Sacher archive.

Edmund Campion remembers Grisey discussing Janáček's *The Cunning Little Vixen* in a composition course at Berkeley. A handwritten rhythmic analysis of the overture to the opera by Grisey sheds light on what he drew from Janáček.[81] At the beginning of the piece, Grisey noted the "confusion [of the] first tempo" which Janáček achieved by contrasting the first, predictable four-bar phrase with a second, five-bar phrase. By doubling a thirty-second-note rhythm in the transition between the phrases, Janáček both weaves the two phrases together and introduces instability into our expectation of what comes next. In bar ten of the overture, two different feelings of time overlap, a technique that appears explicitly in Grisey's *Le temps et l'écume* and *L'Icône paradoxale*. In Janáček's piece, one group of instruments plays in $\frac{4}{8}$ time, emphasizing the downbeat, the other in $\frac{4}{8}$ time with an emphasis on the third beat. The effect is one of subtle rhythmic stereophony. Janáček achieves a similar effect in the following ballet section of the work, "Módrá Vážka," ("The Blue Dragonfly," the children's ballet), in which a notated $\frac{6}{8}$ time signature contains music in $\frac{3}{4}$, $\frac{5}{8}$, *and* $\frac{6}{8}$. For Grisey, after a "destruction" of the $\frac{5}{4}$ music, the section is repeated; Grisey noted that in the reprise of the "three metrical systems, the accents favor a fusion toward $\frac{6}{4}$." Grisey was fascinated by the idea of different levels and layers of time; while Janáček produced this effect more locally than Grisey, the conceptual approach was similar. It defied the traditional, discrete layers of classical music—melody, harmony, rhythm, timbre—to create textures which coalesce despite their delineated vibrancy.

There is a strong current of sexuality in Janáček's music. In Act I of *The Cunning Little Vixen*, when the title character and the Dog discuss their ignorance of making love, the composer adds dissonant non-chord tones to the underlying interplay of major-minor harmonies, illustrating his characters' longing for this aspect of experience.[82] When the Vixen later meets her Fox and they "slip into the burrow" together, Janáček reprises the "Blue Dragonfly" ballet music, but out of regular time, with no bar lines.[83] Time has stopped for the lovers. As Max Brod described it, *The Cunning Little Vixen* is a "dream of the eternity of nature and love-lust."[84] In his letters to Kamila Stösslová that formed the basis of his String Quartet no. 2 "Intimate

---

81   Ibid.
82   Leoš Janáček, *The Cunning Little Vixen* (Universal Edition, piano reduction), 39–41.
83   Ibid, 146.
84   Kaegi, "'Das schlaue Füchslein' von Leos Janacek."

Letters," Janáček makes repeated reference to "bind[ing]" and "tying up" his lover, showing that he, like Grisey, saw love and violence as related.[85]

The critic Benjamin Poore has noted the many connections between Janáček and Freud, whose writings on psychology fascinated Grisey as much as the music of the Czech composer.[86] The two Moravians were fascinated by the mechanisms of the human psyche, the nature of external and internal realities, and the power of sexuality to upend the expectations of society. In 1924, Janáček wrote an essay, "On Naturalism," that Grisey could almost have written himself:

> There exists in each of us an inner environment ... the sequences of all cognitive processes, in general: all consciousness ... All that has fallen into it—even perhaps unnoticed—disintegrates, collects, crisscrosses, pushes through, disappears—but never vanishes ... This seeping—whether conscious or unconscious—is that inner environment. We see through it, we hear through it—through it we more or less even exist.[87]

From his 1970s reading of Carlos Castaneda to this fascination with Janáček, Grisey was preoccupied by a psychological question, the posing of which is maybe incumbent on all artists: is it possible to locate or define the elusive porous boundary between the firing of neurons in our brain which form our subjectivity, and the objective texture of the world?

According to the people who knew Grisey later in his life, starting from the early 1990s, Janáček came to occupy a place in Grisey's pantheon nearly as important as the trinity of Messiaen, Stockhausen, and Ligeti.[88] In 1996, Julian Anderson recalled, Grisey invited him to give a guest seminar at the Conservatoire de Paris, where the two composers discussed Janáček and the power of his "non-pretty orchestration."[89] Grisey introduced Janáček's ravishing Sonata for Violin and Piano (1922) to France Detry.[90] It remains one of her favorite pieces of music.

🐾 🐾 🐾

After the 1984–85 school year, Grisey left the University of California at Berkeley for what was originally intended to be a sabbatical semester in Paris. The purpose of the trip was for him to reconnect with the European

---

85 John Tyrrell (ed.), *Intimate Letters: Leoš Janáček to Kamila Stösslová*, 206–7 and 233.
86 Poore, "Like the Volga Singing."
87 Quoted in Ibid.
88 For example, Christopher Wintle.
89 Interview with Julian Anderson.
90 Interview with Detry.

contemporary music scene: the premiere of *Les chants de l'amour* was coming up in June 1985, and he also needed to finish *Épilogue*, the final work in the cycle *Les espaces acoustiques*, for its first performance at the Venice Biennale on September 28, 1985. He'd also begun the initial work on the as-yet-unnamed *Talea*, for chamber ensemble, commissioned by Radio France.[91]

From Paris, in October 1985, Grisey wrote to Bonnie Wade, the ethnomusicologist and chair of the Berkeley Department of Music. With the benefit of the temporal and physical distance of a sabbatical, Grisey was able to confirm his suspicions about the differences between the American and European new music scenes. His own art was always at the front of his mind: "I realize the damage that the distance, combined with full time teaching, has caused to the promotion of my music," he wrote.[92] Despite the advantages of Berkeley, this letter confirmed the sense that Grisey's students had of his dissatisfaction—the composer felt he had landed in a backwater. A critique of the American approach to the arts was clear in the composer's letter to Wade: "I enclose a program of the last Biennale di Venezia. It is hard to imagine that such a 'little country' as Italy is able to fund such a gigantic contemporary music festival: eight different orchestras and a dozen contemporary music groups were invited."[93]

What followed this lament was a series of five proposals for Grisey to split his time between Berkeley and continental Europe. These ranged from the reasonable—more frequent unpaid leave, fewer courses, an exchange year in France—to the fanciful: a split position with the renowned composer Brian Ferneyhough or a "very flexible permanent visiting position." These ideas made sense from the perspective of Grisey, the artist. But in an academic context, they probably communicated a certain arrogance. Before his departure for France, Wade and Grisey had discussed the possibility of him applying for tenure. Most candidates would use this time to keep their heads down, attend as many faculty meetings as possible, and play nice with their colleagues, maybe taking on some extra administrative duties. Grisey, who at least made the conciliatory gesture of praising Berkeley's generous staff and "very democratic structure," largely adopted a take-me-or-leave-me attitude. "I leave it to you and to the faculty members to decide if the following proposals make it necessary to request a tenure position," he wrote. He continued:

> I know how much trouble all this is going to cause especially for the administration, but I also count on your comprehension and appreciation of my situation which is not at all common or easy. I was hired partly because

---

91 Paul Sacher archive.
92 Ibid.
93 Ibid.

the music department wanted to have an open window to the east and a closer contact with European music. I would like to remain this particular chosen "European composer" and a full time position would make it more and more difficult unless an arrangement with the faculty is possible.[94]

Grisey's obvious identification as a European composer revealed where his sympathies lay. Wade accepted none of his proposals.

Grisey began preparing to settle back to Europe. One day, Detry was at her spacious 1930s-era apartment on the sixth floor at 2 Place Constantin Meunier, in the southern part of Brussels, when boxes containing Grisey's possessions arrived at her doorstep. Though Grisey had neglected to mention the fact to his girlfriend, he was moving in.

Though the composer clearly needed to be close to his new lover, the city of Brussels was not a place where he felt naturally at home. "He was quite miserable because he felt like he was in exile from Paris," Detry said. "He thought that Brussels was dull, and that Belgian people were boring. He couldn't stand the accent." Rather than attempting to integrate into the local culture, Grisey bought a television (ironic considering his piece *Manifestations: pour échapper à la télévision*, though it endeared him to Detry's two sons). They also arranged for a piano, made by Pleyel, which was important to Detry because her great-grandfather had been a builder with the company. Grisey set up his wine collection in the cellar, and cooked delicious meals for the couple (Detry was particularly taken by his Indian recipes).[95] Grisey took an apartment in Paris, too, at 50 Boulevard de la Villette, which he rented from a friend named Simon Krause, in a modern building in orange and white.[96] The neighborhood was a raucous immigrant one, with excellent Vietnamese food, loud traffic, and a busy market for prostitution.

The final composition in Grisey's *Les espaces acoustiques*, titled *Épilogue*, is a peculiar appendage to the cycle that came to define spectral music. Composed in Berkeley and in Paris and completed in 1985, the work is scored as a sort of concerto grosso, with a viola and four horns performing solo parts against the material of the same large orchestra from *Transitoires*. It's the only piece in *Les espaces acoustiques* that may not be played as a stand-alone composition. In a letter to Detry, Grisey described the emotional state he was in as he composed *Épilogue*:

---

94 Ibid.
95 Interview with Detry.
96 Paul Sacher archive.

The music leaks, the music passes. I try to identify some of its palpitations. For *Épilogue*, I reread the diagrams of *Partiels, Modulations* and *Transitoires*: a life of work and patience, as if I wanted to define an inner form, the very skeleton of my soul ...

I am jubilant: great, very great music. After me, they will wonder why, how ...

I'm gloating: *Épilogue*, if I have the energy for it, will make a hell of an ending.

And then, I have my secret (the one that makes me smile like a Buddha with a malicious glint in his eye at all those who would hear this music or who leer at its manuscripts): I am not capable of much. I am capable of ... almost nothing ...[97]

Épilogue begins where *Transitoires* leaves off, with a solo viola reprise of *Prologue*, its fifths signaling a return to the most basic elements of the harmonic spectrum. After this simultaneous conclusion to *Transitoires* and introduction to *Épilogue*, the dual processes that make up the piece proper begin.

The first of these processes is a reprise of *Prologue* with the motivic material transposed to the four solo horns. The neumes from the solo viola work progress in increasing order, as Baillet notes, and reach their climaxes quickly, within individual subsections, creating a more hectic effect than the "slow and progressive evolution" of *Prologue*. As Baillet adds, the music of the solo horns "seems to seek, without succeeding, to move away from an attractor which forces it to return unceasingly on itself."[98] Besides this flailing process, there is something of the bite of irony in the immediate effect of the solo horns. After playing the neumes in *marcato* dissonance, they glissando downwards, as if throwing the motives away—as if insisting on their irrelevance. The horn music of *Épilogue* seems to reprise the slightly cynical humor of the theatrical moments in the earlier pieces *Périodes* and *Partiels*. For Baillet, this part of the final work represents the "monstrous deformation" of the viola solo.[99]

The second process in *Épilogue* takes places in the orchestra and operates independently of the horns. First, it continues a process begun in *Transitoires*, where the instruments outline a rising harmonic spectrum on the central pitch of E. Then, Grisey disintegrates this same spectrum in three stages, through winds, strings, and a mixture of low instruments. An analogously symmetrical process occurs rhythmically as well. "The last sounds are no longer heard at defined pitches, gradually replaced by the percussion,"

---

97 Private archives of Detry.
98 Baillet, *Fondements d'une écriture*, 154.
99 Ibid, 153.

Baillet writes. "The end of *Épilogue* leads irreversibly to noise and the disappearance of all sound events."[100]

The end of *Épilogue*, with its final horn outburst and bass-drum punctuation, is not meant as a tidy ending to *Les espaces acoustiques*. In his program note, Grisey wrote, "Conclusion? I doubt it. Instead, I had to arbitrarily introduce an entropic process that gradually erodes the open system" of the cycle. For Baillet, *Épilogue* also represents an "arbitrary cut" to the cycle;[101] the musicologist Yael Kaduri writes that "*Épilogue* can be heard as a discontinuation, but not as a conclusion."[102] At the end of this majestic work, the horns create an almost mocking texture that both underlines and undercuts the import of an epoch-defining piece.

The complete cycle of *Les espaces acoustiques* was finally premiered on September 28, 1985 at the Venice Biennale, the same venue as the nearly-complete version performed four years earlier. The performers this time were the BBC Symphony Orchestra under the direction of Peter Eötvös.[103]

In 1993, the composer and author Claudy Malherbe wrote to Grisey to praise the piece for its "undeniable success" and "supreme directionality of meaning."[104] More recent performances of *Les espaces acoustiques* underscore its importance for the music of the second half of the twentieth century. In 2000, Paul Griffiths wrote in the *New York Times* that "*Les espaces acoustiques* was a project of the 1970s and can now be seen to have got right much of what that decade got wrong. Grisey heard what was going on around him—repetitive music, the rediscovery of bodily rhythms, especially the rhythm of breathing, the fascination with harmonic spectra, the idea that performing musicians are actors in an abstract drama—and he made it all work."[105] In 2016, *Guardian* critic Andrew Clements wrote, "For all its technical profundity and mathematical precision, Grisey's music has a spectacular physical presence, too."[106]

Les espaces acoustiques exists in two recordings. A version on the Accord label was made in 2001 with many of Grisey's collaborators—the violist Gérard Caussé, the conductors Pierre-André Valade and Sylvain Cambreling, Ensemble Court-Circuit, and the Frankfuter Oper- und Museumsorchester—and is accurate and expressive, though its sound is very dry. A more recent release on Kairos with violist Garth Knox, conductor

---

100 Ibid, 155–165.
101 Ibid, 156.
102 Kaduri, *The Oxford Handbook of Sound and Image in Western Art*, 204.
103 Eötvös declined to discuss Grisey with me.
104 Paul Sacher archive.
105 Griffiths, "A Flutist Makes a Challenge."
106 Clements, "Grisey: Les espaces acoustiques Review."

Stefan Asbury, the Asko Ensemble, and the WDR Sinfonieorchester Köln is slightly more shapely and supple.

That two full recordings of this ambitious, musically and logistically challenging cycle have been made show its status in contemporary music. In his introductory remarks to the 2019 Berlin premiere of the work, the conductor Vladimir Jurowski described *Les espaces acoustiques* as "the first masterpiece of the twenty-first century." He believes its importance rivals that of Wagner's *Ring* cycle, and Stravinsky's *Rite of Spring*.[107]

---

107 I was at the concert.

Chapter Eleven

Absolute Love (1986–88)

In 1986, Grisey finished *Talea*, an eighteen-minute piece for flute and clarinet (with doublings), violin, cello, and piano. *Talea* is a powerful work and an important one in Grisey's oeuvre, his first piece of chamber music to move beyond mature spectralism to something even more personal. It shares many characteristics with the late masterpiece *Vortex Temporum*.

The title *Talea* has a double meaning. The first is musical: in the French polyphonic music of the Middle Ages, including the works of Grisey's beloved Guillaume de Machaut, talea (or isorhythm) refers to a fixed rhythm repeated with different pitches, known as "colors." These are treated initially as separate entities, as de Machaut's contemporary, Johannes Boen, described in his treatise *Ars musicae* from 1355.[1] For Grisey, this conceptual approach had gained new relevance. "In the twentieth century, we again find the dissociation between pitches and durations," he wrote in his program note for *Talea*.[2] For example, the first movement of Messiaen's *Quartet for the End of Time*, "Liturgie de cristal," includes isorhythms in the cello and piano.

The second meaning of the title is its Latin definition, "cutting." This refers to the cut between the two contrasting phrases that structure the work, and the cut between its two overarching sections. The subtitle of *Talea* is "*la machine et les herbes folles*," or "the machine and the wild grass." This subtitle alludes to alternate meanings of the Latin word *talea*: in agriculture, "a cutting, set layer for planting," or, in architecture, "a small beam used for binding together the joints of a wall."[3] The machine-like process and the raucous incursions of the natural world that undermine its rigidity and predictability are essential to the form of the piece.

---

1   Hartt, "Tonal and Structural Implications of Isorhythmic Design in Guillaume de Machaut's Tenors," 59.
2   Lelong, *Écrits*, 161–162.
3   Lewis and Short, *A Latin Dictionary*.

Talea is shaped around two gestures, one fast, loud, ascending; the other slow, soft, descending. Grisey uses Messiaen's term, *personnages*, to describe these gestures. The ones that open the piece are prototypical: tangled, rising microtonal scales in all the instruments, followed by a *dal niente* open C—the sole fundamental of the entire first section—in the cello and piano resonances. The first part of *Talea* is a highly schematic process, the machine. The work begins with a series of staggered entrances that, as Baillet explains, is "close to the formal structure of *Tempus ex Machina*," the percussion piece.[4] Once these entrances are established, Grisey extends the duration of the short, fast, loud, ascending gesture, and shrinks the duration of the soft, quiet, descending one. He does this in a series of integer divisions of the beat which are unique to each instrument, as Baillet shows.[5] For Grisey, this section is an "implacable process" designed to level the difference between the two opposing gestures. This is audible: in the middle of the work, the instruments come close to fusion with ascending and descending swells. Once again, two separate things become one, like lovers locked in a close embrace.

The process of the first section of *Talea* is, for Grisey, a "machine to manufacture the liberty that will emerge in the second section." He described this contrast poetically: "The process [of the second section] is perforated by more or less irrational outgrowths, like reminders of the first part, which gradually become colored by the new context until they are unrecognizable. This wild grass in the interstices of the machine grows in importance …"[6]

This description overstates somewhat the intuitiveness of the compositional process. As Baillet points out, the second section of *Talea* has an important schematic component. The two gestures are extended in duration and their characteristics "amplified," and the process of the first section reverses, with the two contrasting gestures eventually reaching an "extreme differentiation."[7] The second, soft gesture also grows in harmonic complexity, pulled downwards by a chromatic scale of new fundamentals. Then, the wild grass invades the machine in a controlled manner. The scholars Anne Sophie Andersen and Derek Kwan, who produced a beautiful 3D visual model of *Talea*, note that this material "invade[s] and overtake[s] [the second gesture] as the form progresses, dominating the soundscape completely at the end of the piece."[8] But the aural effect is fragmentary, with bits of material coming and going like strange plants briefly examined and tossed aside. *Talea* closes with a descending overtone scale in the violin and a

---

4   Baillet, *Fondements d'une écriture*, 177.
5   Ibid.
6   Lelong, *Écrits*, 162.
7   Baillet, *Fondements d'une écriture*, 181.
8   Andersen and Kwan, "Grisey's *Talea*."

loud, noisy, short pizzicato in the cello: summary distillations of the second gesture, then the first gesture.

Talea fits into Grisey's longstanding interest in contrasting binary structures. It's a more sophisticated version of *D'eau et de pierre*, from 1972, where Grisey referred to "the antinomy of two elements" in his conception of the piece. This reflects the composer's ongoing interest in opposites, in the impossibility of true communication—except under exceptional circumstances, like religious experience and love.

Commissioned by Radio France, *Talea* was premiered on January 13, 1986, at the Maison de Radio France by an ensemble under the conductor Jean-Louis Petit. By now, Grisey was a known quantity in French musical circles. An unsigned review of *Talea* in *Le Monde* describes the composer as "building up a homogeneous and original body of work, through which one can recognize, over the last ten years, not only one of the most exceptional French composers of his generation, but also a particular sensitivity which distinguishes him from those whose aesthetic he shares." The critic wrote of *Talea* itself:

> One is struck by the harshness of the ascending or descending strokes, which the instruments launch one after the other, or almost simultaneously. From time to time, the rain stops and one listens to the resonance. Little by little, the outbursts become organized ... After the disorientation of the beginning, one is surprised to discover the composer's "ear." He makes the Pierrot-Lunaire ensemble sound in an almost unheard-of way ... Only an idea beyond the simple concern for color could give such particular tints.[9]

The critic Isabelle Mili was far less impressed. In a brief but cutting review, she wrote, "The reign of similarity in Gérard Grisey's *Talea*, and the redundancies in the motifs of Michaël Levinas' Concerto for Piano no. 2, raise questions about what leads these lovers of sound to mirror themselves, like Narcissists, in the stagnant products of their imagination."[10] The New York contemporary music group Talea Ensemble was named after the Grisey piece. In an essay for the ensemble, the critic Bruce Hodges sums up the work's appeal. "Somehow when one hears the ensemble ... illuminating Grisey's argument," he writes, "it feels like being exposed to one of life's basic building blocks—like grasping at DNA and holding it in your hands."[11]

On November 13, 1986, Jocelyne and Grisey filed for divorce. Grisey was reluctant to take the legal step, but Jocelyne had insisted, needing the clarity

---

9   "Une création de Gérard Grisey à Radio France."
10 Quoted in Cohen-Levinas, *L'Itinéraire en temps réel*, 486.
11 Hodges, "Listening to Gérard Grisey's *Talea*."

that divorce provided. The two worked out an arrangement where Grisey would spend time with Raphaël when he was in Paris; he noted those dates meticulously in his calendars. "It wasn't easy because I think he felt guilty, and he was always on the defensive," Jocelyne said. "I told him, 'We have a child together, and it's important for us to have a relationship.' But that was hard for him." They had disagreements about child support, made more difficult because Jocelyne assumed that Grisey's income was higher than it really was.[12] Grisey left the apartment to her, which meant a significant financial loss: Grisey felt "dispossessed," and "he was totally broke," France Detry said.[13] Jocelyne still cared about her ex-husband deeply: she continued going to his concerts and is a primary guardian of his musical legacy.

Grisey stayed in touch with Lucie Monna, his mother, who had remarried. He sometimes brought Detry to visit her. She was living in a traditional Alsatian house in a suburb of Belfort called Chèvremont. Detry found Monna tough and stiff, and noted that Grisey "hated Belfort, *oh la la*." Monna was confused by the avant-garde music her son made. Detry recalled that Monna had once wanted to tune into a radio broadcast of his music, but turned it off after a couple of minutes, because the piece was so quiet she thought the broadcast wasn't working.[14] In 1986, maybe hoping to impress Monna with something more tangible, Grisey sent his mother a glowing review of a piece of his in *Le Monde*. "I thought this review might give you pleasure," he wrote.[15]

Since Grisey's time with Raphaël was limited, and France Detry's ex-husband only saw their children on the weekends, the composer took on a role as a sort of surrogate father for Detry's two boys. "He was always insisting that he also raised two kids with France," Raphaël said. "He was sweet, kind, and gentle to me, but also maybe because he didn't have to spend so much time with me."[16] Grisey's relationship with Detry's children was complicated. On the one hand, his presence was enriching: family meals would last for hours, with Grisey expounding on music, architecture, literature, and philosophy. On the other, he was used to being the center of attention. "He was very jealous of my children," Detry recalled. "He was so demanding. He couldn't accept that I would give love to someone else." Sometimes he tried to insist that Detry stay in bed with him instead of making her children breakfast before school. This recalls the jealousy that Jocelyne believes Grisey felt when Raphaël was born.

---

12 Interview with Jocelyne Grisey.
13 Interview with Detry.
14 Ibid.
15 Paul Sacher archive.
16 Interview with Jocelyne and Raphaël Grisey.

Detry was careful to give Grisey the solitude and silence he needed to compose. He would spend time wandering around, listening, searching for sound. "But he would never say, 'Leave me alone, I need to work.' Never," Detry said. "If I was coming to say hello, to give him a kiss on the neck, he was very happy. He was the kind of person who couldn't push away a woman or [her] affection."[17]

By the time of his relationship with Detry, the fervent Catholicism of Grisey's youth was long gone, replaced by a generalized veneration of art. Grisey and Detry visited churches together, but for the beauty of their architecture and artwork—"never because of Jesus or Mary," as Detry put it. One day, Grisey told her, "The most dramatic thing that can happen on this earth is that all these beautiful old buildings, the museums, the paintings disappear."[18] The hesitation he felt at the suggestion to burn down the Opéra in May 1968 had solidified into a deeply held belief.

For Detry, Grisey was a man with two sides, his nature reflected in the dualistic structures of so many of his compositions. He was a little bumbling: Detry vividly remembers buying him a pair of boxers with clouds and musical notes as a joke; mistaking them for normal shorts, Grisey wore them to go on a vigorous hike with her. "He was just like Woody Allen," Detry said. "He would take a shower and use his towel to dry his back, and he would twist his shoulder." Grisey was often bumping into tables and giving himself bruises; one day he left the house wearing shoes that didn't match.

At the same time, Grisey was often effortlessly sophisticated in social situations. "He was a very insecure man. But the funny thing about Gérard was that he could be everywhere," Detry said. "He was like a prince, like a chameleon. He would do and say exactly the right things anywhere in society. He had something so comfortable [in his manner], even though inside he wasn't. Women loved him because he was very charming."[19] Even at the beginning of their relationship, Detry was reconciled to his flirtatiousness. "I don't like to be imprisoned by anyone. So why should he?" she said. "Even though I was a lot more faithful than he was."

In a letter which Grisey had sent to Detry while he was teaching in Berkeley, the composer explained his views on monogamy and polygamy, subjects that concerned not just the practical form of his relationships, but his understanding of the very nature of being:

> For me, the experience of my little life ... has taught me this: when I am monogamous (by choice or by assimilation) I progressively blame the person I love for my blindness. Little by little, I ask her for everything,

---

17 Interview with Detry.
18 Ibid.
19 Ibid.

everything, everything she is not, everything she could be, everything that the others I have excluded could bring me. I become *impossible*, critical, obsessed by imperfections, etc. Monogamy ... I see it as a real disease! As for the other person's monogamy, that's their business but usually they expect monogamy in return or cause guilt. The only time in my life when I found myself totally monogamous—with Jane—turned out to be a real catastrophe for my equilibrium: I rushed into a devouring passion that was exclusive and humorless. I almost died ... Polygamy, on the other hand, [loosens things up] and makes it possible to have a relationship. I accept the other for who she is. I don't ask her to be everything. I am light and in a healthy psychological state.

Don't think (even though ...) that I spend my time flirting or playing leapfrog. I have my phases too: polygamy-monogamy. But monogamy is rarely a positive sign! ...

To summarize: monogamy, a deep tendency in me as in any being. Absolute Love, Romanticism, Tristan and Yseult ... The Idealism of being fifteen years old. I know too well what it hides: the death drive, the impossible, mortal love.

Polygamy, a learned and cultivated tendency. The game of life, the reality of Impermanence, the love of life in its multiple forms, openness (nothing to do with Don Juanism). We love absolute Love; I think we love our feeling of love, our loving self, even more than the person in front of us (you said something like that to me in a letter ...) Tristan needs Yseult ...

What I call polygamy is not the game of Love—passion repeated ad infinitum, the "this time it's for good" of each new beginning, the passionate seriousness of our loves as if heaven depended on it. It's not the cynicism of Don Juan either, a quest never unfulfilled. It is more than all that and my pen fails to describe or to try to explain this ideal in a difficult life ...

Our society doesn't predispose us to [polygamy]. The education that we have received creates endless conflicts with the reality of things and leads to the projection of an ideal that exists only within us.[20]

"He was in love with being in love," Gérard Zinsstag said. "A healthy pathology."[21] The contrasting operatic myths of *Tristan and Isolde* (Wagner) and *Don Giovanni* (Mozart) provided archetypes with which Grisey could understand the polarity of his romantic feelings. But though polygamy may have been the form of relationship best suited to Grisey, his partners often suffered from his affairs, feeling that they intruded on their intimacy.

Grisey applied this research into the possibilities of love to the more explicitly sexual realm as well. Detry recalls receiving a letter containing

---

20   Private archive of Detry.
21   Interview with Gérard Zinsstag.

the composer's sadistic fantasies for their erotic life. Put off, she ultimately burned it. (They also once went to a sex shop together, but Detry found the experience bizarre.[22]) Nevertheless, this interest speaks to Grisey's association between sexuality and violence and death, and his remarks on the violent potential of music as well; in his "Tempus ex Machina" lecture at Darmstadt, the composer had written of the way music penetrates us whether we want it to or not. (There seems to be a common interest among some composers of spectral or spectral-adjacent music in the sexual practices that fall under the umbrella term bondage, discipline, sadism, masochism, or BDSM. Both Grisey's friend Claude Vivier[23] and Georg Friedrich Haas,[24] the Austrian microtonal composer, have spoken about these practices in relation to their music.) Like music, sex can gain power from the interplay of pleasure and pain, violence and gentleness.

A problem, though, came not just from the fact that Grisey had lovers; he had an irresistible urge to seduce the women around him, even when it interfered with his primary relationship. Detry has strong suspicions, at least, that he slept with her cleaning lady and a pianist who was giving one of her sons lessons. She said, "If you touch your truth very acutely, you have so much energy. You don't know what to do with it, you have to use it. But you don't know how. Gérard was a very seductive person who loved women. It was easy for him to use his energy [on seduction]. And that calmed him down." She added that Grisey appreciated "beauty in landscapes, in architecture, in poetry and literature, in music, and of course in women."[25]

On October 1, 1987, Grisey began a new teaching position, at the institution that had contributed so essentially to his own formation as a composer, the Conservatoire National Supérieur de Musique in Paris. In contrast to his position as assistant professor of composition at Berkeley, this job had a more temporary quality to it: Grisey was named interim professor of orchestration. Still, the appointment was important enough to be announced in *Le Monde*.[26] Scheduled for six hours a week at a fee of around 8,000 francs per month, it also had the advantage that Grisey could teach every two weeks for a full day or two, allowing him to spend time with Detry in Brussels and concentrate on composing. In a letter to György Ligeti dated November

---

22   Interview with Detry.
23   Gilmore, *Claude Vivier*.
24   Brown, "Decades."
25   Interview with Detry.
26   "Nominations au Conservatoire de Musique."

1990, Grisey praised this aspect of the job specifically: "I'm teaching composition and orchestration (luckily for me, part-time)."[27]

Grisey's feeling that this job—the title made him sound like an adjunct—was a bit beneath him is palpable in his letters to the director of the Conservatoire (and former May 1968 activist) Alain Louvier. Grisey complained about being placed in the wrong pay category, citing his prestigious previous professorship and "notoriety" as a composer, and lamented the small size of the teaching room assigned to him, as well as its lack of a satisfactory device from which to play musical examples.

Still, the historic institution allowed him more freedom to teach in his preferred style. Grisey took his new duties extremely seriously, and the orchestration course quickly transcended its narrow remit to become, essentially, a composition lecture (as Messiaen's class had as well). Handwritten notes, undated but which Grisey probably wrote around 1987–89, give a sense of his ambitions: Grisey planned to analyze *Talea* and Messiaen's *Couleurs de la cité céleste* (with an emphasis on its Greek, Indian, and Gregorian rhythms); the sonogram of the trombone, so essential to the construction of *Les espaces acoustiques*; and Scelsi's String Quartets, *Anahit*, and *Pranam II*. In the same letter to Ligeti, Grisey wrote, "This year, we will have three orchestra rehearsals devoted to reading the orchestration work of my students and we have imagined orchestrating fragments of your Second Quartet." (Grisey added, "Of course, this will never go beyond the conservatory and I hope you are not too shocked by the idea!"[28]) It was a sign of the prestige of the Conservatoire—and Grisey's place in it—that an orchestration class would be able to arrange for three rehearsals with full orchestra.

In 1989, Edmund Campion came to Paris to study at the Conservatoire, where he participated in Grisey's orchestration class. In a later essay, he summarized this experience, which had an obvious resemblance to the teaching style of Messiaen:

> A typical class with Grisey often lasted from 10 a.m. to 10 p.m. over a single day. It was a ritual that moved between score analysis, eating meals, listening to unusual recordings, drinking coffee, and looking at others' music. Grisey examined his own works as well as odd scores from composers like James Tenney, Conlon Nancarrow, Steve Reich, and even Leoš Janáček. Sometimes the discussions were design related or technological in one way or another. Gérard Grisey and his friend Tristan Murail understood they belonged to an emerging technological generation, one that was changing music forever with science-based approaches to knowledge and communications. Unlike Murail, Grisey was uncomfortable with computers, but he

---

27 Paul Sacher archive.
28 Ibid.

nevertheless considered himself technical, and he enjoyed demonstrating how he used graph paper to do his numeric calculations and procedural transformations on time and spectra.[29]

In another similarity with his teacher, Campion said, Grisey "had several students who were like acolytes ... but a message that he got from Messiaen was that part of a senior, advanced composer's [job] was mentoring people." Many of Grisey's students remember the composer taking them to a particularly outstanding Vietnamese restaurant in his neighborhood of Belleville for phô and conversation. Joshua Fineberg believes that Grisey chose this restaurant because of an especially beautiful waitress; they talked about food, wine, and women. "We would talk about that more than music, which I regret now," Fineberg said. They also talked about "spiritual sex."[30]

The Conservatoire gave Grisey more freedom to choose his students than Berkeley had. Grisey devised a fiendish little test: he would take a short passage from the student's work, play their own harmonies on the piano, and ask the applicant to identify the chords. Most of them couldn't do it.

One who passed the test was Jean-Luc Hervé, who eventually became a close friend. Hervé's first impression of Grisey was that he was quite unfriendly, but he eventually warmed up. "He was very different in public and in private," Hervé said. "In public he was very distant, a little bit pretentious. In private he was very sympathetic." Hervé particularly remembers an observation Grisey made about Boulez's music, which is revealing about Grisey's own, because it was so opposite: in Boulez, "*On n'avance pas*" ("You don't go anywhere").[31]

Grisey was later promoted to Professor of Composition, a post he held for the rest of his life. The composer Fabien Lévy studied with him after quitting a post as an economics researcher. Lévy found Grisey tough, but nice, and not a snob—a quality that stood out in the competitive environment of the Conservatoire. Grisey's penchant for gnomic pronouncements that both disappointed and intrigued his students remained: he told Lévy, "Your music has a problem with rhythm. It has to sing," and encouraged him to study Janáček. Grisey scheduled private lessons on Fridays and held long seminars on Saturdays. He and his students also talked about visual art and architecture, and Grisey encouraged Lévy to leave France and go to Berlin, as he had.

It was an approach that led Lévy to say Grisey was not simply a professor of composition, but a professor of "ethical composition." Lévy remembers his teacher counseling his students not to envy a composer their own age

---

29 Unpublished essay provided by Campion.
30 Interview with Fineberg.
31 Interview with Hervé.

who had become internationally successful. "Don't be jealous," Grisey said. "There are two choices: either you produce [many commissions quickly], or you compose, but you have to decide."[32] Later, a group of his students got together to write a reminiscence of his teaching style:

> Grisey always insisted that the individual lesson take place without an audience, in a kind and intimate face-to-face meeting with the student. This meeting was intended [for him] to look at our compositions. G. Grisey's remarks were pertinent and original ... He also took advantage of this face-to-face meeting to get to know and orient the student's musical personality better, with respect, whatever his or her style and interests, and without any hierarchy other than the one that an experienced elder may have towards a younger student who is in the process of [building his personality].
>
> The next day, we would meet all day for a group lesson that was often full of surprises. The class could consist of orchestrating a piano etude by Ligeti, analyzing in detail Beethoven's *Missa solemnis* or Varèse's *Arcana*, comparing the variation techniques in Stockhausen's *Mantra* with those of Beethoven's *Diabelli Variations*, reflecting on the stretched and unpredictable temporal organization of sound materials in Morton Feldman's music and comparing them with the contracted perception of time in a quartet by Ferneyhough ... Grisey sometimes invited performers and composers to talk about their compositions or their instruments. He also sometimes analyzed his own scores in detail, but always with modesty and without dogmatism, dissecting his craft with rigor while pointing out the intuitive choices he made.
>
> After these technical workshops, which took all morning, we had lunch together. This meal was also a source of learning: Grisey shared with us his knowledge of Nordic mythologies, his reflection on time through his personal experience or his readings of [the chemist Ilya] Prigogine ... On rare occasions, G. Grisey shared with us his concern about the place of artists in an increasingly utilitarian and market-oriented society.[33]

As Grisey once wrote about Scelsi, these courses were "luckily not without humor." At the end of each year, Grisey would give his students an assignment to make a musical joke. Lévy and his colleagues came up with this rewrite of the chorus of Claude François's *chanson* "Comme d'habitude":

> Comme d'habitude
> on est samedi
> Comme d'habitude
> j'ai pas du tout envie

---

32   Interview with Lévy.
33   Text provided by Lévy.

Comme d'habitude
on va spectraliser
Comme d'habitude
on va analyser
Comme d'habitude
c'est le cours de Grisey
Comme d'habitude.[34]

In the summer of 1987, Grisey taught a masterclass at the American Conservatory in Fontainebleau, outside Paris. Established with the intention of introducing American students to French musical education, the Conservatory focused on contemporary music and had played host to many legendary musicians: between 1949 and 1979, its director was Nadia Boulanger. Grisey's student Ellen Fishman-Johnson attended the festival, which began in late July 1987, and took detailed notes.[35] They provide valuable insights into Grisey's musical thought as he began to approach his late style.

Tellingly, Grisey used *Dérives* as the starting point for discussing his spectral techniques. The same work had been a frequent subject for analysis in his Darmstadt lectures; in the five turbulent years since he last presented there, his understanding of the piece as the key to his development—between the proto-spectral *D'eau et de pierre* and the characteristic *Périodes*—hadn't changed. At this later date, he made new connections between *Dérives* and the music that came before it. Grisey noted an overlap between his "intuitive" use of even-numbered overtones in the strings and Debussy's orchestration. Fishman-Johnson's notes don't cite a specific Debussy work here, but there are many possible examples, such as a violin chord in the first movement of *Nocturnes*, "Nuages."[36] Discussing the glissandi of *Dérives*, Grisey quoted Boulez, who said, "Glissando is the white noise of melody." (This supports Cagney's hypothesis that Grisey was not quite as opposed to the musical thought of the elder statesmen as he liked to say he was.[37]) Grisey also still thought of musical form in terms of psychoanalytic metaphors. In the lecture "Tempus ex Machina," he had compared excessive repetition to neurosis; now he said, "For everything we hear, we create a threshold, and when it is exceeded—panic."

Especially interesting in Grisey's Fontainebleau masterclasses were his analyses of three pieces from Debussy's *Images* for solo piano, books one

---

34   Ibid. There is also a complete set of original verses.
35   Provided by Fishman-Johnson.
36   Debussy, *Nocturnes*, "Nuages," rehearsal mark one. The violins, divisi, play a transparent harmony of Gs and Bs against the dissonant D♯ in the English horn.
37   Cagney, "Synthesis and Deviation," 246.

and two. These analyses reveal as much about Grisey's aesthetic priorities as they do about Debussy, showing how the spectral composer found nourishment for his own approach in the French tradition. Grisey began with "Et la lune descend sur le temple qui fut" ("And the moon descends on the temple that was"). He described the effect of anadiplosis in the melodic line of "Et la lune," a term from Greek meter which refers to the "repetition of a prominent and usually the last word in one phrase ... at the beginning of the next."[38] Debussy used an analogous technique right at the beginning of his mysterious and resonant work, giving the melodic line a momentum that belies its profound serenity. (Grisey would use a similar effect in the first song of *Quatre chants pour franchir le seuil*.)

Another one of Debussy's innovations in "Et la lune" with resonances for Grisey's own thinking is structural: Debussy's work has three sections, which are each shortened in the second half of the piece, while still progressing in the same order. Grisey described this effect as the sections being "cut like remembrances," according to Fishman-Johnson's notes. Debussy was composing a process of human perception of the world—the erosion wrought by memory on the image of the temple and the moon. This cutting recalls the theme and structure of *Talea*.

As a student in Messiaen's class, Grisey had analyzed Ockeghem's Requiem with a view to the composer's use of the Golden Section. At Fontainebleau, Grisey showed his own students Debussy's use of this proportion in both "Et la lune" and "Reflets dans l'eau" ("Reflections in the Water"). Grisey cited the research of the musicologist Roy Howat, who presented evidence of Debussy's interest in the Golden Section in his 1983 book *Debussy in Proportion: A Musical Analysis*. The study had helped demolish the cliché that Debussy was a purely intuitive, impressionist composer.[39] Grisey's personal stake in this issue is clear: a rigorous and mathematical composer, he had frequently been dismissed by critics as a mere sound painter. Grisey was showing his students the paradoxical power of using calculations to plan a work, while hiding these calculations to achieve the mirage of the intuitive.

Grisey concluded his course at Fontainebleau with an analysis of Messiaen's *Chronochromie* for large orchestra. Messiaen composed the work in 1960, when Grisey was fourteen years old; it's remarkable for the palette of its percussion timbres, its exotic influences, its clear, almost brutal formal delineations. Discussing the work, Grisey told his students that the premiere had been booed; a woman had supposedly attacked Messiaen with her umbrella. This also seems like an attempt on Grisey's part to retroactively put his own experiences in the context of history.

---

38   Merriam-Webster definition.
39   Nichols, "Disciplined Debussy," 349.

In Strophe I of *Chronochromie*, Messiaen uses chords of contracted resonance to generate rich tapestries of harmony that resemble the harmonic spectrum. There are two "fundamentals," while the harmonics—up to the seventh partial—are transposed down (and notated in the tempered system). Of course, this approach is very different to the spectral understanding of harmony; it strikes the ear as an especially well-composed cluster. Were Messiaen's chords of contracted resonance—Cagney has noted the importance of Boulez's similar resonance chord in *Pli selon pli*—essential for Grisey's interest in the harmonic spectrum?[40] More likely, Grisey was looking backwards for historical parallels to his aesthetic innovations, hoping to secure his place in the music of the twentieth century.

In the fall of 1987, Grisey began working on a curious small project: music for a short film for the centenary of the Eiffel Tower for the Musée d'Orsay in Paris. It was a six-minute commission for two horns and voice at a fee of 30,000 francs.[41] The film was directed by dancer and choreographer Régine Chopinot, with costumes created by the legendary fashion designer Jean Paul Gaultier.

The film, titled *Gustave*, turns the Eiffel Tower into a human figure in the form of a dancer who flirts with the ground below her, slowly rising away to swirl around a model of the city of Paris. According to the program note, "the Tower places itself in the center of the stage and then disintegrates into a pyrotechnic fantasy. An audacious, dreamlike film veiled in a somber, blue, mysterious atmosphere." Unsurprisingly, Gaultier's costume is a highlight, creating a whimsical, "anthropomorphized Eiffel Tower" with both the solidity and the grace of the actual monument.[42]

Grisey's music for the film can be divided into four sections of about a minute and a half each, three of which would be slightly expanded and developed to form movements of a series of five miniatures for two horns, the *Accords perdus* (*Lost chords*). The first section consists of an exploration of the beatings that occur when two notes are close, but not exactly the same, in pitch. These beatings follow a slowly descending scale, audibly influenced by Scelsi. The second plays with the phenomenon of the echo, the scale tending to rise this time, the rhythms subtly offset to create both momentum and a pleasing unpredictability. When the figure of the Eiffel Tower is given a face

---

40   Cagney, "Synthesis and Deviation," 287.
41   Paul Sacher archive.
42   The film is available at https://www.numeridanse.tv/en/dance-videotheque/gustave.

in the film—he is wearing a beard and a defiant expression and holding a small French flag—Grisey's music turns bubbly and complex, with overlapping horn overtone scales. This section takes the patriotic associations of the monument with a certain light irony, as the dancer flies away. In the very short final section, the only part not to reappear in *Accords perdus*, the horns play slow downward glissandi, while a female voice intones overtone scales slowly over them in a vocalise. The film ends on the image of a small explosion, like a firework being released into the atmosphere. While the music to *Gustave* is a minor part of the composer's output, it was the only piece Grisey composed specifically for film, and he clearly saw enough potential in his ideas to develop them into a more complete work shortly thereafter. *Gustave* was first shown on January 11, 1988, at the Musée d'Orsay.

Grisey completed *Accords perdus*, the piece in five movements for two horns based on the music for *Gustave*, quickly by his standards: the premiere of the piece took place six months after the first showing of the film, on May 26, 1988, at the Centre Pompidou, performed by André Cazalet and Hervé Joulin. At the heart of the work is the fact that the horn plays its pitches from natural harmonics, which the player must correct to equal temperament with their lips (a reason why the instrument is more prone to obvious mistakes than most others in the orchestra). Grisey decided to reject this traditional correction: "Here," he wrote in his program note for the piece, "I restore the horn to its origins: the untempered sound and the multiple possibilities of just intonation of the instrument."[43] (Though he was not the only person to do so: György Ligeti's Trio for Horn, Violin, and Piano and *Hamburg Concerto* also use natural harmonics on the horn.) More radical for Grisey, who was so fond of the long process in his compositions, was the miniature structure of *Accords perdus*—a form favored by many twentieth-century composers, but rarely by the spectralists. "As for the short forms, they push me to explore the limits of my own technique by taking uncomfortable, but rewarding risks," Grisey wrote.[44] At this point, even in a small-scale work, the composer was looking for ways to prevent the spectralism of *Les espaces acoustiques* from becoming a calcified style.

The first movement of *Accords perdus*, titled "mouvement," is based on the opening of *Gustave*. Grisey describes it as the expression of a "state of fusion," the two horns creating a "single idealized instrument where the shift from one to the other is perceptible." The form of the three-minute piece is simple: microtonal variations on a pitch—achieved by the hornists fingering the same pitches based on different fundamentals—rub against one another; the musicologist Hans Gebhardt, in his analysis of *Accords perdus*,

---

43   Gérard Grisey, "Accords perdus."
44   Lelong, *Écrits*, 163.

describes the process as an "always returning, downward sliding on quarter- and eighth-tones."[45] As this continues, the rhythmic density and dynamic range of the music increases, and the tessitura slowly descends. The climax is marked by microtonal variations of a B♭, and the movement closes with a long, slow glissando in the first horn.

The second movement, which also features in *Gustave* in a more rudimentary form, is a play of echoes. Titled "accord perdu," Grisey described the movement as a divergent canon, and the echoes, which begin on a unison C, slowly grow apart—they form a sort of melody with one another. This echo has the magical capacity to morph the pitch of the sound that enters it. As the piece progresses, the rhythms of the echo become less predictable, giving the music the quality of an angular dance; toward the middle, the composer adds overtone grace notes. The distinctive, over-an-octave glissandi from *Gustave* close out this two-minute piece. The next movement, "faux mouvement," is a sort of mirror image of the first, the horns playing as a single instrument, and rising in pitch (though only a major second).

The fourth movement is titled "cor à cor," which could be a play on *coeur à coeur* ("heart to heart"), but also on *corps à corps* ("body to body"). The kind of light teasing of clichés about love that Grisey played with in *Les chants de l'amour* resurfaces. The composer understood this movement as a "fallback into the dualistic universe where the two horns are no longer sublimated but assert themselves 'one against the other.'"[46] Marked "savage and very rhythmic," this movement of *Accords perdus* is characterized by fast glissandi at dissonant intervals between the two instruments, and more delineated overtone scales, trills, and pulsations at irregular intervals. The dynamic range increases as the piece goes on, with softer dynamics slowly infiltrating themselves, as this movement, lasting under two minutes, goes straight into the final piece.

This final movement is titled "chute" ("slide"), a programmatic description of the glissandi in the low range of the horn. Grisey also explores multiphonics in this concluding movement. He wonders whether the music calls forth "fusion, return to calm, or entropy?"[47] While *Accords perdus* is a minor work, closer in ambition to *Manifestations* than to the compositions before and after it, it is a non-dogmatic piece that shows the composer continuing to search for an ever-more-personal voice. It was dedicated to the American composer Elliott Carter,[48] who wrote, in a thank-you note, "The title eludes me, but the music does not."[49]

---

45   Gebhardt, *Sepktralismus. Gérard Griseys "Accords perdus."*
46   Lelong, *Écrits*, 164.
47   Ibid.
48   According to Wintle, Grisey was "bored stiff" by Carter's complex serialist music. The goal of the dedication might have been careerist.
49   Paul Sacher archive.

Chapter Twelve

Seduced by the Star (1988–91)

In 1985, while Grisey was a professor at the University of California at Berkeley, he had attended a social function where he made the acquaintance of Joe Silk, a British-American astrophysicist. Silk began teaching at the institution in 1970 and was appointed chair of the astronomy department in 1978. Isolated as Grisey seemed in the music department, it made sense that he went looking elsewhere—beyond the often small-stake aesthetic disputes of musical academia—for intellectual nourishment. Grisey and Silk got to talking about the universe. The astronomer remembered the composer as fascinated by his field, how it explained cosmic "beginnings and endings."[1] Grisey's examination of the births and deaths of sounds was to expand into an investigation of the births and deaths of stars.

Silk introduced the composer to the astronomical concept of pulsars, then still rather new. In 1967, a graduate student at the University of Cambridge named Jocelyn Bell Burnell discovered, almost by accident, a radio transmission that was extremely periodic, emanating a signal every 1.33730133 seconds. The vast majority of astronomical signals are either transient signals, caused by unique and violent events such as the explosion of a star or the formation of a black hole; or erratic signals, radiation emitted irregularly by solar flares and magnetic storms on distant planets. The regularity of this new signal was so stunning that astronomers first guessed the signal was a beacon from an alien civilization. A year later, Franco Pacini and Thomas Gold developed the concept of the pulsar, or "rapidly rotating neutron star." As the French astrophysicist Jean-Pierre Luminet described it in his 1987 book of popular astronomy, *Black Holes*:

> A neutron star is highly magnetized and its magnetic field lines channel electrically charged particles (electrons and protons), enabling it, by "synchrotron radiation," to emit a beam of radio waves which rotates along

---

1   Interview with Silk.

with the star. As the star revolves, a pulse is received at the Earth, at the moment when the beam sweeps across the aperture of the radio telescope.[2]

Neutron stars are formed when the unstable core of a large star collapses, a process that can take billions of years. They are structurally similar to white dwarfs, contracted remnants of stars which become extremely small and incredibly hot. Neutron stars are even smaller and hotter, factors which help explain the extreme speed of their rotations. "The Sun turns on its axis once every 25 days," Luminet explains, "whereas a neutron star completes a revolution in less than a second, in rigid rotation."[3] These extremely rapid movements generate the radio waves that allow astronomers to detect them.

According to Grisey's recollections, Silk introduced the composer specifically to the Vela pulsar, so named because it is located among the remains of the Vela supernova, which exploded some 11,000 to 12,300 years ago. The Vela pulsar rotates at about eleven times per second and is extremely faint, a quality that seemed to have added to its mystery and appeal for the composer. "I was seduced"—note the choice of word—"by the Vela pulsar and immediately asked myself in the manner of Picasso picking up an old bicycle saddle, 'What could I possibly do with it?'" Grisey wrote later.[4] Besides the remarkable periodicity of the pulsar, Grisey was also fascinated by Vela's "glitches," a term astrophysicists adapted from electronics. These glitches occur occasionally in the life of a star and are defined as a "sudden event which acts to accelerate the star," reducing "the period of the pulsar … by a ten millionth of a second over a period of a few days."[5]

As was often the case with Grisey, it took time for these concepts to germinate into a musical idea. On July 27, 1988, Grisey wrote a letter to Luminet, who, besides being an astrophysicist with a large lay following, was also a published essayist and poet and an avid follower of the contemporary arts. (Grisey also wrote to the Canadian astrophysicist Hubert Reeves, but Reeves was unavailable.) In this letter to Luminet, Grisey set out his initial thinking for the piece that became *Le noir de l'étoile* (*The Black of the Star*):

> After many discussions, Joe Silk played me some recordings of pulsars. Since then, the beauty of some of these sounds made me dream and contemplate so much that I decided to compose a rather long piece, probably for orchestra and some electronics, which would use pulsar sounds as material. These will be the starting point and reference point of the musical structure… .

---

2   Luminet, *Black Holes*, 99.
3   Ibid.
4   Lelong, *Écrits*, 166.
5   Luminet, *Black Holes*.

I would like to meet you during my next visit to Paris. Maybe you can suggest other sounds or direct me to interested people or laboratories that have these recordings. The project I would like to talk to you about is a whole evening on the pulsar phenomenon ... Integrating pulsars into a musical composition is an exciting idea, so I am counting on your discretion not to divulge too much about this project![6]

Luminet had already heard of Grisey, being a pianist and a close follower of contemporary music in France. Luminet even owned an LP of Grisey's *Partiels* and *Dérives*. In a letter dated September 13, 1988, Luminet responded to Grisey's idea with enthusiasm. He did note that Grisey's idea was not unique: Luminet had recently been approached by another composer with a similar request for pulsar recordings, and a third artist "gave a concert during which the audience (mostly jaded astrophysicists!) could listen live to the monotonous beat of a pulsar captured by a radio telescope a few thousand kilometers away." Of these compositions, only *Le noir de l'étoile* left a lasting musical impression. As Luminet wrote, "In this case, being first is of little importance compared to the *mis en oeuvre*, and in this I'm sure you will be the best."[7]

In late 1988 or early 1989, Grisey began visiting Luminet at the Observatoire de Paris in Meudon. Founded in 1667 by Louis XIV, the observatory includes a modest park, where the two men would walk and talk, discussing the latest ideas from quantum physics and astronomy as well as music, literature, and the visual arts. Grisey and Luminet quickly became friends.

While the idea for *Le noir de l'étoile* was taking shape in Grisey's mind, he was already in the middle of composing the piece that would eventually becoming *Le temps et l'écume*, and one of the ideas from quantum physics to which Luminet introduced him was the concept of "space-time foam." Conceived by the physicist John Wheeler, it proposes in layman's terms that "spacetime is not constant, but 'foamy,' made up of ever-changing tiny bubbles ... recent work suggests that spacetime bubbles are essentially mini-universes briefly forming inside our own."[8] It's a concept that dovetails with Grisey's philosophical understanding of sounds, their overtone series containing nearly infinite universes in and of themselves. He used the phrase for his next composition, *Le temps et l'écume*, whose title translates literally to *Time and Foam*.[9] By doing

---

6   Lelong, *Écrits*, 347.
7   Paul Sacher archive.
8   Minsky, "The Universe is Made of Tiny Bubbles."
9   Interview with Luminet.

so, as Joshua Fineberg points out, Grisey was blatantly contradicting his famous statement that "We are musicians and our model is sound not literature, sound not mathematics, sound not theatre, plastic arts, *quantum theory*, geology, *astrology* ..."[10]

Grisey and the German composer Helmut Lachenmann first met around 1973 in Boswil, Switzerland, which hosts an artist residency.[11] Their relationship was a rich vein of exchange, with the men swapping personal updates, professional opportunities, and their most recent music. Despite coming from vastly different aesthetics—where Grisey's music is often lush and transcendental, Lachenmann's compositions are frequently disparate, noisy, full of biting historical irony—the two composers had much in common. Lachenmann and Grisey exchanged scores and recordings of their latest pieces, giving one another a sort of aesthetic nourishment. On May 11, 1988, Lachenmann wrote to Grisey, "I don't know *Talea* yet, but I hope to get to know it, sooner or later. Your pieces have always been important experiences for me, for my ears and for my soul." A month later, Lachenmann arranged for Grisey to receive a copy of his pointillistic, thrilling masterpiece *Ausklang* (1984–85) for solo piano and orchestra, a piece which examines the mechanical actions and physical motions required to play the piano with the kind of microscopic precision and care that Grisey trained on sounds themselves. In exchange, Lachenmann asked for a score and recording of *Dérives*. When Lachenmann later received recordings of Grisey's pieces *Le temps et l'écume* and *Talea*, he told Grisey, "This is fantastic, and my admiration is great. I don't know anyone else with such a self-sufficient sense of sound. Thank you."[12]

In 1988, Lachenmann made Grisey an intriguing professional offer. The composer Erhard Karkoschka was leaving his post at the Musikhochschule in Stuttgart, and Lachenmann wanted to know if Grisey would be interested in the position, which would require twenty hours per week of teaching. "It should be an interesting composer with a profile (e.g. you), whom I get along with personally (e.g., you), but who can also lead the electronic music studio (you???)," Lachenmann wrote, praising his friend's combination of aesthetic self-sufficiency and willingness to communicate. In an undated (but likely later) postcard, Lachenmann added: "If you should weaken after

---

10 Brown, "A Gérard Grisey Playlist."
11 Interview with Lachenmann.
12 Paul Sacher archive.

all and take an interest in becoming a professor of composition with us, I would do everything I can to help you come here (I can't make any promises, except that it won't be for lack of me trying)." Grisey's responses to these overtures are lost, but it seems plausible that he declined in order to preserve his time for composition: twenty hours a week of teaching was more than double Grisey's official schedule at the University of California at Berkeley. (This could have included fewer meetings than in California, though German universities are not known for their sleek bureaucracies.) With hindsight, the idea is tantalizing to consider: a composition department with Lachenmann and Grisey as teachers, situated in Germany close to the French border, could have become one of the most exciting places for the development of new music on the European continent.

After this, Grisey and Lachenmann fell out of touch. "We neglected our contact, because each of us was following his own creative 'obsession,'" Lachenmann said. "I love and admire his music, full of intelligent and ingenious sensuality. The superficial 'spectral' label does not do justice to the substance and expressive depth of his work. From my own, vastly different compositional-technical orientation, it never left me indifferent."[13]

Grisey composed *Le temps et l'écume* between 1988 and 1989, at his homes in Brussels and Paris. The piece was commissioned by Radio France and scored for a medium orchestra with two Yamaha synthesizers. Though one of the less prominent pieces in the composer's oeuvre, it is still a brooding, effective composition that marks the first true work in Grisey's "period of different times," in Lelong's term.[14]

In his program note to *Le temps et l'écume*, Grisey named two related questions that he aimed to explore in the work. "Since *Épilogue* and *Talea*, I've been highly preoccupied by acceleration," he wrote. "Is it possible to accelerate a process without returning to a gestural music?"[15] By "gestural music," Grisey meant music with motives and phrases, music that makes an almost linguistic impression. He thought of the term as an opposite pole to the process-based composition that he preferred. Grisey felt that the iconoclastic Mexican-American composer Conlon Nancarrow had succeeded in eliminating gesture while composing acceleration; in works such as the *Study for Player Piano 40A*, descending runs and pseudo-ragtime gestures are sped up to such an extent that the individual pitches which make them up lose all

---

13   Interview with Lachenmann.
14   Lelong, *Écrits*, 427.
15   Ibid, 165.

meaning. But, in another way, these pieces *are* gestural music: they distort and caricature the gestures of traditional piano playing almost beyond recognition. In any case, Grisey wanted to go a step further in his exploration of acceleration, attempting to "surpass the speed of human language" without recourse to mechanical or electronic instruments.

For *Le temps et l'écume*, Grisey modified one of his favorite images, that of a microscope zooming in and out of sounds as it does with living cells, to a temporal one: the various time scales of humans, insects, and whales. (Baillet writes "humans, *birds*, and whales" but the difference seems significant.[16]) To illustrate these three different ways of experiencing time, Grisey uses archetypical material made up of two parts, reusing an important conceptual element of *Talea*. One element is noisy, rhythmical, discontinuous but with the feeling of pulse; the other is harmonic, staggered, continuous without a pulse. Grisey was attempting to walk a difficult line: creating core material that is specific enough to be perceptible and memorable, but broad enough to undergo extreme transformation and that avoids becoming a gesture or even a motive. As the musicologist Ingrid Pustijanac has shown, Grisey used statistical procedures of rhythmic development to structure the pace of passing time in this new work.[17]

The first section of *Le temps et l'écume* is in "human time." Chronometrically, it takes up the first nine or so minutes of the piece. The work opens with what Baillet describes as a "rustling" texture, made up of growling percussion and bass, and repetitive augmented seconds in the synthesizer.[18] This music has the quality of—in the wonderful German phrase—an *Ursuppe*, or "primeval soup." The first part of the overarching gesture emerges from these depths. The archetypical material then appears in thirteen variations and, as in *Talea*, where one gesture gets progressively shorter, the other gets progressively longer. In *Le temps et l'écume*, the two parts of the gesture never really meld. The "spectral" subsection of the gesture slowly takes over, swinging the perceived pendulum of the music to the harmonic. This process is clearly audible, marked by string glissandi and pizzicati at the end of each of the thirteen repetitions.

The next section lasts just 28.5 seconds, a reflection of the incomprehensibility, for humans, of the scale of the life of an insect like a mosquito. This new section is marked by fast ascending-descending runs, most prominently in the winds. Grisey divides his material into two groups, assigning them each a projection of spectra. Baillet notes that Grisey's process is to shorten the length of each group, thereby creating a global acceleration—though one

---

16   Baillet, *Fondements d'une écriture*, 187.
17   Pustijanac, "Un esempio di 'squelette du temps.'"
18   Baillet, *Fondements d'une écriture*, 186.

that doesn't surpass the speed of human language.[19] As Philipp Naumann writes in a study of *Le temps et l'écume*, this section "creates the impression ... of looking through binoculars held the wrong way around. From a long ways away, a macrocosmos of 'flying' melodies is revealed."[20] Despite the new poetic image of insect time, this brief section, with its entangled winds, recalls textures from many previous Grisey pieces, especially from *Les espaces acoustiques*.

The third and final section of *Le temps et l'écume* takes place in the time of whales. Though Grisey refers to "the music of the whales" in his program note, unlike George Crumb's *Vox Balaenae*, from 1971, this piece is less interested in the *sounds* whales make than in the scale of their lives, which can extend to over two hundred years, all spent in the vast ocean. Here, the dual quantum and animal inspirations for Grisey's piece align: Luminet has compared spacetime foam to the foam on the surface of the ocean, imperceptible from an airplane, but vivid at the beach.

This section of the work is stretched so extremely that it consists almost entirely of one long rendition of the single archetypal gesture that undergirds the piece. The first half of this final section is devoted to the noise portion of the gesture and contains, as Baillet shows, two opposite processes, first of deceleration, then of acceleration: an echo of the dual nature of the main gesture itself. These processes gain momentum through periodic bass notes reminiscent of the repetitive synthesizer notes at the beginning. The second half of the final section consists of nine phrases with different fundamentals, with a structure Baillet likens to Russian dolls, with one phrase emerging from the other, now calcifying gradually toward the end of the work. Melodic passages in the flutes, clarinets, trumpets, and horns, recalling the section of "insect time," guide the ear through this process of slowing: they become slower in a way that is more immediately perceptible to our ears than the temporal extension of the monolithic spectral chords.[21]

As Baillet notes, the three-part structure of *Le temps et l'écume* raises more questions than answers: the long final section, for example, is not necessarily heard as a single massive gesture, but "is animated from the inside by microevents."[22] Grisey, such a perfectionist about the aural results of his scores, was uncommonly upfront about this issue in his program note: "There will undoubtedly be once again a slight mismatch between intention and realization, between dream and reality," he writes, "but isn't it this human fragility

---

19 Ibid.
20 Naumann, "Schaum auf den Wellen der Raumzeit," 27.
21 Baillet, *Fondements d'une écriture*, 190–196.
22 Ibid, 198.

and this awkwardness faced with a too-vast project that allows a little of what we call beauty to remain?"[23]

Le temps et l'écume was premiered on December 11, 1989, at the Maison de Radio France by the Nouvel Orchestre Philharmonique de Radio France, conducted by the American David Robertson. It was Robertson's first in-depth engagement with spectral music. "I remember thinking, 'OK, this is complex stuff, let me go to the piano and play it,'" he said. "There were thirteen notes in the first chord that starts the piece off, and I could only play three of them on an equally tempered piano. That left me feeling quite daunted." Robertson had to accept that he would not be able to hear the music in his head before he gave the first downbeat. But he rehearsed with Grisey, whom he found "very calm, but very exacting," and the premiere was a success. The concert was long and had too many new works, Robertson recalled, but the audience could tell that *Le temps et l'écume* "was a serious piece in the repertoire."[24]

In 1983, Claudia Doderer, a German artist and set designer whose mother was one of the initiators of the Darmstädter Ferienkurse, had moved to Brussels to work on projects at the Théâtre Royale de La Monnaie, including a legendary staging of *Wozzeck*. One New Year's Eve, probably from 1986 to 1987, she was invited to a dinner with Louwrens Langevoort and his partner Hervé Boutry, both of whom worked at the opera house. As a gift she brought a sketch she'd made, "a colored structure." The men put it on their mantle.

At the dinner, Doderer was seated next to Grisey. They began to talk in German, which he still spoke well, about Berlin, a city that continued to fascinate him. He noticed Doderer's sketch and asked who it was by. She said it was hers. "Then it burst out of him," Doderer recalled. He told her, "I'm looking for someone, I need someone … I have a vision for a piece."

Grisey and Doderer met again the next day. They spent hours on the tram and in the park, eating ice cream and talking about Ravel, love, and the idea for *Le noir de l'étoile*. "One sees how things mix," Doderer said, "time, love, and the project." A few days later, Doderer came to see Grisey at Detry's home in Brussels, where he noted ruefully that he had the smallest room in the house as his studio. Grisey showed Doderer *Modulations* and explained his idea for *Le noir de l'étoile*, tapping out one of the rhythms of the piece with his finger on his knee.

---

23 Lelong, *Écrits*, 165.
24 Interview with Robertson.

Doderer and Grisey began meeting almost weekly. Although funding for the project came late and piecemeal, they both "burned" for the idea. Doderer came up with a concept for the concert space that involved triangular sails mounted on poles, a structure inspired by the Milky Way. She wanted to underscore Grisey's idea of creating "a communal experience of the abstraction of time." Because the piece was impermanent, it had to be removable after the performance, so Doderer developed the idea of submerging the poles in water instead of fixing them to the ground or the ceiling. They also worked with the light designer Kurt-Rüdiger Wogatzke, from the opera in Stuttgart, choosing to only use reds and blues to give the performance a Constructivist flair.[25]

Meanwhile, Grisey and Luminet continued to discuss other "possible cosmic sounds," as the astrophysicist described them, for the piece. They eventually settled on pulsars because they created more "structured" emissions than shorter-lived phenomena like solar flares.[26] Even when composing with some of the most mysterious acoustic phenomena humans have ever discovered in the universe, Grisey was careful to find the link with musical perception.

Luminet, whose expertise in astronomy lies in the theoretical, set about finding radioastronomers who could help Grisey realize his emerging vision. The sonic world of the piece began to take shape in the composer's mind. After his initial introduction to pulsars through Silk in 1985, Grisey had begun reading popular books on astronomy; he also delved into the historical connections between outer space and music, in works ranging from Pythagoras to those of the seventeenth-century German astronomer Johannes Kepler, who saw God in the motion of the planets, and who developed a concept of the "music of the spheres."[27] As Luminet recalled, Grisey was especially interested in the overlap between astronomical signals and their relationships to frequency and duration, with an emphasis on the slower pulsars, which could be translated more readily into musical rhythms. (We perceive very fast signals as pitch.) As the idea for *Le noir de l'étoile* took shape in Grisey's mind, the composer considered ways of integrating the astronomical phenomena

> without manipulating them, letting them exist simply as reference points within a kind of box or setting, and finally using their frequencies as tempi and developing the ideas of rotation, periodicity, deceleration, acceleration, and "glitches" that the study of pulsars suggests to astronomers. The percussion was necessary because, like the pulsars, it is primordial and implacable and, like them, circumscribes and measures time with a certain

---

25   Interview with Doderer.
26   Luminet, "*Le noir de l'étoile*," 418.
27   Kepler, *Harmonices Mundi*.

austerity. Finally, I decided to reduce the instrumentation to skins and metals and exclude the keyboards.²⁸

In a sense, *Le noir de l'étoile* was less a work "inspired by" the stars, and more a cosmic expansion on acoustic phenomena.

As mentioned, early in the composition process, Luminet had pointed out to Grisey that his idea was not completely new. In Western music history, other composers had also looked to the cosmos for inspiration. In a 1999 lecture, Luminet, the consummate astronomer and musician, summarized this history, which included

> Haydn's and Janáček's operatic voyages to the Moon [and] Holst's planetary orchestral [suite]. In his opera *The Harmony of the World* and the orchestral suite that he drew from it, Hindemith faithfully adopts the correspondences provided by Kepler and uses them as a leitmotif. In *Atlas Eclipticalis*, for chamber orchestra, the mischievous John Cage uses a star chart to determine the pitches of the notes. Stockhausen looks for the path of the stars in Sirius in certain parts of his monumental *Licht*. Gérard Grisey makes the stars sing in a completely different way.²⁹

Although the team was passionate about this project, the lack of institutional support made the organizational work tough at times. On July 25, 1990, Bruno de Beaufort, the manager of Les Percussions de Strasbourg, sent Grisey a letter detailing the conditions of his contract for the work, with a total fee of 80,000 francs, and those of his team, consisting of the set designer Doderer, lighting designer Wogatzke, and the sound designer Orthon Schneider.³⁰ At the end of the month, Grisey responded in a piqued tone about his fee, something which was becoming an increasingly common feature of his correspondence. Grisey insisted that it be set at 80,000 francs excluding an additional commission given by the Ministère de la Culture. (The responses to his appeals have not been preserved and were probably concluded by phone.) Though he agreed to a 5,000-franc honorarium per concert, the same amount as Doderer and Wogatzke, Grisey made it clear to de Beaufort that he saw himself as the main artistic protagonist of this piece. "Do I have to remind you that I'm the author of this project and the composer of the music, without which this spectacle would have no meaning? Do you realize that I've been working on this score for more than a year, five hours a day, and that it's been impossible to accept any other commissions before this project is completed and realized?" In the future, Grisey's negotiations with ensembles would often include this twofold resentment: a sense

---

28 Lelong, *Écrits*, 166.
29 Luminet, "Musiques des Pulsars," 409.
30 Wogatzke died in 2016.

that his work was undervalued, along with a feeling of pressure from being unable to churn out works for money—a trait that led both to the exceptional quality of his small oeuvre as well as his constant need to maximize the fee for every piece. On August 6, 1990, after another back-and-forth with de Beaufort, Grisey agreed to accept the slightly lower sum of 70,000 francs, plus the government commission and additional expenses.[31] *Le noir de l'étoile* "was a hard-fought battle," Doderer said. She remembers that in one meeting with a concert presenter, Grisey got so frustrated that he broke a chair.[32]

The piece is dedicated "to my son Raphaël, affectionately": maybe a nod to Grisey's guilt over his absence from his son during this period, or an expression of his childlike fascination with astronomy, or both. *Le noir de l'étoile* is scored for its six percussionists in a circle around the audience, placing the listener in the star-like position of being orbited around. The work opens with a spoken introduction, written (and read at some performances) by Luminet, who is gifted at explaining astrophysics in layman's terms. After that comes something unusual in Grisey's oeuvre, an instance of outright borrowing. The first twenty-two minutes—the first movement—of *Le noir de l'étoile* are almost exactly the same as *Tempus ex Machina*, from 1979. As Baillet has analyzed, the connection goes further than that. All of *Le noir de l'étoile* is structured according to the same arithmetic scale Grisey used in his earlier work.[33]

The only difference between *Tempus ex Machina* and the first movement of *Le noir de l'étoile* is one of context. As Luminet points out in his own, insightful formal analysis of the piece, we are "waiting for the 'celestial object,'" an anticipation which colors our perception of this section.[34] When the Vela pulsar comes in at last, Grisey smuggles its first entrance in among a mess of wooden percussion. Then he gives it two minutes to sound alone—an appropriate length of time to allow us to appreciate the marvel of the live transmission of the beatings of a star. (This effect took a massive organizational effort, involving telescopes in Australia and France and precise timing for the premiere.)

The Vela beatings become subsumed in the music of the second movement, a process which Luminet describes as the "contamination of the speed of the pulsar by the percussionists." The beginning of this second movement is a complex process of deceleration, marked, as in the first movement, by the interjections of a loud bass drum which function as signposts for the ear.

---

31   Paul Sacher archive.
32   Interview with Doderer.
33   Baillet, *Fondements d'une écriture*, 175.
34   Luminet, "*Le noir de l'étoile*," 422.

Intensity is regained through an interplay between cascading figures in the woods, and groaning sounds created on a variety of unusual instruments, such as the guiro and Waldteufel. The slow, regular beating of another pulsar, named 0329+54, enters at the end of this second movement. Again, it is drowned out at first by the percussion, until its extraterrestrial periodicity is revealed for a full three minutes. The flow of time in the work seems to stop, again allowing us to process our awe.

As Luminet notes, the third movement opens with an interruption of the pulsar by the percussion—a sort of dragging of the listener back to the earth—and the "discovery of another sonic space: the metals."[35] Almost all sensation of regular beatings is lost here, in what the musicologist Dimitris Exarchos terms "spectral polyphony."[36] Archaic, alternating rhythms make a gradual reappearance. As listeners, we need periodicity eventually, and midway through the third movement we get a short return to quasi-chronometric time: soft, regular beatings at the pulse of a second. The wood interjections that structure the first movement and reappear in the second return again, giving a sort of motivic unity to the entire piece and, by now, signaling the increase in textural density and volume to come. Luminet describes this passage as a "progressive unleashing of centrifugal forces [with] variations of speed and intensity."[37] After reaching its last climax, the work ends with a short, deconstructed coda and a hit on an amplified cymbal: the first pitched sound after nearly an hour of music for unpitched percussion. As in *Épilogue*, the ending implies more music could come; it doesn't try to neatly wrap up the piece. As Luminet writes, "Grisey was clearly one of those perceptive observers who finds the light in the black of the night."[38]

On March 15, 1991, the night before the premiere, Grisey and Doderer sat in Les Halles de Schaerbeek in Brussels alone, mostly in silence. The building, since renovated, was then in a state of near collapse; there were no bathrooms. "I was incredibly nervous," Doderer said. "If one of the poles had fallen down ... it was risky." But Grisey seemed satisfied. He told her, "It's beautiful, Claudia. Exactly what I wished for." There was sand on the ground, and to Doderer, the construction and the music combined the archaic with the highly technical.[39] Pulsars have existed since before humans; we have just gained the ability to perceive them.

Le noir de l'étoile premiered at 5:30 p.m. on March 16, by Les Percussions de Strasbourg. Luminet admitted that he found the austerity of the piece

---

35   Ibid.
36   Exarchos, "The Skin of Time in Grisey's *Le noir de l'étoile*," 44.
37   Luminet, "*Le noir de l'étoile*," 422.
38   Ibid, 423.
39   Interview with Doderer.

difficult at first. "I was not completely convinced. It's a difficult work, in fact," he said, "and also, I think it's one of the characteristics of Gérard's compositions that he starts very slowly, very few things happen ... It was not spectacular and cosmic at the beginning."[40] Listening multiple times, Luminet came to love the work. Detry was also unsure about its effect on first hearing. "I felt terribly bad, I felt imprisoned in such a strong noise," she said. "It led to a little disagreement between us."[41]

For Doderer, however, it was a cathartic moment. At the post-concert reception, Grisey gave her a gift of a child's sandbox, with a little shovel. She still remembers him holding it as he made his way through the chic and sophisticated crowd.

In *La Lettre du Musicien*, Guy Lelong praised the "astonishing rhythmic invention of *Le noir de l'étoile*," adding that the listener "gets a strange, undeniable sense of vertigo" from hearing the piece. In *Le Monde*, the critic Anne Rey described hearing the piece as like "being inside a giant stethoscope, listening to the pulse of the universe." She added that the entrance of the pulsars made the audience's "hearts beat faster."[42]

Le noir de l'étoile, created by Grisey with Doderer, Wogatzke, Schneider, and Luminet, traveled throughout Europe. Doderer remembers a performance of the piece at the Huddersfield Contemporary Music Festival in England, where the generator went out and she and Grisey had to sit in a McDonald's all night for warmth. In recent years, however, ensembles have taken to playing it without its most difficult, expensive, and magical aspects: without Doderer's installation and Wogatzke's lighting, using only a recording of Luminet's text, and—most problematically—with recordings of the pulsars rather than the live transmission. "The magic lies in the live transmission," Doderer said. She believes Grisey would not recognize versions of *Le noir de l'étoile* that do not provide the full artistic contribution of the team.[43]

---

40 Interview with Luminet.
41 Interview with Detry.
42 Press clippings in the archive of Les Percussions de Strasbourg.
43 Interview with Doderer.

Chapter Thirteen
Suggestions of the Infinite (1991–96)

In January 1991, Mireille Deguy, a dark-haired, fine-featured mezzo-soprano of Moroccan-Jewish heritage, went to the Maison de Radio France to listen to a concert at the Présence Festival of contemporary music. Deguy, an elegant woman with a certain warm formality, had studied voice in Aix-en-Provence in the south of France and in Lausanne, Switzerland. She worked with singers like the eminent German mezzo-soprano Christa Ludwig and studied at the Academy of the Opéra national de Paris, developing an interest in contemporary music.

Grisey was also at the Maison de Radio France that day, his head in the clouds. He had been overseeing the mix of a recording of *Talea*. But his mind was on something more ambitious: his massive new orchestral work, later to receive the title *L'Icône paradoxale*, for the Los Angeles Philharmonic.

When a mutual friend introduced Deguy to Grisey, she noticed his distraction, but also found him kind, and keenly interested in the singing voice. They discovered that they had a lot to talk about and began spending hours on the phone. "It was very simple, because I had the impression that he was someone I had already known for a long time," Deguy said.

Within two months, Deguy and Grisey were together. "It happened very quickly," Deguy said. "It was fate."[1]

But Grisey was still in a relationship with France Detry. Like Jocelyne, Detry was aware—and to a large extent reconciled—to the fact that Grisey was not the monogamous type. For Detry, it was important to grant Grisey the freedom to be with other women, first when he lived in Berkeley, then as he commuted between Brussels and Paris:

> He liked to conquer the world, especially the world of women ... I couldn't put Gérard in a cage. From the beginning I knew that. It was not an effort for me. Our relationship was built on that basis. When he was in Paris,

---

1   Interview with Deguy.

he could do what he wanted. I told him, "As long as I don't have telephone calls from your girlfriends, as long as you don't bring me any disease—that was very important!—and when you're in Paris it's your world, you're free. But no telephone calls and no diseases." Those were the two [requirements].[2]

Like Jocelyne before, Detry remained a port in the storm of Grisey's erotic life. "Home was very important—he had to have a home somewhere," she said. "I felt that [Brussels] was his home. For me, that was enough."

As a way of explaining his interest in numerous romantic encounters—to Detry and possibly to himself—Grisey turned to Giacomo Casanova's memoir *The Story of My Life*. The eighteenth-century Venetian had a few things in common with Grisey: both were close to their grandmothers, both were avid readers, and both had wrestled hard with sexual morality as teenagers, before becoming convinced that sex was a gift. Casanova also questioned the Christian doctrine that "the soul's dependence on the senses and organs is purely fortuitous and transitory, and that it will be free and happy when the death of the body liberates it from their tyrannical power." In fact, Casanova's attitude toward sex and love fit well with the climate of the late 1960s and 1970s when Grisey forged his mature sexuality: Casanova, the famous libertine, dabbled in all sorts of bisexual and group arrangements; foreswore jealousy; and declared that "any oaths of eternal fidelity [were] absurd oaths indeed, which a man is in no condition to swear to even the most beautiful of women." Detry recalled that Grisey "loved Casanova's *The Story of My Life*. He told me I should absolutely read it. So I did. I thought it was OK. [Grisey said], 'But Casanova was a good man. He really took care of the woman that got pregnant by him.'" Understandably, Detry was not entirely convinced.[3] While certain aspects of Casanova's approach to love were progressive for his time, others were typical of it. In *The Story of My Life*, women "give themselves up" to men, they are "conquered." The man's pleasure is always in the foreground.[4]

Neither Grisey's standing relationship with Detry nor his blossoming one with Mireille Deguy in Paris was simply a tryst, though Grisey had those, too. These relationships were romantic, passionate connections that involved intense feelings on all sides. Though Deguy was spending much of her time with Grisey in early 1991, she also kept her own apartment in Paris. In June, the composer decided to spend his summer vacation with Detry in Italy. Deguy was busy with work that summer, but she continued to correspond with Grisey. It was a painfully unclear situation. France Detry said, "When

---

2 Interview with Detry.
3 Ibid.
4 Casanova, *The History of My Life*.

he was with me, he was totally with me. Except during the last period, when he was with Mireille. I know that when he was with her, he was thinking of me, and when he was with me, he was thinking of her."[5]

Gérard Zinsstag, Grisey's most intimate friend, wrote in a letter to Grisey that it was time for him to decide between the two woman who both clearly loved him:

> I saw Mireille ... She has lost a lot of weight; she doesn't eat anymore and seems to be suffering terribly. Gérard, the time of multiple, parallel liaisons is (or should be) over: you have to decide, because Mireille and France and you are all suffering. Please don't let things get out of hand; of course, it's none of my business, but I am your friend, your faithful friend, and I want you to feel good ... I can see that a deep tenderness binds you to France and that you can hardly get away from her. Anyway, women have changed: they are not so docile anymore. They want, they demand, while men would still be eternal young men looking for the lost pleasure ... [6]

In the fall of 1992, Grisey wrote France Detry a letter asking her to marry him. Stunned, she didn't answer. In November, Zinsstag called Detry and told her that she needed to speak to Grisey. She got in her car and drove to Paris. "I slept overnight there, but I said no," she recalled. "And then he fell apart, but I fell apart, too." After that rejection, for which Detry had so many sound reasons, Grisey seemed unable to face her again. "When we separated, he didn't come to pick up his things," Detry recalled. "He said, 'Put everything in boxes, and I will send a friend.' I had to prepare everything, put everything in boxes by myself. And he didn't even come to pick up his things. He was a bit of a coward."[7] France Detry and Grisey never spoke again. For her part, Detry now sympathized with the heartbreak that Jocelyne had experienced when the Griseys' marriage ended:

> I know that Jocelyne suffered a lot. One day, when I was packing all his things, I found the letters that Jocelyne had sent him. And I was so touched by the love. But for Gérard, Jocelyne was just nonexistent anymore. [I thought], *My turn now*. Even though he said, "You're the love of my life." One nail drives out another.[8]

"Life became impossible between France and Gérard," Mireille Deguy said. "I contributed a little to this misfortune for France." At the same time, she realized that Grisey "had the need to feel free, to have his secret garden.

---

5   Interview with Detry.
6   Ibid.
7   Ibid.
8   Ibid.

He must have felt too invaded with Jocelyne and France" (though Detry sees it differently).

Grisey and Deguy structured their relationship to include space and privacy for both of them. They were each people who needed lots of freedom and who were happy to have time apart. Two weeks together was roughly the right amount. "Then we needed some air," Deguy said. She continued:

> I think I reassured him. I'm Mediterranean. I'm anxious when it comes to myself, but for others I take charge. I brought something soothing for him, he was not very calm. Maybe it's maturity, it's a mixture of things. A couple is an association of two sets of neuroses ... Our two neuroses always managed to soothe this slightly anxious side that he had, he was always a little feverish.[9]

In his vacillation between Detry and Deguy, Grisey was cruel. After the end of his relationship with Detry, he sent her an *eighteen-page* letter detailing what he thought was wrong with her, an act Detry chalked up to his attempt to rid himself of an obsession. "He tried to make dark every part of me," she said. "I burned the letter."[10]

It helped that Mireille Deguy was a musician; her warmth and kindness were essential to Grisey during his bouts of insecurity. Though their relationship started off with suffering, nearly every observer would say that with Deguy, Grisey seemed his happiest.

※ ※ ※

In Saul Bellow's 1964 novel *Herzog*, the protagonist spends much of his time writing furious letters to correspondents such as his ex-wives, Friedrich Nietzsche, and God.[11] In the late 1980s, Grisey began writing letters to more prosaic correspondents that also reflected a deep-seated frustration, even anger. Many of Grisey's friends observe that he felt under-appreciated during his lifetime. As in his rehearsals, he could be harsh in his business dealings. Joshua Fineberg said that Grisey was always unwilling to put himself in the "beggar posture" generally expected of composers, who are supposed to be grateful for the slightest crumb. Grisey never "groveled."[12] This combination of ego and wounded pride was stoked by the composer's financial worries. "He earned very little, with a part-time position at the

---

9   Interview with Deguy.
10 Interview with Detry.
11 Bellow, *Herzog*.
12 Interview with Fineberg.

Conservatoire [and] very little in the way of royalties," Deguy said. "It was very painful for him. He had the impression that he wasn't recognized."[13]

A particularly niggling problem for Grisey was the obtainment of royalties for his performances through the Sacem, the French royalties society. In February 1992, he accused the organization of refusing to issue him payment for pieces performed over the last six years. In March, Grisey wrote to Mimma Guastoni of Ricordi complaining about receiving a smaller sum than he felt he was due for performances of *Dérives* and *Transitoires-Épilogue*. "Mimma, I would like you to take this letter seriously since, without exaggeration, I view all this as an insult to my human dignity and a lack of appreciation of my quality as a composer," he wrote. "The result is catastrophic for my composing, and for the freedom of spirit that is necessary for creativity. I'm exhausted from playing Don Quixote."

In 1994, during contract negotiations for an upcoming work, Grisey noted that "I know, for Ricordi's budget ... the sum of $1,000 is meaningless. Unfortunately, it's not the same for me."

Besides money, Grisey's biggest worry was lack of time to compose. In one letter, Grisey wrote to Guastoni to complain that

> this new notoriety weighs on me, with all the administrative management that it implies and that I am unable to face, alone, without an agent or a secretary.
>
> I'm fighting like a lion to preserve the sacred and silent space necessary for any poetic creation and I confess to you that I fear at any moment being devoured by the administrative hydra ... . How can I avoid becoming little more than the manager of my past?

But Grisey sometimes took time away from composing to dash off piqued letters, not all of which were related to money. In 1992, Grisey signed a joint letter accusing Claude Samuel—the administrator who had given the young composer some of his very first commissions—of intentionally trivializing Radio France's contemporary music program. He wrote to the Sacem to complain about an article on Olivier Messiaen in the organization's newsletter: "One little page and a nasty picture to commemorate the memory of one of the great composers of this century! ... Sacem will still reap the rewards while those honored in the pages of its magazine will be forgotten." (Ironically, Grisey received Sacem's Prix des Compositeurs in April 1993.) In 1995, Grisey complained to the label Erato that his name—he also mentioned other composers—wasn't featured on the front cover of a CD box set. "I would like to express my indignation at a choice that is purely arbitrary or ignorant, and which in any case is detrimental to the above-mentioned

---

13   Interview with Deguy.

composers," he wrote.[14] Grisey was stuck between the contradictory imperatives of having money and having time, focusing on his work and sticking up for what he believed in.

❦ ❦ ❦

Deguy had been raised in Casablanca until the age of seventeen, so she and Grisey traveled to Morocco two or three times together. Their first trip took place in February or March 1992, the others a few years later.[15] On the first trip, they flew into Marrakesh, then traveled out to Erfoud, an oasis town in the Sahara Desert, and finally on to the dunes of Merzouga, in the southeastern part of the country. They took outdoor showers, explored the desert, and met members of the Tuareg people. The owners of their hotel were musicians; one played the violin, and there was percussion music at the restaurant at night. But, Deguy said, Grisey "took the score of [Dufay's] *Missa l'homme armé* with him to study. He was always in music, he never took vacations." A photo from this trip shows Grisey studying a score, his head wrapped in the traditional manner, beneath a palm tree. According to Deguy, these were happy times.[16]

Beginning in 1993, a new type of appointment appears in Grisey's calendar, meetings with a psychologist. Though these were not his first meetings of the kind—as mentioned, he had seen a psychologist in Berkeley at Jocelyne's urging—they appeared to be his first regular sessions, taking place weekly until the end of his life. Grisey's calendars don't make clear who he was seeing or the type of analysis he pursued.[17]

According to Deguy, Grisey's reasons for seeing a psychologist were manifold. The first was his relationship with his mother, because of her "toughness," and the severe environment he grew up in. A dream Grisey wrote down, likely in the early 1990s, implied as much. "A couple. The father takes care of his girlfriend and her children. He seems to completely ignore a sickly, sad little boy: his son, three or four years old. I explain to [the father] that for the child's development, you have to love him, include him, stay in touch with him, and not reject him."[18] But this dream could also have been about Grisey's breakup with France Detry, another reason why Grisey

---

14 All the letters quoted here are in the Paul Sacher archive. There are many more which express such righteous indignation.
15 Deguy remembers this as taking place in February during Ramadan, but the holiday fell in early March in 1992.
16 Interview with Deguy.
17 Paul Sacher archive.
18 Ibid.

went to see a psychologist. (In April 1995 alone, Grisey dreamed of Detry five times.) The third was Grisey's relationship with Raphaël, who was going through a turbulent early adolescence. Then, there were Grisey's tendencies toward despair: he "easily [had] ideas of death or of leaving everything," Deguy said. In August 1991, Grisey had dreamed of a "ritual of death" in a monastery, led by an old woman. "I feel the night, the cold, the forest," he wrote. "The constant sound of my noisy breathing scares me a little."[19]

Another reason may have simply been pure interest in the subject: Grisey began reading Freud at a young age, followed by the works of Jacques Lacan and Carl Jung. As Grisey wrote in April 1993, "Music doesn't have a meaning in and of itself. It is the exact image of the human psyche: conscious or unconscious, logical or intuitive … It's a Sphinx, modeled after human life."[20]

Finally, there was the delicate balance of freedom and security that the new couple was hoping to achieve. "He was thinking of buying a house and starting a family with me, and that scared him," Deguy said. If Grisey was looking for support throughout this process, it was because at least part of him truly wanted this life. He didn't want to sabotage his happiness. The couple tried to have biological children for two years, then began the adoption process. "We dreamed of having a girl," Deguy said.[21]

Even by Grisey's standards, the gestation period for *L'Icône paradoxale* was a long one. The idea came to him in 1988, and he began working on it in earnest in 1991. He composed sections of the piece in Paris, Brussels, San Lorenzo, Schlans; and Saint-Genest-Malifaux and Saint-Polgues, in the Loire region, where he vacationed with Deguy.

When Detry and Grisey were still together, they had taken trips from their San Lorenzo summer home in Umbria to visit churches and artworks in the Italian countryside; this is when the composer first encountered Piero della Francesca's painting the *Madonna del Parto*. At this time, it was held in the church of Santa Maria di Momentana, in the little village of Monterchi, that Grisey visited with Detry.[22] In an interview with Mark Swed of the *Los Angeles Times*, Grisey said that to reach the painting, "You had to go to a farmer and get a key to the church, then get in your car and drive through the woods to try to find the church. And there this great work would suddenly be. Afterwards, you lock the church and drive back to the farmer and

---

19　Ibid.
20　Ibid.
21　Interview with Deguy.
22　Interview with Detry.

give him the key." This effort mirrors a glorious scene in Andrei Tarkovsky's 1983 film *Nostalghia*, where a Russian writer—working on a biography of a composer—and his Italian guide visit the same painting. There is an enigmatic fertility ritual happening in the church, and the guide is overwhelmed with emotion. (The writer stays outside smoking a cigarette and moping.[23])

Grisey wrote in his program note for *L'Icône paradoxale* that he had not been inspired to begin a work based on the *Madonna del Parto* until reading an article about it by the art historian Thomas Martone.[24] Martone had argued that the painting aimed to portray Christ as a fallen, earthly person, by placing the enigmatic Virgin in a tent made according to Old Testament specifications.[25] Grisey told Swed, "If you look carefully at the Virgin, you see her opening her skirt. The gesture tells [the viewer] that the origin of life is not what the two angels in the painting have shown, but the womb." Grisey described the impression the *Madonna del Parto* made on him:

> At once Christian and pagan, ardent and peaceful, virginal and a Mother Goddess ...
>
> The angels part the curtain violently; they are answered by the gesture of [the Virgin] parting her dress, and the roundness of the damask ...
> A space opens on a space which opens on another space, suggesting the infinite.[26]

As with the little Greek village Grisey and Jocelyne visited back in the summer of 1970, Monterchi was not above the imperatives of global commerce. In 1992, "The town realized that it could make some money off this work, so it has now built an awful modern building, put it behind glass," Grisey told Swed. The permanent installation included the worst imaginable background music for the *Madonna del Parto*, Carl Orff's bombastic *Carmina Burana*.

On April 2, 1994, Grisey wrote a letter to the conductor Esa-Pekka Salonen announcing, with unmistakable pride, the completion of *L'Icône paradoxale (Hommage à Piero della Francesca)* for two female voices and large orchestra in two groups, with a length of roughly twenty-three minutes. "If love and patience were sufficient to create masterpieces, this one would certainly be part of the family!" he wrote. "I am extremely pleased with this piece and its form and I expect it to be the best work I have ever done."[27] It would take nearly two more years before *L'Icône paradoxale*

---

23 Edmund Campion sent Grisey a letter urging him to watch the film, but it isn't clear whether he did so. Paul Sacher archive.
24 Lelong, *Écrits*, 167.
25 BookWiki, "Madonna del Parto."
26 Lelong, *Écrits*, 168.
27 Paul Sacher archive.

received its premiere. While this kind of timeframe was not unusual for the orchestral world, it made Grisey anxious, as he waited impatiently to hear the sounding results of his intense labor.

In the summer of 1994, Grisey was an artist-in-residence at La Napoule, a historic fortress in Provence, on the Bay of Cannes. The site had been purchased in 1918 by a wealthy Wall Street heir named Henri Clews and his wife Marie and converted to a retreat for artists in 1951.[28]

At the residency, Grisey became close friends with Jebah Baum, an American visual artist. Baum was struck by Grisey's sophistication and his culture, but also by his unusual personality traits. "He loved women. He was an extremely sexual guy, and he was very open about it," Baum said. "[But] he was very feminine. His masculinity was not that macho style. He was overtly male, but he was very open with his feelings and his mental stuff, which is a typically feminine trait ... His music is so intellectual and conceptual, but it has a physical effect on you."

The two men met frequently for conversation over cups of strong black coffee, glasses of brandy, and cigars. Grisey showed Baum his scores. (*L'Icône paradoxale* was now finished, and he'd already started working on *Vortex Temporum*.) They visited a monastery and the ocean, and even went skinny-dipping with other artists ("He was in paradise," Baum said). They ate well—La Napoule had its own chef, from Morocco—and drank wine, which Grisey eventually began choosing for the entire residency. "At a certain point, the wine got a lot better," Baum laughed.[29]

It was ironic that Grisey's best friend and counterpart for intelligent aesthetic exchange at La Napoule was American, as the composer generally found the Americanness of the program stifling. The first problem was the working conditions, a subject on which Grisey was notoriously picky: he found the environment loud, the musical spaces crowded and inadequate, the other artists unserious, and the management overly miserly, barely willing to pay for him to borrow a synthesizer. But the larger problem was that Grisey felt as if he had been dropped right back in the United States, with what he perceived as its philistinism and cultural insularity. In a complaint to the administration, he wrote:

> I continually felt like I was in a kind of community house or boy and girl scout camp that was inadequately governed in a way that was too often rigid, sometimes even infantile.

---

28   "La Napoule."
29   Interview with Baum.

> As a Frenchman, I can only deplore the excess of American artists. This association was, no doubt wrongly, presented to me as a Franco-American foundation. In reality, during my stay, I felt like the guest of an American foundation, governed in the American way, on French territory. The imbalance between European and American artists was further accentuated by the presence of an American staff and three young interns, also American. The cultural and linguistic imbalance, added to the lack of interest that the majority of the American artists seemed to have for the culture of the "host" country, created a malaise that was felt by all my European colleagues. Two of them even left the castle permanently. I will say nothing of the stupidity of the films, only English and American, rented by the residents, nor of the confinement, of the desire to recreate "home sweet home" at all costs, of the poverty of cultural and intellectual exchanges.
>
> Without a doubt, I only perceived in this microcosm the cultural imperialism of the United States and all the tensions that resulted from it within the European community.[30]

"There were quite a few fairly young Americans from Philadelphia, and he and I were rather irritated, by their amateurism, their being full of themselves, and their resistance to French culture," Baum recalled.[31]

Of course, Grisey tended to exaggerate his sense of personal injury, and neither the Germans (during his year at the Deutscher Akademischer Austauschdienst) nor the Italians (in his interactions with Ricordi), nor the French (throughout his entire life) were spared. Still, the harsh tone of this complaint—it's not clear from his archive whether he ever sent it to the La Napoule administration—was unusual. It suggested that the pain and isolation of his years in Berkeley were not forgotten, but rather transformed into a broader resentment of the unavoidable cultural tentacles of the United States.

Still, it was easy for Grisey to separate his feelings about the country in the abstract from his interactions with people he liked who happened to be American. After the summer of 1994, Grisey and Baum continued to stay in touch. Over the next six years, they exchanged letters, calls, and occasional visits, discussing the tribulations of relationships and the uneven progress of their careers. Baum's letters often featured gorgeous, casual drawings—of abstract symbols, beach scenes, an airplane—that displayed a touching, childlike affection for Grisey. On December 12, 1995, Grisey told Baum that he had been struggling to receive royalties for concerts abroad: "Money is, these days, something of a problem! ... I miss the exchange and quiet castle time so much."

---

30   Paul Sacher archive.
31   Interview with Baum.

An undated letter from Baum shows the mutual appreciation the two artists developed for one another's work. Baum wrote of an unnamed Grisey composition:

> Your piece was very inspirational. Knowing how you work, I was especially impressed with how something created so intellectually could evoke such a physical response. The waves of sound were very effective and the group performed the piece with enthusiasm and intensity. I left wishing that we could have heard it again. The other pieces in the concert were entertaining but clearly not on the same level as your work.[32]

Grisey felt that, in La Napoule, he had attained that rare, valuable prize: an aesthetic ally who was working in an entirely different medium. In advance of a March 22, 1997 performance of *Le noir de l'étoile* at Lincoln Center in New York, Grisey joked to Baum, "It would be nice if you could go so that we could communicate through music. (You can be my secret spy and let me know how it went!)"

Grisey's final letter to Baum, undated but probably from late 1997 or early 1998, showed that the composer missed at least one aspect of life in the United States: cheap Dover Edition scores. He asked if Baum could order him copies of Stravinsky's *L'Histoire du soldat*, *Renard*, and *The Firebird*; Schoenberg's *Verklärte Nacht* and *Pierrot Lunaire*; Monteverdi's *Madrigals, Books IV* and *V*; and Prokofiev's Piano Sonatas and *Shorter Piano Works*. (Grisey didn't say whether he intended to study these compositions for his own inspiration, or for his courses at the Conservatoire.) He added that he was looking forward to Baum's upcoming visit to Paris in November 1998.

With *L'Icône paradoxale* finished, Grisey started focusing on the organization for the performance of the work, scheduled for premiere in January 1996. The choice of singers was of the utmost importance to him, and he made some recommendations to the Los Angeles Philharmonic. Maybe he knew that vocal writing was still one of his weaknesses; maybe he thought he'd finally transcended this weakness and wanted the performance to be perfect. After much back-and-forth, the orchestra and composer settled on two American singers, soprano Lucy Shelton and mezzo-soprano Janice Felty.

Grisey also had specific requests for the rehearsal schedule of *L'Icône paradoxale*, which reflected his ingrained distrust of musical institutions and their willingness to take his pieces seriously. In his letter to Salonen announcing

---

32 Paul Sacher archive.

the completion of the work, he suggested six sectional rehearsals, plus two tutti rehearsals—an unusually rigorous schedule for the well-oiled machine of the Los Angeles Philharmonic.

The Philharmonic did not dedicate itself to this aspect of the premiere until September 20, 1995, despite increasingly anxious pleas from Grisey. (Salonen's father died in July 1995, making the conductor unavailable.) An administrator told Grisey he would have to compromise: "I know that Esa-Pekka will give serious consideration to the question of sectional rehearsals if, having studied the final version of the score, he thinks they are necessary. I can only ask you to trust his judgment on the details of the final rehearsal schedule." On October 1, Grisey made a final plea: "For my score, sectional [sic] rehearsals are indeed more important than anything else." In the end, Salonen came around to this idea.[33]

Grisey remained prickly in his insistence on the number of rehearsals other orchestras needed to perform *L'Icône paradoxale* satisfactorily. On March 2, 1997, in advance of a later interpretation of the work by the orchestra of La Scala in Milan, under the direction of Riccardo Chailly, Grisey wrote to the legendary conductor, "For your information, I enclose a copy of the *Probeneinteilung* [rehearsal schedule] of Frankfurt. Los Angeles had a little [fewer] rehearsals but the American musicians arrive[d] at the rehearsals knowing their parts, which will probably not be the case at La Scala!" (No response from Chailly has been preserved.)

In the interlude between the completion of *L'Icône paradoxale* and the Los Angeles world premiere of the work, Grisey became anxious not just about the conditions of the performance, but also about his remuneration. On August 6, 1994, he wrote a pointed letter to Ernest Fleischmann, the artistic director of the orchestra, asking for his fee to be raised, then transfered to him immediately. Grisey argued that the value of the American dollar had recently decreased against European currencies, saying he'd "already lost 10%" of the Los Angeles Philharmonic's fifty percent share of the total $20,000 fee. He was likely referring to a roughly seven percent depreciation of the dollar against Western European currencies which occurred in 1994; ten percent was a more emotional number, a reflection of Grisey's frustration with not having been paid sooner and a heightened sense of the work he had already done. In a similar tone as his letter to Salonen, Grisey wrote to Fleischmann, "I am extremely pleased and honored to have written a piece which I tend to consider as my favorite child for such an outstanding orchestra."

Despite the slight hyperbole of Grisey's letter, Fleischmann responded favorably, agreeing to raise the Los Angeles Philharmonic's portion of the

---

33 Paul Sacher archive.

fee to $11,000. Carlo Fontana, the artistic director of La Scala Milan, agreed to Grisey's request as well.

Grisey wanted a triumphant return to California after a decade away. In March 1995, he hired an assistant named Anne-Marie Réby.[34] Her job was to organize "the practical and financial organization of the stay, media impact, university residencies and masterclasses and concerts given by the students" for the composer.[35] When Grisey was living in the United States, he had missed the vitality of the European new music scene; back in Europe almost a decade later, he was still deeply concerned with the reach of his music in North America.

Réby quickly got to work, displaying the kind of vigor and ambition in the promotion of Grisey's music that the composer had clearly hoped to get from his publisher, Ricordi. (His expectations might have been unrealistic, though, as publishers generally provide limited promotional services.) By June, Réby had secured invitations for Grisey at the University of California at San Diego and a performance by the New Music Group of Los Angeles, contacted over twenty other institutions, and looped in the cultural attaché from the French consulate. Probably thankful to have another person to answer Grisey's frequent—and frequently anxious—letters and phone calls, Ricordi agreed to pay Réby a fee for her promotional services. Olly Wilson, the chair of Grisey's old composition department at Berkeley, offered a $200 fee for the composer to give a lecture, excluding traveling costs.[36] Réby also secured an invitation for Grisey to teach a composition class at Stanford University, where the eminent English composer Jonathan Harvey, who had reviewed the premiere of *D'eau et de pierre* decades ago, was professor of composition. Réby also realized that she would need help on the ground in California. On September 19, she contacted a French-born, Los Angeles-based publicist named Lena Michals, who promised to "easily" secure interviews with American media and lectures at additional universities. The two women worked together on these aspects of the tour, with Michals receiving an upfront fee. (The relationship between Michals and Grisey ended less than amicably. According to the letters Grisey received, the two agreed that Michals would cash Grisey's lecture fees herself and then transfer them to him, a fee of $600. It took until at least January 1997 for this to happen. Grisey's harshness in their correspondence seemed heightened by his awareness that he really needed such a small sum of money.[37])

---

34 Réby didn't respond to an interview request.
35 All this correspondence is in the Paul Sacher archive.
36 "*$200 c'est une manie*," wrote Réby to Grisey. She couldn't believe the low lecture fees composers earn.
37 Paul Sacher archive.

On November 23, 1995, Grisey had provided Réby with a series of written materials for the program book of *L'Icône paradoxale*, including a text by the Italian musicologist Francesco Leprino, and essays from *Art Press* and *La Musique du XX Siècle* (about which Grisey worried, however, that it might be too "intellectual for the U.S.A."). Despite this obvious progress toward the premiere, the composer confided in Réby, "I have enormous financial problems ... which are making me hesitate to even leave for L.A.!!" The business of composition, even for successful, well-regarded composers like Grisey, rarely results in a net financial gain.

Réby's hard work paid off. She filled Grisey's calendar with important engagements for his trip to California: interviews with the TV station Century Cable and the radio station KPFK; an additional concert at the Japan American Theater; receptions given by the Alliance Française and the French consulate in Los Angeles; and lectures at the University of California at Los Angeles, besides those at San Diego, Stanford, and Berkeley. Shortly before his departure, she wrote him a kind letter, telling him, "I found our collaboration very pleasant and enriching. If, in addition, it brought you some serenity (of organization, I mean), I am satisfied."[38] Réby helped Grisey keep the administrative hydra at bay and paved the way for his triumphant return to California.

* * *

A year earlier, on November 29, 1994, a young composer named Dominique Troncin had died from AIDS at the age of thirty-three. Hailing from Besançon, near Belfort, and fifteen years Grisey's junior, he had been part of the same musical circles as the spectralists, studying composition with Tristan Murail and analysis with Betsy Jolas. Grisey was enlisted to write a memorial work, this time at the request of Ensemble Fa, which was organizing a concert to honor Troncin at Radio France. He finished it in 1995.

After *Anubis et Nout,* this new piece drew again on ancient Egyptian influences, providing Grisey a source of inspiration for the theme of death. Grisey chose an ensemble of a medium and a low bass drum and called the work *Stèle,* after the haunting Egyptian stelae which could be placed both outside and inside tombs to honor the memory of a person who had passed on to the underworld. As he often did, Grisey thought in metaphors while simultaneously applying rigorous structural procedures to his material. For *Stèle,* an idea occurred to him, centering around the *rediscovery* of ancient Egypt. "While composing, an image came to me," he wrote, "that of archeologists discovering a *stèle* and dusting it off until they find a funerary

---

38 Paul Sacher archive

inscription."[39] He would use a similar perspective, a vertiginous telescoping between epochs, to stunning effect in *Quatre chants pour franchir le seuil*.

Lasting around seven minutes, *Stèle* is a miniature by Grisey's standards. The work begins, as does *Jour, contre-jour*, with a sound coming so subtly out of silence that it must begin before the audience falls quiet; in this case, the sound is a slow, circular brushing on the lower of the two bass drums. According to Grisey's program note, the questions animating *Stèle* were, "How to make the rhythm of the duration emerge, a cellular organization of a flow obeying other laws? How to sketch with extreme concision and at the edge of silence a rhythmic inscription—at first indiscernible, then finally hammered in—in an archaic form?"[40] As this text implies, the "rhythmic inscription," the central motive of the work, isn't revealed clearly until the final six bars: a simple rhythmic cell alternating between two timbres in each of the instruments. But once we have heard the end, the beginning makes sense too: it includes a vaguer outline of this rhythm, like a carving covered by sand. The piece follows an archaic A-B-A form which fits the tone of the piece, an imaginary reconstruction of ancient music. The middle section of the work uses a rough-hewn version of one of Grisey's favorite formal techniques, the breath structure. With the first bass drum, he steadily increases and decreases the number of pulsations in a given time frame, while the second drum accompanies with ominous rolls. He also uses permutations from a series of grace notes which increase in number from the first to the second half of the middle section. The whole piece, though structured carefully, often sounds like an enigmatic, antique improvisation—an effect entirely typical of Grisey's style. As the composer Fabien Lévy, Grisey's student, writes, "The composition ... is ingenious: the instrumentalists have to be placed apart to create echo games, ritualistic effects, slow and funereal patterns which become dramatic, in rhythmic and polyrhythmic writing that is extremely precise, clear and effective."[41] For Lévy, the composition was a successful attempt to integrate an important aspect of percussion music from Asia, Africa, and South America: the detailed exploration of the colors of a single instrument.

Stèle was premiered on February 4, 1995, at Radio France's Festival Présences, by Ensemble Fa members Nicolas Piguet and Thierry Miroglio. Though an occasional piece, it remains an effective smaller work in Grisey's oeuvre, analogous to the *Accords perdus* or *Anubis et Nout*. It left a strong impression on Lévy, who was present for the premiere. *Stèle* "stood out from the series of rather anonymous pieces for its originality and depth," he

---

39   Lelong, *Écrits*, 172.
40   Ibid.
41   Lévy, "Stèle by Gérard Grisey."

recalled. Lévy added, "The piece is highly inventive and deep, musically. It uses minimal means that are explored ... in their entirety."⁴²

As Grisey entered a new compositional phase, the time he spent on individual works increased further. He was never content to produce similar pieces for different instrumentations in the spectral style. He was continually reinventing his musical process.

In this sense, his work *Vortex Temporum (The Vortex of Time)* was typical. On September 20, 1993, Grisey had written to Benedikt Föhr, who worked for a company called Art Concept and managed the virtuosic contemporary music group Ensemble Recherche, based in Freiburg, Germany, to propose a new work. It would take at least three, maybe four years to compose the piece, Grisey estimated.⁴³ He was right. The result would become one of his most important pieces, certainly his most powerful piece of chamber music.

Föhr accepted Grisey's proposal on behalf of Ensemble Recherche. He offered Grisey the use of the full ensemble, which the composer accepted, and was also open to the idea of a joint commission, with another ensemble contributing to the composer's fee in return for similar rights to the premiere. This was an important business strategy for Grisey, who, since he wrote so few pieces, was always concerned with getting as much money as possible for each one.

Over a year later, on December 15, 1994, Grisey gave Ensemble Recherche the first hints as to the shape the new piece was taking. The complete piece to be known as *Vortex Temporum* was composed in three separate parts, with Grisey announcing to Föhr that the first movement would be ready in the "first semester of 1995." In the meantime, Grisey sent a sort of program note *avant la lettre*, which provides an effective summary of the ideas in his mind:

> *Vortex Temporum* defines the original material of the piece, a formula of swirling, repeated arpeggios.
>
> Onto this *Gestalt* are grafted two other archetypes: an attack with and without resonance, and a sustained sound with or without crescendo ...
>
> Thanks to an imaginary microphone, a note becomes a timbre, a chord becomes a complex spectrum, and a rhythm becomes a swell of unpredictable duration.⁴⁴

---

42   Lévy, "Composers About Composers."
43   Paul Sacher archive.
44   Ibid.

Meanwhile, the contract negotiations for the new piece, which took place over the holidays between December 1994 and January 1995, were proving problematic. Grisey and Ensemble Recherche had secured the support of the Ministerium für Kunst (Ministry for Art) in the southwestern German province of Baden-Württemberg, where Freiburg is located, and of the Westdeutscher Rundfunk (WDR) in Cologne, through its new music editor Harry Vogt, in exchange for the rights to the premiere of the work at the festival Wittener Tage für Neue Kammermusik in 1995. The partners had also agreed on a total fee of 30,000 Deutsche Mark for *Vortex Temporum*, to be paid in three installments. The sticking point was the ensemble's request for exclusivity with the composition: for the first part, until one year after the premiere, scheduled to take place in 1995; and for the second part, until April 30, 1997, six months after the European premiere. On the contract, Grisey noted by hand, "Is it possible for me to allow exclusivity if at least ten other groups are waiting for the piece? For this reason, I think six months [is fair], and, if not, the ensemble needs to find itself at least ten performances." Once again, Grisey was feeling the financial pressure of being a slow composer.

This financial angst was equally apparent in a letter Grisey wrote to Vogt dated December 10, 1994, in response to a phone call. Vogt had realized that Grisey was unlikely to provide the finished score of *Vortex Temporum* on time and "pulled the emergency brake." Vogt decided to postpone the premiere of the new piece to 1996. Grisey complained that this would ruin his financial planning for 1995, leading to the losses of his commissioning fee, royalties, and income from Sacem, WDR, and Ricordi. "At first, that put Grisey in a bad mood," Vogt recalled. "At the same time, it palpably relaxed the situation. After his initial anger passed, he was able to start again ... and complete the entire work for Witten in 1996."[45]

Probably the greater sin in Grisey's eyes was that Vogt had dared to make an aesthetic recommendation, that the composer make a work that was organized in "fragments." In the composer's response, the injured pride is palpable. "The idea of the composer concerns no one but the composer who I am, and I categorically refuse the idea you mentioned of composing fragments," Grisey wrote. "If I've decided to compose this work in two movements, it is my responsibility ... to compose *two movements which form a coherent whole*."[46] Grisey added, "I hope you understand my attitude, but I feel nothing but mistrust toward an institution which did not hesitate to wait until my fiftieth birthday to produce a few notes of my music." The composer's feeling of being under-appreciated in his lifetime

---

45   Interview with Vogt.
46   Emphasis Grisey's. Paul Sacher archive.

remained true even in his most professionally successful period. "His noticeable hurt was not especially motivating for me," Vogt said. "But I found his music fascinating."

The negotiations continued after the holidays. In March 1995, Grisey told Föhr that he would be willing to grant Ensemble Recherche exclusive performance rights for *Vortex Temporum* for one year, but only within Europe, and on the condition that the ensemble promised to give "around six" performances of the work. Frustrated, but maybe realizing the leverage Grisey had with the option of bestowing the premiere of *Vortex Temporum* on another ensemble, Föhr agreed to change the contract, restricting Ensemble Recherche's exclusivity to Europe and agreeing in principle to six performances of the new work.[47]

Föhr left Ensemble Recherche at the beginning of 1996, replaced by a manager named Sabine Franz. In February 1996, Franz wrote to Grisey. The musicians of the ensemble were anxious to receive the complete score. "When will the second part be ready?" Franz asked. "At least the score. Please let us know *urgently*."

Grisey responded to Franz's message the same day. In the intervening months, *Vortex Temporum* had taken on a new shape; Grisey had composed an additional third section to the initially agreed-upon two movements. But he was conscious of the pressure for everything to be ready for the premiere of the complete work at the Wittener Tage für neue Kammermusik on April 26, 1996. The composer told Franz that eighteen pages were copied, with fifty to go. "As always, it will be tight, but we will manage," he wrote. "As far as possible the score will be ready in mid-March and the parts in early April." A few days later, Franz asked Grisey if he could send the material for *Vortex Temporum III* as it came in, so the musicians could begin practicing it. "We're excited for the third part of *Vortex* and personally, I'm happy that this wonderful piece is becoming a little longer!" Franz wrote.

Grisey had a sense of humor about the delay of the third movement of the work. In a missive announcing that "*Vortex Temporum* is finished!" he dated the letter only "Spring 1996." About ten days later, he labeled an update on the score "Paris, Tuesday ... March." Grisey began sending uncorrected sections of the piece to the ensemble and the conductor engaged by Ensemble Recherche for the project, Kwamé Ryan. On April 24, 1996, Grisey would travel to Freiburg for the final rehearsals with the group, before joining them for the premiere of the entire work in Witten.

With Grisey, however, the financial negotiations were never done. On April 8, he complained about the cost of his hotel in Freiburg. A few days later, Franz wrote, a little annoyed, that "in this case we are talking about a

---

47 Ibid.

really very well-paid commission, in addition to further income thanks to the many performances by Ensemble Recherche. With this sum [30,000 DM]—please allow me to be frank—it should be possible for you to cover the travel expenses."[48]

The work is scored for flute, clarinet, violin, viola, cello, and a piano with four detuned notes spelling out a diminished seventh chord that allow the instrument to generate a surprisingly wide variety of microtonal sounds. The material at the heart of the work is a section from Ravel's ballet *Daphnis et Chloé* with a sinuous piccolo melody, accompanied by a muted trumpet, harp, both violin sections, and violas. For the musicologist Danielle Cohen-Levinas, Ravel's figure is "an anodyne phrase," whose banality Grisey's piece transcends.[49] But Julian Anderson remembers running into Grisey at a Paris performance of *Daphnis et Chloé*, where Grisey said that he'd come to "hear this beautiful piece."[50] Given the reverence he felt for Ravel since he was a young teenager, and the composer's presence on his syllabi, Grisey probably wasn't trying to do what Beethoven did in his *Diabelli Variations*: turn something banal into something transcendent. Grisey's use of Ravel's motive was more likely a genuine tribute.

Ravel's little phrase is never quoted exactly; it's sublimated into the most abstract structures of Grisey's piece. The shape of the melody reminded Grisey of a sine wave, which he then used as a formal model for the first section of *Vortex Temporum I*, analogous to the sound-wave form of *Partiels*. In this section, a "swirling" melodic phrase in the flutes and clarinets is repeated without interruption and in a decrescendo, while being subject to a dual process: "a progressive diminution of its periodicity," as Baillet writes, meaning a movement towards irregularity; and a reduction in its length.[51] This material is also modulated through four different spectra. At the same time, regular accents in the piano give the section a strong sense of pulse, and increasingly common interruptions in the strings make us feel the momentum of this exciting music. George Benjamin remembers a conversation with Grisey during the composition of *Vortex* about the difficulties of composing fast music—but Grisey managed, making one of the most riotous passages in his oeuvre.[52]

The second section of the first movement of *Vortex Temporum* is modeled roughly on a square wave, a type of grating sound only produced by synthesizers. The jerky, robotic, long-short, up-and-down lines of this section

---

48 Paul Sacher archive.
49 Cohen-Levinas, *Le temps de l'écoute*.
50 Interview with Julian Anderson.
51 Baillet, *Fondements d'une écriture*, 215.
52 Interview with Benjamin.

even imitate its shape, if you think of the short notes as representing the vertical lines of a square wave.[53] After a climactic run, this material enters in the viola and cello, coinciding with a sudden drop in tension. Grisey subjects the square wave material to a new series of processes: an undermining of the periodicity, this time through syncopations and intentional non-togetherness; a set of complex rules govern the pitch changes (or lack thereof) in each cell. Two more processes decide the number of instruments to play a given phrase, its tessitura, and which spectra will be applied to it.

The third section is a crazy piano cadenza that is a showstopper in performance. It functions as a summary of *Vortex Temporum I*: the model is that of another synthetic wave, the sawtooth, but the cadenza includes eight blocks of material, including those modeled after the sine and square waves. At the same time, the sequence of these blocks of material is itself constructed to look like a sawtooth wave when drawn on paper. The blocks also have their own associated "reservoirs," in Baillet's term, of harmonic spectra from which they draw, and each is associated with a temporal process as well (usually diminution). Despite this rigor, the effect of the piano cadenza is one of extreme spontaneity. According to Gérard Zinsstag, to whom the first movement was dedicated, the passage used to make Grisey laugh.[54] A constant paradox in his music reaches a high point here. In the first movement of *Vortex Temporum*, Grisey achieves an irresistible current of emotional transcendence using complex mathematical structures and meticulous planning.

Between the two movements there is an interlude of barely audible instrumental noises that recall some works of Lachenmann, and which have the extra benefit of keeping the tension between the two movements: these interludes, which reappear in the *Quatre chants*, are there to prevent people in the audience from coughing. *Vortex Temporum II* is dedicated to Grisey's friend, the Italian composer Salvatore Sciarrino, whom Grisey met through Ricordi in the 1980s and who helped Grisey find the summer house he rented with France Detry.[55] The movement has a melancholy repose that contrasts powerfully with the frenzy of its predecessor. For Baillet, this piece "is conceived as the temporal dilation of the melodic cell of the first movement," and each note of the original *Gestalt* is extended into its own section.[56] (Grisey associated this slowed-down time with the rhythms of sleep.[57]) The structural plan of the piece is a wave or an arch: in its first half, the number of pitches in the piano's

---

53 Baillet, *Fondements d'une écriture*, 217.
54 Interview with Zinsstag.
55 Brown, "Faked Silence." I was unable to reach Sciarrino again for a more detailed interview on Grisey.
56 Baillets, *Fondements d'une écriture*, 221.
57 Lelong, *Écrits*, 170.

lamenting downward line increases, as does the amount of sustained notes in the rest of the ensemble; the process reverses symmetrically in the second half of the movement. Again, Grisey works with a "reservoir" of spectral pitches, but, as Manfred Stahnke points out, "his 'harmonic spectrum' is a personal interpretation, used in a variety of local ways in the work."[58] That makes the choice of pitches more intuitive, and this gorgeous movement benefits from the freedom, with some of the most beautiful melodic writing of the second half of the twentieth century. The premiere of *Vortex Temporum I–II* took place at the Musica festival in Strasbourg on February 4, 1995, with Ensemble Recherche under the direction of the conductor Pascal Rophé.

Vortex Temporum III, dedicated to Grisey's friend Helmut Lachenmann, functions as a temporally warped reprise of *I*. Like *Le temps et l'écume*, there are three "layers" of time in the work. After another cough-inhibiting interlude, the first layer begins. It's an immediately recognizable repetition of the Ravel *Gestalt* and becomes modified over the course of the movement: slowed or sped up, interspersed with silences, or accented in different places to change its contour. The second layer is dilated, to the extent that over the course of the movement it loses all sense of melody or harmonic movement, as Baillet notes.[59] In the third layer, the music is contracted, with bits cut off the beginning and end, a process that recalls the cutting of onset transients off a length of tape in the electronic studio. For the composer Jean-Luc Hervé, the aural effect of this is "of a great novelty." He continues, "Entire sections of the work are contracted into a few bars, resulting in completely new musical sonorities integrating with noisy sounds."[60] Baillet adds that each of these sections progresses toward the most extreme version of itself throughout *Vortex Temporum III*. The piano cadenza is also repeated in a more disjunct form. Baillet claims that the formal scheme of the movement resembles a sine wave, like the first section of the first movement (this is only roughly true).[61] The work ends with regular pulsations in the piano—more heartbeats.

Grisey's friends and colleagues were immediately aware of the importance of *Vortex Temporum*. "It shakes you," Zinsstag said. "It's very powerful, very intense."[62] In 1997, Lachenmann wrote, "The wonderful *Vortex Temporum I–III* arrived and reading and listening [to it] bring me joy." The musicologist Theo Hirsbrunner wrote that "I really like *Vortex* because of its theatrical gestures," and suggested that Grisey compose an opera.[63] The composer Frédéric

---

58   Stahnke, "Die Schwelle des Hörens," 22.
59   Baillet, *Fondements d'une écriture*, 225.
60   Hervé in *Le temps de l'écoute*, 17.
61   Baillets, *Fondements d'une écriture*, 227.
62   Interview with Zinsstag.
63   Both from letters in the Paul Sacher archive.

Durieux found that "it was a decisive work in the evolution of the composer, and a major score of his final years."[64] According to Anderson, as far as he knew, the only colleague of Grisey's who didn't like *Vortex Temporum* was Tristan Murail. But Danielle Cohen-Levinas summed it up best: "The goal of the piece is to get close to the music as you get close to another person."[65] Her interpretation has a clear analogy with sexual union.

The complete *Vortex Temporum* was premiered on April 26, 1996, at the Wittener Tage für neue Kammermusik alongside Hugues Dufourt's *The Watery Star* for octet and Jean-Pierre Guézec's String Trio. For Harry Vogt, the premiere of *Vortex Temporum* was an especially memorable event in his career:

> From the first moment, it was clear that we were hearing a magnum opus. It was a project that outshone many others, and not only because of its long duration. The reactions of the press and the public were admittedly mixed. There was enthusiasm but also distance, cautious confusion, even rejection ...
>
> Much like Grisey's other large, extended pieces— for example, *Les espaces acoustiques* or *Le noir de l'étoile*—*Vortex Temporum* is like a long journey for me. I feel swept up, led through vast landscapes full of epic beauties, with breathtaking transitions, transformations, and metamorphoses.
>
> I was fascinated by the mixture of compositional calculation and sonic sensuality, construction and transcendence, drive and suspense, how everything is derived and unfolded from a small turning formula, the instrumental variety, the virtuosity and musicality ...[66]

An especially striking interpretation of the piece is a version by the Belgian choreographer Anne Teresa De Keersmaeker. It premiered in 2013 and, besides seven dancers, it also involves the musicians moving. At one point, the piano is pushed in a circle around a stage, a surprisingly graceful motion. Her piece demonstrates visually and sensually the spirals of temporal structure that animate Grisey's composition.[67]

❦ ❦ ❦

On January 12, 1996, Grisey and Deguy arrived in Los Angeles. It had been over thirty years since Grisey's first trip to the United States. This time, he was arriving not as a young accordion virtuoso, nor as a talented

---

64   Durieux in *Le Temps de l'Écoute*.
65   Cohen-Levinas, *Le Temps de l'Écoute*.
66   Interview with Vogt.
67   Videos are available at https://www.rosas.be/en/productions/386-vortex-temporum.

young assistant professor, but as an eminent composer at the height of his creative powers.

The potential of this moment was captured in an admiring profile, dated January 18, by Mark Swed of the *Los Angeles Times*. For Swed, Esa-Pekka Salonen and Grisey were similar musical personalities. Both combined intellectual rigor and an interest in complexity with a playful quality:

> A conversation on the phone with Grisey, still a bit jet-lagged from his flight to Los Angeles, reveals a lively and surprisingly amusing attitude toward work that can seem pretty esoteric. It turns out that rather than foisting dry music theory on Music Center audiences tonight with the premiere of "L'Icône paradoxale," the Philharmonic just may be opening a big can of fat, juicy postmodernist worms.[68]

Grisey told Swed he believed there was "a kind of cultural catastrophe occurring in the entire world," a strain of cultural pessimism the composer expressed frequently, from the jokes about mindless television in the youth orchestra piece *Manifestations* to later complaints about the lack of relevance of contemporary classical music in modern society.[69] For that reason, Grisey found it important to reach his audience. "One should be able to grasp something of all this, to perceive it in the music," he said, "and I'm very much concerned that the audience realize this. I hate it when a composer describes things in a piece that you can't hear."

The next few days were busy with further interviews and the rehearsals for *Talea* at the Japan America Theater, performed by a chamber ensemble of musicians from the Los Angeles Philharmonic under Salonen's direction. The concert took place on January 16, 1996, accompanied by David Stoley's reconstruction of *Hoquetus David* by Guillaume de Machaut; Jeffrey Mumford's sensitive *Two Miniatures* for violin and piano; the convulsive and entertaining *Corrente*, by Grisey student Magnus Lindberg; and two Berio *Sequenzas*.[70] Josef Woodard, a critic for the *Los Angeles Times*, reviewed *Talea* enthusiastically:

> Grisey's powerful "Talea" ... is a persuasive example of *musique spectrale*, based on overtones and juxtapositions of opposites—consonance meets dissonance, rhythmic density meets silence, with some microtonal detours around the standard Western scale. Bright flurries of notes erupt out of a bed of soft long tones, and styles are bridged without post-modern flippancy. This is music both coolly objective and visceral, brimming with intrigue.[71]

---

68 Swed, "Finding Harmony in Paradox."
69 Grisey founded CompAct, a sort of composers' political action committee, with Tristan Murail.
70 Paul Sacher archive.
71 Woodard, "Philharmonic's New Music Program Balanced, Timely."

Backed by an advocate as persuasive as Salonen, Grisey's music made a striking impression on the Los Angeles scene.

Sectionals for the main event of the trip, *L'Icône paradoxale,* had begun on January 14. The going was a little rough. The American composer Daniel Rothman said:

> *L'Icône paradoxale* calls for a very large orchestra and between the extras and the stringers, who subbed for the regulars that opted out, the orchestra was poorly equipped for it; players—my friends and colleagues, I'm embarrassed to say—grumbled over the extreme registers, unfamiliar techniques and microtonal tunings ... I knew [Grisey] could not have been very happy and he later expressed it to me.[72]

These sentiments are not preserved in Grisey's letters; maybe Grisey didn't want to anger Salonen and his orchestra.

The world premiere of the work took place on the evening of January 18, 1996, at the Dorothy Chandler Pavilion. The newly commissioned piece opened the program, which also featured a performance of Beethoven's Piano Concerto no. 1 with Radu Lupu as soloist, followed by Sibelius's Symphony no. 7.

L'Icône paradoxale is scored for a large orchestra with a small group of instrumental soloists—similar to *Dérives*—and a soprano and mezzo-soprano. The ambitious work tackles multiple concepts at once. Grisey continued to work with the idea of different "layers" of time. He was also making a new attempt at writing for the human voice and stretching the core concepts of spectral music to their limits.

Le temps et l'écume has three layers of time, *L'Icône paradoxale* four. The two slowest are spectral settings of consonant formants and tectonic harmonic fields based on additional spectra that determine the pitch content of the piece. The "linguistic" or human-time layer governs the progression in the two voices from vowels to consonants, from pitched sounds to noise, and from held sounds to rhythm—ideas from *Les chants de l'amour* that are refined in this later work. The last layer is extremely compressed, taking elements from the other layers and reducing them to one fifty-fourth of their length, as Baillet notes.[73] Listening to the piece, you don't hear these four time scales as distinct, though, as they meld together into its massive textures.

The vocal writing in *L'Icône paradoxale* is improved from *Les chants de l'amour,* a function of its simplicity. The voices, and the small orchestra that serves as their extension, work with short, sleek, graceful melodic motives.

---

72   Interview with Rothman.
73   Baillet, *Fondements d'une écriture,* 199.

Maybe Deguy, a singer, helped Grisey understand the kind of writing that works best for the voice. There are also a few weaker movements, especially the upward chords, which sound awkward, and the mildly cheesy intonation by the singers of the name Piero della Francesca. (Most of the text is vowels and consonants, with the occasional quote from della Francesca's treatise on perspective in painting.)

For Baillet, the global form of the piece "can be summarized as a superposition of two opposite evolutions," with the singers progressing to faster, noisier music, and a roughly opposite process happening in the orchestra. These two processes cross at the middle of the work, a "spiral" of richly intertwined melodic lines. In this section, Baillet sees Grisey abandoning, "consciously or not, the idea of harmonies based on the spectrum in favor of a very free atonality" in a quarter-tone scale.[74] Grisey is still working theoretically with spectra here, but he allows pitches to be transposed to different octaves for his process, a change that really is tantamount to abandoning spectral harmony: since a spectrum contains all pitches if you go high enough, you can use all possible microtonal frequencies if you remove the octave relationships. This change probably *was* conscious: in 1996, Grisey told Julian Anderson, "I'm sick of the harmonic spectrum."[75] Grisey was wary of group projects, as his ambivalence toward Ensemble L'Itinéraire shows, and he was always trying to reinvent himself. The composer François Rose writes that Grisey "may never have considered the harmonic spectrum to be more than a stimulating model for the creative imagination."[76] The harmonic freedom of *L'Icône paradoxale* is as much a return to the quasi-spectral harmonies of early pieces like *Dérives* as it is something completely new. The delicate, haunting coda is based on a harmonic spectrum of a B♭, distorted by various procedures. *L'Icône paradoxale* is also charged with eroticism, from the contemplation of the earthly beauty and fertility of Piero della Francesca's Virgin to the sensual interplay of the two female voices.

The premiere of *L'Icône paradoxale* was a cathartic moment. On the night of the performance, Grisey received well-wishes from around the world, with Ricordi calling the premiere an "important baptism."[77] On January 19, the day after the concert, he wrote in a letter to Réby: "A triumphant premiere last night. Old ladies on their feet to applaud today's music ... that's rare! Except here. The L.A. Phil is the best orchestra in the world. Tonight, it will be even better."[78] After the dust had settled, in March, he wrote to

---

74 Ibid.
75 Interview with Julian Anderson.
76 Rose in *Le temps de l'écoute*, 59.
77 Paul Sacher archive.
78 Ibid.

Fleischmann, the Philharmonic's artistic director, "I would like to thank you again not only for the beautiful performance but also for the human quality of the crew and for the kindness of the welcome both my wife and I received in L.A." (Grisey and Deguy never actually married.) It seemed that Grisey's return to California was every bit as triumphant as he had hoped and planned for.

But not everyone saw it that way. In the *Los Angeles Times*, the critic Martin Bernheimer quoted several Gilbert and Sullivan lines to skewer what he considered Salonen and Grisey's pretentious descriptions of the music. When it came to the piece itself, he wrote:

> Grisey's means may be novel and his procedures may be forbidding. But his ends tend to suggest easy modernist clichés.
>
> That doesn't have to be taken as a negative judgment. Originality isn't everything these days. One doesn't have to memorize an eccentric cookbook to savor a conventional meal. Predictability still has a place in the scheme of things.
>
> Any innocent listener could appreciate Grisey's clever manipulation of sound clusters, his fine melding of instrumental and vocal timbres, his abstraction of lyrical impulses and delayed sense of crashing drama. "L'Icône paradoxale" actually dares to be subtle when it isn't making a mighty noise.
>
> The first hearing did not inspire an overwhelming desire for a second. For the intellectual minority this essay actually may be more compelling as music for the eyes than as music for the ears.[79]

The text seemed calculated to puncture what Bernheimer clearly considered the composer's inflated self-importance. (No reaction to the review from Grisey has been preserved.)

After repeat performances of *L'Icône paradoxale* on January 19 and 20, Grisey and Deguy traveled to northern California. The composer held his lecture at Stanford on January 22, then another at Berkeley on January 23. After their return to L.A., they had another week off and took some time to explore, going to Redwood National Park. On February 1, 1996, the two returned to Paris.

After the fact, Grisey tried to obtain a copy of the recording of his new piece—fruitlessly, as American orchestra-union rules generally prevent the sharing of archival recordings. In a letter to Fleischmann, Grisey wrote, "Speaking with the *Konzert-Meister*, he mentioned that if there were some difficulties, he could ask the Union to vote an exception for the 'poor composer going back home with only the memories of his piece!!!'"[80] Grisey

---

79 Bernheimer, "Icon and Iconoclast at the Philharmonic."
80 Paul Sacher archive.

soon had a chance to hear the piece again in Europe. This trip would be the composer's last visit to the United States. "For him, this concert was the moment when he entered history," Deguy said. "It was a very happy time."[81]

---

81 Interview with Deguy.

Chapter Fourteen

Nut
(1996–98)

As Grisey's new girlfriend, Mireille Deguy became an essential part of his family life. When Raphaël was going through a tough phase as a teenager, he came to stay with them. Deguy fell into the role of disciplinarian by default. "Gérard wasn't able to be firm with his son because he felt guilty for leaving him when he was small," she said. Raphaël recalled that he and his father had their "first real conversations" at this time. But Grisey didn't pass his love of classical music on to his son.[1]

Like France Detry, Deguy also went to visit Lucie Monna, Grisey's mother, with him. She remembers the house as having a small interior but a large garden. They only went into the town of Belfort once; Grisey preferred to walk around the small hills, forests, and ponds by the village of Chèvremont. They enjoyed the view of what Alsatians call *la ligne bleue des Vosges*, the silhouette of the mountain range that separates the region from its neighbors. Deguy recalls that in this time, Grisey was thinking of leaving Paris for a place in the country, a desire strengthened by the time spent in the natural environment of his childhood home.[2]

Like Detry before her, Deguy picked up on Monna's strictness. She realized Grisey and his mother couldn't interact on an intellectual or musical level. In photographs from these visits, Monna is as well put together as always, her clothes and her hair orderly, but her gaze is a little slack.[3] In about 1995, Monna began to suffer from dementia. One day, she had a stroke and fell. Grisey felt he had no choice but to bring her to a nursing home, though he did so unwillingly. Claudia Doderer remembers Grisey calling her after a visit to the home in Belfort, shocked and sad, and saying, "Claudia, now I understand how the world works."[4]

---

1 Interview with Raphaël and Jocelyne Grisey.
2 Interview with Deguy.
3 Photographs in Deguy's collection.
4 Interview with Doderer.

According to Deguy, life in the nursing home was too difficult for Monna and she died after only six months. "In spite of everything, he was close with his mother," Deguy said. To process his loss, Grisey began reading texts by the ancient Tibetans, Greeks, and Romans on death, and planning for the composition of *Quatre chants pour franchir le seuil*. In 1962, at the age of sixteen, Grisey had composed his first piece for his mother, the *Petite Caprice en La*. Now he would compose for her again.

🙟 🙟 🙟

In June 1996, Grisey celebrated his fiftieth birthday. Deguy organized a garden party, which took place at the home of a friend outside Paris. "It was a really happy celebration," said Paol Keineg, a French poet and friend of Grisey's who had spent a long time in the United States. Around fifty people showed up, most of them musicians. "I thought the whole opera choir was there," Keineg added. It felt like a culmination.

The year of Grisey's fiftieth birthday was a high point in his career, with many musical institutions acknowledging the importance of his oeuvre. 1996 had begun with the triumphant performance of *L'Icône paradoxale* in Los Angeles; it ended with a festival dedicated largely to the performance of his works at the Musica festival in Strasbourg, the Alsatian city not far from Belfort. Performances took place through September and October 1996 and included, of Grisey's music: a full performance of *Les espaces acoustiques* by Ensemble Court-Circuit under Pierre-André Valade (for the smaller movements) and the Frankfurt Opera Orchestra under Sylvain Cambreling (for the larger ones); *Le temps et l'écume*, with Ensemble intercontemporain; *Tempus ex Machina* with Les Percussions de Strasbourg; *Les chants de l'amour* with the BBC Singers; and the complete *Vortex Temporum* with Ensemble Recherche.[5]

In *Le Monde*, Gérard Condé was thrilled with the cycle of *Les espaces acoustiques*:

> If each of the six stages of this extremely subtle journey through sound and its metamorphoses can be performed alone, it is only in continuity ... that the work acquires its true dimension ...
>
> It invites us to follow its minute evolutions like the mobile forms of clouds. If you relax your attention, you discover that the landscape has changed, but if you concentrate on the becoming of a single metamorphosis, you forget where you came from. You are both regularly lost, and regularly amazed.[6]

---

5   Programs from past performances are archived on the Musica website.
6   Condé, "Ouverture brillante pour le Festival Musica."

Condé was less excited about *L'Icône paradoxale*: "The composer has doubtlessly gone further than in *Les espaces acoustiques*, but that's also why we understand him less well [in this piece]."

Rounding out the program were works by Grisey's heroes, composers like Messiaen, Scelsi, Varèse, and Ravel, as well as aesthetic comrades such as Michaël Levinas, Helmut Lachenmann, Hugues Dufourt, George Benjamin, and Jonathan Harvey. As Grisey's letter to Harry Vogt during the planning for *Vortex Temporum* showed, the fiftieth birthday celebrations for the composer did not completely assuage his insecurity about the lack of recognition for his music. But, maybe even more than the Los Angeles Philharmonic premiere, the Musica festival was the event that made Grisey enter music history.

In 1995, Grisey had received a commission from Ensemble intercontemporain to compose a work of about twenty minutes in length in honor of its twentieth anniversary, for either the 1997–98 or 1998–99 concert season. Grisey had suggested a fee of 100,000 francs, an amount which Hervé Boutry, formerly at the Théâtre Royal de La Monnaie in Brussels and later the manager of Ensemble intercontemporain (until 2017), noted "exceeds what we usually pay even composers of great renown."[7] (Grisey clearly considered himself a composer of such status.) On a copy of Boutry's note, Grisey sketched out his idea for the initial instrumentation—with significantly smaller forces than would eventually be required—for what became *Quatre chants pour franchir le seuil*.

On January 23, 1996, Boutry made Grisey a counteroffer of a fee of 70,000 francs and raised the possibility of a joint commission with the new-music ensemble London Sinfonietta. But Grisey didn't budge on the fee, meaning that his work could not be included in Ensemble Intercontemporain's twentieth-anniversary celebrations. In a letter dated July 1996, Grisey insisted on this high honorarium, adding that he would like the new composition to be performed as part of a composer-portrait concert of himself, alongside *Le temps et l'écume, Modulations*, or *Les chants de l'amour*.[8]

Some specifics of the new piece were beginning to take shape in the composer's mind. Now using the working title *Chants de mort et d'éternité* (*Songs of Death and Eternity*), he told Boutry the work would last twenty-five to thirty minutes and be scored for twelve or thirteen musicians with female voice and electronics.

---

7   Paul Sacher archive.
8   Ibid.

The lack of specificity in this indication—soprano, mezzo-soprano, or alto—suggests that the piece was originally composed with Deguy in mind, and only later changed to a virtuosic soprano part. As he composed, Grisey told Deguy that he was sorry, but he needed high notes.

"Don't worry," she answered. "You'll write another piece for me."[9]

In November 1996, Boutry told Grisey that IRCAM would be unable to support the development of an electronics part, but that, in exchange, he would be able to expand the instrumentation to sixteen or seventeen musicians. Meanwhile, Boutry negotiated with the artistic director of the London Sinfonietta, Paul Meecham, and Richard Steinitz, the director of the Huddersfield Festival, who was considering a twenty-five percent stake in the commission.

As the work began to take its final form, the logistics of the project became increasingly difficult. Grisey had selected two additional saxophones and an additional tuba for the *Quatre chants*, a choice that adds to the unusual, ominous color of the work, but which gave Boutry practical headaches. On September 9, 1997, Boutry asked Grisey, "Could you please avoid the three supplementary sopranos?" This suggests that Grisey had at least considered composing the piece for multiple female voices.

He eventually dropped that idea and chose the Anglophone Canadian soprano Valdine Anderson for the premiere. He and Anderson met in the lounge of the Cité de la Musique in Paris to discuss the composer's vision for the soprano part. Anderson recalls that Grisey had ideas of the utmost clarity for the realization of the piece. "He was so very specific," she recalled. "My score is full of notes, little things that he would have said."[10]

With hindsight, it is almost frightening to realize how close the project of *Quatre chants* was to being canceled. On October 1, 1997, Boutry sent Grisey a pointed letter, saying he found Grisey's financial demands unreasonable. Boutry nearly scrapped the performance; the composer's recalcitrance had brought a prestigious commission to the brink.[11] Luckily for music history, Boutry and Grisey eventually managed to reach an agreement.

At the beginning of their relationship, Deguy had been shy about singing in front of Grisey.[12] That shyness eventually eased and, in 1997, Grisey made an orchestration of four songs by the Austrian Romantic lied composer

---

9   Interview with Deguy.
10 Interview with Valdine Anderson.
11 Paul Sacher archive
12 Interview with Deguy.

Hugo Wolf for her. It was the first such orchestration he had made since the exercises of his student days, and the only one to be officially published. The *Wolf Lieder* are true orchestrations, rather than the sort of creative reworkings of classical works popular with contemporary composers. Their purpose was clearly practical: to be performed. But the subtleties of the arrangement shows an artist grappling with the implications of more traditional text setting, where the composer's reading of a poem is underlined by musical means.

The ensemble for the *Wolf Lieder* consists of mezzo-soprano, clarinet, Mozart's beloved basset horn, two French horns, two violins, viola, cello, and bass. The first three songs are from Wolf's *Mörike-Lieder*, a set of fifty-three pieces in four volumes by the eponymous poet; the final song is a folk rhyme from the *Spanisches Liederbuch*. Grisey's first compositional decision was therefore a curatorial one, to focus on a theme of night and day.

The first song in Grisey's collection, titled "In der Frühe" ("In the early morning"), is a powerfully condensed treatment of insomnia and fear which is eased by the arrival of the morning bells. The most striking idea in this song is his use of stopped horns, clarinets, and pizzicato violins at the beginning; the color has a dark richness that illustrates the night, but also a disconcerting quality. Sul tasto strings and muted horns accompany the transition to dawn described in the poem, shifting subtly from tension to relief. But the very similar instrumentation suggests that these two states are not quite as far from one another as the narrator of the poem claims.

The second piece, "Um Mitternacht" ("At Midnight"), takes place in a friendlier night, rendered calm by the lullaby of a bubbling stream. Grisey uses mixtures of arco and pizzicato in the strings, and the quick physical changes required of the instrumentalists between these ways of playing, to suggest the kind of pleasant, mild rushing of water in Mörike's poem. The horns, alternating in accents, also suggest the "brash" movement of the water.

In the third song, titled "Das verlassene Mägdlein" ("The Abandoned Maiden"), the sound world of Grisey's original compositions shines through the most, though only in the form of masterfully orchestrated string harmonics. The poem is written from the perspective of a peasant girl whose lover hasn't appeared for their meeting. Grisey's string harmonics evoke the "disappearing stars," and the analogous images of the sparks from the fire and the maiden's tears. The narrator of the poem describes a feeling that was familiar to many of Grisey's lovers:

> Suddenly I realize,
>   Faithless boy,
>   That in the night
>   I dreamt of you.

> Tear after tear
> Then tumbles down;
> So the day dawns –
> O would it were gone again![13]

At this point, Grisey divides Wolf's already-short melodic motive into even smaller fragments. This illustrates the disorientation the narrator feels as she suddenly remembers the cause of her suffering. The song closes as it began; the maiden begs the day to pass and the night to come. As she finishes singing, the stars, orchestrated in harmonics, appear again.

"Nun Wandre, Maria" ("Wander Now, Maria") is Christian in theme, in contrast to the previous three songs, which draw on conventional Romantic imagery. Like the previous song, it also makes use of the image of crowing roosters—an image this text has in common with the D.H. Lawrence novella *The Man Who Died*. Grisey uses a spatial effect which also recalls his original compositions: the cello and bass, realizing Wolf's march-like ostinato, repeat their lowest G for the first two bars; the cello changes strings each time, switching from the C string to the open G string. This makes the introduction sound like footsteps, as if the protagonist is alternating between her left and right feet on her wanderings. The clarinets and violins wind around the vocal line like a twisting path. *Wolf Lieder* closes on a single, lonely cello C.

Grisey's orchestrations of Wolf's four songs are beautiful on their own terms and would not be out of place on a traditional chamber music program. Taken alone, the pieces are not milestones in Grisey's compositional development. But in the *Quatre chants*, Grisey deployed a mode of text-setting with certain similarities to Wolf's style. This concession to the vocal tradition reappeared in Grisey's final masterpiece to shattering effect.

The *Wolf Lieder* premiered on November 23, 1997, by Ensemble Fa and Mireille Deguy, at the Maison de Radio France in Paris. After a performance of the work in November 2001, the critic Pierre Gervasoni wrote in a brief review that the piece "achieved a real emotion."[14]

❧ ❧ ❧

In July 1996, Grisey began the process of composing *Quatre chants pour franchir le seuil*. He started with the structure of the first movement. This work already had him dreaming about a larger work to follow:

> If I compose an opera: bring out the stakes and the tragedy not from the external situation or the relationships between the voices, but from the relationship between the voices and the sound of the cosmos. To signify

---

13   Translations of these poems from the *Oxford Lieder*.
14   Gervasoni, "Des compositeurs curieux du monde."

human time, facing—or inside, or carried by, or rebelling against—cosmic time, nothing is better than the human voice, so radically different from instrumental or electronic sounds. The voice as radical otherness. Yet it emits sound too.[15]

The following summer, Grisey went to Schlans to continue working on the first movement of the piece and start the second. He was flush with his accomplishment so far. He wrote of the end of the first movement, "One minute of disconcertingly simple music in three parts, with microtones integrated into a harmonic language of great purity. May this minute of music reconcile Man with Death." Of the second, he added:

> The following movement, on Egypt, frightens me a little and bewitches me—like everything related to ancient Egypt.
> I don't think I've ever done anything so simple.
> Reduction is a virtue that is acquired in silence and absolute isolation. For eight days I have been completely alone in these mountains and the music has become like a flower that only needs to be plucked.[16]

In the summer of 1998, Grisey returned to Schlans again to finally finish the piece, making *Quatre chants* the work with the strongest imprint of the place in the composer's output. He wrote, "After three months in Schlans in the utmost silence and concentration, I finished *Quatre chants* with the lullaby of the dawn." He added that he'd spent six, even eight hours a day composing in a trance. When he returned to Paris on October 2, 1998, he found the city extremely strange. He didn't elaborate.[17]

The final instrumentation of *Quatre chants pour franchir le seuil* is an unusual one: flute, two low clarinets, two low saxophones, trumpet, and tenor tuba (all with doublings), as well as one bass tuba, harp, three percussionists, violin, cello, bass, and soprano. The setup, heavy on winds, requires careful orchestration. But, as Grisey wrote, it is necessary for the content of the piece: "The choice of the instrumentation was dictated by the musical requirement to oppose the lightness of the soprano with a low, heavy, but still sumptuous, colorful mass."[18]

The first song of the *Quatre chants pour franchir le seuil* is based on a short but potent textual fragment. In late October 1987, the poet Guez Ricord (later known as Christian Gabriel/le), whom Grisey met during his stay at the Villa Médicis, was hospitalized at Sainte Marguerite in Marseille, where he composed a series of brief but rich stanzas under the title *Le sujet de ma poésie,*

---

15 Lelong, *Écrits*, 374.
16 Paul Sacher archive.
17 Ibid.
18 Ibid.

c'est ma poésie (*The Subject of My Poetry is My Poetry*). This poem, which Guez Ricord's editor, Bernar Mialet, later collated into the prose-poem *Les heures à la nuit* (*The Hours at Night*), contains much Christian imagery and references to the Egyptian goddess Isis, with the image of blood flowing through the text. It crossbreeds the religious with the sexual in a way destined to attract Grisey's interest. The eighth section, for instance, reads:

> So I sign the cross
> > for mother, father, holy ghost
> > I drink the ashen milk
> > the milk of deaths
> > from an amorous, adventurous
> > voyage[19]

Less than a year later, in June 1988, Guez Ricord was found dead in his apartment, surrounded by eight empty bottles of the cardiac regulator Sotalex. It's unclear when Grisey first encountered this work of Ricord's, but Mialet received his request for permission to use the text in the first half of 1997.[20]

The poem that Grisey set, a short, untitled collection of lines composed on two pages and marked with mysterious symbols, was written at the same time as the seventeen sections of *Le sujet de ma poésie*, though its place within this work is unclear. Prefaced with a drawing of a dot within a circle, and dated October 22, 1987, they read as follows:

> For whom is it right
> > to die
> > like
> > an angel ... .
>
> As it is right to die
> > like an angel
> > it's my right
> > to die
> > myself
>
> It is his right to die,
> > his angel and to die
> > like
> > his becoming death
> > like an angel

---

19 Ricord, *Les heures à la nuit*. My translations. Guez Ricord's work has never been published in English.
20 Paul Sacher archive.

In this mysterious poem, with its ritualistic repetitions of the reflexive in the original French, a sense of the all-encompassing extinction of death is prevalent. In his program note, Grisey wrote, "The death of the angel is the most horrible of all, because it forces us to mourn our dreams."[21]

The first movement of *Quatre chants* opens with descending scales in the ensemble, divided into three groups. As Baillet points out, Grisey began with a rhythmic analysis of Ricord's poem, counting the number of times similar phrases reoccur in the text and noticing a form in which these repetitions decrease, from six to one.[22] These relationships, recalling the whole number relationships of the harmonic spectrum, reappear in the rest of the composition. In the soprano, Grisey sets the text in a short-long structure, with the last syllable of each line given the only long, held pitch (an abstraction of the rhythm of the heartbeat). He then looked to the number of lines in each verse—three, five, and four—and set the three groups of instruments in these rhythmic relationships to one another.

From the beginning of the movement, the stark contrast between the ornamented, wrenching declamations of the soprano and the sinking scales of the ensemble makes clear the gruesome indifference of the world to this terrible death. A brilliant bit of orchestration is Grisey's combination of the soprano with the trumpet and violin, which takes place on the long syllables and lends these moments a terrifying heraldry; the intervals are often neutral thirds, poised strangely between major and minor, and resisting categorization by our ears in a way that recalls a miniaturization of the instrumental synthesis technique. Joshua Fineberg said of this music, "You have the trumpet and the voice always coming together in the first movement, and he sets it up in such a way that, when the voice comes in later without the trumpet, you hear the trumpet anyway."[23]

As Baillet explains, the pitch material of the first movement is based on five harmonic spectra, with portions of the overtone spectrum divided among the three groups. These pitches fall progressively lower throughout the movement.[24] The rhythm of each phrase is determined by a process based again on Grisey's analysis of the poem, with the order of the abstracted verses varied by the composer.[25] Against these structural games, the perceptible form is strikingly traditional. The piece starts calmly, builds to a climax about two-thirds through the piece, and then gives way to a transparent, bereft conclusion.

---

21 Lelong, *Écrits*, 176.
22 Baillet, *Fondements d'une écriture*, 232–33.
23 Interview with Fineberg.
24 Baillet, *Fondements d'une écriture*, 236.
25 Ibid, 235.

Grisey told Valdine Anderson that the vocal part of the first movement should sound light. "Even though the intervals for each one of those little outbursts get progressively larger and more dramatic, they still had to be sung as though they were a bird uttering a sound," she said. "He wanted it humanized, but not sentimental."[26]

The second movement of the *Quatre chants* is preoccupied by the leveling effects of time. By now Grisey's fascination with Egyptian mythology is well-documented. This piece, lasting just seven minutes, is the composer's most powerful integration of Egyptian themes into his oeuvre. The composer Julian Anderson and the musicologist Christopher Wintle both remember a telling anecdote that shows the depth of Grisey's involvement with this long-lost civilization, as well as his impish sense of humor. In 1993 or 1994, Grisey was visiting London, and went to see the Egyptian exhibit at the British Museum. Wintle remembers that they spent the entire day there, with Grisey taking notes on the inscriptions on the sarcophagi.[27] The next day, Anderson invited Grisey to go to the same exhibit with him. Without telling Anderson he'd just visited, Grisey lectured the younger composer on the artifacts, leading the Englishman to believe he was a great expert on the material. Anderson was completely fooled. Grisey "couldn't resist playing a prank," Anderson recalled.[28]

The actual texts of the piece are fragments from the Egyptian Coffin Texts, rendered in French in a 1986 translation by the Egyptologist Paul Barguet, in his *Les Textes des sarcophages égyptiens du Moyen Empire*. They are chosen for their potent illustration of the lacerating effect of time on human endeavor:

Nos. 811 and 812: (Almost entirely faded away)

No. 814: "Grant that you rest in eternity ..."

No. 809: (destroyed)

Nos. 868 and 869: (Almost entirely destroyed)

No. 870: "I've been through ... I've been flourishing ... I've made a lamentation ... the Luminous falls [within ..."

Nos. 961 and 963: (destroyed)

No. 972: (Almost entirely erased)

No. 973: "Who goes all over the sky ... to the confines of the sky ... to her whose arms are outstretched ... [Make me a path of light, let me pass ..."

---

26 Interview with Valdine Anderson.
27 Interview with Wintle.
28 Interview with Julian Anderson.

No. 903: (destroyed)

No. 1050: "Spell for being a god ..."[29]

This is a remarkable text, heightened in performance by the neutral, recitative character of the soprano line, and it results in some of the most powerful music Grisey ever composed.

Two additional points about Grisey's setting are worth noting. First, on February 6, 1997, Grisey wrote a letter to Barguet mentioning that he was hoping to compose a piece based on these fragments. He asked the Egyptologist if it would be possible to receive "the original, in Egyptian, even if the pronunciation of the consonants is uncertain and fragmentary," adding that "it is very important for me to use these fragments in the original language."[30] If Barguet responded, his letter is not preserved. It would be a fascinating musicological exercise to put together a version of this movement with a version of the text in the original Egyptian. But the work derives much of its unsettling power from the immediate comprehensibility of the text, especially considering the careful scoring Grisey used in the ensemble to make the words audible. Just as the effects of time are inescapable, so too is the meaning of this song.

Second, Grisey did not follow Barguet's translation slavishly; while his changes are small, they have an outsized impact on the effectiveness of the text. Grisey collated and combined different spells together and, in some places, took even smaller fragments from the little that remained. The lines "the Luminous falls within" and "make me a path of light, let me pass ..." are not actually contained in the given spells. In spell 973, the entire surviving text reads as follows:

> The representatives of Ra who go all over the sky in [...] forever [...]. Sky and earth come to you, the deserts of them of Kenzet come to you [...] Maret [...] before the wind [...] her whose arms are outstretched. I have lain on my right side.[31]

Grisey edited the Coffin Texts with a sure literary hand, making an already powerful source text even more so.

As in *Vortex Temporum*, Grisey uses soft instrumental interludes to maintain the silence and concentration between the movements of *Quatre chants*, allowing the listeners to rest briefly while preventing them from making noise. What follows is the most heartrendingly simple music the composer ever wrote. Over quasi-tonal chords and soft swells in the ensemble, the

---

29   Barguet, *Textes des Sarcophages*, 612–13.
30   Paul Sacher archive.
31   Barguet, *Textes des Sarcophages*, 612–13.

soprano declaims the text, lamenting, as Grisey described it, "the death of a civilization." The vocal style for the destroyed or defaced coffin texts is matter-of-fact and almost spoken, while the composer allows the singer modest lyrical flights—whose scope and intensity, as Baillet points out, increase throughout the movement—for the text that remains.[32] The plucked chords, intoned in the harp, cello, and bass, are based on a rhythm of two short and one long syllable, a sequence Baillet locates in the last line of Guez Ricord's poem. Throughout the movement, the duration of this repeated figure increases, but flexibly and "non-linearly," as Baillet puts it.[33] Grisey also increases the density of tempo changes, putting the listener on increasingly uncertain footing, like the shifting sands that covered so many of the remnants of Egyptian civilization.[34] The harmony of the piece is similarly effective. Ulrich Alexander Kreppein describes a "harmonic dualism [that] is used again to support the text: dense, inharmonic chords accompany the fragments–the poetic stratum–while harmonic, rather simple chords are combined with the prosaic stratum of the text."[35] The music sucks the air out of the concert hall, leaving the audience in a state of heightened silence.

Deguy still has books that Grisey trawled through for material for the third movement of the *Quatre chants* with his markings: *La Sagesse grecque* by Giorgio Colli; Louise Mistral's translation of the *Odyssey*; poetry by Ovid, Sappho, and Alcaeus of Mytilene. The text he eventually settled on for "D'après Erinna" creates a through-line with the preceding movement. This text is taken without changes from its source material. In most other ways, though, it exists in a very similar aesthetic cosmos to the Coffin Texts. According to Marguerite Yourcenar, the first woman elected to the Académie Française and author of *La Couronne et la Lyre: Anthologie de la poésie grecque ancienne*, from which Grisey took this text, Erinna was a poet, or two poets, from somewhere between the sixth and fourth centuries BC, originating from Rhodes, Lesbos, the Peloponnese, or elsewhere in Greece. All that is known for certain about the author is that she died at the age of nineteen, and that the work attributed to her was found during an archeological excavation in Egypt. As with the Coffin Texts, nearly everything about the origin of the material is in doubt.

Grisey chose these lines for the movement:

... In the emptiness below, the echo propagates in vain,
And all is silent among the dead. The voice expands in the shadow ...[36]

---

32 Baillet, *Fondements d'une écriture*, 240.
33 Ibid.
34 Kreppein, "In the Labyrinth of Time," 13.
35 Ibid, 15.
36 Yourcenar, *La Couronne et la Lyre*, 90–91.

In this text, sound—the material that Grisey considered to make up his soul—is prevented from echoing by the airless atmosphere of the underworld. The line in French is *"Dans le vide d'en bas l'écho en vain dérive,"* and maybe Grisey read an allusion to his early composition *Dérives* here. At the same time, sound is not completely dead in this mysterious place, as the spectrum of the voice achieves what the echo can't—it expands. Grisey's programmatic title for the movement is "The Death of the Voice," a clear allusion to the death of his grandmother all those years ago, when he wondered, "Where is that voice?" This movement is an attempt to evoke that lost voice, or at least to mourn it.

The third movement of the *Quatre chants* makes explicit use of the musical and metaphorical effect of the echo. The soprano intones four phrases, each of which dissipates into the vast emptiness in poignant, alternating major thirds. The loneliness of this process is emphasized by the fact that the echo takes longer each time; the musicologist Lukas Haselböck notes a proportional relationship to the metrical structure of Guez Ricord's poem in this movement. He describes the poetic effect of the process: "The voice echoes unheard. It is drowned out by its own echo and must finally fall silent. It is lost in the kingdom of shadows."[37] The harmonies of this movement are generated using a technique Grisey developed during the composition of *Les chants de l'amour*, an analysis of the formants of vowels, which he gives over to the melismatic, lamenting violin line, which coils around the voice. He also uses the shadow sound process, which, as Haselböck points out, "demonstrates an analogy to the content [of the poem]: the voice gets lost in the shadows of its own sound." The movement ends with a downward melodic interval one quarter-tone higher than a minor second and flows without a break into the final two movements. Grisey was hoping to evoke a kind of universal grief; in his program note, he wondered if, in all the centuries since Erinna, "has nothing changed in our mourning?"[38]

The fourth movement of the *Quatre chants* is based on Jean Bottéro's 1992 French translation of the *Epic of Gilgamesh*; Deguy still has Grisey's copy of that book, too. The passage that Grisey sets comes after the death of Gilgamesh's companion Enkidu and takes place during the Flood, the story that was repeated in the Bible. (Grisey makes the connection between the two stories in his program note.) Gilgamesh, who has become afraid of death, learns the secret of immortality. This allows him to survive an apocalypse:

… Six days and seven nights
    Squalls, beating rains,

---

37   Haselböck, *Unhörbares hörbar machen*, 315–19.
38   Lelong, *Écrits*, 176.

> Hurricanes and deluge
> > Continue to
> > Pillage the earth.
> > The seventh day comes,
>
> Tempest, deluge, and
> > Carnage cease.
> > After having spread
> > Their random blows,
>
> Like a woman
> > In her pains,
> > The Sea becomes
> > Calm and immobile.
>
> I look around:
> > Silence reigns!
> > All the men
> > Have turned to clay:
>
> And the liquid
> > Looks like solid ground.[39]

The previous movement closes and the coming one opens with a "Faux Interlude" that tricks us into feeling at rest, but which is actually preparing us for a coming storm: soft percussion tremoli allude to the previous two interludes, while the less-than-minor-second motive of the third movement continues to echo.

When the fourth movement proper, "D'après l'épopée de Gilgamesh" opens, it does so with a process that closely recalls *Tempus ex Machina*, even down to the bass-drum hits which mark the entrance of a new instrument or a change in rhythmic structure. What follows is music of unprecedented violence in Grisey's oeuvre, "first as rain and the soft roll of thunder, announcing the catastrophe, then as the deluge, which breaks over the listener with the full violence of the ensemble," Haselböck writes.[40] He adds, using Grisey's sketches, that the composer explicitly intended the groaning tubas in quarter-tones to evoke the straining of elephants against the storm—another reference to the story of Noah. These tubas play the same melodic motive that ended the third movement and echoed in the "Faux Interlude," a motive the singer picks up before erupting into a panicked flight made more heart-rending by the thinning instrumental texture. It is not until the flood lets up that we begin to process its devastation.

---

39   Bottéro, *L'épopée de Gilgameš*.
40   Haselböck, *Unhörbares hörbar machen*, 324.

After this climax of both the movement and the entire *Quatre chants*, the musical process works in the opposite direction, with, as Haselböck shows, "active" phrases of the texture being reduced in number and length, and "calm" phrases being added and stretched out.[41] The harmonic density of the work is also gradually reduced, according to Grisey's meticulous plan. The movement winds down with an aching canon on the now-central interval of the minor second reduced by a quarter-tone, between the voice, violin, and cello. It ends with a long pause of complete immobility.

The final movement of the *Quatre chants* is not its own song, but a coda and a lullaby. The text continues where the previous movement left off:

I open a window
    And the day strikes my cheek,
    I fall on my knees, immobile,
    and I cry ...
    I look at the horizon
    of the sea, the world ...

It's an apocalyptic text with obvious parallels to the environmental catastrophes of our time. "I dare to hope that this lullaby will not be one of those we will sing tomorrow to the first human clones," Grisey wrote, "when it will be necessary to reveal to them the unbearable genetic and psychological violence which was committed against them, by a humanity desperately in search of foundational taboos [to break]."[42] Anxieties about cloning now seem a distant relic of the 1990s. To today's listeners, Grisey's allusions to the terrors of climate change are harder to shake.

While the text of the "Berceuse" continues directly from the previous movement, Haselböck notes that the structure of this movement is all its own. The vocal part gains in intensity and density toward the middle of the movement, becoming increasingly elaborate (even on the word "immobile"). Grisey sets a harmonic spectrum he calls "the *Berceuse* spectrum" as the central pole of the movement. Rhythmic patterns repeat throughout the work, lending the whole a remarkable calm, while the short measures accelerate and the long measures slow down, drifting apart from one another. "At the same time, the sonority rises, as if leaving the body and approaching the sphere of the inaudible," Haselböck writes, an effect strengthened by the ethereal timbres of the ensemble.[43] In the middle of the piece, the voice becomes calmer again, singing the words "the sea, the world" with quiet poise. The ending of the "Berceuse" and the *Quatre chants* as a whole

---

41   Ibid, 324.
42   Lelong, *Écrits*, 177.
43   Haselböck, *Unhörbares hörbar machen*, 332.

is stunning because the piece doesn't come to a traditional conclusion. It simply stops, with sustain lines touching the double bar in the score. In one millisecond there is sound and life, and in the next there is death, and vast silence.

❦ ❦ ❦

Documents in Grisey's archive show the beginnings of a new work taking shape to follow the *Quatre chants pour franchir le seuil*, probably the fulfillment of his promise to compose an original piece for Mireille Deguy.[44] The instrumentations he considered included duos of mezzo-soprano and bass clarinet or mezzo-soprano and lute, an idea that was accompanied by the reminder to "re-listen to the music of Guillaume Du Fay." Grisey also made some very general harmonic sketches for the piece, including a chart of overtones based on C.

Beyond these early considerations, the most fixed part of the composition is the text, a rich fragment from Samuel Beckett's French-language poem *mirlitonnades*. Beckett composed the work between 1976 and 1978. The title is an invented word based on the term *mirliton*, or kazoo—the title is something akin to "kazooations"[45]—and the stanzas of the twelve-page poem are by turns darkly comic and existential, making heavy use of slang, vulgar rhymes, over-alliteration and repetition. The scholar Mar Garre García writes that the poem

> ... . recall[s] the old tradition of the nightwatchmen offering their "doggerel or trashy verse" to citizens on New Year's Eve: the "vers de mirliton." Beckett appropriated this custom for a new poetic concept which intentionally lacked literary sophistication and had connotations of fragility and brightness, while not quite succumbing to the pejorative "vers de mirliton" and which alluded to "a bad poetry, common, vulgar, unpretentious." These short verses repeatedly suggest the confrontation with nothingness through the shape of a blackbird's song.[46]

The *mirlitonnades* have a tossed-off, transient character. As Dirk Van Hulle writes, the *mirlitonnades* were "explicitly conceived as minor or 'throwaway' poetry ... jotted down on 'throwaway' material and everyday objects, such as envelopes, letters, a piece from a box of cigars, pages torn

---

44 Paul Sacher archive.
45 A German translation by Barbara Köhler renders the title, effectively, as *Trötentöne*.
46 Translation from García, "The Translation of Samuel Beckett's 'mirlitonnades' by Three Spanish Authors," 83.

from notebooks and coloured notepads."[47] Fittingly, Grisey jotted down the passage he planned to set on his appointment planner.

This passage consists of four lines toward the middle of the poem, following a section which is saturated by absurd repetitions. In the lines that interested Grisey, these repetitions give way to a stanza of striking beauty:

night that brings such
longing for the dawn
night of grace
fall[48]

This excerpt is biblical in the power of its evocatively compressed language,[49] a quality it shares with the Guez Ricord poem Grisey set. It also explores the theme of night and day as metaphors for death and life, ideas present in Grisey's works from *Jour, contre-jour* and *Sortie vers la lumière du jour* to the *Wolf Lieder*. This duality becomes clearer with the inclusion of the stanza just before the lines Grisey had planned to set to music:

Each day wants
To become a living day
Not sure to lack regret
A day of being born

The composer's intention to set a stanza from the *mirlitonnades* shows that his interest in the opposite states of existence called life and death, represented in the image of night and day, had remained.

In preparation for the never-titled composition, Grisey made some rhythmic sketches based on these four lines and wrote a note to himself to "see the formants" of the various vowels and consonants in the text, a technique reminiscent of his treatment of the phrase "I love you" in *Les chants de l'amour*.[50] Besides these few clues, there is little left of Grisey's last idea, and almost certainly not enough from which to build a completion of the piece.

In November 1998, Grisey went to Milan for a business meeting with his publisher Ricordi. While he was there, he met his friend and former student, the composer Atli Ingólfsson. They went out for dinner, and Ingólfsson noticed that Grisey seemed grounded. He didn't complain about the food,

---

47   Van Hulle, "Beckett's Art of the Commonplace."
48   My translations of Beckett.
49   Robert Alter is the expert on the potent compression of Biblical Hebrew.
50   Paul Sacher archive.

as he sometimes did, nor did the cigar smoke at the next table bother him, as it usually would have. Grisey told his friend how calm he felt. "I feel good. Maybe I won't compose anymore," he said.[51]

On the early morning of November 10, Grisey returned to Paris, bearing a gift from Ricordi: an original engraving plate from the score of Puccini's opera *Manon Lescaut*. After breakfast, Mireille Deguy went to work, then to the gym. Grisey, without unpacking his suitcases, left for a meeting at the Conservatoire. He came home at lunchtime. Deguy returned to their apartment at about 7 p.m. that evening; in the meantime, Grisey had made an unusual number of calls to his friends.

They had plans for dinner. Grisey suggested having a drink before leaving. He wanted to savor the early-evening contentment with her.[52] Deguy remembers that he removed his watch and asked her to do the same before he collapsed, the result of an aneurism. He fell into a coma, and was brought to the Kremlin-Bicêtre hospital, a few miles outside Paris. He crossed the threshold the following morning, at dawn.

---

51   Interview with Ingólfsson.
52   Interview with Deguy.

Chapter Fifteen

Berceuse

Grisey's death followed the composition of his masterpiece on death. Originally a requiem for his mother, it became an autorequiem. It's an unsettling circumstance, made more so by the frequent references to death in his writings. In June 1998, he had said of the *Quatre chants*, "Why are the final decisions the most painful ones? Saying goodbye? Attachment? To what, from what?"[1] Friends had memories of things that seemed prophetic in hindsight. "He was fascinated by death, as a symbol and as a fact," Zinsstag said.[2] Claudia Doderer remembered his flushed face after a particularly intense lesson, Wintle a surprisingly full medicine cabinet for what seemed to be such a healthy man.[3] Jocelyne thought there might have been a connection between his mental anguish at the end of their relationship and the brain aneurism that ended his life.[4]

But there is also evidence that *Quatre chants* was the beginning of a new stylistic era in Grisey's life, and that he never thought of the piece in connection with his own death. One example is the unfinished work based on the *mirlitonnades*. Many of Grisey's friends recalled that after completing the *Quatre chants*, he was exhilarated about the possibilities he had discovered. "He was going on and on about that piece, really the only time I'd ever heard him go on about his music," Joshua Fineberg said. "He'd figured out what he needed to do."[5] A letter to the artistic director of the Donaueschinger Musiktage, Armin Köhler, shows that Grisey was already planning commissions past the year 2000.[6] After the completion of *Quatre chants*, Grisey told George Benjamin how excited he was about this newfound stylistic independence; he called his friend Jean-Pierre Luminet and said he had found "a new language that begins with this composition." He

---

1 Paul Sacher archive.
2 Interview with Zinsstag.
3 Interviews with Doderer and Wintle.
4 Interview with Jocelyne Grisey.
5 Interview with Fineberg.
6 Paul Sacher archive.

also spoke with Jean-Luc Hervé, who remembered something Grisey told him. "We are like onions," Grisey said. "We shed our skin."[7] At the time of his death, the composer was the closest he'd ever been to his true self. He was fifty-two years old. "He died just as he was coming into focus," Christopher Wintle said.[8]

The French musical scene was stricken, having lost one of its leading artistic personalities. For the critic Cestin Cazaban, Grisey's death "opened a breach in a generation."[9] In *Le Monde*, Gérard Condé wrote, "Sudden, unexpected, the announcement of his death leaves us distraught. Many still considered him a young composer, probably because he never gave the impression of an artist who had arrived, but of a musician whose demands did not let him rest."[10] Guy Lelong added that because Grisey "considered listening to be one of the factors of composition, because his music is at once learned, playful, and extremely seductive, he represented—for those of us who admired him—a kind of latter-day Debussy."[11] It's an appropriate comparison. Like Debussy, Grisey composed music of structural rigor and spine-tingling sensuality, controlled by form and enlivened by delirium, changing the history of music as he went.

The one thing everyone remembers about Grisey's funeral is the bitter cold of November 1998. The mood was one of devastation, his survivors surveying a world wiped out, like Gilgamesh pondering the end of the Flood and the remains of the earth.

Deguy felt that an ecumenical ceremony would be appropriate for Grisey's funeral, grounded in the Catholic faith. While she set about looking for a priest who would agree to give the last rites to a divorced man and allow elements from other religious traditions to be included in the ceremony, Grisey's body was stored for ten days in the cold before he could be cremated.

Once Deguy found a priest who was willing to preside over this unusual service, she decided on a little chapel, the Église Sainte-Marie des Batignolles, as the venue.[12] The priest read the Catholic rites, Michaël Levinas the kaddish, a third friend a Buddhist poem: a universal ceremony that would have

---

7   Interview with Hervé.
8   Interview with Wintle.
9   Cazaban, "Salut de l'artiste."
10 Condé, "Gérard Grisey: Un observateur attentive de la matière sonore."
11 Lelong, *La lettre du musicien*.
12 Newspaper clipping in the private archive of Lanza.

brought the composer joy. Jocelyne and Raphaël were there; Zinsstag said a few words. Jean-Pierre Luminet came but couldn't bring himself to speak. There were many beautiful women, weeping.[13] Jebah Baum, the artist Grisey had met at La Napoule, came with his daughter, who lay in her carriage, wrapped in layers of blankets, and slept peacefully through the service.

After the ceremony, the group retired to a room close to the famous Père Lachaise Cemetery in Paris. It was freezing, but they sat for two or three hours listening to their friend's music. They could not listen to the *Quatre chants*. It would be another decade before Paol Keineg could face hearing the piece; his grief was too raw. He dedicated a book to the memory of his friend, called *There and Not There*.[14] Many musical tributes followed.[15]

France Detry has never listened to the *Quatre chants*, and she could not face going to the funeral alone. But, one day, she was at her cousin's having lunch. Suddenly she started feeling unwell. She went outside to get some air. It was freezing outside, but Detry felt like she was burning. "I know Gérard is hot," she thought. "I can't do anything." She realized later that this feeling intersected precisely with the timing of his cremation.[16]

In the early nineties, probably 1992, Deguy had given a concert in central France that Grisey came to hear. They went for a picnic at the Chartreuse du Liget, a monastery near the ancient town of Loches, located in the clearing of a forest. Grisey told her he could imagine his ashes being scattered in a place like this. After his death, Deguy went to spread them at the monastery by the roots of a chestnut tree.

Quatre chants pour franchir le seuil was premiered on February 3, 1999, at Queen Elizabeth Hall, along with Wolfgang Rihm's *Gedrängte Form* (premiered in December 1998) and Boulez's *Sur incises* (1996). The ensemble was the London Sinfonietta under the direction of George Benjamin. A team based around Fabien Lévy and the conductor Pierre-André Valade corrected the harp part and other details in Grisey's composition, which was not quite ready for performance.[17] The critic Andrew Clements wrote that it was "a wonderfully strange and haunting piece, full of beguiling imagery and unclassifiable sounds."[18] Fiona Maddocks wrote, "That a man in the prime of life feels an imperative to write his own elegy without realizing it, raised questions yet more disturbing than the potent work itself."[19]

---

13 Interview with Keineg.
14 *Là et pas là* in French.
15 Lelong, *Écrits*, 418.
16 Interview with Detry.
17 Interview with Lévy.
18 Clements, "Man of the Future."
19 Maddocks, "Mayfair Festival."

Two recordings of the *Quatre chants* have since been made, a version on the label Kairos with Klangforum Wien, Sylvain Cambreling, and the soprano Catherine Dubosc; and a slightly more elegant and more effortless version by Barbara Hannigan and the Ludwig Orchestra. In 1999, Mireille Deguy recorded the "Berceuse." The piece Grisey had promised her would never materialize.

A group of those close to Grisey traveled to London for the premiere. A quarter-century later, words still seem to fail them: none of Grisey's eloquent colleagues, friends, and lovers seemed able to talk about the concert at all. This story must end like the *Quatre chants pour franchir le seuil* itself, with the sudden, gaping silence.

Appendix

Recordings of Music by Gérard Grisey

Boulez, Pierre. *Modulations*, recorded 1984. Erato.
Cambreling, Sylvain, SWR Sinfonieorchester, *Paris Compositions*, recorded 1997. Hänssler Classic.
Deguy, Mireille, Alessandro de Curtis, Maurizio Longoni, Michele Fait, and Lorenzo Meneghetti, *Wolf Lieder, Charme, Accords perdus*, recorded 2000. SMC.
Dubosc, Catherine. Klangforum Wien, *Quatre chants pour franchir le seuil*, recorded 2001. Kairos.
Duhamel, Antoine, Jean-François Jenny-Clark, Spiros Sakkas, *Initation, Yod, Alternances, Hevel*, recorded 1972. LP. Point-Radiant.
Ensemble Court-Circuit, Gérard Caussé, Frankfurter Museumsorchester, Pierre-André Valade, Sylvain Cambreling. *Les espaces acoustiques*, recorded 1999. Accord Una Corda.
Ensemble Fa, *Stèle pour 1 percussionnistes*, recorded 1995. MFA.
Ensemble L'Itinéraire, Gérard Caussé, Claude Delangle, Mark Foster, Pascal Rophé. *Talea, Prologue, Jour, contre-jour*, recorded 1993. Accord.
Ensemble Recherche, *Vortex Temporum*, recorded 1996. Accord Una Corda.
Ensemble Risognanze, Tito Ceccherini. *Vortex Temporum, Périodes*, recorded 2007. Stradivarius.
Ensemble S, WDR Sinfonieorchester Köln, Emilio Pomárico, Schola Heidelberg, Walter Nußbaum. *Le temps et l'écume, Les chants de l'amour*, recorded 2008. Kairos.
Hannigan, Barbara, Ludwig Orchestra, *La Passione*, recorded 2020. Alpha Classics / Outhere Music.
KammerensembleN live, *Talea*, recorded 1998. Caprice.
Knox, Garth, *Spectral Viola*, recorded 2002. Edition Zeitklang.
Knox, Garth, ASKO Ensemble, WDR Sinfonieorchester Köln, Stefan Asbury, *Les espaces acoustiques*, recorded 2005. Kairos.
Luoma, Mikko, *The Virtuoso Accordion*, recorded 2017. Bridge Records Inc, New Rochelle, NY.

Molinari, Ernesto, Uwe Dierksen, Ensemble S, *Solo pour deux, Anubis-Nout, Stèle, Charme, Tempus ex Machina*, recorded 2005. Kairos. Liner notes by Wolfgang Hofer.

Les Percussions de Strasbourg, *Le noir de l'étoile*, recorded 2004. Accord Una Corda.

Published Scores by Gérard Grisey

Échanges. Milan: Ricordi, 1968.
Charme. Milan: Ricordi, 1969.
Mégalithes. Milan: Ricordi, 1969.
Initiation. Milan: Ricordi, 1970.
Vagues, Chemins, le Souffle. Paris: Henri Lemoine, 1972.
D'eau et de pierre. Milan: Ricordi, 1972.
Dérives. Milan: Ricordi, 1974.
Périodes. Milan: Ricordi, 1974.
Partiels. Milan: Ricordi, 1975.
Manifestations. Milan: Ricordi, 1976.
Prologue. Milan: Ricordi, 1976.
Modulations. Milan: Ricordi, 1977.
Sortie vers la lumière du jour. Milan: Ricordi, 1978.
Jour, contre-jour. Milan: Ricordi, 1979.
Tempus ex machina. Milan: Ricordi, 1979.
Transitoires. Milan: Ricordi, 1980.
Solo pour deux. Milan: Ricordi, 1981.
Anubis et Nout. Milan: Ricordi, 1983.
Les chants de l'amour. Milan: Ricordi, 1984.
Épilogue. Milan: Ricordi, 1985.
Talea. Milan: Ricordi, 1986.
Accords perdus. Milan: Ricordi, 1987.
Le temps et l'écume. Milan: Ricordi, 1989.
Anubis et Nout (saxophone version). Milan: Ricordi, 1990.
Le noir de l'étoile. Milan: Ricordi, 1990.
Stèle. Milan: Ricordi, 1995.
Vortex Temporum. Milan: Ricordi, 1995.
L'Icône paradoxale. Milan: Ricordi, 1996.
Wolf Lieder. Milan: Ricordi, 1997.
Quatre chants pour franchir le seuil. Milan: Ricordi, 1998.

Bibliography

Primary Sources

Interviews with the author (in English unless otherwise noted)

Anderson, Julian. By phone, April 15, 2019.
Anderson, Valdine. By phone, June 13, 2019.
Bade, Franz-Josef. By phone, June 11, 2021. In German.
Baum, Jebah. By phone, February 5, 2022.
Benjamin, George. By phone, May 5, 2019.
Boone, Charles. By phone, August 12, 2021.
Boudreau, Walter. By phone, February 20, 2021.
Campion, Edmund. By phone, May 10, 2019.
Deguy, Mireille. In person, December 5, 2021. In French.
Delnon, Georges. By phone, April 8, 2020.
Dennehy, Donnacha. By email, April 30, 2019.
Detry, France. In person, August 13–14, 2019, and December 6–7, 2021, with Noel Schneider.
Doderer, Claudia. In person, September 15, 2020. In German.
Dufourt, Hugues. In person, March 8, 2022. In French. With Carine Kuntz.
Febel, Reinhard. In person, July 23, 2019. In German.
Fineberg, Joshua. In person, June 19, 2019.
Fishman-Johnson, Ellen. By phone, April 7, 2020.
Grisey, Jocelyne. In person. With Raphaël Grisey on May 10, 2019. In person with Jocelyne Grisey, December 8, 2021, and March 1, 2022. In English and French.
Haas, Georg Friedrich. By phone, April 4, 2020. In German.
Hein, Folkmar. By phone, May 11, 2020. In German.
Hervé, Jean-Luc. By phone, April 22, 2020.
Imbescheid, Albrecht. By email, September 19, 2019. In German.
Ingólfsson, Atli. By phone, April 27, 2021.
Jacobs, Edward. By phone, June 15, 2021.

Jolas, Betsy. In person, November 4, 2021.
Keineg, Paol. By phone, April 28, 2021.
Kim, Hi-Kyung. By phone, June 7, 2019.
Klanac, Petar. By phone, September 10, 2021. In French.
Lachenmann, Helmut. By email, November 15, 2022. In German.
Lanza, Josienne. In person, March 9, 2022. In French. With Carine Kuntz.
Lefebvre, Noémi. By Twitter DMs, August 4, 2020.
Lejet, Édith. By email, April 28, 2020.
Lelong, Guy. In person, November 6, 2021. In French. With Carine Kuntz.
Lévy, Fabien. In person, August 19, 2019.
Lieberman, David. By phone, August 25, 2021.
Louvier, Alain. By email, August 6, 2020. In French.
Luminet, Jean-Pierre. By phone, January 22, 2021.
Maiguashca, Mesías. By email, May 15, 2019. In German.
McAdams, Stephen. By phone, January 4, 2021.
Mialet, Bernar. By email, December 20, 2022. In French.
Paris, François. By phone, January 18, 2021.
Robertson, David. By phone. October 7, 2022.
Rothman, Daniel. By email, August 22, 2021.
Rose, François. By phone, May 20, 2019.
Rouan, François. By email, June 8, 2021.
Schimmel, William. By Facebook Messenger, July 17, 2021.
Shelton, Lucy. By email, August 27, 2021.
Silk, Joe. By phone, January 14, 2021.
Tenzer, Michael. By phone, June 9, 2020.
Vogt, Harry. By email. September 20, 2022. In German.
Wildman, Leslie. By email, July 2, 2021.
Wintle, Christopher. By phone, August 10, 2019.
Wit, Antoni. By email, February 15, 2021.
Zinsstag, Gérard. In person, May 23, 2019, and January 13, 2022. In German.
Ziporyn, Evan. By phone, May 11, 2020.

Archives

Archiv Internationales Musikinstitut Darmstadt, Darmstadt, Germany.
Archiv Deutscher Akademischer Austauschdienst, Berlin, Germany.
Médiathèque Musicale Mahler, Paris, France.
Paul Sacher Stiftung, Gérard Grisey Collection, Basel, Switzerland.
Private archives of France Detry, Les Valarèdes, France.
Private archives of Mireille Deguy, Lyon, France.

Private archives of Jocelyne Grisey, Paris, France.
Private archives of Josienne Lanza, Champigneulles, France.

Secondary Sources

Books on Gérard Grisey

Baillet, Jérôme. *Gérard Grisey: Fondements d'une écriture*. Paris L'Harmattan, 2006.

Bauer, Amy, Liam Cagney, and William Mason (eds). *The Oxford Handbook of Spectral Music*, online edition, Oxford Academic, December 8, 2021, https://doi.org/10.1093/oxfordhb/9780190633547.001.0001, accessed November 10, 2022.

Cohen-Levinas, Danielle (ed.). *Le temps de l'écoute: Gérard Grisey, ou la beauté des ombres sonores*. Paris: L'harmattan, 2013.

Gebhardt, Hans. *Spektralismus. Gérard Griseys "Accords perdus – Cinq Miniatures Pour Deux Cors En Fa."* GRIN Publishing (September 13, 2009). www.grin.com/document/134205, accessed November 10, 2022.

Grisey, Gérard and Guy Lelong. *Écrits*. Paris: Editions Mf, 2018.

Haselböck, Lukas. *Gérard Grisey - Unhörbares Hörbar Machen*. Freiburg, Rombach, 2009.

Newspaper and magazine articles

Anderson, Julian. "A Provisional History of Spectral Music." *Contemporary Music Review* 19 (2): 7–22. https://doi.org/10.1080/07494460000640231.

Bernheimer, Martin. "Icon and Iconoclast at the Philharmonic." *Los Angeles Times*. January 20, 1996. https://www.latimes.com/archives/la-xpm-1996-01-20-ca-26611-story.html.

Besada, José L., and Cristóbal Pagán Cánovas. "Timelines in Spectral Composition: A Cognitive Approach to Musical Creativity." *Organised Sound* 25, no. 2 (August 1, 2020): 142–155. https://doi.org/10.1017/s1355771820000059.

Brown, Jeffrey Arlo. "A Gérard Grisey Playlist." *VAN Magazine*. August 17, 2017. https://van-magazine.com/mag/gerard-grisey-playlist/.

Brown, Jeffrey Arlo. "Decades." *VAN Magazine*. February 4, 2016. https://van-magazine.com/mag/georg-friedrich-haas/.

Brown, Jeffrey Arlo. "Faked Silence." *VAN Magazine*. July 5, 2018. https://van-magazine.com/mag/salvatore-sciarrino/.

Cagney, Liam. "On Vagues, Chemins, Le Souffle (1970–72) and the Early Use of Resonance Chords in Grisey's Oeuvre." *Mitteilungen der Paul Sacher Stiftung* 28 (April 2015): 49–54. https://www.paul-sacher-stiftung.ch/de/forschung-publikationen/publikationen/mitteilungen/nr-28-april-2015.html.

Cazabin, Costin. "Salut l'artiste." *Le Monde de la Musique*. No. 228, January 1998. Médiathèque Musicale Mahler, Paris.

Clements, Andrew. "Spectral Songs." *Guardian*. January 11, 2002. https://www.theguardian.com/lifeandstyle/2002/jan/11/shopping.artsfeatures4.

Clements, Andrew. "Grisey: Les espaces acoustiques CD Review–Profound and with a Huge Physical Presence." *Guardian*. August 3, 2016. https://www.theguardian.com/music/2016/aug/03/grisey-les-espaces-acoustiques-cd-review-garth-knox-stefan-asbury-wdr-sinfonieorchester-koln.

Clements, Andrew. "Man of the Future." *Guardian*. February 6, 1999. https://www.theguardian.com/books/1999/feb/06/books.guardianreview2.

Condé, Gérard. "Gérard Grisey." *Le Monde*. November 14, 1998. https://www.lemonde.fr/archives/article/1998/11/14/gerard-grisey_3693492_1819218.html.

Condé, Gérard. "Oeuvres contemporaines à la Biennale de Venise." *Le Monde*. October 20, 1981. https://www.lemonde.fr/archives/article/1981/10/20/uvres-contemporaines-a-la-biennale-de-venise_2711295_1819218.html.

Condé, Gérard. "Recherches de musique contemporaine: La nouvelle école de Darmstadt." *Le Monde*, August 5, 1978. https://www.lemonde.fr/archives/article/1978/08/15/recherches-de-musique-contemporaine-la-nouvelle-ecole-de-darmstadt_3132650_1819218.html.

Condé, Gérard. "Ouverture Brillante Pour Le Festival Musica, Le Rendez-Vous Strasbourgeois Des Compositeurs." *Le Monde*, September 24, 1996. https://www.lemonde.fr/archives/article/1996/09/24/ouverture-brillante-pour-le-festival-musica-le-rendez-vous-strasbourgeois-des-compositeurs_3751460_1819218.html.

Condé, Gérard. "La Dernière Charrette de La S.I.M.C." *Le Monde*, November 1, 1975. https://www.lemonde.fr/archives/article/1975/11/01/la-derniere-charrette-de-la-s-i-m-c_2583565_1819218.html.

Condé, Gérard. "Sympathies." *Le Monde*, June 3, 1986. https://www.lemonde.fr/archives/article/1986/06/03/sympathies_2914373_1819218.html.

Condé, Gérard. "Retour à l'Évidence Musicale," *Le Monde*, March 7, 1978. https://www.lemonde.fr/archives/article/1978/03/07/retour-a-l-evidence-musicale_2983579_1819218.html.

Condé, Gérard. "Gérard Grisey voix et ordinateur." *Le Monde*. June 10, 1985. https://www.lemonde.fr/archives/article/1985/06/10/gerard-grisey-voix-et-ordinateur_2755131_1819218.html.

Cyr, Gordon C. "Roger Sessions at Berkeley: A Personal Reminiscence." *Perspectives of New Music* 23, no. 2 (1985): 131–138. https://doi.org/10.2307/832716.

Downey, Sally A. "Jacob C. Neupauer, 93, a Musician and Educator." *Philadelphia Inquirer*. Accessed March 8, 2022. https://www.inquirer.com/philly/obituaries/20110419_Jacob_C__Neupauer__93__a_musician_and_educator.html.

Exarchos, Dimitris. "The Skin of Spectral Time in Grisey's *Le noir de l'étoile*." *Twentieth-Century Music* 15 (1): 31–55 (2018). https://doi.org/10.1017/s1478572218000051.

Féron, François-Xavier. "The Emergence of Spectra in Gérard Grisey's Compositional Process: From Dérives (1973–74) To Les espaces acoustiques (1974–85)." *Contemporary Music Review* 30 (5): 343–75 (2011). https://doi.org/10.1080/07494467.2011.665582.

Féron, François-Xavier. L'organisation rythmique dans la première section de *Modulations. Mitteilungen der Paul Sacher Stiftung* 25 (April 2012): 41–48.

Garre García, Mar. "The Translation of Samuel Beckett's 'mirlitonnades' by Three Spanish Authors." *Complutense Journal of English Studies* 28 (November 2020): 71–80. https://doi.org/10.5209/cjes.65523.

Gervasoni, Pierre. "Des compositeurs curieux du monde." *Le Monde*. November 17, 2001. https://www.lemonde.fr/archives/article/2001/11/17/des-compositeurs-curieux-du-monde_4148276_1819218.html.

Godin, Emmanuel, and Christopher Flood. "French Catholic Intellectuals and the Nation in Post-War France." *South Central Review* 17 (4): 45 (2000). https://doi.org/10.2307/3190166.

Goldman, Jonathan. "Gérard Grisey, Accordionist." *Twentieth-Century Music* 15 (1): 11–29 (2018). https://doi.org/10.1017/s147857221800004x.

Goldman, Jonathan. "Boulez and the Spectralists between Descartes and Rameau: Who Said What about Whom?" *Perspectives of New Music* 48, no. 2 (2010): 208–32. http://www.jstor.org/stable/23076972.

Griffiths, Paul. "Music Review; a Flutist Makes a Challenge, and a Climax Goes Uncrashed." *New York Times*, February 2, 2000, sec. Arts. https://www.nytimes.com/2000/02/02/arts/music-review-a-flutist-makes-a-challenge-and-a-climax-goes-uncrashed.html.

Hartt, Jared C. "Tonal and Structural Implications of Isorhythmic Design in Guillaume de Machaut's Tenors." *Theory and Practice* 35 (2010): 57–94. http://www.jstor.org/stable/41784451.

Harvey, Jonathan. "The ISCM Festival." *The Musical Times* 117 (1595): 33 (1976). https://doi.org/10.2307/958922.

Hennessy, Jeffrey J. "Beneath the Skin of Time: Alternative Temporalities in Grisey's 'Prologue for Solo Viola.'" *Perspectives of New Music* 47, no. 2 (2009): 36–58. http://www.jstor.org/stable/25753696.

Hodges, Bruce. "Listening to Gérard Grisey's Talea." March 5, 2021. http://taleaensemble.org/listening-to-gerard-griseys-talea/.

Hulle, Dirk Van. "Beckett's Art of the Commonplace: The 'Sottisier' Notebook and Mirlitonnades Drafts." *Journal of Beckett Studies* 28 (1): 67–89 (2019). https://doi.org/10.3366/jobs.2019.0254.

Humięcka-Jakubowska, Justyna. "The Spectralism of Gérard Grisey: From the Nature of the Sound to the Nature of Listening." *Interdisciplinary Studies in Musicology*, no. 8 (October 2017): 227–52. http://cejsh.icm.edu.pl/cejsh/element/bwmeta1.element.ojs-issn-2657-9197-year-2009-issue-8-article-14916.

Jakubowski, Joseph R. "Embodied Form in Grisey's *Prologue*: Variation, Opposition, Tension." *Intégral* 34:1–23. https://www.esm.rochester.edu/integral/34-2020/jakubowski/.

Kaegi, Gabriela. "'Das schlaue Füchslein' von Leos Janacek." *SRF*. October 29, 2012. https://www.srf.ch/audio/diskothek/das-schlaue-fuechslein-von-leos-janacek?id=10245960.

Kohda, Claire. "Boulez in His Own Words." *Guardian* March 26, 2015. https://www.theguardian.com/music/musicblog/2015/mar/26/boulez-in-his-own-words.

Krier, Yves. "Partiels, de Gérard Grisey, Manifestation d'une Nouvelle Esthétique." *Musurgia* 7, no. 3/4 (2000): 145–72. http://www.jstor.org/stable/40567133.

Laspière, Victor Tribot. "Mai 68 au Conservatoire de Paris, un mois et demi d'utopie musicale." *Radio France*. April 23, 2018. https://www.radiofrance.fr/francemusique/mai-68-au-conservatoire-de-paris-un-mois-et-demi-d-utopie-musicale-4527760.

Lelong, Guy. Untitled obituary for Gérard Grisey. *La lettre du musicien*. No. 216. December 15, 1998. Médiathèque Musicale Mahler, Paris.

Le Monde. "L'Itinéraire de Murail à Méfano," January 30, 1974. https://www.lemonde.fr/archives/article/1974/01/30/l-itineraire-de-murail-a-mefano_2519963_1819218.html.

Le Monde. "Musique-Plus," November 2, 1974. https://www.lemonde.fr/archives/article/1974/11/02/musique-plus_2530240_1819218.html.

Le Monde. "Une Création de Gérard Grisey à Radio-France 'Talea': le pas en avant," January 18, 1987. https://www.lemonde.fr/archives/article/1987/01/18/une-creation-de-gerard-grisey-a-radio-france-talea-le-pas-en-avant_4024938_1819218.html.

Le Monde. "Nominations au Conservatoire de Musique," November 18, 1987. https://www.lemonde.fr/archives/article/1987/11/18/nominations-au-conservatoire-de-musique_4076253_1819218.html.

Lonchampt, Jacques. "Partiels, de Gérard Grisey à L'Itinéraire." *Le Monde*. March 8, 1976. https://www.lemonde.fr/archives/article/1976/03/09/partiels-de-gerard-grisey-a-l-itineraire_2962667_1819218.html.

Lonchampt, Jacques. "Dufourt, Boulez, Grisey, Messiaen une apothéose contemporaine," *Le Monde*, May 28, 1986. https://www.lemonde.fr/archives/article/1986/05/28/dufourt-boulez-grisey-messiaen-une-apotheose-contemporaine_3117598_1819218.html.

Maddocks, Fiona. "Turgenev Adored Her. She Was the Toast of Paris Society. And Then She Had a Revival in Northampton ..." *Guardian*. February 7, 1999. https://www.theguardian.com/theobserver/1999/feb/07/featuresreview.review14.

Marshall, Robert. "The Dark Legacy of Carlos Castaneda." *Salon*. April 12, 2007. https://www.salon.com/2007/04/12/castaneda/.

McClary, Susan. "Music and Sexuality: On the Steblin/Solomon Debate." *19th-Century Music* 17 (1): 83–88 (1993). https://doi.org/10.2307/746783.

Minsky, Carly. "The Universe Is Made of Tiny Bubbles Containing Mini-Universes, Scientists Say." *Vice*. October 24, 2019. https://www.vice.com/en/article/j5yngp/the-universe-is-made-of-tiny-bubbles-containing-mini-universes-scientists-say.

Nichols, Roger. "Disciplined Debussy, by Roy Howat." *The Musical Times* 126, no. 1708 (1985): 349. https://doi.org/10.2307/964032.

Otto, Randall E. "The Use and Abuse of Perichoresis in Recent Theology." *Scottish Journal of Theology* 54 (3): 366–84 (2001). https://doi.org/10.1017/s0036930600051656.

Parouty, Michel. "Boulez, L'inflexible." *Les Echos*. January 28, 2005. https://www.lesechos.fr/2005/01/boulez-linflexible-1064576.

Poore, Benjamin. "Like the Volga Singing." *VAN Magazine*. July 29, 2021. https://van-magazine.com/mag/janacek-kata-kabanova-freud/.

Pustijanac, Ingrid. "Un Esempio Di 'Squelette Du Temps': Aspetti Ritmici in Le temps et l'écume Di Gérard Grisey.' *Mitteilungen der Paul Sacher Stiftung* 17 (March 2004): 42–47.

Rey, Anne. "Musique-plus." *Le Monde*. November 2, 1974. https://www.lemonde.fr/archives/article/1974/11/02/musique-plus_2530240_1819218.html.

Rigaudière, Pierre. "De l'esprit au spectre: mysticisme et spiritualité chez les compositeurs du courant spectral." *Circuit* 21 (1): 37–44 (2011). https://doi.org/10.7202/1001161ar.
Service, Tom. "Lucerne Gets to Grips with the Alphorn." *Guardian*. August 18, 2009. https://www.theguardian.com/music/tomserviceblog/2009/aug/18/lucerne-festival-switzerland.
Simms, Bryan R. "Schoenberg's Program Notes and Musical Analyses, Ed. by J. Daniel Jenkins." *Notes* 74 (4): 633–35 (2018). https://doi.org/10.1353/not.2018.0045.
Stahnke, Manfred."Die Schwelle des Hörens: 'Liminales' Denken in 'Vortex Temporum' von Gérard Grisey." *Österreichische Musikzeitschrift* 54 (6) (1999). https://doi.org/10.7767/omz.1999.54.6.21.
Swed, Mark. "Finding Harmony in Paradox." *Los Angeles Times*. January 18, 1996. https://www.latimes.com/archives/la-xpm-1996-01-18-ca-25822-story.html.
Taylor, Ben. "The Acoustic Ensemble as Spectral Synthesizer: Gérard Grisey's Jour, Contre-Jour" (2013). http://taylorbf.github.io/articles/grisey-jour.pdf.
"Who Cares If You Listen: An Evolving Dialogue on Public Musicology." *College Music Symposium* 56 (2016). https://doi.org/10.18177/sym.2016.56.ca.11237.
Woodard, Josef. "Philharmonic's New Music Program Balanced, Timely." *Los Angeles Times*. January 17, 1996. https://www.latimes.com/archives/la-xpm-1996–01–17-ca-25375-story.html.

Websites

"Accords perdus, Gérard Grisey." n.d. Brahms.ircam.fr. Accessed March 21, 2022. https://brahms.ircam.fr/works/work/8946/.
"Bio | Richard Felciano." n.d. www.richardfelciano.com. Accessed March 21, 2022. http://www.richardfelciano.com/bio.html.
"Biography of Richard Felciano | CNMAT." n.d. Cnmat.berkeley.edu. Accessed March 21, 2022. https://cnmat.berkeley.edu/content/biography-richard-felciano.
"Composers about Composers." n.d. www.ricordi.com. Accessed March 21, 2022. https://www.ricordi.com/en-US/News/2014/06/Levy-Grisey.aspx.
"Das Verlassene Mägdlein | Song Texts, Lyrics & Translations." n.d. Oxford Lieder. Accessed March 21, 2022. https://www.oxfordlieder.co.uk/song/244.

"David L. Wessel." n.d. Senate.universityofcalifornia.edu. Accessed March 21, 2022. https://senate.universityofcalifornia.edu/_files/inmemoriam/html/DavidL.Wessel.html.

"Felciano, Richard | Encyclopedia.com." n.d. www.encyclopedia.com. Accessed March 21, 2022. https://www.encyclopedia.com/arts/dictionaries-thesauruses-pictures-and-press-releases/felciano-richard.

"Gustave." 2014. www.numeridanse.tv. Accessed March 21, 2022. https://www.numeridanse.tv/en/dance-videotheque/gustave.

"Henri Clews." n.d. Accessed March 21, 2022. https://www.lnaf.org/Henri-clews/.

"Historique | Institution Sainte-Marie Belfort." n.d. Accessed March 7, 2022. https://www.sainte-marie-belfort.fr/accueil/historique.

"History." n.d. Marianist. https://www.marianist.com/history. Accessed March 7, 2022.

"Les Lauréats | Fondation de la Vocation." n.d. Fondationdelavocation.org. Accessed March 11, 2022. https://fondationdelavocation.org/les-laureats.

"Listening to Gérard Grisey's Talea | Talea Ensemble." n.d. Accessed March 21, 2022. http://taleaensemble.org/listening-to-gerard-griseys-talea/.

"Mick Finch – François Rouan." n.d. Mickfinch.com. Accessed March 11, 2022. http://mickfinch.com/texts/rouan.html.

"Olly Wilson's Biography." n.d. The HistoryMakers. Accessed March 21, 2022. https://www.thehistorymakers.org/biography/olly-wilson-41.

"Rilke, Rainer Maria (1875–1926) – Duino Elegies." n.d. Accessed March 11, 2022. www.poetryintranslation.com. https://www.poetryintranslation.com/PITBR/German/Rilke.php.

"The Man Who Died." n.d. Gutenberg.net.au. Accessed March 21, 2022. https://gutenberg.net.au/ebooks07/0700631h.html.

"The Map Is Not the Territory." 2015. Farnam Street. Accessed November 11, 2015. https://fs.blog/map-and-territory/.

"The Music of Sound: Analysis of Grisey's 'Partiels' by Chris Arrell." Issuu.com. Accessed March 12, 2022. https://issuu.com/chrisarrell/docs/arrellpartielsanalysis.

Ackerman, Susan. "Astarte: Bible." Accessed May 12, 2021. https://jwa.org/encyclopedia/article/astarte-bible#:~:text=Astarte%20is%20the%20Greek%20form,also%20has%20associations%20with%20war.

Andrews, Richard, Johanna Devaney, and Kathleen Maclay. "In Memorial: David L. Wessel." Accessed April 26, 2021. https://senate.universityofcalifornia.edu/_files/inmemoriam/html/DavidL.Wessel.html.

Augemus Musikverlag, "Der Pianist und Komponist Hans Brehme (1904–1957)." Accessed December 4, 2022. https://www.augemus-shop.de/buecher/geschichte-gegenwart/897/der-pianist-und-komponist-hans-brehme-1904-1957.

BookWiki, "Madonna del Parto." Accessed May 18, 2021. https://boowiki.info/art/peintures-de-piero-della-francesca/madonna-del-parto.html.

Chang, Ed. "Stimmung." Accessed June 8, 2021. https://stockhausenspace.blogspot.com/2014/07/opus-24-stimmung.html.

Cummings, Simon. "Gérard Grisey – Mégalithes (UK Première)." June 7, 2014. Accessed April 6, 2022. https://5against4.com/2014/06/07/gerard-grisey-megalithes-uk-premiere.

Discogs, "Stanley Darrow, Gérard Grisey, Mogend Ellegaard – Contemporary and Original Music for the Accordion." Accessed December 4, 2022. https://www.discogs.com/release/12129362-Stanley-Darrow-Gerard-Grisey-Mogens-Ellegaard-Contemporary-And-Original-Music-For-The-Accordion.

Féron, François-Xavier. "Gérard Grisey—*Prologue*." Accessed March 12, 2022. https://brahms.ircam.fr/analyses/Prologue/.

Guastoni, Mimma. "LinkedIn – Mimma Guastoni." Accessed February 22, 2021. https://it.linkedin.com/in/mimma-guastoni-404b7832.

Knauer, "Der Pianist und Komponist Hans Brehme." https://www.augemus-shop.de/buecher/geschichte-gegenwart/897/der-pianist-und-komponist-hans-brehme-1904-19572.

Kreppein, Ulrich Alexander. "Im Labyrinth Der Zeit: 'Wie la Mort de la Civilisation' aus Quarte Chants Pour Franchir Le Seuil von Gerard Grisey von der Zeit erzählt." Accessed March 21, 2022. http://www.ulrich-kreppein.de/wp-content/uploads/2019/10/Im-Labyrith-der-Zeit.pdf.

Lévy, Fabien. "Stèle by Gérard Grisey." Accessed August 12, 2021. https://www.ricordi.com/en-US/News/2014/06/Lévy-Grisey.aspx

Pavlović, Aleksandra. "Messiaen on Debussy and Colour," February 22, 2014. Accessed March 5, 2021. https://www.youtube.com/watch?v=cTtz76AFfw4.

Schott Music Group, "Hans Brehme." Accessed December 4, 2022. https://www.schott-music.com/de/person/hans-ludwig-wilhelm-brehme.

Vaughan, Alex. "Variation, Transformation and Development in Gérard Gisey's Les espaces acoustiques." Accessed June 15, 2021. https://alexvaughan.com/pdfs/variation_transformation_and_development_in_gerard_grisey%27s_les_espaces_acoustiques.pdf.

Other Sources

Abidor, Mitchell. *May Made Me: An Oral History of the 1968 Uprising in France*. London: Pluto Press, 2018.
Alain-Fournier. *Le Grand Meaulnes*, translated by Robert Gibson. London: Grand & Cutler, 1986.
Alter, Robert. *The Book of Psalms: A Translation with Commentary*. New York; London: W.W. Norton, 2009.
Andersen, Anne Sophie, and Derek Kwan. "Grisey's 'Talea': Musical Representation as an Interactive 3D Map." NIME 2021. Accessed March 21, 2022. https://doi.org/10.21428/92fbeb44.27d09832.
Barguet, Paul. *Les Textes des sarcophages égyptiens du Moyen Empire*. Paris: Cerf, 1986.
Bataille, Georges. *Eroticism*. San Francisco: City Lights Books, 1986.
Beckett, Samuel. *Poèmes*. Paris: Les Éditions De Minuit, 1978.
Bellow, Saul. *Herzog*. London: Penguin, 2007.
Bergier, Lauren. "Paul Claudel's Cinq Grandes Odes: A Translation and Commentary." University of Chicago, 2016.
Boivin, Jean. *La Classe de Messiaen*. Paris: Bourgois, 1995.
Bischoff, Georges, and Yves Pagnot. *Belfort, 1307–2007: Sept Siècles de Courage et de Liberté*. Strasbourg: Editions Coprur, 2007.
Bottéro, Jean. *L'épopée de Gilgameš: Le Grand Homme Qui Ne Voulait Pas Mourir*. Paris: Gallimard, Cop, 1997.
Budge, Sir Wallis, and John Baldock. *The Egyptian Book of the Dead*. London: Arcturus Publishing Limited, 2011.
Cagney, Liam. "Synthesis and Deviation: New Perspectives on the Emergence of the French Courant Spectral, 1969–74." City University London, 2015.
Carroll, Lewis. *Through the Looking-Glass and What Alice Found There*. Church Hanborough, Oxford: Inky Parrot Press, 2018.
Castaneda, Carlos. *Tales of Power*. New York: Pocket Books, 1992.
Casanova, Giacomo. *History of My Life*. New York: A.A. Knopf, 2007.
Claudel, Paul. *Cinq Grandes Odes*. Paris: Gallimard, 1936.
Cohen-Levinas, Danielle. *Vingt-Cinq ans de création musicale contemporaine: L'itinéraire en temps réel*. Editions L'Harmattan, 1998.
De la Fontaine, Jean. *Toutes les fables de La Fontaine*. Paris: Azou, 2007.
Dostoyevsky, Fyodor. *The Idiot*. Translated by Kris Martin.
Drott, Eric. "Spectralism, Politics, and the Post-Industrial Imagination." In *The Modernist Legacy: Essays on New Music*, edited by Björn Heile, 39–60. Surrey: Ashgate, 2019.
Dufourt, Hugues. *Musique, Pouvoir, Écriture*. Sampzon: Éditions Delatour France, 2014.

Fenby, Jonathan. *France: A Modern History from the Revolution to the War with Terror*. New York: St. Martin's Press, 2016.
Flaubert, Gustave. *Madame Bovary*. New York: New American Library, 1979.
Gervasoni, Pierre. *Henri Dutilleux*. Arles; Paris: Actes Sud, 2016.
Gilles Deleuze. *Difference and Repetition*. London: Bloomsbury, 2014.
Gilmore, Bob. *Claude Vivier: A Composer's Life*. Rochester: University of Rochester Press, 2014.
Griffiths, Paul. *Olivier Messiaen and the Music of Time*. Ithaca: Cornell University Press, 1985.
Guez Ricord, Christian Gabriel/le. *Le Cantique qui est à Gabriel/le*. Edited by Bernar Mialet. La Sétérée. L'Isle sur la Sorgue: Les Bois d'Orion, 2002.
Heusser, Lars. "Il Est Donc Temps de Rendre La Complexité Efficace": In *Musik-Konzepte 176/177: Gérard Grisey*, edited by Ulrich Tadday. Edition Text und Kritik, 2017.
Ikram, Salima. *Ancient Egypt: An Introduction*. Cairo: American University in Cairo Press, 2011.
Isherwood, Christopher, and Alan Cumming. *Goodbye to Berlin*. New York: New Directions Pub. Corp, 2013.
Janáček, Leoš. John Tyrrell, translator and editor. *Intimate Letters: Leos Janácek to Kamila Stösslová*. Princeton: Princeton University Press, 2014.
Kaduri, Yael. *The Oxford Handbook of Sound and Image in Western Art*. Oxford: Oxford University Press, 2016.
Keineg, Paol. *Là, et Pas Là*. Cognac: Le Temps Qu'il Fait, 2015.
Kepler, Johannes, Ptolemy, and Robert Fludd. *Ioannis Keppleri Harmonices Mundi*; Libri V. Bruxelles, Culture et Civilisation. 1968.
Kurtz, Michael. *Stockhausen: Eine Biographie*. Kassel: Bärenreiter, 1988.
Johnson, Charles, *The Brihadaranyaka Upanishad*. CreateSpace Independent Publishing Platform, trans 2016.
Lefevbre, Noémi. "Mai 1968 au Conservatoire National Superieur de Musique." April 3 and 4, 2008. La musique en mai 68 / Mai 68 dans la musique.
Leipp, Émile. *Acoustique et Musique*. Paris: Masson, 1971.
Lewis, Charlton T, William Freund, E.A. Andrews, and Charles Short. *A Latin Dictionary: Founded on Andrews' Edition of Freund's Latin Dictionary*. Chapel-en-le-Frith: Nigel Gourlay, 2020.
Luminet, Jean-Pierre. *Black Holes*. Cambridge; New York. Cambridge University Press, 1999.
Luminet, Jean-Pierre. "Le noir de l'étoile: la musique des pulsars. In hommage à Gérard Grisey." Hommage à Gérard Grisey, pour une esthétique de la creation musicale. Paris, 1999.

Mason, William. "Feeling Machines: Immersion, Expression, and Technological Embodiment in Electroacoustic Music of the French Spectral School." Columbia University. https://academiccommons.columbia.edu/doi/10.7916/d8-k4nh-zd64, 2019.

McQuinn, Julie. "Exploring the erotic in Debussy's music." In S. Trezise (ed.), *The Cambridge Companion to Debussy* (Cambridge Companions to Music, 117–36). Cambridge: Cambridge University Press, 2003.

Moles, Abraham. *Information Theory and Esthetic Perception.* Urbana: University of Illinois Press, 1968.

Nabokov, Vladimir. *Ada, Or Ardor: A Family Chronicle.* New York: Mcgraw-Hill, 1969.

Naumann, Philipp. "Schaum auf den Wellen der Raumzeit. Eine Studie über Gérard Griseys Le Temps et L'Écume." Hochschule für Musik und Theater Felix Mendelssohn Bartholdy Leipzig. https://slub.qucosa.de/api/qucosa%3A613/attachment/ATT-0/, 2009.

Pascal, Blaise. *The Thoughts of Blaise Pascal*: Translated from the Text of M. Auguste Malinier by C. Kegan Paul. London: Bell, 1890.

Potter, Caroline. *Henri Dutilleux: His Life and Works.* London: Routledge, 2016.

de Saint-Exupery, Antoine, *Wind, Sand, and Stars.* Translated by William Reese. New York: Penguin Books, 1995.

Singer, Daniel. *Prelude to Revolution: France in May 1968.* Chicago: Haymarket Books, 2013.

Stendhal. *The Red and the Black.* Translated by Roger Gard. London: Penguin Books, 2002.

Stockhausen, Karlheinz. *Texte zur Elektronischen und Instrumentalen Musik.* Cologne: M.D. Schauberg, 1963.

Sudlow, Brian. *Catholic Literature and Secularisation in France and England, 1880–1914.* Manchester; New York: Manchester University Press, 2011.

Taylor, Rhonda Janette. "Gérard Grisey's Anubis et Nout: A Historical and Analytical Perspective." The University of Arizona, 2005. https://repository.arizona.edu/bitstream/handle/10150/194938/azu_etd_1076_sip1_m.pdf?sequence=1&isAllowed=y.

Teilhard de Chardin, Pierre. *Hymn of the Universe.* New York: Harper & Row, 1965.

Weil, Simone, Emma Crawford, Mario Von, and Gustave Thibon. *Gravity and Grace.* London; New York: Routledge, 2008.

Weil, Simone. *Waiting for God*, translated by Emma Crawford. London: Routledge & K. Paul, 1951.

Winckel, Fritz, and Thomas Binkley. *Music, Sound and Sensation: A Modern Exposition.* New York: Dover Publications, 1967.

Von Ehrenfels, Christian. "Über 'Gestaltqualitäten.'" Leipzig: Reisland, 1890.

Yourcenar, Marguerite. *La Couronne et La Lyre*: *Poemes.* Paris: Gallimard, 1984.

Index

Académie de Besançon, 12
Accademia Chigiana, 65–66
accordion, 6–10, 15, 18–19, 21–23, 25–28, 32–34, 57–58, 96, 98, 111, 114, 126, 139, 141, 181, 252
Accords perdus, 215–17, 245
acoustics, 20, 23, 27, 62, 78, 99, 109, 118, 147, 162, 167, 172–73
Acoustique et Musique, 78, 109
Alsace, 9
alto, 27, 261
Anahit, 95, 100, 210
Andersen, Anne Sophie, 204
Anderson, Julian, 7, 37, 39, 50, 98, 103, 197, 249, 252, 255, 267
Anderson, Valdine, 261, 267
The Annunciation, 75
Anthony (Paris), 72, 143
antinomy, 52, 87, 205
Anubis et Nout, 107, 179, 180–81, 244–45
aperiodicity, 112, 122
Appels, 84, 168
Arrell, Chris, 112
Asbury, Stefan, 201
Asko Ensemble, 201–2
astronomy, 218–20, 226, 228
Atelier I, 84–85
Austria, 1, 29, 80, 148, 186, 209, 261

Bade, Franz–Josef, 19
Baden-Baden, 18
Baden-Württemberg, 21, 247
Baillet, Jérôme, 85–86, 98, 101, 103, 116–17, 121, 123, 129–30, 136–37, 162–64, 200–1, 204, 223–24, 228, 249–51, 254–55, 266, 269
Baroque Era, 14, 31, 75
Barguet, Paul, 267–68
Bartholdi, Frédéric-Auguste, 1, 49
bass clarinet, 34, 47, 68, 83, 111, 179–81, 273
bass drum, 136–37, 201, 228, 244–45, 271
bassoon, 25–26, 96
BBC Symphony Orchestra, 201
Beaufort, Bruno de, 227–28
Beckett, Samuel, 273
Beiträge zur Analyse der Empfindungen, 117
Belfort, 1–5, 8, 15, 17–21, 25, 28, 32, 39–40, 42, 44–47, 54, 59–60, 109, 206, 244, 258–59
Berlin, 3, 148–49, 158–60, 162, 165–66, 190, 202, 211, 225
Besada, José L., 128
Besançon, 2, 244
Biafra, 56, 63–64
Black Forest, 21
bongos, 83, 127
Bossis, Bruno, 191
Boulanger, Lili, 28, 52
Boulanger, Nadia, 213
Brehme, Hans, 22
Brihadaranyaka Upanishad, 80

Cagney, Liam, 5, 7, 9, 18, 24, 37–39, 45, 62–64, 67–68, 73, 75, 77, 80–83, 85–88, 93, 100, 102–3, 105–6, 109, 213, 215

Camus, Albert, 55
Canada, 18, 57, 60, 89, 147, 178, 190, 195, 219, 261
carnal shell, 16
Carroll, Lewis, 138
Carter, Elliott, 217
Casa Ricordi, 53, 105–6, 120, 235, 240, 243, 247, 250, 255, 274–75
Cathédrale Saint-Alexandre-Nevsky, 104
Catherine of Siena, 65
cello concertos, 38, 61
Châlons-en-Champagne, 29
chamber ensemble, 198, 253
chamber music, 203, 246, 263
chamber orchestra, 59, 63, 121, 169, 227
champagne, 18, 43
chapel, 72, 277
Charme, 66–68, 73, 105, 179–80
Charon, Guylaine, 24–25
Chicago (Illinois), 74
Chopin, Frédéric, 15, 18, 60
Christianity, 13, 16, 31, 41, 43, 67, 70–72, 78–79, 95, 105, 194, 232, 238, 263, 265
Christmas, 6, 45, 61
Chronochromie, 76, 214–15
Cinq Grandes Odes, 40–41, 43
Cité des Arts in the Marais, 72
clarinet, 47, 60, 67–68, 78, 81, 83, 86, 96, 99, 111, 160–61, 179, 195, 203, 224, 249, 262–64
Claudel, Paul, 9, 13–14, 22, 24, 43, 55, 58; *Paul Claudel poète-musicien*, 43
Cleveland Orchestra, 37
Clews, Henri, 239
C minor seventh chord, 44
Columbus, Christopher, 36
Concerto de Varsovie, 17
concerto grosso, 199

Conservatoire National Supérieur de Paris, 27–29, 36–37, 39, 46, 49–52, 57–59, 61–62, 68–69, 72–74, 77, 79, 85–86, 89, 104, 106, 108–9, 172, 181, 197, 209–11, 235, 241, 275
Contemporary and Original Music for the Accordion, 21
contralto, 191–92
contrabass clarinet, 179, 181

Darmstadt, 88–91, 119, 131–33, 148, 150–52, 156, 166–70, 172, 178, 189, 209, 213
Darmstadt Festival, 131–33, 149, 151
Darmstädter Tagblatt, 133, 158
Darrow, Stanley, 25
D'eau et de pierre, 36, 41, 82, 85–88, 96–97, 105, 205, 213, 243
de Beauvoir, Simone, 55
Denfert-Rochereau, Aristide, 1
Dérives, 7, 36, 74, 83, 96–103, 105–6, 109, 112, 115, 126, 132, 162, 188, 213, 220–21, 235, 254–55, 268, 270
Detry, France, 5, 143–44, 185–89, 197, 199, 206–9, 225, 230–34, 236–37, 250, 257, 278
Deutscher Akademischer Austauschdienst (DAAD), 148–49, 158–60, 240
Deux Madrigaux, 42–45, 53, 104
D harmonic minor, 44
Diabelli Variations, 212, 249
dissonance, 64, 124, 154, 167, 191, 200, 253
"Dissonance" Quartet (Mozart), 55
Doderer, Claudia, 225–30, 258, 276
duality, 54, 66, 72–73, 75, 84, 129, 180, 274
Dubosc, Catherine, 279
Dukas, Paul, 69

Dutilleux, Henri, 36, 39; Second Symphony, 36

Échanges, 45, 48, 53–54, 64–65, 68
Échos, 84
École Municipale de Musique de la Ville de Belfort, 18
écriture, 27–28, 39, 42, 46, 59, 61
Egypt, 40, 107, 127, 244, 264, 269; ancient civilization of, 127–28, 269; art, 43; *Book of the Dead*, 128; *Book of the Two Ways*, 79; and goddess Isis, 194, 265; influences, 244, 267–68; mythology, 267; pantheon, 72, 129, 179–80, 194; rituals, 105
Éluard, Paul, 45
ensemble, 42, 44, 59, 72, 78, 82, 84, 88, 93, 97, 112, 114, 116, 136–37, 227, 230, 262, 266, 268, 271–72, 278; chamber, 198, 253; instrumental, 149; *petit ensemble*, 96; sound, 190; sympathetic vibration, 119
Ensemble Ars Nova, 132, 220
Ensemble Court-Circuit, 201, 259
Ensemble Fa, 244–45, 263
Ensemble L'Itinéraire, 93, 100, 102, 115, 130, 134, 149, 169, 179, 255
Ensemble Intercontemporain, 121, 124, 130, 160, 181, 259–60
Ensemble Musica Negativa, 130
Ensemble Recherche, 246–49, 251, 259
Épilogue, 164–65, 187, 198–201, 222, 229, 235
Europe, 128, 173, 186, 198–99, 230, 246, 248, 256

Ferneyhough, Brian, 131, 133, 198, 212
Festival Pontino di Musica, 179, 181

Fête en Alsace, 10
Fett, Armin, 22, 27
First French Army, 3
flute, 13, 25–26, 34, 47, 68, 78, 81, 83, 96, 99, 111, 113–14, 126, 195, 203, 224, 249, 264
France, 1–3, 9, 23, 37, 39–40, 57, 76, 93, 108, 153, 160, 165, 173, 175, 182–83, 198, 206, 211, 228, 278; and contemporary music, 220; French Resistance, 2; and May 1968, 64; northern, 78, 94; north-east, 85; occupation of, 20; provincial, 42; and Russian Orthodoxy, 104; and secularism, 63; and sexual revolution, 48; southern, 231; and working class, 49
Franche-Comté, 1, 12
Frankfurter Allgemeine Zeitung, 131
Franz, Sabine, 248
French Alps, 110
French Resistance, 2–3, 9, 20, 50

Gaultier, Jean Paul, 215
Germany, 1, 9, 19, 21, 23, 58, 130, 148–49, 222, 246
Gregorian chant, 45
Grisey, Gérard Henri: and accordion, 8, 23, 27, 57, 139, 141; and *Accords perdus*, 216; and American Conservatory in Fontainebleau, 213–14; and André Malraux, 54–55; and Anne-Marie Réby, 243–44; and *Antigone*, 47, 65; and *Anubis et Nout*, 179–81, 244; and *Autoportrait avec L'Itinéraire*, 95; in Belfort, 20, 42; and Bernadette, 16–17, 21–22; and Bonnie Wade, 198; and *Charme*, 66–67; and Christiane, 34–35; and Claude Debussy, 185, 214, 277; and Claude Vivier at Darmstadt, 178;

Grisey, Gérard Henri—*cont'd*
and Claudia Doderer, 225–26, 258; and composition, 1, 10–11, 14–15, 17–18, 22, 26, 28, 32, 35, 41–42, 45, 48, 52–54, 77–79, 90–91, 101, 120, 262, 265–66; and Conservatoire National Supérieur, 28–29, 39, 46, 108; and Darmstädter Ferienkurse, 166; and *D'eau et de pierre*, 36, 41, 82, 88, 96; and *Dérives*, 7, 83, 96–100, 106, 109, 132, 235; and Deutscher Akademischer Austauschdienst (DAAD), 148–50, 158–60, 240; and *Deux Madrigaux*, 42–45; and D.H. Lawrence, 193, 263; and diaries, 12, 16, 37–39, 71–72; and duality, 84; and *École Normale de Musique*, 36; and *Échanges*, 65; and Edgard Varèse, 174; and Egypt, 107, 127–28; and Ensemble Intercontemporain, 260; and Ensemble Recherche, 247–48; and *Épilogue*, 199–201, 229, 235; and Esa-Pekka Salonen, 238, 253–54; and *Étude harmonique*, 10; father of, 1–2, 20; and "fear of homosexuality," 11–12; and Fondation de la Vocation prize, 65; and France Detry, 5, 143–44, 186, 199, 206–7, 232–34, 236–38; and François Rouan, 93–94; and Gérard Zinsstag, 158–60, 166, 210; and German culture, 19; and Giacinto Scelsi, 95; and grandmother, 7, 20; and *Gustave*, 215–17; and Guylaine Charon, 24–25; and Helmut Lachenmann, 221–22; and Henri Dutilleux, 36–39; and Hohner-Konservatorium, 20–23, 27; and *Initiation*, 60, 72–74; and Institut de recherche et coordination acoustique/musique (IRCAM), 147–48, 160, 172; and Jean-Luc Hervé, 51; and Jean-Pierre Luminet, 219–20, 226, 229–30; and Jocelyne Simon, 29–31, 43, 46–47, 49, 71–72, 92, 107, 110, 143, 182–84, 232, 238; and Joe Silk, 218; and *Jour, contre-jour*, 128–30; and Julien Sorel, 40; and La Napoule, 239, 241; and lectures, 156–58, 167; and Leoš Janáček, 195–97; and *Les chants de l'amour*, 188–92, 260; and *Les espaces acoustiques*, 115, 162, 165; and *L'Icône paradoxale*, 231, 242, 254–56; and *Le noir de l'étoile*, 168, 227–30; and *Le temps et l'écume*, 222–25, 260; and love, 13–14, 16–17, 20, 22, 29–30, 32, 35–36, 40, 44, 55, 127, 134–35, 156, 160, 182–83, 185, 187–94, 196–97, 205–6, 208, 217, 225, 232–33, 236, 238, 258, 274; and Lycée Fénelon Sainte-Marie, 28; and Magnificat, 32; and *Manifestations*, 125–26; and marriage, 135; and martyrdom, 13; and *Mégalithes*, 64–65; and Mireille Deguy, 7, 233–36, 252, 255–56, 258–59, 261, 278; and *Modulations*, 121–24, 150–52, 158–60, 180, 225, 260; musical philosophy of, 53–54, 88; and nature, 56; and numerical structures, 136; and Olivier Messiaen, 15, 34, 38–39, 43, 49–51, 57–59, 61–62, 76–77, 153, 214, 235; and Paris, 23, 28, 36, 45, 51, 54, 93, 142, 148, 165–66, 175, 177, 179, 184–86, 198–99, 206, 220, 222, 233, 241, 248, 256, 258–59; and *Partiels*, 36–37, 112–16, 131, 162, 174,

178; and *Passacaille*, 33–34; and *Perichoresis*, 68–69, 105; and *Périodes*, 99, 102–4, 109, 111, 131, 190; and periodicity, 154; and *Petit Caprice*, 15; and Pierre Boulez, 76, 147, 153; and Prezman, 32; and Prix Hervé Dugardin, 106; and Prix de la Vocation, 74; and *Prologue*, 115–20, 131, 133–34, 164; psyche of, 2; and *Quatre chants*, 267–70, 272–74, 276, 279; and Raphaël Grisey, 258; and religion, 9, 13, 15, 22, 45, 50, 70, 75, 104–5, 140, 174, 234; and *Répons*, 63; and Schlans, 264; and sexuality, 29; and Simone de Beauvoir, 55–56; and *Solo pour deux*, 160–62; and *Sortie vers la lumière du jour*, 129–30, 150; and *Talea*, 203–5; and teaching, 169–70, 175–78, 211–13; teenage years of, 9, 13, 16–20, 26, 29, 41, 43, 46, 59, 104, 110, 183, 249; and Teilhard de Chardin, 43–44; and *Tempus ex Machina*, 136–38, 150, 168, 228; and Toronto, 24; and *Transitoires*, 162, 164, 180, 200, 235; and Tristan Murail, 92–93, 155, 169, 210; and University of California, Berkeley, 165–66, 171–74, 184, 187–88, 197–98, 218; and University of California, San Diego, 243; and the United States, 24–25; and *Vagues, Chemins, le Souffle*, 79–82, 85, 87, 89; and Villa Médicis, 85, 92, 105; and *Vortex Temporum*, 246, 248–51, 268; youth of, 3–5, 7–10, 19
Grisey, Jules Henri, 2, 4, 9, 13, 20, 109–10, 135; and Lucie Monna, 3
Grisey, Raphaël, 2, 135, 143, 145, 148, 159, 165, 171, 182–86, 206, 228, 237, 278; teenage years, 258
Guderian, 2

Hannigan, Barbara, 279
harmonics, 7, 77, 97, 100, 115, 161, 192, 215–16, 223, 263; harmonic complexity, 204; harmonic density, 272; harmonicity, 112–13, 121–22, 128, 161; harmonic resonances, 119; harmonic series, 79, 135–36, 150, 163, 180, 191; harmonic thinking, 64; high, 73; inharmonicity, 112–13, 118, 121–23, 129, 154, 269; inharmonic spectrum, 78; natural, 95; string, 262. *See also* spectrum
harmonies, 62, 126, 129, 191, 196, 211, 255, 270
harp, 68, 76, 119, 121, 249, 264, 269, 278
Hein, Folkmar, 149
Hennessy, Jeffrey J., 117
Hindemith, Paul, 26
Hofer, Wolfgang, 161
Holy Spirit, 41, 68
Holy Trinity, 68, 105
Hohner-Konservatorium, 19–22, 27
Hohner Morino, 8, 57, 139
Hohner, Matthias, 21
homophobia, 12
homosexuality, 11
horn, 34, 64, 68, 83–84, 96, 103, 111, 115, 126, 155, 199–201, 215–17, 224, 262
Huddersfield Contemporary Music Festival, 230, 261

Imbrie, Andrew, 171–72
inhalation, 101, 112–14, 117, 190
Initiation, 60, 72–74, 80, 189
Institut de recherche et coordination acoustique/musique (IRCAM), 119, 147–48, 160, 172, 188–89, 192, 261

Jacobi, Wolfgang, 26

Jesus, 194–95, 207
Jews, 1, 16, 89, 173, 182, 231
Jour, contre-jour, 105, 128, 130, 149, 160, 169, 179, 245, 273

Keersmaeker, Anne Teresa De, 252
Krakow Radio Symphony Orchestra, 150
Kreppein, Ulrich Alexander, 269
Krier, Yves, 111–12, 114–15

La présence du Christ dans le Monde, 43
Lanza, Pierre Frédéric, 3–4
Latin, 32, 34, 136, 150, 203
Latin Quarter, 31, 48–49, 109
"Le devenir des sons" (The Becoming of Sound), 12, 167
Lefort, Bernard, 195
Le fou d l'île, 25
Lelong, Guy, 11, 195, 230, 277
Le Monde, 67, 82, 99, 103, 115, 124, 130, 152, 164, 192, 205–6, 209, 230, 259, 277
Le noir de l'étoile (The Black of the Star), 119, 168, 187, 219–20, 225–30, 241, 252
Les chants de l'amour, 156, 187–93, 198, 254, 259–60, 270, 274
Les espaces acoustiques, 26, 102, 115, 121, 123, 127, 148, 151, 162, 164–65, 168, 171, 180, 198, 201–2, 210, 216, 224, 252, 259–60
Les Portes (The Gates), 94
Le temps et l'écume, 47, 196, 221–25, 254
Lewinski, Wolf-Eberhard von, 158, 169
l'Hôtel de Ville, 72
L'Icône paradoxale, 168, 196, 231, 237–39, 241–42, 244, 253–56, 259–60
Linaia-Agon, 88
Lion de Belfort, 1, 49

Loire (France), 237
Lorenzetti, Ambrogio, 65, 75
Los Angeles Philharmonic, 231, 241–42, 253, 260
Louvier, Alain, 50–51, 100, 210
Lucerne Festival, 64
Ludwig Orchestra, 279
Luminet, Jean-Pierre, 218–20, 224, 226–30, 276, 278
Luoma, Mikko, 33

Madonna del Parto, 237–38
Magnificat, 15, 32–34, 36, 45, 104
major sevenths, 44
Manifestations (Incantations), 125–27, 199, 217, 253
Meecham, Paul, 261
Méfano, Paul, 88
Mégalithes, 56, 63–65, 67–68
Messiaen, Olivier, 15, 34, 38–39, 43, 50–51, 54, 57–62, 67, 69, 72–73, 76, 79, 81, 85, 92, 96, 98, 105, 116–17, 121–22, 132, 153, 157, 165, 171, 174, 176, 197, 210–11, 214–15, 235, 260
Metz Festival, 105
Mialet, Bernar, 265
Miereanu, Costin, 169
misterioso, 33
Modulations, 121–24, 127, 129, 131, 150–52, 158, 160, 162–63, 168, 180, 200, 225, 260
Mörike-Lieder, 262
mouth harmonica, 27
Mumford, Jeffrey, 253
Murail, Tristan, 73, 76, 92–94, 95, 100, 102–4, 133, 135, 150, 153, 155, 157–58, 166, 169, 174, 210, 244, 252
Musica Festival, 251, 259–60
musicologists, 7–8, 18, 36, 43, 50, 52, 54, 59, 62, 85, 97, 104, 111–12,

117, 119–20, 122, 130, 132, 136, 166–67, 185, 191, 201, 214, 216, 223, 229, 244, 249, 251, 267, 270
music scenes, 58, 151, 164, 176, 181, 198, 243, 277

Nazis, 1–3, 20, 22, 58, 65

Olivier Messiaen et les Oiseaux (Olivier Messiaen and the Birds), 60
orchestra, 7, 15, 27, 36, 76–77, 80–81, 96–97, 99, 103, 122–23, 125–26, 151–52, 156, 162–63, 199–200, 210, 214, 216, 219, 221–22, 227, 238, 241–42, 253–56, 259; chamber, 59, 63, 121
Orchestra Sinfonica Siciliana, 164
Orchestre National de France, 99, 220

Paris (France), 23, 36, 45, 51, 54, 93, 148, 165–66, 175, 177, 179, 184–86, 198–99, 206, 220, 222, 233, 241, 248, 256, 258–59, 261, 263–64, 275, 278; and Bagneux, 32; Biennale de Paris, 74; and Boulevard de la Bastille, 120; and Centre Pompidou, 147; and Claude Vivier, 178; and *Daphnis et Chloé*, 249; and *écritures*, 28, 39; and Edmund Campion, 210; and Jean-Marie de Miscault, 44; and Jocelyne Simon, 182–83; and Karlheinz Stockhausen, 63; and Marianist Institution, 72; and May 1968, 50; and Mireille Deguy, 232, 237; and Musée d'Orsay, 215; and music schools, 108; and Nouveau Carré, 115; and *Périodes*, 102; suburbs of, 86, 143; and universities, 29, 92.
See also Grisey, Gérard Henri
Paris Match, 39
Paris Opéra, 48–50, 195

Partiels, 36–37, 96, 111–16, 121, 126, 131–32, 137, 147, 151, 153, 155, 162–63, 165, 168, 174, 178, 181, 200, 220, 249
Passacaille, 25, 33–34, 42
Pelléas et Mélisande, 17, 60
percussion, 34, 42–44, 47–48, 68, 76–78, 111, 114–15, 121, 127, 132, 136–37, 200, 204, 214, 223, 226–29, 236, 245, 264, 271
Percussions de Strasbourg, Les, 136, 227, 229, 259
Périodes, 96, 99–103, 105, 109, 111–12, 114–16, 121, 131, 147, 165, 189–90, 193, 200, 213
Petit Caprice, 15
Philadelphia Orchestra, 23
piano, 10, 14, 20, 22, 27–28, 31–34, 38, 42–46, 48, 53–54, 57, 59–61, 64–67, 83, 119, 127, 156, 175, 196–97, 199, 203–5, 211–13, 216, 221–23, 225, 241, 249–54
piano concertos, 156, 205, 216, 254
Piano Sonatas (Prokofiev), 241
Piano Sonata in C Minor op. 111 (Beethoven), 22
Piano Sonata no. 3 (Boulez), 61, 64
Pierrot-Lunaire Ensemble, 205
Pinacoteca Nazionale, 65
pitch, 26, 33, 37, 42, 44, 48, 63–64, 67–69, 79–81, 84–88, 100–2, 111–13, 116–18, 126, 128–29, 132, 136, 147, 161, 163–64, 168, 174, 179–81, 191, 200, 203, 215–17, 222, 226–27, 229, 250–51, 254–55, 266
Potard, Yves, 188
pour trouver le silence, 125–26
Présence Festival, 231, 245
Prix Paul Valéry, 94
Prologue, 115–21, 123, 131–34, 163–64, 180, 200

Prussia, 1, 3, 9

Quatre chants pour franchir le seuil, 70, 105, 107, 214, 245, 259–60, 263–64, 273, 278–79

Rabinovitch-Barakovsky, Alexandre, 100, 106–7
Radio France, 99, 127, 130, 198, 205, 222, 225, 231, 235, 244–45, 263
Radio Symphony Orchestra Berlin, 160
rape, 12, 160, 168, 194
Réby, Anne-Marie, 243
reference points, 82, 219, 226
"relative durations," 84, 152
Renaissance, 16, 41, 65, 92
repetitions, 67, 87, 94, 113, 118, 162, 223, 266, 274
Rey, Anne, 230
rhythm, 29, 40, 54, 59, 64, 67, 71, 78, 80–81, 113, 116, 122, 126, 132, 136–37, 153–55, 196, 201, 202, 211, 245–46, 254, 266, 269; aperiodic, 79, 101, 163; periodic, 79, 101, 163, 189; training, 23
rhythmic analysis, 196, 266
rhythmic cells, 26, 68, 195, 245
rhythmic complexity, 10, 42
rhythmic density, 80, 127, 217, 253
rhythmic structure, 54, 60, 71, 97, 122, 132, 152–53, 271
Rihm, Wolfgang, 132, 158, 165, 278
Robertson, David, 225
Royan Festival, 79, 85

Saarbrücker Zeitung, 88
Salonen, Esa-Pekka, 238, 241–42, 253–54, 256
Sartre, Jean-Paul, 49
saxophone, 34, 96, 181, 261, 264
Schenker, Heinrich, 173
Schneider, Orthon, 227, 230
Schoenberg, Arnold, 22, 47, 99, 160, 241
seventh partial, 118, 215
Simon, Jocelyne, 2, 29–35, 39–41, 43–49, 51, 53–56, 60, 64–67, 71–72, 74, 79, 87, 143, 199
Solo pour deux, 160–62
Sonata for Violin and Piano (Janáček), 197
Sorbonne, 48–50, 77, 92, 108–9
Sortie vers la lumière du jour, 105, 107, 127, 129–30, 150, 160, 179, 274
"sounding sculptures," 84, 119
Spanisches Liederbuch, 262
Sparnaay, Harry, 179, 181
spectral movement, 52, 103
spectral music, 23, 62, 83, 91, 93–94, 103–4, 109, 116, 126, 135, 150, 153, 174, 199, 224–25, 254
spectrograms, 101, 109, 162–63
spectrum, 78–79, 86, 97, 101, 113, 116, 118, 122, 150, 180, 191, 246, 255, 270, 272; harmonic, 37, 78–79, 82–83, 86, 88–90, 94, 96–98, 100–2, 111–12, 114–17, 121, 123, 125–26, 129, 155, 157–58, 162, 163, 167, 169, 174, 179–80, 190, 200–1, 215, 250–51, 255, 266, 272; overtone, 111–12, 266; trombone, 161–62
Stèle, 244–45
Stockhausen, Karlheinz, 61, 68, 77, 96–98, 102–3, 115, 121, 133, 153, 157–58, 161, 165, 170–71, 178, 190, 192, 197, 212, 227; and *Charme,* 66; and Gérard Grisey, 57, 59, 63, 80–81, 88–90; and Olivier Messiaen, 87; and Pierre Boulez, 42, 52, 81; and *Trans,* 76
Stoley, David, 253
Stravinsky, Igor, 44, 157, 202, 241

Süddeutsche Zeitung, 151, 169
Suite en mi, 25–26, 33
Swiss Alps, 166
Switzerland, 1, 21, 146, 158, 166, 221, 231
symphonies, 36, 150, 160, 254
Symphony no. 7 (Sibelius), 254
Symphony no. 9 (Bruckner), 156
Symphony no. 40 in G Minor (Mozart), 156
Symphony Orchestra of the Westdeutscher Rundfunk, 168

Talea, 198, 203–5, 210, 214, 221–23, 231, 253
Talea Ensemble, 205
Technische Universität, 149
Teilhard de Chardin, Pierre, 9, 19, 39, 43
Tempus ex machina, 136–38, 148, 150, 156–57, 167–68, 204, 209, 213, 228, 259, 271
Tenzer, Michael, 177
Théâtre de la Ville, 124
timbre, 71, 79, 81, 85, 87, 113, 129, 137, 168, 196, 246, 272; clarinet, 86; and dissonance, 154; dynamism of, 99, 115, 179–80, 245; human perception of, 162; instrumental, 80; percussion, 137, 214; and piano, 53; vocal, 256
timpani, 34
tonality, 15, 42, 52, 169
tonal seventh chord, 153, 156, 249
tonal ninth chord, 153
transients, 111–12, 162–63, 251
"transitional space," 84
Transitoires, 123, 127, 159, 162–64, 180, 199–200, 235
translation, 32, 40, 128, 167, 226, 267–70

tritone-seventh chords, 53
Trossingen (Germany), 19–23, 25–27, 58

University of California Berkeley, 5, 165, 171–72, 174–75, 177, 179, 181–82, 184–87, 196–99, 207, 209, 211, 218, 222, 231, 236, 240, 243–44, 256
Upanishads, 80, 83, 86

Valade, Pierre-André, 201, 259, 278
Vagues, Chemins, le Souffle, 36–37, 41, 78–83, 85–87, 89, 97, 122
variations, 3, 15, 17, 33, 117, 122, 223, 229; melodic, 116; microtonal, 96, 216–17, 161; quarter tone, 77; rhythmic, 163; techniques, 212; timbral, 95
Variations for Orchestra, 47
Varèse, Edgard, 96, 105, 108, 157, 174, 260
Vichy France, 1, 3, 9
Villa Rojo, Jesús, 66
violin concertos, 61, 216
Virgin Mary, 65, 75, 238, 255
Vortex Temporum, 195, 203, 239, 246–52, 259–60, 268
Vosges Mountains, 1, 110, 135, 258

Wade, Bonnie, 198–99
Weberian chords, 34, 53, 63
Wehrmacht, 2, 20
Weil, Simone, 70
Wessel, David, 147, 172
Winckel, Fritz, 112
Wintle, Christopher, 267, 276–77
Wolf Lieder, 262–63, 274
World War II, 1–2, 9, 17, 20, 54, 63

www.ingramcontent.com/pod-product-compliance
Lightning Source LLC
Chambersburg PA
CBHW070308230426
43664CB00015B/2669